The Consumer Credit and Sales Legal Practice Series

AUTOMOBILE FRAUD

Odometer Tampering, Lemon Laundering, and Concealment of Salvage or Other Adverse History

2006 Supplement

With CD-Rom

Carolyn L. Carter
Jonathan Sheldon

Contributing Author: Elizabeth De Armond

National Consumer Law Center

77 Summer Street, 10th Floor   Boston, MA 02110

www.consumerlaw.org

About NCLC

The National Consumer Law Center, a nonprofit corporation founded in 1969, assists consumers, advocates, and public policy makers nationwide who use the powerful and complex tools of consumer law to ensure justice and fair treatment for all, particularly those whose poverty renders them powerless to demand accountability from the economic marketplace. For more information, go to www.consumerlaw.org.

Ordering NCLC Publications

Order securely online at www.consumerlaw.org, or contact Publications Department, National Consumer Law Center, 77 Summer Street, Boston, MA 02110, (617) 542-9595, FAX: (617) 542-8028, e-mail: publications@nclc.org.

Training and Conferences

NCLC participates in numerous national, regional, and local consumer law trainings. Its annual fall conference is a forum for consumer rights attorneys from legal services programs, private practice, government, and nonprofit organizations to share insights into common problems and explore novel and tested approaches that promote consumer justice in the marketplace. Contact NCLC for more information or see our web site.

Case Consulting

Case analysis, consulting and co-counseling for lawyers representing vulnerable consumers are among NCLC's important activities. Administration on Aging funds allow us to provide free consulting to legal services advocates representing elderly consumers on many types of cases. Massachusetts Legal Assistance Corporation funds permit case assistance to advocates representing low-income Massachusetts consumers. Other funding may allow NCLC to provide very brief consultations to other advocates without charge. More comprehensive case analysis and research is available for a reasonable fee. See our web site for more information at www.consumerlaw.org.

Charitable Donations and Cy Pres Awards

NCLC's work depends in part on the support of private donors. Tax-deductible donations should be made payable to National Consumer Law Center, Inc. For more information, contact Suzanne Cutler of NCLC's Development Office at (617) 542-8010 or scutler@nclc.org. NCLC has also received generous court-approved *cy pres* awards arising from consumer class actions to advance the interests of class members. For more information, contact Robert Hobbs (rhobbs@nclc.org) or Rich Dubois (rdubois@nclc.org) at (617) 542-8010.

Comments and Corrections

Write to the above address to the attention of the Editorial Department or e-mail consumerlaw@nclc.org.

About This Volume

This is the 2006 Supplement to *Automobile Fraud* (2d ed. 2003) with a 2006 CD-Rom. Retain the 2003 Second Edition, this Supplement, and the 2006 CD-Rom. Discard all prior volumes, supplements, and CDs. Continuing developments can be found in periodic supplements to this volume and in NCLC REPORTS, *Deceptive Practices & Warranties Edition*.

Cite This Volume As

National Consumer Law Center, Automobile Fraud (2d ed. 2003 and Supp.).

Attention

ISBN-13: 978-1-931697-92-7
ISBN-10: 1-931697-92-2 (this Supplement)
ISBN 1-931697-36-1 (main volume)
ISBN 0-943116-10-4 (Series)

Library of Congress Control Number 2003104843

About the Authors

Carolyn L. Carter is NCLC's deputy director for advocacy, and was formerly co-director of Legal Services, Inc., in Gettysburg, Pennsylvania, and director of the Law Reform Office of the Cleveland Legal Aid Society. She is the editor of *Pennsylvania Consumer Law*, editor of the first edition of *Ohio Consumer Law*, co-author of this volume's second edition, *Consumer Warranty Law* (3d ed. 2006), *Unfair and Deceptive Acts and Practices* (6th ed. 2004), *Repossessions* (6th ed. 2005), *Fair Credit Reporting* (5th ed. 2002), contributing author to *Fair Debt Collection* (5th ed. 2004), *Truth in Lending* (5th ed. 2003) and *The Cost of Credit* (3d ed. 2005), and the 1992 recipient of the Vern Countryman Consumer Award.

Jonathan Sheldon has been an NCLC staff attorney writing and consulting on automobile fraud, deceptive practices law and other consumer law topics since 1976. Previously he was a staff attorney with the Federal Trade Commission. His publications include the first two editions of this volume, *Unfair and Deceptive Acts and Practices* (1982, 1988, 1991, 1997, 2001, 2004), *Consumer Warranty Law* (1997, 2001, 2006), *Consumer Arbitration Agreements* (2001, 2002, 2003, 2004), *Consumer Class Actions* (1999), and *Repossessions* (1982, 1988, 1995, 1999, 2002, 2005).

Elizabeth De Armond is on the faculty of the Chicago-Kent College of Law. She is a frequent contributor to NCLC publications and is a contributing author to the second edition of this volume, *Unfair and Deceptive Acts and Practices* (6th ed. 2004), *Consumer Warranty Law* (3d ed. 2006), and *Fair Credit Reporting* (5th ed. 2002). Previously, she was in private practice in Texas and a clerk for the Hon. Cornelia Kennedy of the United States Court of Appeals for the Sixth Circuit. She is a member of the Illinois, Massachusetts, and Texas bars.

Acknowledgments: We want to thank Robert Eppes and Richard Morse for their advice and Ariel Patterson, Denise Lisio, Allen Agnitti, and Mary Kingsley for legal research and writing. We are particularly grateful to Eric Secoy for editorial supervision; Nathan Day for editorial assistance; Shirlron Williams for assistance checking the citations; Shannon Halbrook for production assistance; Xylutions for typesetting services; and Neil Fogarty of Law Disks for developing the CD-Rom.

What Your Library Should Contain

The Consumer Credit and Sales Legal Practice Series contains 17 titles, updated annually, arranged into four libraries, and designed to be an attorney's primary practice guide and legal resource in all 50 states. Each manual includes a CD-Rom allowing pinpoint searches and the pasting of text into a word processor.

Debtor Rights Library

2004 Seventh Edition, Special Guide to the 2005 Act, and 2005 CD-Rom, Including Law Disks' 2005 Bankruptcy Forms

Consumer Bankruptcy Law and Practice: the definitive personal bankruptcy manual, from the initial interview to final discharge, including consumer rights as creditors when a company files for bankruptcy. The Special Guide to the 2005 Act includes a redlined Code, Interim Rules, a date calculator, new forms, pleadings, and software, means test data, and a new questionnaire and client handout.

2004 Fifth Edition, 2006 Supplement, and 2006 CD-Rom

Fair Debt Collection: the basic reference, covering the Fair Debt Collection Practices Act and common law, state statutory and other federal debt collection protections. Appendices and companion CD-Rom contain sample pleadings and discovery, the FTC Commentary, *all* FTC staff opinion letters, and summaries of reported and unreported cases.

2005 First Edition with CD-Rom

Foreclosures: a new volume covering VA, FHA and other types of home foreclosures, workout agreements, servicer obligations, and tax liens. The CD-Rom reprints key federal statutes, regulations, interpretations, and handbooks, and contains numerous pleadings.

2005 Sixth Edition with CD-Rom

Repossessions: a unique guide to motor vehicle and mobile home repossessions, threatened seizures of household goods, statutory liens, and automobile lease and rent-to-own default remedies. The CD-Rom reprints relevant UCC provisions, summarizes many other state statutes, and includes many pleadings covering a wide variety of cases.

2002 Second Edition, 2005 Supplement, and 2005 CD-Rom

Student Loan Law: student loan debt collection; closed school, false certification, disability, and other discharges; tax intercepts, wage garnishment, and offset of social security benefits; repayment plans, consolidation loans, deferments, and non-payment of loan based on school fraud. CD-Rom and appendices contain numerous forms, pleadings, letters and regulations.

2004 Third Edition, 2006 Supplement, and 2006 CD-Rom

Access to Utility Service: the only examination of consumer rights when dealing with regulated, de-regulated, and unregulated utilities, including telecommunications, terminations, billing errors, low-income payment plans, utility allowances in subsidized housing, LIHEAP, and weatherization. Includes summaries of state utility regulations.

Credit and Banking Library

2003 Fifth Edition, 2005 Supplement, and 2005 CD-Rom

Truth in Lending: detailed analysis of *all* aspects of TILA, the Consumer Leasing Act, and the Home Ownership and Equity Protection Act (HOEPA). Appendices and the CD-Rom contain the Acts, Reg. Z, Reg. M, and their Official Staff Commentaries, numerous sample pleadings, rescission notices, and two programs to compute APRs.

National Consumer Law Center ■ **77 Summer Street** ■ **10**th **Floor** ■ **Boston MA** ■ **02110**
(617) 542-9595 ■ **FAX (617) 542-8028** ■ **publications@nclc.org**
Order securely online at www.consumerlaw.org

2002 Fifth Edition, 2005 Supplement, and 2005 CD-Rom

Fair Credit Reporting: the key resource for handling any type of credit reporting issue, from cleaning up blemished credit records to suing reporting agencies and creditors for inaccurate reports. Covers credit scoring, privacy issues, identity theft, the FCRA, the new FACT Act, the Credit Repair Organizations Act, state credit reporting and repair statutes, and common law claims.

2005 Third Edition, 2006 Supplement, and 2006 CD-Rom

Consumer Banking and Payments Law: unique analysis of consumer law (and NACHA rules) as to checks, money orders, credit, debit, and stored value cards, and banker's right of setoff. Also extensive treatment of electronic records and signatures, electronic transfer of food stamps, and direct deposits of federal payments. The CD-Rom and appendices reprint relevant agency interpretations and pleadings.

2005 Third Edition, 2006 Supplement, and 2006 CD-Rom

The Cost of Credit: Regulation, Preemption, and Industry Abuses: a one-of-a-kind resource detailing state and federal regulation of consumer credit in all fifty states, federal usury preemption, explaining credit math, and how to challenge excessive credit charges and credit insurance. The CD-Rom includes a credit math program and hard-to-find agency interpretations.

2005 Fourth Edition, 2006 Supplement and 2006 CD-Rom

Credit Discrimination: analysis of the Equal Credit Opportunity Act, Fair Housing Act, Civil Rights Acts, and state credit discrimination statutes, including reprints of all relevant federal interpretations, government enforcement actions, and numerous sample pleadings.

Consumer Litigation Library

2004 Fourth Edition, 2005 Supplement, and 2005 CD-Rom

Consumer Arbitration Agreements: numerous successful approaches to challenge the enforceability of a binding arbitration agreement, the interrelation of the Federal Arbitration Act and state law, class actions in arbitration, collections via arbitration, the right to discovery, and other topics. Appendices and CD-Rom include sample discovery, numerous briefs, arbitration service provider rules and affidavits as to arbitrator costs and bias.

2006 Sixth Edition with CD-Rom

Consumer Class Actions: A Practical Litigation Guide: makes class action litigation manageable even for small offices, including numerous sample pleadings, class certification memoranda, discovery, class notices, settlement materials, and much more. Includes a detailed analysis of the Class Action Fairness Act of 2005, recent changes to Rule 23, class arbitration, and other contributions from experienced consumer class action litigators around the country.

2005 CD-Rom with Index Guide: ALL pleadings from ALL NCLC Manuals, including Consumer Law Pleadings Numbers One through Eleven

Consumer Law Pleadings on CD-Rom: Over 1000 notable recent pleadings from all types of consumer cases, including predatory lending, foreclosures, automobile fraud, lemon laws, debt collection, fair credit reporting, home improvement fraud, rent to own, student loans, and lender liability. Finding aids pinpoint the desired pleading in seconds, ready to paste into a word processing program.

Deception and Warranties Library

2004 Sixth Edition, 2005 Supplement, and 2005 CD-Rom

Unfair and Deceptive Acts and Practices: the only practice manual covering all aspects of a deceptive practices case in every state. Special sections on automobile sales, the federal racketeering (RICO) statute, unfair insurance practices, and the FTC Holder Rule.

2003 Second Edition, 2006 Supplement, and 2006 CD-Rom

Automobile Fraud: examination of title law, odometer tampering, lemon laundering, sale of salvage and wrecked cars, undisclosed prior use, prior damage to new cars, numerous sample pleadings, and title search techniques.

2006 Third Edition with CD-Rom

Consumer Warranty Law: comprehensive treatment of new and used car lemon laws, the Magnuson-Moss Warranty Act, UCC Articles 2 and 2A, mobile home, new home, and assistive device warranty laws, FTC Used Car Rule, tort theories, car repair and home improvement statutes, service contract and lease laws, with numerous sample pleadings.

National Consumer Law Center ■ 77 Summer Street ■ 10th Floor ■ Boston MA ■ 02110
(617) 542-9595 ■ FAX (617) 542-8028 ■ publications@nclc.org
Order securely online at www.consumerlaw.org

NCLC's CD-Roms

Every NCLC manual comes with a companion CD-Rom featuring pop-up menus, PDF-format, Internet-style navigation of appendices, indices, and bonus pleadings, hard-to-find agency interpretations and other practice aids. Documents can be copied into a word processing program. Of special note is *Consumer Law in a Box*:

July 2006 CD-Rom

Consumer Law in a Box: a double CD-Rom combining *all* documents and software from 17 other NCLC CD-Roms. Quickly pinpoint a document from thousands found on the CD through keyword searches and Internet-style navigation, links, bookmarks, and other finding aids.

Other NCLC Publications for Lawyers

issued 24 times a year

NCLC REPORTS covers the latest developments and ideas in the practice of consumer law.

2006 Second Edition with CD-Rom

The Practice of Consumer Law: Seeking Economic Justice: contains an essential overview to consumer law and explains how to get started in a private or legal services consumer practice. Packed with invaluable sample pleadings and practice pointers for even experienced consumer attorneys.

First Edition with CD-Rom

STOP Predatory Lending: A Guide for Legal Advocates: provides a roadmap and practical legal strategy for litigating predatory lending abuses, from small loans to mortgage loans. The CD-Rom contains a credit math program, pleadings, legislative and administrative materials, and underwriting guidelines.

National Consumer Law Center Guide Series are books designed for consumers, counselors, and attorneys new to consumer law:

2006 Edition

NCLC Guide to Surviving Debt: a great overview of consumer law. Everything a paralegal, new attorney, or client needs to know about debt collectors, managing credit card debt, whether to refinance, credit card problems, home foreclosures, evictions, repossessions, credit reporting, utility terminations, student loans, budgeting, and bankruptcy.

2006 Edition

NCLC Guide to the Rights of Utility Consumers: explains consumer rights concerning electric, gas, and other utility services: shut off protections, rights to restore terminated service, bill payment options, weatherization tips, rights to government assistance, and much more.

First Edition

NCLC Guide to Mobile Homes: what consumers and their advocates need to know about mobile home dealer sales practices and an in-depth look at mobile home quality and defects, with 35 photographs and construction details.

First Edition

Return to Sender: Getting a Refund or Replacement for Your Lemon Car: find how lemon laws work, what consumers and their lawyers should know to evaluate each other, investigative techniques and discovery tips, how to handle both informal dispute resolution and trials, and more.

Visit **www.consumerlaw.org** to order securely online or for more information on all NCLC manuals and CD-Roms, including the full tables of contents, indices, listings of CD-Rom contents, and **web-based searches of the manuals' full text**.

National Consumer Law Center ■ 77 Summer Street ■ 10ᵗʰ Floor ■ Boston MA ■ 02110
(617) 542-9595 ■ FAX (617) 542-8028 ■ publications@nclc.org
Order securely online at www.consumerlaw.org

Finding Aids and Search Tips

The Consumer Credit and Sales Legal Practice Series presently contains seventeen volumes, twelve supplements, and seventeen companion CD-Roms—all constantly being updated. The Series includes over 10,000 pages, 100 chapters, 100 appendices, and over 1000 pleadings, as well as hundreds of documents found on the CD-Roms, but not found in the books. Here are a number of ways to pinpoint in seconds what you need from this array of materials.

Internet-Based Searches

www.consumerlaw.org

Electronically search every chapter and appendix of all seventeen manuals and their supplements: go to www.consumerlaw.org/keyword and enter a case name, regulation cite, or other search term. You are instantly given the book names and page numbers of any of the NCLC manuals containing that term, with those hits shown in context.

www.consumerlaw.org

Current indexes, tables of contents, and CD-Rom contents for all seventeen volumes are found at www.consumerlaw.org. Just click on *The Consumer Credit and Sales Legal Practice Series* and scroll down to the book you want. Then click on that volume's index, contents, or CD-Rom contents.

Finding Material on NCLC's CD-Roms

Consumer Law in a Box CD-Rom

Electronically search all seventeen NCLC CD-Roms, including thousands of agency interpretations, all NCLC appendices and over 1000 pleadings: use Acrobat's search button* in NCLC's *Consumer Law in a Box CD-Rom* (this CD-Rom is free to set subscribers) to find every instance that a keyword appears on any of our seventeen CD-Roms. Then, with one click, go to that location to see the full text of the document.

CD-Rom accompanying this volume

Electronically search the CD-Rom accompanying this volume, including pleadings, agency interpretations, and regulations. Use Acrobat's search button* to find every instance that a keyword appears on the CD-Rom, and then, with one click, go to that location on the CD-Rom. Or just click on subject buttons until you navigate to the document you need.

Finding Pleadings

Consumer Law Pleadings on CD-Rom and Index Guide

Search five different ways for the right pleading from over 1000 choices: use the *Index Guide* accompanying *Consumer Law Pleadings on CD-Rom* to search for pleadings by type, subject, publication title, name of contributor, or contributor's jurisdiction. The guide also provides a summary of the pleading once the right pleading is located. *Consumer Law Pleadings on CD-Rom* and the *Consumer Law in a Box CD-Rom* also let you search for all pleadings electronically by subject, type of pleading, and by publication title, giving you instant access to the full pleading in Word and/or PDF format once you find the pleading you need.

Using This Volume to Find Material in All Seventeen Volumes

This volume

The Quick Reference at the back of this volume lets you pinpoint manual sections or appendices where over 1000 different subject areas are covered.

---

* Users of NCLC CD-Roms should become familiar with "search," a powerful Acrobat tool, distinguished from "find," another Acrobat feature that is less powerful than "search." The Acrobat 5 "search" icon is a pair of binoculars with paper in the background, while the "find" icon is a pair of binoculars without the paper. Acrobat 6 and 7 use one icon, a pair of binoculars labeled "Search," that opens a dialog box with search options.

Contents

Chapter 3

Automobile Title Law

Chapter 4

Compliance with Federal and State Odometer Acts

Chapter 5   Remedies for Federal and State Odometer Act Violations

Chapter 6   Other Statutes Specifically Relating to Automobile Fraud

new subsection

Chapter 7 — Common Law Fraud, Deceit, and Misrepresentation

Chapter 8   Warranty, Mistake, UDAP, RICO, and Unconscionability Claims

replacement subsection

new subsection

Chapter 9

Litigating Automobile Fraud Cases

new subsection
new subsection

new subsection

new subsection

Appendix A   Federal Statutes

Appendix B   Federal Regulations

Appendix C   State Laws Relating to Automobile Fraud

Appendix D   State-by-State Information on Requesting Title Histories
replacement appendix

Appendix F   State Automobile Dealer Licensing Offices
replacement appendix

Appendix G   Sample Complaints

Appendix H   Sample Discovery

Appendix I   Sample Jury Trial Documents

Appendix J   Sample Motions and Briefs
replacement appendix

CD-Rom Contents

How to Use/Help

CD-Rom Text Search (Adobe Acrobat 5 and 6)
Searching NCLC Manuals
Ten-Second Tutorial on Adobe Acrobat 5
Two-Minute Tutorials on Adobe Acrobat 5 and 6
>   Navigation: Bookmarks
>   Disappearing Bookmarks?
>   Navigation Links
>   Navigation Arrows
>   Navigation: "Back" Arrow
>   Adobe Acrobat Articles
>   View-Zoom-Magnification: Making Text Larger
>   Full Screen vs. Bookmark View
>   Copying Text in Adobe Acrobat
>   How to Copy Only One Column
>   Printing
>   Other Sources of Help

Microsoft Word Files
About This CD-Rom
How to Install Adobe Acrobat Reader, with Search
Finding Aids for NCLC Manuals: What Is Available in the Books

Map of CD-Rom Contents

Adobe Acrobat 6.0 Problem

Statutes, Agency Interpretations

Introduction (Appendix A.1.1)
Federal Odometer Act (Appendix A.1.2)
Federal Odometer Act, Prior to Re-Codification
Conversion Table
>   15 U.S.C. to 49 U.S.C. (Appendix A.1.3.1)
>   49 U.S.C. to 15 U.S.C. (Appendix A.1.3.2)

Odometer Act Legislative History (Appendix A.1.4)
Federal Odometer Regulations (Appendix B.1.1)
Supplementary Information to Federal Odometer Regulations
>   July 17, 1987 (Appendix B.1.2.1)
>   Aug. 5, 1988 (Appendix B.1.2.2)
>   Aug. 1988 (Appendix B.1.2.3)
>   Aug. 30, 1989 (Appendix B.1.2.4)
>   Sept. 20, 1991 (Appendix B.1.2.5)

Titles, Title Histories

Dealer/Manufacturer Information

Car Pricing Guides
Vehicle Financing
Consumer Organizations and Advocacy Groups
Industry Trade Associations
Others

Contacts/Links

State Automobile Dealer Licensing Offices (Appendix F, 2006 Supplement)

new material   **State-by-State Information on Requesting Title Histories (Appendix D, 2006 Supplement)**

new material   **Websites Related to Automobile Fraud (Appendix M, 2006 Supplement)**

Automobile Fraud Appendices on CD-Rom

Table of Contents
Appendix A, Federal Statutes (and 2006 Supplement)

new material   **Appendix B, Federal Regulations (and 2006 Supplement)**
new material   **Appendix C, State Laws Relating to Automobile Fraud (and 2006 Supplement)**
new material   **Appendix D, State-by-State Information on Requesting Title Histories (2006 Supplement)**

Appendix E, Sample Documents
Appendix F, State Automobile Dealer Licensing Offices (2006 Supplement)
Appendix G, Sample Complaints (and 2006 Supplement)
Appendix H, Sample Discovery (and 2006 Supplement)

new material   **Appendix I, Sample Jury Trial Documents (and 2006 Supplement)**
new material   **Appendix J, Sample Motions and Briefs (2006 Supplement)**
new material   **Appendix K, Sample Class Action Pleadings in an Odometer Rollback Case (and 2006 Supplement)**

Appendix L, Sample Attorney Fee Papers (and 2006 Supplement)

new material   **Appendix M, Websites Related to Automobile Fraud (2006 Supplement)**

Cumulative Index
Microsoft Word Pleadings & Practice Aids
Quick Reference to the Consumer Credit and Sales Legal Practice Series
What Your Library Should Contain

Microsoft Word Files on CD-Rom

Complaints
Discovery
Class Actions
Voir Dire, Opening and Closing Statements, Other Trial Documents
Expert Reports, Expert Witnesses
Jury Instructions, Verdict Forms
Briefs, Memoranda
Attorney Fee Documents

Contents of NCLC Publications

Internet-Based Keyword Search of All NCLC Manuals
Detailed and Summary Tables of Contents for Each Manual
Short Description of Each Manual's Features with Link to Manual's Detailed Index
Short Index to Major Topics Covered in the Seventeen-Volume Series
Descriptions of Other NCLC Books for Lawyers and Consumers
Features of *Consumer Law in a Box* (Seventeen CD-Roms Combined into Two CD-Rom Set)

Printer-Friendly Three-Page Description of All NCLC Publications, Latest Supplements
Printer-Friendly Twenty-Five-Page Brochure Describing All NCLC Publications
Printer-Friendly Order Form for All NCLC Publications
Secure On-line Order Form

Consumer Education Brochures, Books

Legal and General Audience Books Available for Order from NCLC
   The Practice of Consumer Law
   STOP Predatory Lending: A Guide for Legal Advocates, with CD-Rom
   Return to Sender: Getting a Refund or Replacement for Your Lemon Car
new material   **The NCLC Guide to Surviving Debt (2006 Ed.)**
new material   **The NCLC Guide to the Rights of Utility Consumers**
   The NCLC Guide to Consumer Rights for Immigrants
   The NCLC Guide to Mobile Homes
   Printer-Friendly Order Form
   Secure On-line Order Form
Brochures for Consumers on This CD-Rom
   General Consumer Education Brochures
   Consumer Concerns for Older Americans
   Immigrant Justice in the Consumer Marketplace

Order NCLC Publications, CD-Roms

NCLC Manuals and CD-Roms
Order Publications On-line
Printer-Friendly Order Form
Consumer Law in a Box CD-Rom
Credit Math, Bankruptcy Software
Printer-Friendly Publications Brochure
NCLC Newsletters
Case Assistance
Conferences, Training
Books for Lawyers, Consumers
Consumer Education Pamphlets
Consumer Weblinks

About NCLC, About This CD-Rom

National Consumer Law Center
   Mission Statement
   Contact Information: Boston, Washington Offices
   Go to NCLC Website
   What Your Library Should Contain
   Order NCLC Publications On-line
   Learn More About NCLC Manuals, CD-Roms
   Order Form: Order NCLC Publications Via Mail, Phone, Fax
About This CD-Rom
   What Is Contained on This CD-Rom
   Finding Aids for NCLC Manuals: What Is Available in the Books?
   Disclaimers—Need to Adapt Pleadings; Unauthorized Practice of Law
License Agreement, Copyrights, Trademarks: Please Read
Law Disks: CD-Rom Producer, Publisher of Bankruptcy Forms Software

Adobe Acrobat Reader 5.0.5 and 7.0.7

Chapter 1   Introduction and Practice Checklist

1.1 About This Manual

Page 2

1.1.3 Clearinghouse Cases

Replace "National Center on Poverty Law" in subsection's first sentence with:

Sargent Shriver National Center on Poverty Law

Replace address in subsection's first sentence with:

50 E. Washington St., Suite 500, Chicago, IL 60602

1.3 Automobile Frauds Analyzed in Other NCLC Manuals

Page 3

1.3.2 Automobile Warranties and Repairs

Replace NCLC UDAP citation in subsection's final sentence with:

Unfair and Deceptive Acts and Practices § 5.4.1 (6th ed. 2004)

1.3.3 Deceptive Pricing and Sales Techniques

Replace NCLC UDAP citation in subsection's first sentence with:

Unfair and Deceptive Acts and Practices (6th ed. 2004)

Replace third bulleted item with:

• Dealer misrepresentations and sharp practices (§ 5.4.4.6); and

1.3.4 Trade-ins, Yo-Yo Sales, and Financing

Replace subsection's third paragraph with:

The best place to look for information on these various abuses is NCLC's *Unfair and Deceptive Acts and Practices* (6th ed. 2004 and Supp.), particularly §§ 5.1.4–5.1.7 on oppressive credit practices, § 5.4.4.4 on trade-in practices, § 5.4.3.7 on dealer financing practices, § 5.4.7.6 on dealer kickbacks when financing is assigned, and § 5.4.5 on yo-yo sales.

Replace NCLC Truth in Lending citation in subsection's last paragraph with:

National Consumer Law Center, *Truth in Lending* (5th ed. 2003 and Supp.)

1.3.5 Credit Insurance, GAP Insurance, and Service Contracts

Replace first NCLC UDAP citation in subsection's second paragraph with:

Unfair and Deceptive Acts and Practices §§ 5.3.9, 5.4.3.6, 5.4.3.7 (6th ed. 2004)

1

Replace NCLC Truth in Lending citation in subsection's second paragraph with: *Truth in Lending* (5th ed. 2003 and Supp.)

Replace second NCLC UDAP citation in subsection's second paragraph with: *Unfair and Deceptive Acts and Practices* § 5.3 (6th ed. 2004 and Supp.)

1.3.6 Documentary Fees, Other Charges, Add-Ons, and Options

Replace NCLC citation with: *Unfair and Deceptive Acts and Practices* §§ 5.4.3, 5.4.3.8 (6th ed. 2004 and Supp.)

Page 4

1.3.7 Leasing

Replace NCLC Truth in Lending citation in subsection's first paragraph with: National Consumer Law Center, *Truth in Lending* Ch. 10 (5th ed. 2003 and Supp.)

Replace NCLC citation in subsection's final sentence with: *Unfair and Deceptive Acts and Practices* § 5.4.8 (6th ed. 2004 and Supp.)

1.3.10 Forced-Placed Automobile Insurance

Replace NCLC citation with: *Unfair and Deceptive Acts and Practices* § 5.3.11 (6th ed. 2004 and Supp.)

Chapter 2

Investigatory Techniques

2.1 Automobile Frauds Described

2.1.2 Odometer Fraud

Page 12

2.1.2.2 What Is an Odometer?

Add to text at end of subsection:

Technological changes have led to a variety of odometer types and to a variety of possible methods to alter an odometer. The following discussion is based on material provided by two automobile fraud experts, Richard Diklich of Liberty, Missouri and Robert Eppes of Shawnee, Kansas.

For the past several years there has been a patchwork quilt of mileage generating devices and storage units used to produce odometer readings. The systems have changed rapidly from year to year, and from model to model. They continue to do so. It is beyond the scope of this manual to identify how each of the myriad makes and models store mileage, or to describe each of the number of ways that the odometer reading can be altered. In the past, for example, simply pulling a fuse or disconnecting a sensor would keep the mileage from accumulating past the last recorded number in some models.

Regulatory authorities do not specify how a manufacturer collects and holds mileage. Manufacturers are concerned about mileage for the purposes of warranty administration, but manufacturers may retain proprietary information about storage that is not readily available to anyone outside a select few in their engineering departments.

Over-the-road trucks record mileage in their engine computer, and only the engine factory can alter it in the event a new computer is installed. Heavy truck technicians performing routine maintenance can read the engine computer mileage and often note a discrepancy between the odometer reading and the stored mileage. The dashboard module does retain mileage, and if replaced the mileage goes to zero, but the engine computer will keep on accumulating. Truck-type engines in motor homes operate in the same manner.

As consumers become more comfortable with electronic digital display odometers, older mechanical or electro-mechanical roll-type odometers will be completely phased out. There is still some activity in the field altering such older roll-type units, but at this point the vehicles involved are older vehicles on smaller lots. Some of the same dealers will move into altering electronic odometers that hold information in a computer module called a "cluster," and just change clusters on a volume basis. There are also individuals who will reprogram the cluster when it is sent in to them. A reprogrammed storage unit will not leave a trace that can be detected through normal means.

Reprogramming equipment is available on the Internet for purchase by individuals who purport to "repair" clusters or systems that retain mileage. The reprogramming devices are designed separately for the systems they are advertised to "repair," and go to all places in the vehicle that mileage is stored, erase it, and replace it with the desired number. Some work through the vehicle repair diagnostic port, and others clamp onto the back of the chip that holds the mileage. Odometer information is kept in an EEPROM, which stands for Electronically Erasable Programmable Read Only Memory. It is a common practice for a dealer or some private shops to reprogram the engine and transmission modules for enhanced performance, or when a new module is required.

The process of producing an odometer reading begins with an electronic signal that is produced by some rotating component, such as an anti-lock brake sensor or the transmission output shaft. The vehicle has to know how fast it is going and how far it has traveled for several reasons other than the odometer display. Some examples of the multiple uses for this signal include: odometer, speedometer, transmission shifting, engine timing and fuel metering, active suspension systems, oil change notification programs, cruise control, Exhaust Gas Recirculation systems, fuel mileage and trip information, and anti-lock brake self-testing.

The management of the vehicle's systems is largely electronically controlled, with very few mechanical devices in constant use. An anti-lock brake sensor produces a sine-wave voltage that changes polarity a specified number of times per wheel revolution, and thus can be used to determine how far the tires have traveled. The transmission output shaft could also produce the voltage; it used to be produced by the speedometer cable circa 1975. There are some low-end models that use one anti-lock sensor for odometer/speedometer purposes even when the vehicle does not have anti-lock brakes.

Registered importers bring in vehicles from other countries, and must convert kilometers to miles. These importers had to learn to reverse engineer and reprogram odometer storage devices for themselves, because the manufacturers would not release information to enable them to perform the conversion.

For the individual or attorney who suspects that they have an odometer fraud case involving an electronic odometer, discovery and research is absolutely necessary. Often, a vehicle's electronic diagnostic system may record a code when triggered by a fault in one of the vehicle systems and a mileage number will be recorded at the time of the fault. However, in some instances the mileage generated is not accurate, and can be misleading. A better list to use may be one that includes all the times a paper odometer reading has been generated during the life of the vehicle. A check with a dealer's service department is the first step to see if the odometer reading is stored in an alternate location that can be accessed. Most service managers want to combat odometer fraud, and will assist the customer all they can. Although some dealer service personnel have been involved in altering odometer readings, the frequency is relatively low. Simply go to a dealer other than the selling dealer to make the inquiry.

Page 13

Add to text at the end of the subsection:

2.1.2.7 Most Common Forms of Odometer Fraud Today

As older cars become more valuable, another form of odometer fraud is to reset an odometer to around 60,000 miles even though the car actually has several hundred thousand miles of use. Then the odometer disclosure is listed as "not actual mileage." The impression is that the mileage is somewhat higher, without disclosing that the mileage is much much higher. Although this practice violates the federal Act, fraud perpetrators mistakenly believe this tactic insulates them from liability.

Page 15

Add new subsection to text after § 2.1.4:

2.1.4a Hurricane Cars

It is estimated that at least half a million cars were ruined by the disastrous 2005 Gulf Coast hurricanes Katrina, Wilma, and Rita. Many vehicles that sat in the sewage and fuel contaminated floodwaters in New Orleans are in fact biohazards.[24.1] Other vehicles may have been flooded both by salt and by fresh water, each posing its own problems. Vehicles that were flooded include private passenger vehicles that were insured against flood damage and others that were not, commercial vehicles that are often self-insured, and many brand new vehicles that were sitting on dealer lots waiting to be sold, whose flood damage may or may not have been covered by the dealer's insurance policy.

Because of the sheer numbers of flood vehicles involved, any loopholes in state auto salvage laws that allow these cars to be resold without disclosure are certain to be exploited, by at least some dealers, insurers, and other companies. At the time of the hurricanes, Louisiana's law required a vehicle to be branded as salvage only if it was declared a total loss as a result of an insurance settlement.[24.2] If the vehicle was not covered by insurance, or not covered for this particular hazard, the branding requirement would not apply.

Vehicles also were not branded where the insurer did not declare the vehicle a total loss. Since flood damage is not as visually apparent as wreck damage, insurers may be tempted to increase the resale value of flood-damaged cars by not declaring them to be total losses.

After the hurricanes, the Louisiana salvage statute was amended[24.3] to define a water-damaged vehicle as one whose power train, computer, or electrical system has been damaged by flooding as the result of a gubernatorially declared disaster or emergency, where the damage equals at least 75% of the vehicle's market value. When an insurance company acquires ownership of such a water damaged vehicle as a result of an insurance settlement, a certificate of destruction must be obtained, the vehicle can never be licensed to be used in Louisiana or resold as a retail unit, and the vehicles should be either sold for parts or destroyed.

This statute still applies only to insurance settlements, and only where the insurer determines that the loss exceeds 75%. Moreover, if past history is a guide, some of these water-damaged vehicles will be transported out-of-state to avoid the Louisiana law.

24.1 According to the Coordinating Committee for Automotive Repair, which advises the auto industry on pollution, health, and safety issues. *See* www.ccar-greenlink.org.

24.2 La. Rev. Stat. Ann. § 32:707.3(A).

24.3 La. Rev. Stat. Ann. §§ 32:702, 32-707.3, *as amended by* 2005 La. Sess. Law Serv. 1st Ex. Session Act 42 (H.B. 11).

Page 16

2.1.5 Undisclosed Prior History of Mechanical Problems and Lemon Laundering

Add to text at end of subsection:

A similar technique for concealing a vehicle's lemon history is to give the original buyer a trade-in bonus as an incentive to trade the lemon in for a replacement car. For example, in one case the manufacturer gave the original buyers an "owner appreciation certificate" for a credit of $1500 on any trade-in transaction as a means of resolving their concerns about the car.[28.1] Evidence that the manufacturer had a policy of offering trade-in incentives as a means of evading the state's lemon laundering prohibition supported the award of punitive damages in that case.

28.1 Johnson v. Ford Motor Co., Johnson v. Ford Motor Co., 35 Cal. 4th 1191, 113 P.3d 82, 86–87 (2005), *rev'd in part, remanded on other grounds*, 113 P.3d 82 (Cal. 2005) (ruling on punitive damages issues).

2.1.9 Undisclosed Canadian or Other Foreign Origin

Page 17

2.1.9.1 Introduction

Add to text at end of subsection's first paragraph:

The National Highway Traffic Safety Administration (NHTSA) has detailed standards for the importation of vehicles.[36.1]

36.1 49 U.S.C. § 30112 (imported vehicles must meet U.S. safety standards and be certified); 49 U.S.C. § 30141 (when certification is necessary); 49 U.S.C. § 30146 (certification requirements); 49 C.F.R. § 519 (procedures for importation of vehicles); 49 C.F.R. § 592.6 (bond and record keeping requirements). NHTSA's website, www.nhtsa.gov (click on "International Activities," then on "Importation of Vehicles"), has forms and guidelines for the importation of vehicles.

2.1.9.2 Odometer Discrepancies in Canadian Vehicles

Add note 36.2 at end of subsection's second paragraph.

36.2 *See, e.g.*, Tuckish v. Pompano Motor Co., 337 F. Supp. 2d 1313 (S.D. Fla. 2004).

Add to text after third sentence in subsection's fifth paragraph:

NHTSA keeps the photos for only two years, so they should be requested promptly.

2.1.9.3 Warranty and Other Problems

Add to text after subsection's first sentence:

Sometimes the manufacturer will offer goodwill warranty coverage, but some manufacturers are reported to be adopting a stricter policy and refusing all coverage.

Page 18

Add note 36.3 to end of subsection's second-to-last sentence.

36.3 *See* § 8.2.4.2, *infra.*

2.1.9.4 Identifying a Vehicle As Not Manufactured for the United States Market

Replace "United States" in second sentence of subsection's first paragraph with:

"United States" or refer to "federal" standards

Add to text at end of subsection's last sentence:

and provide a copy of its vehicle compliance package, including any photos of the vehicle.[37.1] But there is some concern that many of the requirements as to a registered importer, VIN numbers, and even stickers may be avoided if the Canadian manufacturing plant transfers the vehicle to a United States subsidiary, such as Fleetmax.

37.1 The office that actually maintains the records is the Vehicle Safety Compliance Office, 400 7th St. S.W., Room 6111, Mail Code NSA-30, Washington, DC 20590.

2.2 Investigating Fraud Based on Information Within the Consumer's Control

2.2.2 Stickers and Paperwork Found on and in the Car

Page 19

Add to text after first sentence of subsection's last paragraph:

It states the year and month of production and the country of origin.

Replace "United States," in second sentence of subsection's last paragraph with:

"United States" or refers to "federal" standards,

Add to text at end of subsection:

Sellers have been known to tear off a Canadian sticker to conceal a vehicle's origins. If it is suspected that a vehicle is a gray market vehicle, the vehicle identification number should also be checked.[38.1]

38.1 *See* § 2.1.9.4, *supra.*

2.2.4 The Vehicle Identification Number (VIN)

2.2.4.2 How to Check a VIN

Page 20

Add to text after sentence containing note 46:

A Ford Motor Co. website offers a similar program for free.[46.1] It decodes vehicle identification numbers not just for Ford vehicles, but for all makes.

46.1 The website may be found at www.fleet.ford.com/maintenance/vin_tools/default.asp.

2.2.9 *Expert Inspection of the Vehicle*

2.2.9.1 Finding an Expert

Page 23

Add to text at end of subsection:

One underutilized source is the automobile theft detective with the local police. These individuals are often extremely knowledgeable and are rarely contacted for advice. Many serious automobile theft detectives are members of the International Association of Automobile Theft Investigators. They will often volunteer much useful information even on a salvage vehicle. For example, they can often identify stolen parts, cloned vehicles, and other problems. If police department policy permits, they can be excellent expert witnesses when not on duty, or can provide referrals to other experts.

2.2.9.2 What the Expert Should Check

Page 24

Add to text at end of subsection:

Mileage in modern cars is registered on the power train control module and can be reprogrammed, in effect spinning the odometer. In that case, a specialized expert will be required to spot the reprogramming. As one expert put it, one has to look "for magnetic shadows in the storage EEPROM." Moreover, some vehicles may store the mileage information in two different places in the vehicle, such as both the instrument cluster and the ignition module. An expert finding two different mileage readings for the same car should indicate an odometer problem.

2.2.9.3 Inspection Procedures and Techniques

Addition to note 60.

60 *See* Lockhart v. Cmty. Auto Plaza, Inc., 695 N.W.2d 335 (Iowa Ct. App. 2004) (citing expert testimony that problems would have been obvious with even the most cursory inspection); Cohen v. Express Fin. Services, 145 S.W.3d 857 (Mo. Ct. App. 2004) (citing expert testimony that damage would have been obvious to a person with training and experience).

Page 25

Add to text at end of subsection.

If the opposing side is present during an inspection, the expert may want to give them the opportunity to photograph each part that is removed from the vehicle, especially in the case of destructive testing.

2.2.9.4 Defense Inspections

Add note 62.1 at end of subsection.

62.1 *See* Parks v. Newmar Corp., 2005 WL 2071722 (W.D. Va. Aug. 26, 2005) (ordering that defense inspection be coordinated with counsel for all parties so that all experts may be present and participate); Canter v. Am. Cyanimid Co., 5 A.D.2d 513, 173 N.Y.S.2d 623 (ordering that party who produces item for testing be allowed to observe tests), *as modified by* 6 A.D.2d 847, 174 N.Y.S.2d 983 (1958); State *ex rel.* Remington Arms Co. v. Powers, 552 P.2d 1150, 1153 (Okla. 1976) (as general rule, plaintiff or representative should be permitted to observe opponent's testing of item produced by plaintiff); Miller v. Goodyear Tire & Rubber Co., 40 Pa. D. & C.3d 430 (C.P. 1985) (defendant has right to test physical evidence but plaintiffs need not surrender custody and control; plaintiffs may send representative to monitor testing but must avoid overhearing conversations); Rea v. Schmocker, 5 Pa. D. & C.3d 434 (C.P. 1978) (ordering that plaintiffs' representative be allowed attend defendant's testing to retain control of item during testing).

2.3 Summary Title History

2.3.2 *Carfax*

Page 27

Add to text after "incidents" in second sentence of subsection's second paragraph:

from consumer protection agencies that handle lemon law claims, from extended warranty companies,

Replace "two billion" in third sentence of subsection's second paragraph with:

four billion

Delete "although Rhode Island's data is only now being added" from fourth sentence of subsection's second paragraph.

Replace "most" in fifth sentence of subsection's second paragraph with:

all

Page 28

Replace "seventeen" in sentence containing note 77 with:

a number of

Addition to note 77.

77   *Replace first two words of note with*: The states include Alabama, Arizona, California,

Replace in note 78 with:

78   The guarantee is the purchase price of the vehicle up to 10% over the Kelley Blue Book value.

Replace "www.carfax.com/ reports" in first sentence of subsection's fifth paragraph with:

www.carfax.com/cfm/purchase_options.cfm

Replace last sentence of subsection's fifth paragraph with:

As of 2005, Carfax was offering a single report for $19.99, and an unlimited number of reports over a thirty-day period for $24.99.

Replace note 79 with:

79   In early 2006, Carfax's website stated that it had 14,000 dealer subscribers.

Add to text after third sentence of subsection's seventh paragraph:

If the dealer has represented to a consumer that the Carfax report can be relied on to show whether a car has been in an accident, the consumer's attorney should obtain the dealer's application and subscription agreement with Carfax through discovery. These documents reportedly prohibit such representations.

Page 29

2.3.3 AutoCheck

Replace "300 million" in subsection's second sentence with:

500 million

Add to text after third sentence of subsection's first paragraph:

It claims to receive data from most of the automobile auctions in the country.

Replace subsection's second paragraph with:

AutoCheck will provide a free report showing how many records it has on a particular vehicle. A full report costs $19.99, and unlimited reports may be purchased over a sixty-day period for $24.99. Sample reports are available on-line. Insurance coverage of up to $50,000 for protection against defective titles and transfer problems may be purchased with Auto-Check's Unlimited report for $59.99. If the vehicle has a branded title that was not revealed by the report the insurance policy will pay the full purchase price plus up to $500 for accessories to buy the vehicle from the buyer.

2.3.4 CarFraud.com

Add to text at end of subsection:

However, in 2005 its website was no longer functioning and efforts to locate it were unsuccessful.

Replace § 2.3.5 heading with:

2.3.5 Information Sources for Canadian Vehicles

Replace first six words of sentence following sentence containing note 82 with:

For $39.95 Canadian (about $32 U.S.)

Replace subsection's last sentence with:

The completed report can be sent by mail, facsimile, or e-mail to the customer. A sample report is available on-line.

Add to text at end of subsection:

When checked in April 2006, however, it was discovered that Auto Facts no longer provides vehicle history reports. Instead, Auto Facts directs interested consumers to CarProof, another Canadian business providing such reports.[82.1] CarProof offers four different reports to consumers and claims that it is able to provide lien information and live registration status checks from every jurisdiction in Canada, accident claim and coverage information from 90% of private insurance companies in Canada, and insurance claim data from the Insurance Corporation of British Columbia. In addition, Car Proof is able to access additional information within Experian Automotive's database of more than 20 billion records, which also contains U.S. vehicle history information. CarProof's reports range in cost from $24.99 to $59.99 Canadian for its most comprehensive report.

Another company, A Plus Registry Services, retrieves title and registration documents in Alberta for a fee.[82.2]

82.1   www.carproof.com.
82.2   Its website is www.aplusregistry.com.

2.3.6 Insurance Databases

Add to text after subsection's second sentence:

ISO's records include the date of a claim, the claim number, the names of the insured and the insurance company, the policy number, the amount and type of damage, and the telephone number of the claims office.

Page 30

Add to text at end of subsection:

Any request for information should include the car's vehicle identification number. Not all insurance companies are members of NICB, however, so some claims information may not be in its database. NICB's website includes a list of its members.

NICB supplies manufacturer shipping information to Carfax for some cars. If a Carfax report refers to NICB, it may be worthwhile to subpoena the rest of NICB's information on the vehicle from NICB. The subpoena should seek all of NICB's files on the vehicle, including any information about theft, impoundment, damage estimates, and claims. NICB's data is in electronic form and will identify where the physical files are located. Some auto auctions may have access to this database, and therefore could be charged with knowledge of any problems it reveals.

2.3.7 Other Quick Search Procedures

Replace third and fourth sentences of subsection's third paragraph with:

As of 2006 early, twenty four states participate in the system. Arizona, Florida, Indiana, Iowa, Kentucky, Massachusetts, Nevada, New Hampshire, Ohio, South Dakota, Tennessee, Virginia, Washington, and Wisconsin (Montana also participates in theft inquiries only) have integrated NMVTIS on-line transactions into their titling systems. Alabama, Idaho, Louisiana, Nebraska, Nevada, New Jersey, North Carolina, Pennsylvania, Texas, and Wyoming also participate, but only by providing regular updates to the system's central files.

Add to text at end of subsection's third paragraph:

Some experts in 2005 predict that the whole system will be abandoned due to lack of funding and involvement by the states.

2.4 Detailed Title Histories

2.4.2 How a Chain of Title Works

Page 32

2.4.2.4 How the DMV Stores Title Information

Add to text at end of subsection:

National Highway Traffic Safety Administration (NHTSA) regulations do not require the states to retain title information after vehicle ownership has been transferred, but NHTSA has stated that "retention of these records by the States is a valuable enforcement tool."[101.1] NHTSA also opined that digital imaging is a preferable method for storing information compared to using microfilm.[101.2]

101.1   Opinion Letter from Nat'l Highway Traffic Safety Admin. to Ab Quillian, Comm'r, Virginia Dep't of Motor Vehicles (Apr. 2, 2002) (reproduced on the CD-Rom accompanying this volume).

101.2   *Id.*

2.4.5 How to Use Title Information to Uncover Fraud

2.4.5.4 Flood-Damaged, Wrecked, Rebuilt, and Other Salvage Vehicles

Page 35

2.4.5.4.1 General

Add to text after first sentence of subsection's second paragraph:

Some but not all state laws have a mechanism to require these owners to obtain salvage titles, but it is unclear how effective these mechanisms are.

Page 36

2.4.5.4.4 When salvage brand is removed from title

Add to text after subsection's fourth paragraph:

A few states, including New York, Alabama, and Nevada, will issue certificates of title for older vehicles when the owner has only a bill of sale, not a title. There are companies in these states that will obtain titles for these older vehicles even if the vehicle is never physically present in the state. The owner sends the company the bill of sale, the company "purchases" the vehicle, obtains a certificate of title in its name, and then sells the vehicle back to the owner. The owner can use the new certificate of title to re-register the vehicle in other states. While these companies claim that they handle only legitimate transactions, a fraudulent operator could take advantage of this procedure as a way of washing a brand off a title or obtaining a certificate of title for a stolen or non-existent car.

Page 38

2.4.5.6 Number of Prior Owners; Demonstrators; Lease or Rental Cars, Taxis, Police Cars, and Other Unusual Prior Owners

Add to text after fourth sentence of subsection's third paragraph:

If there is a duplicate Manufacturer's Statement of Origin in the title history, the dealer may have requested the duplicate to conceal the fact that the vehicle is not new but was previously sold.

2.4.5.7 Duplicate Titles; Laundered Titles; Powers of Attorney

Add to text at end of subsection:

Typically, the existence of a manufacturer's statement of origin (MSO) is evidence that the car is still "new," while titling a vehicle indicates that it is "used." But dealers have been known to take back a vehicle after it has been titled, and then request a replacement MSO from the manufacturer, misrepresenting that they have lost the old MSO or that it had to be discarded because of a paperwork mistake. The dealer than sells the vehicle again, using the replacement MSO, and the vehicle then has two titles. This practice should result in two different titles showing up in the department of motor vehicles and Carfax's records for the same VIN number.

Another suspicious circumstance is a duplicate Manufacturer's Statement of Origin in the title history. This may indicate that the dealer sold the car once and had a title issued to the buyer, but then the deal fell through and the dealer retook the car. Sometimes in this circumstance the dealer obtains a duplicate MSO in order to conceal the fact that the vehicle was already sold and titled once.

2.5 Obtaining Information from Others Involved in Car's History

2.5.1 Contacting the Prior Consumer Owners

Page 39

Add to text at end of subsection's fourth paragraph:

Other key questions to ask are what the prior owner told the dealer about the car, how the paperwork was handled, and whether the dealer had the prior owner sign any of the disclosure documents in blank.

Sometimes prior owners are more willing to talk to the new owner than to the new owner's attorney. Having the client contact the prior owner also minimizes the risk that the attorney will be drawn into the case as a fact witness. The client should be carefully prepared before contacting the prior owner, however. In the alternative, an office assistant or private investigator may contact the prior owner.

2.5.2 Automobile Dealers

2.5.2.2 Other Dealer Records

Replace note 126 with:

126   National Consumer Law Center, *Unfair and Deceptive Acts and Practices* § 5.4.2 (6th ed. 2004 and Supp.).

Page 41

2.5.2.4 Former Dealer Employees

Add to text at end of subsection:

Prior to any interview, some attorneys ask former dealership employees to sign a statement that they understand the attorney does not represent them, that the former employee is being interviewed only as a potential witness, that the attorney will not compensate the former employee or pay for information or referral of clients, and that the attorney can use any documents the former employee provides for any purpose including passing them on to a reporter.

Add new subsection to text after § 2.5.2.4:

2.5.2.4a Speaking the Dealer's Language on Odometer Rollbacks

In deposing or cross-examining dealer employees, it helps to be familiar with typical dealer slang. The very fact that the employee is familiar with the slang may make an impression on the jury. For example, odometer rollbacks have their own code language.

A "mile buster" or "mile hitter" is a dealer that sells vehicles with altered odometers or an individual that alters odometers. The person who alters odometers can also be referred to as the "clocker," "spinner," "twister," "cutter," "clipper," "odo guy," or "rollback guy." To alter an odometer is called to "clock," "bust," "spin," "cut," "clip," "twist," "roll," "hit," "knock it in the head," or "hit the miles of" an odometer.

The dealer and cutter will often speak in code when discussing how many miles to roll an odometer back. For example, a horse race code system would sound something like this:

> [*Dealer asking cutter how many miles can safely be removed from the odometer.*] Dealer: "How do you think this horse will finish in the race?" Cutter: "It's an old pony, but it will probably finish 5th or 6th." Dealer: "I'll put $50.00 on that horse to finish 5th in the race."

The meaning of the conversation is that the dealer wants the odometer altered to 50,000 miles for a known fee of $50.00. The term "5th race" meant the "cutter" should alter the first digit of the odometer to the number five making the odometer read 50,000 miles.

There are many variations in the words used, but there is usually a common theme to the verbal dialogue. The terms to disguise the topic of altering the odometer may be "race car numbers," "lucky numbers," "horses," "dollars for gas" or a host of other topics. It will seldom be as blatant as "Hey, odometer buster! Will you reset my odometer to a lower mileage of 50,000?"

Usually such transactions involve few words. Similarly to drug deals, everyone knows what they are supposed to do, and they do not have to verbally go over the details. Sometimes instructions are given in notes left in vehicles or offices that show the vehicle year, make, and desired mileage, or sometimes on small pieces of paper, similar to "bookie sheets," showing only a number to guide the person altering the odometer.

2.5.2.5 Contacting the Selling Dealer and Prior Servicing Dealers Concerning Mechanical Problems

Replace note 132 with:

132   *See* National Consumer Law Center, Consumer Law Pleadings No. 2, § 6.1 (Cumulative CD-Rom and Index Guide).

2.5.2.6 When New Car Damaged Before Delivery

Add to text at end of subsection's second paragraph:

In this case, the receipt the dealer signed when the manufacturer delivered the car will show no damage.

Page 42

2.5.4 Auctions

Replace last sentence of subsection's first paragraph with:

Sometimes a search through Carfax or a similar service will show that the car has been through an auction, as certain auctions have agreed to report information to these services. An auction sale can not be ruled out even if no such sale appears on the summary title report, however. Further, the summary title report may show only one auction sale for a car that went through several auctions. For these reasons, the consumer's attorney should also use formal or informal discovery methods to determine how each owner in the chain of title acquired the car.

Add to text after sentence containing note 137:

These sheets may also contain codes that give information about the vehicle's origins.

Add to text after sentence containing note 138:

The auction's invoice typically records the sale price, the seller, the vehicle identification number, and what announcements were made at the sale about the condition of the vehicle. A copy of the invoice often serves as a gate pass, allowing the dealer to take the vehicle away.

Add to text at end of subsection's third paragraph:

The auction may also have records of services it performed, such as inspections, repair estimates, repairs, clean-up, and detailing, and the price it charged for these services. These documents will help verify the vehicle's history and condition.

Add to text at end of subsection's fourth paragraph:

It is important to get both the front and back of the title.

Add to text after sentence containing note 139:

Auctions are likely to inspect cars that are being sold off after the expiration of a lease.

Add to text at end of subsection:

An auction may also have arbitration files, created to resolve a dealer's request for a price concession after buying a particular vehicle. A dealer's request for arbitration on a vehicle because it had wreck damage or an odometer discrepancy will dispel any claim that the dealer was unaware of the problem. The auction may also have a repair division that will have additional records on the vehicle, or the auction may have records showing that it arranged for an outside repair shop to work on the vehicle. Auctions also have valuable information about the dealer's assets, such as checks and drafts from the dealer, floor plan financing arrangements, and bridge contracts with the dealer.

Additional information about auctions can be found in § 2.6.4, *infra*.

Page 43

2.5.6 Floor Plan Financers

Add note 142.1 at end of first sentence of subsection's third paragraph.

142.1 It is also sometimes called an "envelope draft." *See* Flanagan v. Redland Ins. Co., 2003 WL 193080 (Tex. App. Jan. 30, 2003) (unpublished).

Addition to note 143.

143 *Add at end of note*: The exchange of drafts and documents through this system is described in Lawyers Sur. Corp. v. Riverbend Bank, 966 S.W.2d 182 (Tex. App. 1998).

Page 44

Add to text at end of subsection's next-to-last paragraph:

Withdrawals from the reserve account can also lead to pattern evidence, as they may have occurred on other occasions when the dealer bought problem vehicles.

2.5.7 Lessors and Lessees

Add to text at end of subsection:

If the car was previously leased by a consumer who then returned it at the end of the lease, the dealer that accepted it at lease end will have inspected it and recorded its condition at that time. Typically the car is then transported to an auction. The company that transports it will probably have recorded its condition at the time of pickup and at the time of delivery, to protect itself from damage claims. Once the vehicle gets to the auction, the auction will also inspect it.[148.1] All of these records can help establish whether a particular vehicle was damaged and who knew about it.

Daily rental companies are usually self-insurers, so an insurance company will not be involved in repairing damage to a rental car.

148.1 *See* § 2.5.4, *supra*.

Add new subsection to text after § 2.5.7:

2.5.7a Rental Car Companies

When a car was formerly a daily rental car, the car rental company will have records not only of major collisions, but also of dents, scrapes, and other minor damage it repaired. Even if the vehicle never gets in a wreck, the typical rental car suffers more incidents of minor damage than non-rental cars. This record of damage can help persuade a judge or jury that prior use as a rental vehicle is a material fact that the dealer should have disclosed. Other important records to demand are the rental car company's odometer records and its records showing how it disposed of the vehicle, including the identity and date of any auction sale and any records or information disclosed at the time of disposition.

Page 45

2.5.9　Manufacturer Records

Replace note 151 with:

151　*See* National Consumer Law Center, Consumer Law Pleadings No. 2, § 6.1 (Cumulative CD-Rom and Index Guide).

Add to text at end of subsection:

One example of manufacturer records is General Motors's vehicle inquiry system (GMVIS). This system is a nationwide database. The service managers of all General Motors (GM) dealerships have access to the system, and vehicle owners can often obtain this information from the service manager. This record will provide information on warranty repairs made to the vehicle by GM-franchised dealers anywhere in the country. It does not record repairs performed outside of the warranty.

The GMVIS captures the date of repair, the dealership name or code, and the labor operation as to what was replaced. The information is retrievable using the last eight digits of the vehicle identification number. The GMVIS also captures mileage information.

Sometimes mileage information has been entered incorrectly, so the GMVIS report should not always be taken at face value concerning odometer issues. Of course, if warranty service was refused because of a mileage discrepancy, this is a good indication that GM thinks the mileage found in its records involves fraud, and not a mere clerical error.

2.5.11　Information About Whether the Dealer Obtained a Vehicle History Report

Add to text at end of subsection's first paragraph:

Even if the dealer does not get vehicle history reports on all the cars it buys at auction, it may get them on all the vehicles it accepts as trade-ins, because it can use this knowledge to reduce the trade-in allowance.

Add to text at end of subsection's second paragraph:

A telephone deposition of a Carfax employee may be necessary to decipher the entries on the documents. Since the company frequently changes the nature and format of its reports, it is best to describe the desired information in the subpoena, rather than specifying a report by name. It may also be helpful to discuss the information needed with the company's in-house counsel before issuing the subpoena.

Add new subsection to text after § 2.5.11:

2.5.11a　Absence of Information from Vehicle History Report

The information that is *not* included in a vehicle history report can be just as significant as the information that is included. If a person or organization that was involved with the car reported some information to Carfax or a similar service but did not report adverse history that it knew, the consumer should explore that person or organization's motivation. Keeping adverse information out of a publicly-accessible database may enable a downstream seller to conceal it from a consumer, which in turn increases the price the downstream seller is willing to pay to acquire the vehicle.[152.1] By keeping the adverse information out of the public record, the upstream seller facilitates the downstream seller's fraud.

If a dealer argues that it should be exonerated because it ordered a Carfax report but the report did not show the negative history, the consumer's attorney should subpoena the application the dealer filed to become a Carfax certified dealer and the subscription agreement between it and Carfax. These documents reportedly detail the gaps in the Carfax database and prohibit dealers from asserting such a defense.

152.1　*See also* § 2.6.4.3, *infra*.

Page 46

Add to text at end of subsection's second paragraph:

NHTSA also keeps compliance packages on vehicles that were legally imported from other countries, such as Canada. To obtain a copy of a vehicle's compliance package, send a Freedom of Information Act (FOIA) request for it and any photographs of the vehicle to NHTSA, Office of Chief Counsel, 400 7th St., Room 5219, Washington, DC 20950. The request should identify the vehicle's year, make, model, and vehicle identification number.[153.1]

153.1   *See* § 2.1.9.4, *supra.*

Add to text after first sentence of subsection's fourth paragraph:

Notifying these government agencies creates a permanent record that other litigants may be able to obtain. The state attorney general's complaint form may, for example, have a box that the consumer can check to allow the complaint to be released to others. In addition, these agencies are more likely to take action against a fraudulent dealer if they receive a large number of consumer complaints.

Add to text at end of subsection's fifth paragraph:

The licensing department's files may also include information about the dealer's insurance, bond, premises lease, and general financial worthiness.

Add to text after third sentence of subsection's sixth paragraph:

In the alternative, this information may be found in the dealer's annual application for renewal of its license, or in the motor vehicle department's records of temporary tags issued by the dealer.

Add to text at end of subsection's eighth paragraph:

The state may have a statewide police agency that maintains copies of motor vehicle accident reports. Many local police and sheriff departments and state police forces collect accident information in a standard format and submit it to a central repository agency in the state as part of a nationwide program known as the Statewide Traffic Accident Reporting System. To identify the state repository agency, ask a local police traffic unit. The state repository agency may have a policy of refusing to release information to the public. However, even repository agencies that will not release the information themselves may, if provided the VIN, year, and make of the vehicle, provide enough information so that the accident report can be located at a local police department. Summary title services such as Carfax also sometimes include enough information about an accident to identify the municipality where it occurred so that the report may be obtained.

Add to text at end of subsection:

The Secretary of State for the state in which the dealer is incorporated will also have information about the dealer such as the articles of incorporation, annual reports, and fictitious name filings. These filings may reveal the identities of the officers of the corporation, who are sometimes relatives of the dealer.

Page 47

2.5.15 On-Line Resources

Replace second bulleted item after bulleted item containing note 162 with:

• Links to state motor vehicle departments' public records websites: www.pimall.com/nais/dmv.html, www.virtualgumshoe.com, and www.carprice.com/dmvdot;

Page 48

Replace bulleted item before bulleted item containing note 166 with:

• The Florida Attorney General's list of lemon buybacks: http://myfloridalegal.com;
• Lists of New Jersey buybacks, flood damaged vehicles, and salvage vehicles, sorted by vehicle identification number: www.state.nj.us (click on Law and Public Safety, then on Division of Consumer Affairs, then on Lemon Law Unit); and

Replace first bulleted item following bulleted item containing note 166 with:

• National Automobile Dealer Association (NADA): www.nada.org;

Add to text after bulleted item containing note 167:

- www.internetautoguide.com has a search feature for vehicle recalls;
- www.AA1Car.com provides links to technical resources, sources of service bulletins, service manuals, vehicle associations, organizations and manufacturers, and other automotive sites;
- www.pacer.uspci.uscourts.gov is a litigation database which can be searched to find other lawsuits against a company or individual;

Replace bulleted item containing note 168 with:

- www.FinanCenter.com, www.TValue.com, www.auto-loan.com, and www.fairlanecredit.com, all of which offer information about vehicle financing;[168]

168   *Retain as in maid edition.*

2.6 Uncovering a Party's Special Culpability

2.6.2 The Culpability of the Selling Dealer

2.6.2.2 Title Documents Known to the Dealer

Page 50

Add to text after sentence containing note 172:

The mere presence of an insurance company in the title documents gives an automobile dealer reason to know that a vehicle has been involved in an accident.[172.1]

172.1   Lockhart v. Cmty. Auto Plaza, Inc., 695 N.W.2d 335 (Iowa Ct. App. 2004).

Add to text at end of subsection's second-to-last paragraph:

Helpful guidelines for evaluating forgeries may be found at an FBI website.[172.2]

172.2   www.fbi.gov/hq/lab/handbook/intro12.htm.

2.6.2.4 Dealer's Inspection or Duty to Inspect Car

Add to text after sentence containing note 176:

The manufacturer may also have a database with information about the history of its cars which it requires that the dealer check before certifying a car. Some private companies also provide warranties on cars if the dealer gives them a multi-point inspection.

Page 51

Add to text after subsection's sixth paragraph:

If the dealer inspected the vehicle, the consumer should utilize discovery to obtain the original inspection sheet and the names of the technicians who inspected the vehicle. If the dealer inspected the vehicle pursuant to a "certified used car" program, the consumer should also request in discovery the policy and procedures manual issued by whatever entity created the certification program. Some manufacturers' websites include information about their certified used car programs.

2.6.2.6 Dealer Knowledge of Carfax Report; Other Title Searches

Add to text after subsection's fourth paragraph:

If a "Carfax certified" dealer argues that it should be exonerated because it ordered a Carfax report but the report did not show the negative history, the consumer's attorney should subpoena the application the dealer filed to become a Carfax certified dealer and the subscription agreement between it and Carfax. These documents reportedly detail the gaps in the Carfax database and state that the dealer can not represent to anyone that the Carfax report is reliable for showing accident information.

2.6.2.7 Wholesaler or Other Seller's Reputation

Page 52

Add to text after first sentence of subsection's last paragraph:

The companies that provide insurance to auctions may also maintain a list of dealers that have been barred from doing business with member auctions because of rollbacks, selling stolen cars, failing to pay the auction, or other misdeeds.

Add to text at end of subsection:

Companies that provide insurance to auctions give auctions a list (often called a "knock-out" list and usually provided electronically) of dealers who have a history of fraud and should not be allowed to register with the auction. Finding that a dealer, either under its current name or in a prior incarnation, is on a knock-out list can provide some evidence of its reputation and can also lead to pattern evidence.

2.6.2.9 Warnings from Dealer Associations or State Regulators

Add to text at end of subsection:

Dealer association bulletins about changes in the law are useful to dispel dealers' claims that they did not know the law required certain disclosures or records.

Page 53

Add new subsection to text after § 2.6.2.11:

2.6.2.12 Access to Computer Read-Out of True Mileage

It is becoming increasingly common for vehicles to come equipped with computer modules that measure the odometer mileage. Even if the odometer has been tampered with the computer module will reflect the true mileage. Many factory-authorized repair shops now have equipment that can read the odometer reading from this module.

Experts have indicated that the standard industry practice today is *not* to check for true mileage using readily available diagnostic equipment in a dealer's repair shop. For example, when a dealer buys a vehicle from a consumer or at wholesale, it would be easy to verify the mileage before reselling the vehicle to a consumer. The fact that a dealer had the means to easily determine the true mileage and decided not to do so indicates that at a minimum the dealer did not want to know the vehicle's true mileage. Experts have pressed dealers to explain why they do not perform this simple check of the computer read-out, and have not received any reasonable response, other than that the dealers would just as soon not know.

2.6.4 Automobile Auctions

Page 54

2.6.4.1 Dealer-Only Automobile Auctions Described

Add to text after subsection's sixth paragraph:

Many auctions have several different types of sales or have several different lanes of vehicles at the same sale. One lane or sale date may be for "factory sales," generally including a manufacturer's leased vehicles, repurchased rental vehicles, company service vehicles or "executive driven" vehicles, vehicles damaged in transit, and lemon buybacks. The manufacturer may allow only franchised dealers to attend these sales. Other auctions will have a lane or sale date for vehicles coming off lease, another for wrecked or damaged vehicles, and another for vehicles consigned to the auction by dealers. About forty percent of vehicles offered through auction are dealer consignments.

Add to text after subsection's eighth paragraph:

Most auctions are traditional live auctions, with all bidders present in person, but some auction sites allow dealers to participate remotely through a terminal at the dealership. A few auctions even have simulcast centers, where the dealer can sit at a desk and watch simulcast auctions in a half-dozen cities on screens. These dealers will have had less of an opportunity to inspect the car before the auction, but the dealer can pay the auction to inspect the car after the sale, and can also invoke the arbitration procedures after its own inspection. A 2005 industry trade publication reported that all major auction companies and many independent companies use the Internet to remarket consigned vehicles and that, of 10 million used cars and trucks sold at wholesale in 2004, 500,000 to 750,000 were sold on-line.[195.1]

195.1　*Company's Goal: Push More Auctions Online,* Automotive News, Mar. 28, 2005.

2.6.4.2 Salvage Auctions

Add to text after second sentence of subsection's first paragraph:

These auctions may clean up the cars and remove loose parts, but few perform any significant repairs.

Add to text after first sentence of subsection's second paragraph:

In some cases, the insurance company has the insured take the wrecked vehicle directly to the salvage auction, and the insurance adjuster inspects it there. The auction then may take responsibility for obtaining the salvage title.

Add new subsection after § 2.6.4.2:

2.6.4.2a Public Auctions

Unlike dealer-only auctions, public auctions are open to the public. These auctions lack even the minimal self-regulation that the arbitration system provides for dealer-only auctions, by which dealers are able to object to defective vehicles for a few days after the auction. As a result, public auctions tend to attract vehicles with defects that would make them unattractive to dealers.

In investigating a public auction, it is important to find out what its disclosure rules are: what it requires sellers to disclose, what the seller in question actually did disclose to the auction, and what the auction communicated to buyers.

2.6.4.3 Auction Culpability for Car Fraud

Add to text at end of subsection's third paragraph:

Auctions often perform thorough inspections for sellers, particularly when cars are being auctioned off at the end of a lease. Even in the absence of one of these more thorough inspections, the auction will have checked the vehicle identification number of each car and evaluated whether it needs mechanical repairs, body work, or detailing before it is sold.

Records of a car's condition are generated even before it arrives at an auction. Cars that are transported to the auction by rail are inspected beforehand to protect the rail carrier from damage claims. The condition report is usually kept in the vehicle's glove compartment. Similar reports are often prepared when a car is transported by truck. If a car is simply driven to the auction, many auctions require the driver to fill out a condition report. In addition, if a car is damaged while being moved around the auction lot, there will be an in-house accident report and possibly an inspection report.

Add to text after subsection's fourth paragraph:

In addition, an auction's actions, while not deceiving the immediate buyer, may enable that buyer to conceal the car's history from the next buyer. For example, auctions often know because of their own inspections that certain vehicles have frame damage, and this damage is announced before the sale. Yet many auctions, even though they submit other information about the vehicle to a summary title service such as Carfax, do not submit the information that the vehicle was sold with an announcement of frame damage. This omission enables the buyer who purchases at the auction to resell the vehicle without disclosing this crucial information, knowing that the new buyer will not be able to discover it by running a Carfax check. By keeping this information out of the summary title services' databases, the auction enables its buyers to resell vehicles at higher prices, which means that the auction will have more buyers and can command higher prices.

Add to text after fourth sentence of subsection's fifth paragraph:

A yellow light indicates that the vehicle has certain specified defects.

Add to text after seventh sentence of subsection's fifth paragraph:

A representative of the seller may stand next to the auctioneer during the sale to represent the vehicle.

Page 56

Add to text before last sentence of subsection's fifth paragraph:

The invoice the buyer gets from the auction may also show the problems with the car that were announced when it was auctioned. Many auctions audiotape and videotape each sale.

2.6.5 Insurance Companies

Addition to note 202.

202   *Delete Gridley v. State Farm citation.*

Add to text after subsection's second paragraph:

In a dramatic example of this type of practice, State Farm Mutual Automobile Insurance Co. has admitted that it improperly failed to seek salvage titles on tens of thousands of vehicles that were later sold to consumers, and has approached the state attorneys general in an attempt to work out a deal concerning liability. Consumers will be notified that they are driving salvage vehicles, and be offered what critics claim is a very small monetary settlement to give up their claims against State Farm. Some critics also wonder whether the number of vehicles State Farm failed to mark as salvage might number in the hundreds of thousands, and not the tens of thousands State Farm alleges.[202.1]

202.1   Press Release, States Reach Settlement with State Farm Insurance That Will Result in $40 Million to Consumers (Jan. 10, 2005), *available at* www.iowaattorneygeneral.org/latest_news/releases/jan_2005/State_Farm.html.

Page 57

Addition to note 206.

206   *Add after O'Brien citation*: *See also* Brannon v. Munn, 68 P.3d 224 (Okla. Civ. App. 2003) (reversing dismissal of insurer on UDAP claim).

Add to text at end of subsection's second-to-last paragraph:

Helpful guidelines for evaluating forgeries may be found at an FBI website.[208.1]

208.1   www.fbi.gov/hq/lab/handbook/intro12.htm.

2.6.6 Manufacturers

Add to text at end of subsection:

The manufacturer may also be liable if the dealer who defrauded the consumer was acting as its agent.[210.1]

210.1   Owens v. Mitsubishi Motors Sales of Am., Inc., 2004 WL 2433353 (N.D. Ill. Oct. 28, 2004) (manufacturer may be liable for dealer's misrepresentation of mileage).

2.6.7 Secured Creditors in the Chain of Title

Add to text after sentence containing note 211:

A secured creditor is also culpable when it obtains possession of a vehicle because of odometer fraud, but then sells the vehicle again to an auction without disclosing that odometer problem.[211.1]

211.1   *See* Clevenger v. Bolingbrook Chevrolet, Inc., 401 F. Supp. 2d 878 (N.D. Ill. 2005).

2.6.8 Creditor Financing the Sale to the Consumer

Replace note 214 with:

214   16 C.F.R. § 433; *see* National Consumer Law Center, Unfair and Deceptive Acts and Practices § 6.6 (6th ed. 2004 and Supp.).

Replace note 216 with:

216   *See* §§ 9.4.4, 9.7.4, *infra*; National Consumer Law Center, Unfair and Deceptive Acts and Practices § 6.6.3 (6th ed. 2004 and Supp.).

Add new sections to text
after § 2.6.8:

2.6.9 Prior Private Owners

Sometimes a prior consumer owner of a vehicle trades it in to a dealer or sells it privately without disclosing known damage or other problems with it. Some of the laws discussed in this manual do not apply to individual consumers. For example, some state UDAP statutes impose obligations only on companies and individuals that are regularly engage in consumer transactions. Many state motor vehicle laws apply only to dealers, manufacturers, or auctions. On the other hand, common law fraud is an action that applies to anyone, so an individual consumer who knowingly misrepresented or fraudulently concealed a vehicle's history may be liable. In addition, the common law doctrine of mistake may enable the buyer to rescind the transaction.[217] The Odometer Act does apply to a prior private owner,[218] but there is a stricter intent standard for such an individual, as compared to a dealer.[219]

2.7 A Special Case: Cloned and Retagged Vehicles

2.7.1 Introduction

Much of the discussion in this chapter assumes that a vehicle's identification number (VIN) and title belong to that vehicle, and the focus is on using that information to uncover the vehicle's true history. But in an increasing number of cases the VIN itself is phony and, at some point in the car's history, a counterfeit or otherwise bogus title was inserted into the chain of title. The vehicle loses its past identity and assumes a new identity.

This practice is particularly common with stolen vehicles that, instead of being sold for parts, are resold, eventually landing in the hands of an unsuspecting consumer. Over a million cars are stolen in the United States each year, and some significant percentage of these vehicles are not recovered and eventually are sold to unsuspecting consumers. In addition, a growing number of vehicles stolen in Canada and other countries eventually are resold in the United States to consumers unaware of the vehicle's background. But giving a vehicle a new identity is a strategy that will hide not only stolen vehicles, but almost any type of fraud, from lemon laundering to undisclosed salvage history.

Cloning a vehicle occurs when someone replicates a VIN number plate belonging to another vehicle and places that duplicate VIN number plate on the cloned vehicle. One

investigator reports that VIN number plates with the same exact number have been found on as many as twenty different vehicles.

Retagging a vehicle occurs when someone physically takes a VIN number plate from a junked vehicle and uses that plate to replace the VIN number plate on another car. Because the VIN indicates the vehicle's year, make, and model, a careful fraud operator will take the VIN number plate off a junked vehicle that has the same year, make, and model as the retagged vehicle.

When a vehicle is stolen and a new vehicle identification number created, a dealer receiving the stolen vehicle will have to create a new title if the dealer wants to optimize the vehicle's resale price. Because the dealer almost never has the old title, this necessity will require that the dealer, in effect, manufacture a phony title out of thin air. As a result, cloning and retagging will both be accompanied by title fraud.

Cloned and retagged vehicles present unique investigative challenges. Carfax reports or title searches must be looked at with a new level of complexity, because some of the information produced may relate to one vehicle and other information may relate to another, both having the same VIN. Discovering a laundered salvage title may not indicate a true salvage history, but instead the fact that a vehicle was stolen and then given the identity of a salvage vehicle.

These vehicles also present unique avenues for consumers to obtain legal redress. If a dealer can be shown to have participated in or even have knowledge of the change of vehicle identity, the dealer should be subject to both criminal prosecution and, in most states, a civil action for punitive damages. Whether a dealer should be aware of the bogus VIN and title will depend on the sophistication of the cloning and retagging operation, but in many cases there will be clear signs visible to a knowledgeable dealer that either the VIN or the title is bogus.

Even if a dealer had no knowledge of the fraud, showing that a vehicle has a false identity means the consumer has an iron-clad case to have all payments returned from the dealer. A vehicle with a false VIN is subject to law enforcement seizure, and thus has no value to the consumer.[220] Unlike lemon laundering, where actual damages are the difference between the purchase price and what the vehicle would have been worth if its provenance was properly disclosed, in these cases the actual damages are the full purchase price, as the consumer will not be allowed to keep the car.

In addition, because the consumer has a claim for breach of the warranty of title, the consumer need not show mali-

---

217 *See* § 8.3, *infra.*
218 *See* § 4.2.1, *infra.*
219 *See* § 4.8.13, *infra.*

220 *Cf.* Citifinancial v. Messer, 606 S.E.2d 453 (N.C. Ct. App. 2005) (seizure of cloned vehicle).

cious intent, knowledge, reliance, or anything else other than that the title is defective.[221] Nor can the dealer disclaim this warranty by selling the vehicle "as is," because, unlike warranties of merchantability or fitness for a particular purpose, warranties of title can not be disclaimed (except in circumstances not relevant to this discussion). As a result, one of the best ways to get out of an "as is" sale is to find a bogus VIN. The dealer, faced with a potential law enforcement investigation and with no defenses, should immediately give the consumer a full refund. Unfortunately, many vehicles with a false identity are sold by curbstoners and other fly-by-night dealers, so the consumer's legal recourses are severely limited, particularly if the consumer arranged for financing independently of the seller.

This section will outline various ways that both the VINs on a vehicle and the related title documents can be falsified. It will also provide some investigative techniques to uncover and prove the vehicle's false identity.

2.7.2 Falsifying the VIN

The VIN can appear in numerous places on a vehicle, with those locations varying with the make and model. Depending on the sophistication of the fraud operator some, but not all, of those VINs will be replaced with the false VIN. In general, if a vehicle has a particularly high value, one can expect an astonishingly expert job of falsifying most of these VINs. In other cases, the fraud will be obvious to anyone looking for it.

The public/primary VIN plate is usually located on the left side of the dashboard, visible through the windshield, or on the inside of the left windshield pillar. This plate will be a metal plate riveted to the vehicle. Certain vehicles will also have stickers ("mylars") bearing the VIN located on a number of vehicle parts. These vehicles are designated as high theft vehicles[222] by NHTSA and have very visible stickers on twelve components, including the fender, hood, trunk lid, and doors. Domestically produced vehicles will also often have a derivative of the VIN (the last six VIN digits plus three digits signifying the make and manufacturer) stamped on the engine and transmission. Foreign-made vehicles tend to have the full VIN stamped on the firewall. In addition, most vehicles have "secret VINs" stamped in hidden places where only a limited number of law enforcement investigators know to look. Finally, the VIN may be indicated on the car's computer, called the body control module or the electronic control module.

Consequently, there is an enormous range in the degree of sophistication used when falsifying a vehicle's VIN. At one extreme, only the public/primary VIN plate will be crudely replaced by a false plate that bears obvious damage marks. At the other extreme, foreign companies advertise packages on the Internet whereby an individual can order extensive material and instructions on how to falsify a particular vehicle's VIN, for approximately $150. A crook can request a particular VIN number and obtain a corresponding VIN plate and rivets, matching VIN stickers to place at various locations on the vehicle, and even directions detailing how to alter the control module to change the VIN to the new number.

As a result, even if a number of VINs found on a vehicle match with each other, the careful investigator will not assume that the identity is accurate. Only the secret VINs are virtually impossible to counterfeit. VINs stamped on the engine and transmission are also hard to reach and difficult to alter.

2.7.3 Falsifying the Title

Typically a falsified VIN will be accompanied by a falsified title. A thief will not be in possession of the vehicle's title, and the old title will have the true VIN anyway. There are any number of complicated schemes to create a bogus title. One increasingly common approach is to steal blank titles from the state department of motor vehicles (DMV) and then fill them in with fake information. For example, one report found that 1700 blank titles were recently stolen from the Arizona department of motor vehicles.

Another approach is to counterfeit the title. Although title documents often have hidden features that make exact duplication difficult, busy state DMVs will often not notice such discrepancies in the title or will be unfamiliar with these features from another state's titles. These difficulties are heightened if the title document comes from Canada or some other foreign country. The same outfits that supply bogus VIN plates and stickers may even supply the bogus titles.

A more complicated scheme involves taking a legitimate title from one car and switching it to another vehicle. For example, when a vehicle is junked, a fraud operator could take both the VIN and the title from the junked car and use them for another vehicle of the same make, model, and year. A salvage title can easily be laundered and then, as far as the state DMV is concerned, the title is legitimate, and can pass any paperwork inspection. Only if the true VIN is discovered would the scheme unravel.

When the title is either a counterfeit or based on a stolen blank form, the fraud scheme faces another challenge: turning the title in to the state to obtain a new title when the car is sold at retail. Of course this danger is not an issue for a fly-by-night crook who has no interest in keeping the fraud secret after receiving the cash. More commonly, however, the fraud operator will prefer that the identity switch never come to light. The operator may be a dealer wishing to duplicate the scheme for many other vehicles.

---

221 *See* § 8.2.2, *infra.*
222 *See* Appx. B.2, *infra.*

In that case the crook will need to overcome DMV scrutiny of the old title. The DMV may note that it has two titles with the same VIN or it may find an old title being turned in for a new title, when it has no record of ever issuing the old title. Of course, critics frequently complain that DMVs do not perform the most cursory inspection of title requests, so such problems may go unnoticed.

A safer approach for the crook is to transfer titles from state to state. But even that runs risks, as states have increasing access to interstate, electronic databases of titled vehicles. The preferred approach appears to be to transfer a vehicle with a phony identity from country to country. There is a growing trend of sending vehicles back and forth between the United States and Canada, taking advantage of differences in the titling systems and lack of communication between the two countries as to title information. Hundreds of thousands of vehicles from Canada are titled in the United States each year, and there is a suspicion that many of these transfers are fraudulent.

2.7.4 Investigatory Techniques

2.7.4.1 Examining the VIN on the Vehicle

The difficulty of proving and spotting VIN fraud will depend on the sophistication of the fraud operator. Look at the VIN plate that has been replaced. Scratches, warping, and loose rivets are a dead giveaway. Manufacturers also use special rivets, and these should be compared with the rivets used to attach the VIN plate. For example, General Motors cars have a rosette pattern on the VIN plate rivets.

A vehicle identification number also indicates extensive information about the particular vehicle, and discrepancies between what the VIN indicates and the nature of the car itself are a sure sign of fraud. The ninth digit is a check digit, and is mathematically derived from the VIN's other digits. If this check digit is off, then the VIN is counterfeit. The vehicle's country of origin, manufacturer, make, type, year, plant of manufacture, line, series, body type, engine type, and restraint system type are all identified by the VIN. Section 2.2.4.2, *supra*, sets out various ways and services that aid in checking the information provided by the VIN.

The VIN on the plate by the windshield should also be compared with every other VIN sticker or stamp on the vehicle and with any documentation related to the vehicle, either accompanying the vehicle or in the hands of third parties. Inconsistencies are a dead giveaway. In addition, a trained investigator can look for traces left by old VIN stickers when they are removed—the adhesive may leave a cross-hatch effect on the surface.

It is generally easier to replicate stickers with a phony VIN than to change the numbers stamped into the transmission, engine, or firewall. It may take a mechanic to inspect for these latter VINs. A factory-authorized repair facility should have equipment to read the control module to determine if that VIN matches the VIN on the plate. But the fact that it matches does not guarantee that the VIN is accurate.

The only failproof way to check a vehicle's identity is to have a specialized law enforcement officer, or perhaps a retired officer, check for the secret VIN. This highly skilled task may only be performed by certain individuals. Taking a vehicle into a state police office or other state automobile fraud enforcement office will probably result in a qualified individual looking for the secret VIN, as these offices can call in outside experts if they are not able to do the search themselves. Doing so however may lead to confiscation of the vehicle before the consumer is ready to turn the vehicle over. Another approach would be to hire an expert from the ranks of a state's retired auto fraud investigators. If state rules allow, an active investigator may be able to testify on days when the investigator is not working for the state.

2.7.4.2 Checking Title History and Other Paperwork

Ordering a Carfax or other summary vehicle history report will produce much useful information. It may reveal a VIN alert or show other inconsistencies indicating a phony VIN. More commonly, the investigator will have to look carefully through the report for anything suspicious. For example, has the car been titled in more than one state, and is it possible that Carfax is actually reporting on two different cars under the same VIN? What about odometer discrepancies? Has the mileage gone up dramatically from one title to the next or has it gone down—a sure giveaway that something is amiss? Does Carfax or the other service indicate a salvage history, and does a mechanic see no evidence of this history?

Because of the frequency with which vehicles with false VINs are originating from Canada, it is also helpful to use a database with information on Canadian vehicles: www.autofacts.ca. For a discussion of how to identify a vehicle's Canadian origin, see § 2.1.9, *supra*.

The manufacturer's warranty service records may also indicate an unusual sequence of events or inconsistent information. For example, they may show a 30,000 mile check up before a 24,000 mile check up, and in two different states. Do the manufacturer's records indicate a vehicle modification done pursuant to a recall notice, and has that modification been made to the vehicle at issue?

A complete title search can also produce information not available from Carfax, such as the names and addresses of prior owners, and reassignments from consumers to dealers, dealers to dealers, and dealers to consumers. This information may help pinpoint that more than one vehicle is listed under the same VIN. A complete title search may also produce fictitious individuals listed as owners and may lead to information as to when the bogus VIN was placed on the vehicle and what parties were involved in the fraud.

Tracing the title back from a vehicle should be done carefully, because there may be two title trails for the same VIN. What the investigator wants to do is trace back the trail leading to the vehicle with the false VIN. Following this trail back should eventually lead to a dead-end, where there is no evidence of a manufacturer's statement of origin or other title being turned in for the title. The title at the end of that trail should then be the original counterfeit title. Hopefully, an expert examining that title could uncover evidence of the fraud. The reassignments indicated on that title may also lead back to the individuals who either were involved in the fraud or should have had knowledge that a phony vehicle was being transferred to them.

2.8 Another Special Case: Used Cars Sold Without Airbags

As a higher and higher percentage of cars on the road contain air bags, a growing problem is the sale of used vehicles without disclosing that their air bags are missing. One study estimates that four percent of deployed air bags are not replaced, meaning that about 40,000 cars are returned to the road each year without air bags.

Given that a replacement air bag can cost approximately $2000, it is not surprising that unscrupulous buyers of wrecked cars have seen an opportunity to make a higher profit by not replacing the air bag and hiding this fact from the purchaser. It is a simple matter to disconnect the wiring that indicates an air bag malfunction on the dashboard, and it is impossible to tell if an air bag is present without opening up the air bag panel.

Even when a consumer keeps a vehicle after the air bag has deployed, the consumer may fail to replace the air bag because of cost considerations or simple negligence. A dealer taking the car as a trade-in may be told about the missing air bag or may notice an air bag malfunction light, but may not pass this information on to a subsequent purchaser and instead disconnect the malfunction light.

There is also a booming business in stealing air bags. Some experts view air bags as a higher risk target than car stereos, because the air bag may be worth more and car stereos increasingly feature anti-theft devices. A rogue repair shop could steal the air bag and disconnect the air bag malfunction light, and no one would be the wiser. Someone breaking into a car to steal the air bag may leave obvious evidence of the theft, but again the consumer may decide not to replace the air bag. A repair shop can also make a quick profit by telling the consumer the stolen air bag has been replaced when it has not.

When the air bag indicator light shows a malfunction, or when the consumer has any fear that an air bag is missing from a vehicle or that something is fishy about a vehicle, a mechanic can simply pop the panel and inspect for the air bag, replacing the panel upon finding that all is well.

Of course, fraud relating to missing air bags may result in significant punitive damages because of the safety hazards involved. In addition, a number of states have enacted legislation specifically prohibiting the sale of vehicles without all air bags intact, or at least requiring disclosure that they are not. These statutes are examined in § 6.3bS, *infra*.

Chapter 3   Automobile Title Law

3.2 How Automobile Titles Work

Page 59

3.2.2 Titling a New Vehicle

Add to text at end of subsection:

Typically, the existence of an MSO is evidence that the car is still "new," while titling a vehicle indicates that it is "used." But dealers have been known to take back a vehicle after it has been titled, and then request from the manufacturer a replacement MSO, misrepresenting that they have lost the old MSO or that it had to be discarded because of a paperwork mistake. The dealer than sells the vehicle again, using the replacement MSO, and the vehicle then has two titles. Uncovering this practice will prove that a deceptive sale of a used vehicle as new was intentional and may result in an award of punitive damages.

Page 60

3.2.4 Title Transfers to Dealers and Others Purchasing for Resale

Add to text after subsection's third sentence:

In some states a dealer must obtain a new title before it transfers an out-of-state title.

3.3 Transferee Must Sign Title Documents

3.3.1 Importance of the Issue

Page 61

Add to text at end of subsection:

The information available to the consumer signing the existing title document means that a dealer bent on fraud will evade this requirement. One common approach is simply to forge the consumer's signature on the title assignment. The new title will often be sent directly to the lienholder, and the consumer may not see the new title for years, if ever. Moreover, certain important information will be found only on the old title, not on the new title.

The dealer will simply offer to handle all the title issues for the consumer. The dealer will often obtain the consumer's signature on an application for a new title, giving the consumer a copy of that version. The dealer may then place another copy of this version in its files, to show dealer regulators or the Internal Revenue Service. But the dealer will then destroy the original, and instead forge the consumer's signature on another title application, which will be the one it sends to the state department of motor vehicles. This approach is necessary to make sure that the forged signature on the title assignment matches the forged signature on the application for a new title.

A fraudulent dealer who has forged the consumer's signature on the title application may not stop there. When the consumer has paid the sales tax to the dealer (that is, has not cut a separate check made out to the state), the dealer can alter the title application to reduce the sales tax obligation by reducing the sales price or increasing the trade-in value, and pocket the difference.

3.3.5 When Transferee Signature Allowed to Be on Power of Attorney Instead of on Title

Page 65

3.3.5.6 Use of Part A Allowed in Only Two Situations

Addition to note 39.

39 *Add at end of note*: An April 10, 2003 letter from Chief Counsel Jacqueline Glassman, National Highway Traffic Safety Administration, to Lawrence Highbloom, VINtek, Inc., states the opposite of the 1989 Supplementary Information, opining that a secure power of attorney can be used when the state maintains the vehicle title subject to a lien in electronic form and generates a paper title only upon being notified that the lien is satisfied. The letter is reprinted on the CD-Rom accompanying this volume.

Page 66

Add new subsection to text after § 3.3.5.7:

3.3.6 Fallacious Argument That Buyer Can Not Legally Review All Information on the Title

Certain dealers allege that the federal Driver's Privacy Protection Act (DPPA) prohibits car buyers from reviewing all the information on the title, because this statute prohibits release of the names and addresses of prior owners. This claim is certainly false, and one can expect it to be used to hide information on the title that would otherwise uncover a fraudulent transaction.

The argument is clearly fallacious. Section 3.8, *infra*, analyzes the DPPA. In brief, the DPPA allows the state to release title and other motor vehicle information from its files only under enumerated circumstances. The prohibition on release of information applies to a state department of motor vehicles (DMV) and its employees, not to private individuals transferring titles.[49.1] In addition, the Act lists permissible uses for disclosure of information and the buyer of a vehicle's purposes might fall within several of these permissible uses.[49.2] Nor is the dealer someone who is redisclosing information the dealer obtained from the DMV under a permissible use.[49.3] Instead, the dealer obtained the title from the prior owner. The DPPA also prohibits any person from disclosing personal information from a motor vehicle record for any use not permitted by the Act.[49.4] A buyer's review of the title to a vehicle is a use permitted by the Act, and the Act in this section can not be referring to a transferor handing over the title to a vehicle. Instead it only refers to disclosing information obtained from the DMV.

49.1 18 U.S.C. § 2721(a).
49.2 18 U.S.C. § 2721(b).
49.3 18 U.S.C. § 2721(c).
49.4 18 U.S.C. § 2722(a).

3.6 When Must Transfer Be Completed on Title Documents?

Page 68

3.6.1 Introduction

Add to text at end of subsection:

Bear in mind that dealers often finance their purchase of vehicles through floor plan financers. The way floor plan financers operate is that they hold onto a vehicle's title as security that the dealer will repay the loan. Thus, regardless of state law, floor plan financers generally will not hand over a vehicle's title to a dealer until they have been paid. This practice is one of the common reasons why dealers never have possession of the title at the time they sell vehicles to consumers.

3.6.2 Federal Requirements

Replace note 71 with:

71   Ferrari v. Howard, 2002 WL 1500414 (Ohio Ct. App. July 11, 2002).

3.6.3 Explicit State Requirements As to Timing

Addition to note 75.

75   *See also* Werdann v. Mel Hambelton Ford, Inc., 79 P.3d 1081 (Kan. Ct. App. 2003) (transfer void when title not handed over within thirty days).

Page 69

3.6.4 Requirement That Dealer Possess the Title at the Time of Sale

Addition to note 79.

79   *Cf.* N.M. Stat. Ann. § 57-16A-3 (Michie) (effective Jan. 1, 2004) (for sellers who are *not* dealers, title must be in seller's possession at time of sale and made out in the name of the seller).

Add new subsection to text after § 3.6.6:

3.6a Electronic Titling

After a paper title is transferred, when the consumer applies for a new title that title is often mailed directly to the lienholder. A number of states have agreed to send the lienholder an electronic version of the title to be held by the lienholder. When the lien is paid off, the lienholder notifies the state department of motor vehicles, which then issues a paper certificate to the consumer. From the consumer's perspective, nothing has changed from the traditional paper title system.

No state has applied to the National Highway Traffic Safety Administration (NHTSA) for permission to adopt, and no state has adopted, a truly electronic titling system whereby the title remains electronic, and an electronic procedure is used to initiate the transfer of ownership. It is unlikely that any such system would comply with existing federal requirements. A state may petition NHTSA for approval of an alternative system,[83.1] but no state has done so.

83.1   *See* 49 C.F.R. § 580.11.

3.8 Privacy of Title Information

3.8.1 The Driver's Privacy Protection Act

Page 70

Add to text at end of subsection:

Those requesting information must be careful to have a proper basis for the request. The individual to whom the information pertains can bring a federal court action against any person who knowingly obtains, discloses, or uses personal information from a motor vehicle record for a purpose not permitted under the DPPA.[87.1] The individual can seek actual damages, but not less than liquidated damages in the amount of $2500.[87.2] To recover statutory damages, no actual damages need be proved.[87.3] The wronged individual can also seek punitive damages for willful or reckless disregard of the law, reasonable attorney fees, and preliminary or equitable relief as appropriate.[87.4]

87.1   18 U.S.C. § 2724(a).
87.2   18 U.S.C. § 2724(b).
87.3   Kehoe v. Fid. Fed. Bank & Trust, 421 F.3d 1209 (11th Cir. 2005).
87.4   18 U.S.C. § 2724(b).

3.8.2 DPPA Allows DMV to Release Names and Addresses in Selected Circumstances

Add to text after sentence containing note 89:

One federal court has explained that the litigation exception applies to information when there is a reasonable likelihood that the decision maker would find the information useful in the course of the proceeding.[89.1] The investigation in anticipation of litigation exception is applicable when 1) there is an actual investigation, 2) at the time of the investigation litigation appeared likely, and 3) the information obtained would be of use in the litigation, as described in the preceding sentence.[89.2]

> 89.1 Pichler v. UNITE, 339 F. Supp. 2d 665 (E.D. Pa. 2004).
> 89.2 *Id.*

Add to text at end of subsection's third paragraph:

Case law appears to allow a reseller approved by the state to obtain DMV information without a permissible purpose, as long as it forwards the information to individuals only when those individuals have permissible uses.[90.1]

> 90.1 *See* Russell v. Choicepoint Services, Inc., 302 F. Supp. 2d 654 (E.D. La. 2004).

3.9 Remedies for Title Violations

Page 71

3.9.1 Scope of This Section

Addition to note 103.

> 103 *Replace NCLC UDAP citation with*: National Consumer Law Center, Unfair and Deceptive Acts and Practices (6th ed. 2004 and Supp.) (regarding remedies in a yo-yo or spot-delivery sales context).

3.9.2 MVICSA Remedies

3.9.2.1 Utility of a MVICSA Claim

Add note 103.1 at end of subsection's first sentence.

> 103.1 At least one court has disputed that the Act should be called the Motor Vehicle Information and Cost Savings Act. *See* Hamilton v. O'Connor Chevrolet, Inc., 2004 WL 1403711 (N.D. Ill. June 23, 2004). The court incorrectly relied on the fact that, in the recodification of transportation legislation, the MVISCA provisions were grouped under a chapter called "Odometers." This placement of course does not change the fact that Congress, in first enacting those provisions, labeled the legislation the Motor Vehicle Information and Cost Savings Act. Moreover, Congress explicitly stated that the recodification was not making any substantive changes and that, if any such changes were found, the meaning of the earlier statute controls. *See* § 4.1.3, *infra.*

Replace note 104 with:

> 104 *See* National Consumer Law Center, Unfair and Deceptive Acts and Practices § 9.2 (6th ed. 2004 and Supp.).

Page 72

3.9.2.2 MVICSA Claim Need Not Relate to Odometer Violation

Addition to note 106.

> 106 *Replace Gourrier citation with*: 115 S.W.3d 570 (Tex. App. 2002); *add*: Owens v. Samkle Auto. Inc., 425 F.3d 1318, (11th Cir. 2005); Tuckish v. Pompano Motor Co., 337 F. Supp. 2d 1313 (S.D. Fla. 2004); *see also* Krogull v. Woodfield Chevrolet, 2004 WL 1429963 (Ill Cir. Ct. June 22, 2004). *But see* Ioffe v. Skokie Motor Sales, Inc., 2005 WL 1592955 (7th Cir. July 7, 2005), *cert. denied* 126 S. Ct. 1432 (2006); Hunter v. Riverside Ford Sales, Inc., 2005 WL 1529541 (E.D. Mich. June 23, 2005); Lewis v. Horace Mann Ins. Co., 410 F. Supp. 2d 640 (N.D. Ohio 2005); Hamilton v. O'Connor Chevrolet, Inc., 2004 WL 1403711 (N.D. Ill. June 23, 2004), *reconsideration denied*, 2005 WL 1189589 (N.D. Ill. Mar. 23, 2005); Locascio v. Imports Unlimited, Inc., 309 F. Supp. 2d 267 (D. Conn. 2004).

Add to text after sentence containing note 106:

As the Eleventh Circuit has stated:

> On its face, this statute's meaning is direct, clear and unambiguous. No language limits the meaning of the clause "with intent to defraud." Absent any such limitation, the statute's meaning is clear—if you violate the Odometer Act, and you do so with the intent to defraud your victim in any respect relating to the Odometer Act or the regulations passed pursuant to it, you are liable. Thus, the statute's plain language does not admit to the district court's limiting construction, which reads words into the statute that do not exist.[106.1]

It further found that:

The identity of former owners, of critical import to the consumer, is also critical to law enforcement, who rely on the chain of title to ascertain the true ownership and mileage of a vehicle. *See* Odometer Disclosure Requirements, 53 Fed. Reg. at 29468–69 ("Congress noted that '[o]ne of the major barriers to decreasing odometer fraud is the lack of evidence or "paper trail" showing incidence of rollbacks[.]' . . . Under [the title disclosure requirements], the integrity of the paper trail has been maintained since the disclosure will be on the title and consumers will be able to see the disclosures and examine the titles for alterations, erasures, or other marks. Furthermore, consumers will learn the names of previous owners that appear on the title.") (quoting H.R. Rep. No. 99-833, at 18 (1986) (committee report for the Truth in Mileage Act of 1986, Pub. L. No. 99-579, 100 Stat. 3309 (1986), which modified the original federal odometer laws in the Motor Vehicle Information and Cost Savings Act of 1972, Pub. L. No. 92-513, §§ 401–13, 86 Stat. 947, 961–63)).

Thus, the success of the complex remedial scheme Congress has created depends on compliance with a multitude of interdependent and seemingly "technical" provisions, such as those Samkle allegedly violated. Violations of these "technical" regulations can defeat the entire remedial scheme-even if they are not committed with the intent to defraud with respect to the vehicle's mileage-by creating gaps in the vehicle's "paper trail" that: (1) thwart investigation of future violations; and (2) make it difficult for future purchasers of a vehicle to spot odometer fraud by preventing them from accurately assessing the vehicle's ownership history.[106.2] An excellent brief supporting the view taken by the Eleventh Circuit is found in a certiorari petition in *Ioffe v. Skokie Motor Sales, Inc.*, written by Public Citizen, and found on their website.[106.3]

106.1 Owens v. Samkle Auto. Inc., 425 F.3d 1318, (11th Cir. 2005).

106.2 *Id.*

106.3 *See* Petition for Writ of Certiorari, *available at* www.citizen.org/litigation/consumer/.

Add note 106.4 after the comma in sentence following sentence containing note 106.

106.4 Of course, the consumer must show some intent to defraud. *See* § 4.8, *infra*. For example, where the dealer provides a separate, accurate odometer statement, but does not provide the title to the consumer, there is no intent to misrepresent the odometer mileage, and the consumer must find some other intent to defraud in the failure to promptly turn over the title. *See* Werdann v. Mel Hambelton Ford, Inc., 79 P.3d 1081 (Kan. Ct. App. 2003).

Add note 107.1 at end of subsection's second paragraph.

107.1 *See* Tuckish v. Pompano Motor Co., 337 F. Supp. 2d 1313 (S.D. Fla. 2004).

Add note 109.1 at end of first sentence of subsection's fifth paragraph.

109.1 At least one court has disputed that the Act should be called the Motor Vehicle Information and Cost Savings Act. *See* Hamilton v. O'Connor Chevrolet, Inc., 2004 WL 1403711 (N.D. Ill. June 23, 2004). The court incorrectly relied on the fact that, in the recodification of transportation legislation, the MVISCA provisions were grouped under a chapter called "Odometers." This placement of course does not change the fact that Congress, in first enacting those provisions, labeled the legislation the Motor Vehicle Information and Cost Savings Act. Moreover, Congress explicitly stated that the recodification was not making any substantive changes and that, if any such changes were found, the meaning of the earlier statute controls. *See* § 4.1.3, *infra*.

Page 73

Add to text at end of subsection:

Another helpful strategy may be to provide some kind of nexus between the violation and odometer mileage. For example, in one case the dealer hid the fact that a car sold as new was previously titled in Canada. The dealer improperly had the consumer sign a power of attorney instead of the actual title, which would have shown the prior ownership. The court found an intent to defraud by hiding the prior Canadian ownership. But the court also noted that the complaint stated that importing a vehicle into the United States required kilometers to be converted to miles on the odometer, and that this changeover presented an opportunity for tampering.[113.1]

113.1 *See* Tuckish v. Pompano Motor Co., 337 F. Supp. 2d 1313 (S.D. Fla. 2004).

3.9.3 Remedies Under the State Motor Vehicle Title Statute

Replace note 114 with:

114   Gourrier v. Joe Myers Motors Inc., 115 S.W.3d 570 (Tex. App. 2002) (no private remedy under Texas law).

Addition to note 115.

115   Werdann v. Mel Hambelton Ford, Inc., 79 P.3d 1081 (Kan. Ct. App. 2003); *see* Chief Eagle v. C & G Auto, 88 P.3d 807 (Kan. Ct. App. 2004); Werdann v. Mel Hambelton Ford, Inc., 79 P.3d 1081 (Kan. Ct. App. 2003); Jackson v. Cannon, 147 S.W.3d 168 (Mo. Ct. App. 2004); *see also* Jackson v. Cannon, 147 S.W.3d 168 (Mo. Ct. App. 2004).

3.9.4 MVICSA and State Motor Vehicle Title Statute Violations As UDAP Violations

Replace NCLC citation in subsection's first paragraph with:

Unfair and Deceptive Acts and Practices Ch. 3 (6th ed. 2004 and Supp.)

Add note 118.1 at end of subsection.

118.1   *See* Locascio v. Imports Unlimited, Inc., 309 F. Supp. 2d 267 (D. Conn. 2004).

Page 74

Add new subsection to text after § 3.9.5:

3.9.6 Securities Fraud

Placing false information on a title is securities fraud. The United States Supreme Court has ruled that titles are securities and that false information placed in a title violates federal criminal statutes that regulate falsely made or forged securities.[121] Consequently title fraud may involve securities fraud under federal or state law, which may provide a private right of action.

121   Moskal v. United States, 498 U.S. 103, 111 S. Ct. 461, 112 L. Ed. 2d 449 (1990).

Compliance with Federal and State Odometer Acts

Page 80

4.4 Repair or Replacement of an Odometer

Add to text at end of section:

Many modern vehicles are also equipped with backup modules that continue to record accurate mileage in the event the odometer on the dashboard fails to operate properly. NHTSA has stated that a repair shop can transfer the mileage reading from the backup module to the dashboard odometer, and will not be required to reset the odometer to zero and place a label on the door frame.[60.1]

60.1   Opinion Letter from Nat'l Highway Traffic Safety Admin. to Erika Jones, Mayer, Brown & Platt (Jan. 31, 2000) (reproduced on the CD-Rom accompanying this volume).

4.6 Disclosure Requirements

4.6.2 Parties Responsible for Making Disclosures

Page 81

4.6.2.1 General

Add to text at end of subsection:

On the other hand, the Act prohibits any person from conspiring to violate the disclosure requirements.[76.1] Consequently even those not responsible for making disclosures are still liable under the Act if they assist in the making of improper disclosures. For example, when an auction fills out the title transfer information for the seller and improperly discloses the mileage, then the auction can be held liable under the Act for statutory and treble damages.

76.1   49 U.S.C. § 32703(4); *see also* § 4.7, *infra.*

4.6.3 Transfers for Which Disclosures Must Be Made

Page 83

4.6.3.1 Transfers Broadly Defined

Addition to note 89.

89   Kennedy v. BMW Fin. Services, N.A., 2003 WL 22305163 (D. Conn. Oct. 3, 2003).

Add to text at end of subsection:

Similarly, if title is never signed over and the transfer is void under state law, one court has found no requirement to make odometer disclosures.[90.1]

90.1   Werdann v. Mel Hambelton Ford, Inc., 79 P.3d 1081 (Kan. Ct. App. 2003).

Page 84

4.6.3.3 Auction Companies As Transferors

Add to text after subsection's first paragraph:

On the other hand, the Act prohibits any person from conspiring to violate the disclosure requirements.[97.1] Consequently even those not responsible for making disclosures are still liable under the Act if they assist in the making of improper disclosures. Thus, if an auction fills out the title transfer information for the seller and improperly discloses the mileage, then the auction can be held liable under the Act for statutory and treble damages.

97.1   49 U.S.C. § 32703(4); *see also* § 4.7, *infra.*

4.6.4 Transfers NHTSA Exempts from Disclosure Requirements

Page 85   **4.6.4.1 General**

Addition to note 104.   104   *See also* Coleman v. Lazy Days RV Ctr., Inc., 2006 WL 889736 (M.D. Fla. Mar. 31, 2006).

Page 86   **4.6.4.3 Can the Transferor Waive the Exemption?**

Addition to note 117.   117   Coleman v. Lazy Days RV Ctr., Inc., 2006 WL 889736 (M.D. Fla. Mar. 31, 2006).

4.6.4.6 Exemptions for Heavy Trucks, Trailers, Mobile Homes, and Government Vehicles

Addition to note 123.   123   *See also* Coleman v. Lazy Days RV Ctr., Inc., 2006 WL 889736 (M.D. Fla. Mar. 31, 2006) (NHTSA exemptions applied to a motor home).

4.6.5 Method of Making Disclosures

Page 89   **4.6.5.4 Use of Separate Disclosure in Transfer of Used Vehicle**

Replace note 145 with: 145   *See* § 8.4.3, *infra*; National Consumer Law Center, Unfair and Deceptive Acts and Practices § 4.2.17 (6th ed. 2004 and Supp.).

4.6.6 Content of Mileage Disclosures

Page 96   **4.6.6.5 When Lessor Transfers Ownership Without First Recovering Possession from the Lessee**

Add to text after subsection's third paragraph:

It is prudent to also review any oral or written information sent to the lessee in conjunction with this disclosure. Lessors have been known to tell the lessee not to check boxes that the odometer is inaccurate because those boxes "do not apply."

Replace subsection's fifth paragraph with:

A trade association of lessors has requested that NHTSA allow the disclosures from the lessee to the lessor to be made electronically. The lessee would be given a secure password and identification number. At the end of the lease, the lessee would go to a website, complete the disclosures, and send them to the lessor electronically. A NHTSA letter has granted this request.[222.1]

222.1   Opinion Letter from Nat'l Highway Traffic Safety Admin. to Edwin Huddleson, II, General Counsel, Am. Auto. Leasing Ass'n (Apr. 25, 2003) (reproduced on the CD-Rom accompanying this volume).

Page 97   **4.6.6.7 When a Used Vehicle Is Assembled from Parts or Restored**

Addition to note 232.   232   Opinion Letter from Nat'l Highway Traffic Safety Admin. to John Kelly, Office of Motor Vehicle Enforcement, Iowa Dep't of Transp., Clearinghouse No. 43,095Q (Oct. 15, 1980) (reproduced on the CD-Rom accompanying this volume). *But see* Adkins v. Crown Auto, Inc., 2005 WL 1278948 (W.D. Va. May 27, 2005) (where sheet metal of another car was used to repair tail end of vehicle, the odometer mileage of the vehicle contributing the sheet metal need not be disclosed).

4.6.7 Non-Mileage Disclosures

Page 99

4.6.7.1 Content of Non-Mileage Disclosures

Add to text at end of subsection's fourth paragraph:

Neither do rubber-stamped signatures or signatures sent by facsimile.[250.1]

> 250.1   Opinion Letter from Nat'l Highway Traffic Safety Admin. to Enoch Whitney, Gen. Counsel, State of Florida Dep't of Highway Safety & Motor Vehicles (June 20, 2003) (reproduced on the CD-Rom accompanying this volume).

Add to text after subsection's sixth paragraph:

An issue which may soon arise is the nature of the signature requirement when a state switches to electronic titling. Because the title will be in electronic form, it will not be practical to have the parties sign the title with pen and ink. NHTSA has been asked its opinion on whether electronic signatures will be permitted, and has responded with a qualified yes, as long as the regulation's requirements are otherwise met. NHTSA has stated that the electronic signature must:

> (1) provide a means to validate and authenticate the signatures of the transferor and transferee; (2) provide a level of security equivalent to that of a disclosure on a secure title document; and (3) be available to the transferee at the time ownership of the motor vehicle is transferred.[253.1]

> 253.1   Opinion Letter from Nat'l Highway Traffic Safety Admin. to Enoch Whitney, Gen. Counsel, State of Florida Dep't of Highway Safety & Motor Vehicles (June 20, 2003) (reproduced on the CD-Rom accompanying this volume); Opinion Letter from Nat'l Highway Traffic Safety Admin. to Ab Quillian, Comm'r, Virginia Dep't of Motor Vehicles (Apr. 2, 2002) (reproduced on the CD-Rom accompanying this volume).

4.8 The Intent Requirement

Page 102

4.8.2 Need Intent Be Proven Under State Odometer Statutes?

Add to text at end of subsection's first paragraph:

Even a clerical error involving a *de minimis* mileage discrepancy gives rise to liability.[295.1]

> 295.1   Hubbard v. Bob McDorman Chevrolet, 662 N.E.2d 1102 (Ohio Ct. App. 1995); Rubin v. Gallery Auto Sales, 1997 WL 1068459 (Ohio Ct. Com. Pl. June 9, 1997).

Page 103

4.8.3 General Standards Concerning Proof of Intent

Addition to notes 305, 308.

> 305   Harris v. Jamaica Auto Repair, Inc., 2005 WL 1861730 (E.D.N.Y. Aug. 1, 2005); Daluz v. Acme Auto Body & Sales, Inc., 814 F. Supp. 242 (D. Conn. 1992).

> 308   *Add to Nigh citation*: rev'd on other grounds, 125 S. Ct. 460 (2004).

Add to text at end of subsection:

Consumers will need to be very careful in proving intent to defraud when the dealer failed to make mileage disclosures on the title, but has made an odometer disclosure on a separate document and that disclosure is accurate. In general courts will find no intent to defraud,[308.1] unless the consumer can show special circumstances.

> 308.1   Werdann v. Mel Hambelton Ford, Inc., 79 P.3d 1081 (Kan. Ct. App. 2003).

Page 105

4.8.6 Intent Inferred from Failure to Disclose or Dealer's Circumvention of Disclosure Requirement

Add to text after sentence containing note 326:

Similarly, intent to defraud can be inferred from the dealer forging the consumer's signature on the title and not disclosing that the title stated "not actual mileage."[326.1] Altering the odometer disclosure after it is provided to the consumer, so that the later disclosure is accurate, is evidence that the dealer knew of the problem with the initial disclosure, and shows intent.[326.2]

> 326.1   Barrett v. Brian Bemis Auto World, 2006 WL 140543 (N.D. Ill. Jan. 17, 2006).
> 326.2   Small v. Savannah Int'l Motors, Inc., 2005 WL 1863407 (Ga. Ct. App. Aug. 8, 2005).

Page 106

4.8.8 Intent Inferred from Dealer's Failure to Investigate

Addition to note 339.

339   *See also* Harris v. Jamaica Auto Repair, Inc., 2005 WL 1861730 (E.D.N.Y. Aug. 1, 2005).

Add to text at end of subsection:

One court has found that the fact that a vehicle was imported from Canada is not enough to require the dealer to pursue a more extensive investigation of the accuracy of a vehicle's odometer.[340.1]

Dealers may also argue that their employees may have an intent to violate the Act, but the dealers themselves do not. But their culpability can be shown from their gross negligence, in their failure to provide oversight or supervision of their agents.[340.2]

340.1   Nelson v. Cowles Ford, Inc., 2003 WL 22293597 (4th Cir. Oct. 7, 2003).
340.2   *See* Westside Investments, Inc. v. Rabizadeh, 2004 WL 1045923 (Cal. Ct. App. May 10, 2004).

4.8.10 When Dealer Makes Same "Clerical Error"

Add to text at the end of the subsection:

A court has also questioned why a clerical error on the title held by the dealer for a number of months was never found and corrected.[342.1]

342.1   Vang v. Reda Auto Port, 2005 WL 2304792 (N.D. Ill. Sept. 20, 2005).

Page 108

4.8.11 Dealer's Correction May Show No Fraudulent Intent

Add to text at end of subsection:

On the other hand, after a consumer's attorney writes a demand letter alleging Odometer Act violations, the defendant's offer to settle the matter is not evidence of the defendant's lack of intent, and is not admissible under the Federal Rules of Evidence.[346.1]

346.1   Clevenger v. Bolingbrook Chevrolet, Inc., 401 F. Supp. 2d 878 (N.D. Ill. 2005).

Page 109

4.8.13 Courts Are Less Likely to Infer a Consumer's Intent to Defraud

Add to text after sentence containing note 357:

In a surprising number of cases, after a dealer is sued by a buyer for odometer fraud, the dealer turns around and demands payment from the consumer who traded in that vehicle to the dealer. Often the dealer knew of the odometer discrepancy when it bought the vehicle, and the consumer trading in the vehicle had no intent to deceive the dealer. The dealer, though, who controls all the paperwork in the transaction, makes it appear that the dealer is the innocent victim and that the consumer trading in the vehicle was at fault. It may require investigation and looking behind the paperwork to uncover the true facts.

Chapter 5   Remedies for Federal and State Odometer Act Violations

5.4 Statute of Limitations

Page 114

5.4.1 The Two-Year Rule Under the Federal Act

Addition to notes 40, 41.

40   Edmonds v. Newman Chrysler, Inc., 2005 WL 293493 (D. Conn. Feb. 4, 2005); Small v. Savannah Int'l Motors, Inc., 2005 WL 1863407 (Ga. Ct. App. Aug. 8, 2005).

Page 115

41   *See* Edmonds v. Newman Chrysler, Inc., 2005 WL 293493 (D. Conn. Feb. 4, 2005).

5.4.2 Statute of Limitations Under State Odometer Acts

Replace note 49 with:

49   *See* National Consumer Law Center, Unfair and Deceptive Acts and Practices § 7.3 (6th ed. 2004 and Supp.).

5.4.3 Use of Counterclaim or Recoupment When Statute of Limitations Has Run

Addition to note 50.

50   *Replace NCLC Truth in Lending citation with*: National Consumer Law Center, Truth in Lending § 7.2.5 (5th ed. 2003 and Supp.); *replace NCLC UDAP citation with*: National Consumer Law Center, Unfair and Deceptive Acts and Practices § 7.3.5 (6th ed. 2004 and Supp.).

Replace note 51 with:

51   *See* § 9.4.4, infra; *see also* National Consumer Law Center, Unfair and Deceptive Acts and Practices § 6.6 (6th ed. 2004 and Supp.).

5.6 Choosing Federal or State Act Claims; Impact on Choice of Federal Versus State Court

Page 117

5.6.2 Staying in State Forum When Federal Act Claim Is Preferred

Replace note 64 with:

64   *See* § 9.4.4, *infra. See generally* National Consumer Law Center, Unfair and Deceptive Acts and Practices § 6.6 (6th ed. 2004 and Supp.).

Addition to note 65.

65   *Replace NCLC citation with*: National Consumer Law Center, Unfair and Deceptive Acts and Practices § 6.6.3.4.3 (6th ed. 2004 and Supp.).

Page 118

5.6.3 Benefits of Adding State Odometer Claim to Federal Act Claim

Replace note 68 with:

68   *See* National Consumer Law Center, Unfair and Deceptive Acts and Practices § 7.3 (6th ed. 2004 and Supp.).

5.7 Drafting the Complaint

Addition to notes 78, 79.

78   *Add to Nigh citation*: rev'd on other grounds, 125 S. Ct. 460 (2004).
79   *Add to Nigh citation*: rev'd on other grounds, 125 S. Ct. 460 (2004).

5.8 Private Remedies

5.8.1 Treble Damages

Page 119

5.8.1.1 General

Addition to note 82.

82   *See also* Roberts v. Korn, 2006 WL 509103 (D. Kan. Mar. 1, 2006).

Page 120

5.8.1.2 Diminished Value of the Vehicle

Add to text after subsection's third paragraph:

One expert has indicated that diminution in value in most cases will be forty to fifty percent of fair market value.[88.1] Dealers may refuse to accept the vehicle as a trade-in. Automobile financers may refuse to lend money on a not-actual-mileage vehicle. Extended service contract companies may not provide coverage for not-actual-mileage vehicles. Most manufacturers will not honor a warranty claim on a not actual mileage vehicle, which is increasingly becoming an issue as manufacturer warranties cover more years and miles. Insurance companies will not pay out full value on a total loss settlement for such vehicles, as well. *Ad valorem* taxes on the vehicle may be higher than appropriate because the state uses a low mileage assumption.

88.1   Declaration of Richard Diklich, Auto. Technical Support Services, Liberty, Mo. *See also* Declaration of Robert L. Eppes, United States Attorneys' Manual, tit. 4, No. 175, Eppes Declaration, *available at* www.usdoj.gov/usao/eousa/foia_reading_room/usam/title4/civ00000.htm.

Page 122

5.8.1.7 Repair Costs and Substitute Transportation Expenses

Addition to notes 102, 103.

102   *See also* Castillo v. Autokirey, Inc., 379 F.3d 4 (1st Cir. 2004).
103   *See also* Castillo v. Autokirey, Inc., 379 F.3d 4 (1st Cir. 2004).

Page 123

5.8.1.9 Other Consequential Damages

Addition to notes 112, 113.

112   Castillo v. Autokirey, Inc., 379 F.3d 4 (1st Cir. 2004).
113   *See also* Castillo v. Autokirey, Inc., 379 F.3d 4 (1st Cir. 2004) (finding non-economic damages award excessive, but seeming to accept a lower amount of non-economic damages).

5.8.1.10 Pre-Judgment Interest

Addition to note 115.

115   Roberts v. Korn, 2006 WL 509103 (D. Kan. Mar. 1, 2006).

5.8.2 $1500 Statutory Damages Awards Under the Federal Act

5.8.2.1 General

Add to text at end of subsection:

Nor does the consumer have to prove reliance. Similarly, it is no defense if the odometer's mileage in plain sight is correct, if the disclosure is inaccurate, and the requisite intent to defraud is proven.[118.1]

118.1   Buechin v. Ogden Chrysler-Plymouth, Inc., 511 N.E.2d 1330 (Ill. App. Ct. 1987).

5.8.2.2 Statutory Damages Awarded Against Each of Multiple Defendants

Add to text after sentence containing note 123:

At least one case has held that each defendant's liability for all damages is separate and individual, not joint and several. Thus the amount paid in settlement by certain defendants is not set off against the liability for actual and treble damages of those remaining in the lawsuit.[123.1]

123.1   Roberts v. Korn, 2006 WL 509103 (D. Kan. Mar. 1, 2006).

5.8.4 Attorney Fees

Addition to notes 139, 143, 148, 154.

139   *Replace Williams citation with*: Williams v. Fin. Plaza, Inc., 78 S.W.3d 175 (Mo. Ct. App. 2002).

143   *Replace Williams citation with*: Williams v. Fin. Plaza, Inc., 78 S.W.3d 175 (Mo. Ct. App. 2002).

148   *Replace NCLC Truth in Lending citation with*: National Consumer Law Center, Truth in Lending § 8.9 (5th ed. 2003 and Supp.).

154   *Eighth Circuit*: Roberts v. Korn, 2006 WL 509103 (D. Kan. Mar. 1, 2006) ($135,000 in attorney fees; $275 an hour for lead counsel).

Chapter 6

Other Statutes Specifically Relating to Automobile Fraud

6.1 Introduction

Violation of a motor vehicle statute may also be negligence per se.[0.1] An Ohio decision defines negligence per se as failure of a person to observe a special duty imposed by a statute for the protection of others.[0.2] The plaintiff must also show proximate cause and damages.[0.3] Applying these standards, the court held that a consumer buyer could assert a negligence per se claim against an insurer that violated the applicable salvage title statute.

0.1 Lewis v. Horace Mann Ins. Co., 2005 WL 3962818 (N.D. Ohio Aug. 23, 2005) (violation of state salvage title law or state odometer law is negligence per se, but only salvage title claim survives summary judgment); Werremeyer v. K.C. Auto Salvage Co., 2003 WL 21487311 (Mo. Ct. App. June 30, 2003), *aff'd in relevant part, rev'd in part on other grounds*, 134 S.W.3d 633 (Mo. 2004) (reversing denial of prejudgment interest but affirming award in all other respects). *See also* Elder v. Allstate Ins. Co., 341 F. Supp. 2d 1095 (D. Minn. 2004) (elements of negligence per se claim are same as negligence, but reasonable person standard is supplanted by standard of care established by statute; plaintiff must show, *inter alia*, that harm suffered was type statute intended to prevent; not shown here).

0.2 Lewis v. Horace Mann Ins. Co., 2005 WL 3962818 (N.D. Ohio Aug. 23, 2005).

0.3 *Id.*

6.2 Statutes Dealing with Disclosure of Vehicle's Prior Physical Damage

6.2.1 State Salvage Vehicle Statutes

6.2.1.2 Constitutionality

An intermediate appellate court in Michigan upheld the state requirement that "distressed" vehicles be issued salvage certificates against a challenge that the definition was unconstitutionally vague.[5.1]

5.1 Royal Auto Parts v. State, 324 N.W.2d 607 (Mich. Ct. App. 1982).

6.2.1.3 Persons Covered

An insurer may be liable for violation of a salvage title law even when it does not deal directly with the consumer, but sells the vehicle to a dealer who then sells it to a consumer. By violating the salvage title law, the insurer enables the dealer to sell the car without disclosing its history.[6.1]

6.1 Lewis v. Horace Mann Ins. Co., 2005 WL 3962818 (N.D. Ohio Aug. 23, 2005).

6.2.1.4 Definition of Salvage Vehicle

Add to text after sentence following sentence containing note 9:

Sometimes a repair shop inspecting a wrecked vehicle will prepare an estimate with "open items," meaning that if additional problems are discovered once the work begins the repair cost will be higher. In such a case, the estimate may not be an accurate measure of the likely repair costs.

Add to text after sentence containing note 10:

A decision from Ohio holds that sales tax is not to be included in the calculation of the vehicle's pre-accident value.[10.1] For example, the statute may specify the retail cost of repair,[10.2] which means that any repair discount negotiated by the insurance company must be disregarded.

The California statute defines a "total loss salvage vehicle" as one that has been damaged to the extent that the owner considers the vehicle uneconomical to repair. A California court held that the reference to the owner's subjective belief was intended only to identify which person or entity had to make the objective determination of whether the cost to repair the vehicle exceeded its predamage retail value.[10.3]

> 10.1   Lewis v. Horace Mann Ins. Co., 2005 WL 3962818 (N.D. Ohio Aug. 23, 2005).
> 10.2   *See* Stone v. Clifford Chrysler-Plymouth, Inc., 775 N.E.2d 92 (Ill. App. Ct. 2002) (question of fact whether repair cost exceeded six percent of manufacturer's suggested retail price, when statute specified actual retail repair cost).
> 10.3   Martinez v. Enterprise Rent-A-Car Co., 119 Cal. App. 4th 46, 13 Cal. Rptr. 3d 857 (2004).

6.2.1.5 Requirement That Title Be Exchanged for Salvage Certificate

Replace "self-insurers" in sentence containing note 13 with:

self-insurers, other owners,

Addition to note 13.

> 13   *But see* Martinez v. Enterprise Rent-A-Car Co., 119 Cal. App. 4th 46, 13 Cal. Rptr. 3d 857 (2004) (requirement does not apply when one dealer sells to another dealer).

6.2.1.6 Titling, Resale, and Disclosure

Page 133

Addition to note 20.

> 20   *Replace parenthetical after citation to Conn. Gen. Stat. § 42-225 with*: (must disclose whether title stamped "totalled," "salvage," or comparable designation, or vehicle has been declared constructive total loss). *Add:* S.D. Codified Laws § 32-3-51.18 (Michie) (salvage vehicle must display sticker, decal, or notice that discloses the damage); *see also* Freeman v. A & J Auto MN, Inc., 2003 WL 22136807 (Minn. Ct. App. Sept. 16, 2003) (unpublished) (no duty of disclosure when buyer failed to prove seller knew vehicle had sustained damage in excess of seventy percent of value).

Page 134

Replace note 24 with:

> 24   *See* Locascio v. Imports Unlimited, Inc., 309 F. Supp. 2d 267 (D. Conn. 2004); § 8.4.6, *infra*.

Add new subsection to text after § 6.2.1.7:

6.2.1.7a State Vehicle Identification Number Laws

State vehicle identification number (VIN) laws should also be consulted in cases involving the sale of salvage vehicles.[28.1] These laws prohibit alteration, removal, falsification, or defacement of VINs. They also may prohibit knowing sale of a vehicle with a VIN discrepancy.[28.2] State VIN laws typically require a legitimate VIN before the vehicle can be titled or registered, and allow the police to seize any vehicle that has a VIN discrepancy.

VIN discrepancies often mean that a salvage vehicle was rebuilt with parts from stolen vehicles or is a "clipped" vehicle composed of the halves of two different vehicles welded together. Or it may mean that the vehicle is a cloned or retagged vehicle,[28.3] or a thief may have altered the VIN to conceal the fact that the vehicle is stolen. The VIN discrepancy will give rise to a claim for breach of warranty of title.[28.4] It may also lead to express and implied warranty claims because a vehicle with VIN discrepancies will not pass without objection in the trade and probably fails to conform to the contract description.[28.5] As most VIN discrepancies will be apparent to a dealer, their existence can also help establish the *scienter* required for a fraud claim[28.6] or the deception required for a UDAP claim.[28.7] One decision holds that selling a car with an altered VIN, in violation of state law, is negligence per se even if the seller is unaware of the altered VIN.[28.8]

28.1 *See* § 2.2.4, *supra* (significance of VINs and how to check them).

28.2 *See, e.g.,* Werremeyer v. K.C. Auto Salvage Co., 134 S.W.3d 633 (Mo. 2004) (upholding damage award based on dealer's sale of vehicle with altered VIN; sale need not be knowing).

28.3 *See* § 2.7, *supra.*

28.4 *See* § 8.2.2, *infra.*

28.5 *See* Terrell v. R & A Mfg. Partners, 835 So. 2d 216 (Ala. Civ. App. 2002) (seller breached express warranty when contract was for 2000 vehicle but VIN was for 1999 vehicle). *See generally* §§ 8.2.3, 8.2.4, *infra.*

28.6 *See* Mobile Dodge, Inc. v. Alford, 487 So. 2d 866 (Ala. 1986); Regency Nissan, Inc. v. Taylor, 391 S.E.2d 467 (Ga. Ct. App. 1990); Bill Spreen Toyota, Inc. v. Jenquin, 294 S.E.2d 533 (Ga. Ct. App. 1982).

28.7 *See* Ramirez v. C.L.A.S., Inc., 2000 WL 46119 (Mass. App. Ct. Jan. 13, 2000); Whittenberger v. Tom O'Brien Nissan, Inc., 1995 WL 809835 (Mass. Super. Ct. Jan. 27, 1995), *as amended by* 1995 WL 809484 (Mass. Super. Ct. Mar. 16, 1995). *See generally* § 8.4, *infra.*

28.8 Werremeyer v. K.C. Auto Salvage Co., 2003 WL 21487311 (Mo. Ct. App. June 30, 2003), *aff'd in relevant part, rev'd in part on other grounds,* 134 S.W.3d 633 (Mo. 2004).

Page 135

6.2.1.9 Remedies

Addition to notes 33–35.

33 Locascio v. Imports Unlimited, Inc., 309 F. Supp. 2d 267, 271–72 (D. Conn. 2004) (violation of statute requiring buyer to be given certificate of title, which would have revealed rebuilt brand, is UDAP violation); Freeman v. A & J Auto MN, Inc., 2003 WL 22136807 (Minn. Ct. App. Sept. 16, 2003) (unpublished) (remote prior owners can be held liable under UDAP statute for placing wrecked car in stream of commerce, without obtaining salvage title as required by law).

34 Utah Code Ann. § 41-3-702(4) (affording private cause of action to purchaser for $1000 or treble damages plus attorney fees and costs if dealer violates certain motor vehicle laws, including those prohibiting sale of salvage vehicle without disclosure).

35 Del. Code Ann. tit. 21, § 6909(d) (purchaser has right to rescind contract if dealer fails to disclose in writing that title has been branded reconstructed, flood damaged, salvage, or as former taxi); S.D. Codified Laws § 32-3-51.18 (Michie).

Add to text after sentence containing note 36:

Under Georgia statute, any person injured by a used vehicle dealer's violation of the laws regarding titling and inspection of wrecked or salvage motor vehicles has a private cause of action for actual, consequential, and punitive damages, plus costs and attorney fees.[36.1]

36.1 Ga. Code Ann. §§ 43-47-15, 43-47-21.

6.2.2 Used Car Damage Disclosure Statutes

Page 136

6.2.2.2 Requirements and Interpretations

Add to text at beginning of subsection:

In Colorado, it is a deceptive trade practice for a person, in the course of the person's business, vocation, or occupation, to fail to disclose in writing, prior to sale, that a motor vehicle has sustained material damage at any one time from any one incident.[49.1] The statute does not define "material damage" or make any distinction between new and used vehicles. This is part of the state UDAP statute, so UDAP remedies are available.

49.1 Colo. Rev. Stat. § 6-1-708(b).

Replace first two sentences of subsection's third paragraph with:

The former version of the Iowa statute required disclosure of damage costing more than $6000 to repair that was caused by fire, vandalism, collision, water, falling objects, submersion in water, or flood. In 2004 the statute was amended to require only that the transferor disclose whether the vehicle was damaged to the extent that it was a wrecked or salvage vehicle and whether any prior owner had made such a disclosure.[54]

54 Iowa Code § 321.69.

Replace sentence following sentence containing note 55 with:

Disclosure is not required for new vehicles with mileage of 1000 miles or less that have not sustained $6000 in damage, vehicles with certain salvage designations, motor trucks and truck tractors with a gross vehicle weight of 16,000 lbs. or more, vehicles more than seven model years old, motorcycles, motorized bicycles, and special mobile equipment.

Page 137

Addition to note 60.	60 *Add at end of note*: By virtue of a 2003 statutory amendment, the dealer is excused from obtaining this information if it buys the car at an out-of-state dealer-only auction from an out-of-state seller, and in that case the dealer is to disclose to the buyer that the vehicle was acquired at an out-of-state auction and that historical information regarding mechanical defects and substantial damage is not available.
Add note 61.1 to end of sentence preceding sentence containing note 62.	61.1 Me. Rev. Stat. Ann. tit. 10, § 1477. *See* Tanguay v. Seacoast Tractor Sales, Inc., 494 A.2d 1364 (Me. 1985) (affirming award of attorney fees; company that sold at least 12 vehicles over 20 years was "dealer" subject to the statute).

Add to text at end of subsection's sixth paragraph:

A trial court has held that compliance with the disclosure rule immunizes the dealer from liability under one of Maine's UDAP statutes, but not under the other one.[62.1]

62.1   Laing v. Clair Car Connection, 2003 WL 1669624 (Me. Super. Ct. Jan. 29, 2003).

Addition to note 73.

73   *Delete Blankenship opinion. Add*: Blankenship v. Town & Country Ford, Inc., 622 S.E.2d 638 (N.C. Ct. App. 2005) (upholding award of treble damages and attorney fees, but plaintiffs cannot recover treble damages on both UDAP and damage disclosure law claims).

Page 138

Replace "transfer, or trade-in" in sentence containing note 81 with:

transfer, trade-in, or titling

Replace "$3000" in sentence containing note 81 with:

$5000

Add to text after sentence containing note 81:

If the vehicle has incurred damages more than once, only those damages that occurred at one time are considered in determining whether the damages exceed the threshold.

Replace "nine model years old" in sentence following sentence containing note 81 with:

six model years old or weighing more than 16,000 lbs.

Replace note 82 with:

82   Wis. Admin. Code Trans. § 139.04(6).

Addition to note 83.

83   *Replace Wis. Admin. Code citation with*: Wis. Admin. Code Trans. § 139.04(6)(a)(1); *add at end of note*: Wis. Admin. Code Trans. § 139.04(6)(a)(2), (3).

Replace notes 84, 85 with:

84   Wis. Admin. Code Trans. § 139.04(4).
85   Wis. Admin. Code Trans. § 139.04(5).

6.2.3 New Car Damage Disclosure Statutes

Page 139

6.2.3.2 Threshold Amounts of Damage Requiring Disclosure

Addition to note 92.

92   *See also* Jeter v. M&M Dodge, 634 So. 2d 1383 (La. Ct. App. 1994) (dealer violated damage disclosure statute even though it claimed damage was less than 6%, where expert testified that damages actually cost more than 6% to repair).

Page 140

6.2.3.5 Actual Knowledge Precondition

Addition to note 101.

101   Hart v. Boehmer Chevrolet Sales, Inc., 337 Ill. App. 3d 742, 787 N.E.2d 350 (2003).

Replace second sentence of subsection's first paragraph with:	Some statutes and courts authorize revocation or rescission of the sale in some circumstances.[101.1]

101.1 *See, e.g.,* Tesch v. Best Motors, Inc., 539 N.W.2d 338 (Wis. Ct. App. 1995) (table, text at 1995 WL 478413) (rescission is proper remedy for dealer's failure to disclose damage to new vehicle purchased).

6.2.3.6 Remedies

Addition to note 104.	104 *Replace "N.H. Rev. Stat. Ann. § 357-C:16" with*: N.H. Rev. Stat. Ann. § 357-C:15. *Replace "Ohio Rev. Code Ann. 4517.99(A)" with*: Ohio Rev. Code Ann. 4517.99.

Replace notes 107, 108 with:	107 *See* Hart v. Boehmer Chevrolet Sales, Inc., 337 Ill. App. 3d 742, 787 N.E.2d 350 (2003). *See generally* National Consumer Law Center, Unfair and Deceptive Acts and Practices § 3.2.7 (6th ed. 2004 and Supp.).
	108 Pa. Stat. Ann. tit. 73, § 1970.8 (West). *See also* Colo. Rev. Stat. § 6-1-708 (UDAP statute requiring damage disclosure); Fla. Stat. Ann. § 501.976(19) (West) (damage disclosure provision of UDAP statute); Ohio Admin. Code § 109:4-3-16(B)(14) (UDAP regulation requiring damage disclosure).

6.2.3.7 Statutes Shield Dealers from Consumer Remedies When Threshold Damage Amount Is Not Reached

Addition to notes 109, 111.	109 Ark. Code Ann. § 45.25.510(b).
	111 *See* Check v. Clifford Chrysler-Plymouth, 342 Ill. App. 3d 150, 794 N.E.2d 829 (2003) (jury's verdicts finding that dealer committed fraud but did not violate damage disclosure law are irreconcilable, so new trial must be held on both claims, but warranty verdict for plaintiff stands).

Replace note 113 with:	113 *See* § 8.4, *infra*; National Consumer Law Center, Unfair and Deceptive Acts and Practices § 5.4.7.4 (6th ed. 2004 and Supp.).

Add to text after sentence containing note 114:	Dealers may also be liable under UDAP statutes for acts other than nondisclosure of the damage, such as performing poor repairs, selling a repaired car as new without inspecting the repair work, or making affirmative misrepresentations about the repairs.[114.1]

114.1 *See, e.g.,* Check v. Clifford Chrysler-Plymouth, 342 Ill. App. 3d 150, 794 N.E.2d 829 (2003).

Page 141

Add to text at end of subsection:	If the statute is silent about warranty claims, it should be construed to preserve them. As warranty claims are not based on misrepresentation, they are distinct from damage disclosure, fraud, and deception claims.[115.1]

115.1 *See* Check v. Clifford Chrysler-Plymouth, 342 Ill. App. 3d 150, 794 N.E.2d 829 (2003) (upholding warranty verdict for buyer even though jury found no violation of damage disclosure law).

6.2.4 Dealer Responsibility to Inspect Vehicles

Addition to note 124.	124 *See also* Mo. Rev. Stat. § 407.020 (emissions inspection).

Add to text after sentence containing note 127:	New Jersey prohibits retail sale of a used passenger motor vehicle to be registered in the state unless it meets state inspection standards.[127.1] If the vehicle fails inspection because of defects that are not the fault of the buyer, the seller must either refund the purchase price or make the necessary repairs at no cost to the buyer.[127.2] These duties can only be waived by a separately signed waiver.[127.3]

127.1 N.J. Stat. Ann. § 39:10-26 (West).
127.2 N.J. Stat. Ann. § 39:10-27 (West).
127.3 N.J. Stat. Ann. § 39:10-29 (West).

6.3 Statutes Dealing with Disclosure of Vehicle's Prior Use

Addition to note 134.	134 *Delete see also* Wis. Admin. Code *citation; add*: Wis. Admin. Code § Trans. 139.04(6) (dealer must provide prospective purchasers of used vehicles with a Buyer's Guide that discloses all material history, prior use, and title brands, or that history and prior use are unknown if dealer could not find them using reasonable

care); *see also* People v. Condor Pontiac, Cadillac, Buick & GMC Trucks, Inc., 2003 WL 21649689 (N.Y. Sup. Ct. July 2, 2003) (enforcing voluntary assurance requiring restitution to consumers who were sold cars without disclosure of prior use as rental cars).

Page 142

Replace note 136 with:

136   *See* Diaz v. Paragon Motors of Woodside, Inc., 2006 WL 802289 (E.D.N.Y. Mar. 29, 2006). *See generally* § 8.4.6, *infra*.

Add to at end of subsection's second paragraph:

In addition, a few states explicitly provide a private cause of action for failure to disclose a vehicle's prior use.[136.1]

136.1   Del. Code Ann. tit. 21, § 6909(d) (buyer has right to rescind sale if dealer fails to disclose in writing that vehicle has been branded as a former taxi); N.Y. Veh. & Traf. Law § 417-a (McKinney) (treble damages or $100, plus attorney fees, for failure to disclose principal prior use of vehicle).

Add to text after sentence containing note 137:

If the statute or regulation requires the disclosure to be made in the contract of sale, it is a violation to include the disclosure in a separate document given to a buyer who has already signed a retail installment sales contract and paid a deposit.[137.1]

137.1   Diaz v. Paragon Motors of Woodside, Inc., 2006 WL 802289 (E.D.N.Y. Mar. 29, 2006).

Addition to note 139.

139   Colo. Rev. Stat. § 6-1-708(b).

Add new subsections to text after § 6.3:

6.3a   State Laws Requiring Disclosure of Gray Market Origin

Gray market vehicles are vehicles that are sold in the United States even though they were manufactured for sale elsewhere. They may not meet federal emissions and safety standards.[140.1] As a result, it may be difficult or impossible to title the vehicle in the United States.[140.2] Odometer issues also arise because the odometer must be converted from kilometers to miles when the vehicle is brought into the United States.[140.3]

Some states have special motor vehicle laws that require disclosure that a vehicle was manufactured for a foreign market.[140.4] Even without a special statute, fraud and deceptive practices (UDAP) claims are viable.[140.5]

6.3b   State Airbag Laws

Sale of cars without functioning airbags is a growing problem in light of the expense of replacement airbags and their attractiveness to thieves.[140.6] A number of states have enacted laws addressing this problem. Many of these laws create a new criminal offense of installing a fake or inoperative airbag or a replacement airbag that does not comply with federal safety standards for the make, model, and year of the vehicle.[140.7] One state prohibits the sale, lease, trade, or transfer of a vehicle with a non-complying airbag,[140.8] but others merely require disclosure to the consumer.[140.9] Some limit the circumstances in which airbags that are not newly-manufactured can be used to replace a deployed or stolen airbag.[140.10] Several states require repair shops to disclose to the owner or lessor of the car if a used or salvage airbag is installed.[140.11] Colorado specifically requires airbags to be replaced after an insurer pays a claim for a stolen or deployed airbag.[140.12] In addition, some states have identified airbag theft or tampering as a special criminal offense, and impose record-keeping requirements upon businesses that salvage, sell, or install airbags.[140.13]

140.1   *See* § 2.1.9.3, *supra*.
140.2   *See* § 8.2.2.2, *infra* (warranty of title issues).
140.3   *See* § 2.1.9.2, *supra*.
140.4   Cal. Civ. Code §§ 1797.8 to 1797.86 (West) (violation is a UDAP violation); Conn. Gen. Stat. § 42-210 (violation is a UDAP violation); N.H. Rev. Stat. Ann. § 357-C:3 (must disclose if vehicle is "direct import," give details as to modifications performed to comply with federal or state law, and state whether manufacturer's warranty and state lemon law apply); N.Y. Gen. Bus. Law § 218-aa (McKinney) (applies to any gray market merchandise, not just vehicles); N.Y. Veh. & Traf. Law § 471 (McKinney) (applies to

vehicles; includes private cause of action); 75 Pa. Cons. Stat. § 110(b)(9) (requiring title to be branded if vehicle was originally manufactured for distribution outside the United States).

140.5   *See* § 8.4.8.7, *infra.*

140.6   *See* § 2.8, *supra.*

140.7   Ala. Code § 13A-11-270(a)(1); Colo. Rev. Stat. §§ 6-1-710, 42-9-111; Conn. Gen. Stat. § 53a-119(16); Del. Code Ann. tit. 6, § 4903A; Del. Code Ann. tit. 21, § 4802(e); Fla. Stat. Ann. § 860.146 (West); Ga. Code Ann. § 16-9-111; 720 Ill. Comp. Stat. § 5/17-11.2; Ind. Code § 9-19-10.5-2; Iowa Code § 321.71A; Ky. Rev. Stat. Ann. § 434.415 (Michie); Miss. Code Ann. § 63-7-62; Neb. Rev. Stat. § 28-635; N.H. Rev. Stat. Ann. §§ 358-D:11-a, 358-D:11-b; N.C. Gen. Stat. § 20-136.2; Ohio Rev. Code Ann. § 4549.20 (West); Okla. Stat. tit. 15, § 902 (but allows installation of non-complying airbag with owner's consent); Or. Rev. Stat. § 167.822; Tenn. Code Ann. § 55-9-108; Tex. Transp. Code Ann. § 547.614 (Vernon); Vt. Stat. Ann. tit. 13, § 2026; Va. Code Ann. § 46.2-1088.3 (Michie) (allows installation of non-complying airbag if owner knows); Wash. Rev. Code § 46.37.660; W. Va. Code § 17C-15-50; *see also* Nev. Rev. Stat. § 487.520 (requires garage or body shop to replace airbag with one that complies with federal standards); Utah Code Ann. § 41-6-145.5 (if vehicle to be used on highway is repaired and repair facility knows airbag is damaged or has been deployed, it must restore it to operating condition; repair facility that knows airbag is damaged or has been deployed must inform owner).

140.8   Ind. Code § 9-19-10.5-3.

140.9   Ala. Code § 13A-11-271 (criminal offense for owner to knowingly and intentionally fail to disclose absence of airbag when selling vehicle, if airbag deployed but owner did not replace it); Ariz. Rev. Stat. § 28-2091(M) (person who sells vehicle that formerly had salvage title and who has actual knowledge that airbag or components were deployed and removed must disclose this fact unless airbag is repaired or replaced); Ind. Code § 49-967 (unlawful to sell or transfer ownership of vehicle without giving prior written notice if seller knows or should reasonably know that airbag is inoperable unless this fact is visible); Iowa Code § 321.69(10); Vt. Stat. Ann. tit. 13, § 2027; *see also* Wis. Stat. § 347.475 (may not sell, install, reinstall, or distribute any previously deployed airbag, but may sell vehicle with previously deployed airbag if deployment is not concealed or disguised; may not install cover to conceal missing or previously deployed airbag).

140.10 Cal. Veh. Code § 27317 (West) (criminal offense to knowingly install or reinstall for compensation, or distribute or sell, any previously deployed airbag); Colo. Rev. Stat. § 42-9-109.5 (may use salvage airbag only if it is acquired from vehicle dismantler or auto parts recycler); N.Y. Veh. & Traf. Law § 398-d (McKinney) (may use salvage airbag if use is prominently disclosed and certain requirements are met); W. Va. Code § 17C-15-50 (misdemeanor to install or reinstall anything other than a not previously deployed airbag); Wis. Stat. § 347.475 (may not sell, install, reinstall, or distribute any previously deployed airbag, but may sell vehicle with previously deployed airbag if deployment is not concealed or disguised).

140.11 Ala. Code § 13A-11-270(a)(2); Colo. Rev. Stat. § 42-9-109.5 (must disclose prominently on face of invoice that salvage airbag was used); Fla. Stat. Ann. § 860.145(3) (West) (person who sells or installs salvaged airbag must disclose to buyer); N.Y. Veh. & Traf. Law § 398-d (McKinney); Va. Code Ann. § 46.2-1088.3 (Michie) (misdemeanor to install airbag that was previously installed in another vehicle, unless owner knows); Wash. Rev. Code § 46.37.650 (misdemeanor to knowingly install for compensation or distribute previously deployed airbag).

140.12 Colo. Rev. Stat. § 10-4-614 (insured must replace airbag after receiving payment from insurer).

140.13 *See, e.g.*, Fla. Stat. Ann. § 860.145 (West); Mich. Comp. Laws §§ 257.1318a, 750.356a; 9 P.R. Laws Ann. §§ 2074, 2076; Wis. Stat. §§ 347.475 (airbag tampering), 347.50 (penalty); *see also* Utah Code Ann. § 41-6-145.5 (no person may remove or disable airbag unless acting under a dismantling permit).

6.4 State Lemon Laundering Statutes

6.4.1 *General*

Page 143

Add to text at end of subsection's first paragraph:

Another major benefit of a lemon laundering claim is that a consumer who wins may be entitled to an attorney fee award under the state lemon laundering law.[142.1]

142.1   *See, e.g.*, Johnson v. Ford Motor Co., 2003 WL 22794432 (Cal. Ct. App. Nov. 25, 2003) (unpublished) (affirming $379,348 attorney fee award; actual damages were $17,800.60 and punitive damages on fraud claim were reduced from $10 million to $53,435), *rev'd in part, remanded on other grounds*, 113 P.3d 82 (Cal. 2005) (ruling on punitive damages issues).

Add to text at end of subsection's second paragraph:

Lemon laundering laws typically require that the consumer give the manufacturer notice and an opportunity to resolve the problem before suing. Even though this requirement is more appropriate for repairable warranty problems, a trial court has required the consumer to give the manufacturer notice before bringing a lemon laundering claim.[143.1]

143.1   Alexander v. DaimlerChrysler Corp., 2004 WL 179369 (N.C. Super. Ct. Jan. 30, 2004).

Add to text after subsection's fourth paragraph:

Some lemon laundering laws go beyond disclosure and impose an affirmative duty on the manufacturer to repair the defects before reselling the car. Violation of this duty may give the consumer a cause of action regardless of disclosure.

Add note 144.1 at end of first sentence of subsection's last paragraph.

144.1   Lee v. Chrysler Corp., 2005 WL 449762 (Ohio Ct. App. Feb. 22, 2005) (unpublished) (failure to make statutorily-required disclosure that vehicle was a lemon buyback can be basis of fraud claim).

Addition to note 145.

145   Johnson v. Ford Motor Co., 2003 WL 22794432 (Cal. Ct. App. Nov. 25, 2003) (unpublished) (affirming fraud verdict and punitive damages, reduced to comply with constitutional limits, when manufacturer had practice of evading lemon laundering laws), *rev'd in part, remanded on other grounds*, 113 P.3d 82 (Cal. 2005) (reversing reduction of punitive damages and remanding for redetermination of maximum award allowed by constitution).

Add note 145.1 at end of sentence following sentence containing note 145.

145.1   Alexander v. DaimlerChrysler Corp., 2004 WL 179369 (N.C. Super. Ct. Jan. 30, 2004) (allowing UDAP claim against dealers who failed to give statutorily required lemon disclosure).

6.4.2 Application to "Goodwill" and Other "Voluntary" Buybacks

Add to text after third sentence of subsection's second paragraph:

Another way to conceal that a vehicle is a lemon is to give the original buyer a monetary bonus for trading the vehicle in on a new replacement car.[145.2]

145.2   *See, e.g.,* Johnson v. Ford Motor Co., 2003 WL 22794432 (Cal. Ct. App. Nov. 25, 2003) (unpublished), *rev'd in part, remanded on other grounds*, 113 P.3d 82 (Cal. 2005) (reversing reduction of punitive damages and remanding for redetermination of maximum award allowed by constitution).

Add to text at end of subsection:

The dealer's and manufacturer's files on the vehicle may also contain the original buyer's complaints and the manufacturer's acknowledgment of the problems with the car.[145.3]

145.3   *See, e.g.,* Johnson v. Ford Motor Co., 2003 WL 22794432 (Cal. Ct. App. Nov. 25, 2003) (unpublished), *rev'd in part, remanded on other grounds*, 113 P.3d 82 (Cal. 2005) (reversing reduction of punitive damages and remanding for redetermination of maximum award allowed by constitution).

Page 144

6.4.4 Lack of Privity Should Not Be a Defense to a Lemon Laundering Claim

Replace note 150 with:

150   *See* National Consumer Law Center, Unfair and Deceptive Acts and Practices § 4.2.15 (6th ed. 2004 and Supp.).

Add to text at end of subsection:

A North Carolina trial court, however, found that the manufacturer was not required to ensure that dealers who bought buybacks at auctions gave the required disclosures to buyers.[154.1] The manufacturer's duty was to give the disclosure to the dealers. If a dealer failed to pass along the disclosure to a consumer buyer, the dealer would be liable under the state UDAP statute.[154.2]

154.1   Alexander v. DaimlerChrysler Corp., 2004 WL 179369 (N.C. Super. Ct. Jan. 30, 2004).
154.2   *Id.*

6.5 Dealer Licensing Statutes

6.5.1 Relevance of Dealer Licensing Statutes to Consumer Claims

Page 145

Replace "fraud" in sentence containing note 162 with:

fraud, negligence,

Addition to note 162.

162   *See also* Getz v. Mercedes-Benz of Bakersfield, 2004 WL 902119 (Cal. Ct. App. Apr. 27, 2004) (unpublished) (consumer has negligence claim against dealer, who should have been aware that deal with unlicensed fraudulent broker was irregular).

Page 146

6.5.3 Scope

Add to text at end of subsection:

The administrative agency that enforces the licensing law may have authority to impose sanctions only against licensees, not against others involved in the fraud.[168.1]

When an Indiana vehicle dealer worked out a tentative agreement by telephone with an Ohio consumer but then brought the vehicle to Ohio for the consumer to test drive, and the parties signed a lease agreement there, the dealer had to comply with Ohio dealer licensing laws.[168.2] The court also rejected the dealer's claim that requiring an Ohio license would violate the United States Constitution's Commerce Clause.

168.1   *See* Pretzer v. Motor Vehicle Bd., 138 S.W.3d 908 (Tex. 2004).

168.2   Arnold v. Volkswagen of Am., Inc., 2005 WL 844968 (Ohio Ct. App. Apr. 8, 2005) (unpublished).

Page 148

6.5.7 *General Prohibition of Fraud and of Misrepresentation in Advertising*

Addition to note 179.

179   N.M. Stat. Ann. § 57-16-4 (Michie) (prohibiting false, deceptive, or misleading advertising, representing a used vehicle or demonstrator as new); N.M. Stat. Ann. § 57-16-13 (Michie) (providing cause of action for actual damages (trebled if malicious) and attorney fees to "any person who shall be injured in his business or property" by reason of a violation; although law is part of Motor Vehicle Dealers Franchising Act, private cause of action appears to extend to consumers and such a claim was allowed in Salmeron v. Highlands Ford Sales, Inc., 271 F. Supp. 2d 1314 (D.N.M. 2003)); *cf.* Pretzer v. Motor Vehicle Bd., 138 S.W.3d 908 (Tex. 2004) (fraud is ground for sanctions, but only licensees can be sanctioned, not owner and general manager).

Page 150.

Add new section to text after § 6.6.4:

6.7 Special Statutory Causes of Action for Automobile Fraud

A number of states have special motor vehicle statutes that give the consumer a cause of action for automobile fraud. Some of these statutes provide better remedies or have fewer preconditions than the state unfair and deceptive practices (UDAP) statute.

Colorado gives consumers the right to sue licensed motor vehicle dealers and their salespersons for any fraud or fraudulent representations.[202] The remedies are inferior to those under the state UDAP statute in that they do not include multiple damages or attorney fees. On the other hand, the motor vehicle statute does not require that the consumer show a significant impact on the public as a precondition of suit, which Colorado's courts have imposed as a precondition of a UDAP suit.[203] The motor vehicle statute also explicitly allows the consumer to sue the dealer's bonding company.[204]

Delaware requires dealers to disclose in writing if a vehicle title has been branded "reconstructed," "flood damaged," "salvage," or as a former taxi. If the dealer does not make this disclosure, the statute gives the buyer the right to rescind the contract at any time and receive a full and complete refund of all purchase moneys, including interest and fees.[205]

Georgia allows any person damaged by a violation to bring a private cause of action for actual, consequential, and punitive damages, plus attorney fees and court costs, against any licensed used vehicle dealer or used vehicle parts dealer who purchases or rebuilds a wrecked or salvage motor vehicle without complying with the state laws regarding titling and inspection.[206] A claim under this statute may offer advantages over the state unfair and deceptive practices (UDAP) statute, which requires notice thirty days before suit and has been interpreted to require a showing of public impact.[207]

Idaho extends a private cause of action to any person who suffers loss or damage by reason of any fraud, fraudulent representation, or violation of certain motor vehicle laws by a licensed dealer or a dealer's salesperson who is acting for the dealer.[208] Damages and equitable relief are authorized.[209] This cause of action applies to, *inter alia*, prohibi-

202   Colo. Rev. Stat. § 12-6-122(1).

203   *See* National Consumer Law Center, Unfair and Deceptive Acts and Practices § 7.5.3.3 (6th ed. 2004 and Supp.).

204   Colo. Rev. Stat. § 12-6-122(1).

205   Del. Code Ann. tit. 21, § 6909(d).

206   Ga. Code Ann. §§ 43-47-15, 43-47-21.

207   *See* National Consumer Law Center, Unfair and Deceptive Acts and Practices § 7.5.3.6 (6th ed. 2004 and Supp.).

208   Idaho Code § 49-1610(1) (Michie).

209   Idaho Code § 49-1610(2) (Michie).

tions against misleading or inaccurate advertising and the knowing sale of a stolen vehicle.[210] For odometer tampering claims in which the seller or the seller's employees knew or had reason to know that the odometer had been tampered with or replaced, but failed to disclose that knowledge to the buyer prior to the sale, the buyer is also entitled to recover costs and a reasonable attorney fee.[211]

Illinois allows any person injured by a violation of its laws regarding vehicle dealers, transporters, wreckers, and rebuilders, or any interested person, to seek an injunction to prevent violations.[212] This cause of action applies to the state's requirement that vehicle dealers disclose that a vehicle has been rebuilt[213] or is a lemon buyback.[214]

Kentucky grants a private cause of action for an injunction against further violations, actual damages, costs, and attorney fees to any person who suffers an injury to business or property as a result of a violation of certain motor vehicle laws.[215] These laws include Kentucky's new car damage disclosure requirement,[216] the state's prohibition against selling a used or demonstrator vehicle as new,[217] its general prohibition against false or fraudulent representations in connection with the operation of a new motor vehicle dealership,[218] and its requirement that dealers disclose the identities of prior owners.[219] Suit under this section must be filed in the Franklin Circuit Court.[220]

Nebraska extends a private cause of action for damages and equitable relief to any person injured by a violation of the state's motor vehicle industry licensing laws.[221] These laws prohibit, *inter alia*, various types of false advertisements and the representation of used vehicles as new.[222]

New Hampshire grants a private cause of action for actual damages, costs, and attorney fees to any person whose business or property is injured by a violation of certain state motor vehicle laws.[223] The substantive prohibitions to which this private cause of action applies include the sale of gray market vehicles without disclosure.[224]

New Mexico prohibits motor vehicle dealers from, *inter alia*, using any false, deceptive, or misleading advertisements; willfully defrauding any retail buyer; failing to perform their obligations under a manufacturer's warranty; and misrepresenting demonstrators or other used vehicles as new.[225] "Fraud" is defined broadly to include the intentional failure to disclose a material fact and misrepresentations that result from gross negligence.[226] The consumer has a private cause of action for damages and attorney fees.[227] In addition, if the defendant acted maliciously, the court or jury may award punitive damages of up to three times actual damages.[228]

New York grants a special private cause of action to any person aggrieved by a dealer's sale of a gray market vehicle without a prominent label disclosing that it was manufactured for distribution outside the United States. The plaintiff may recover "any additional margin obtained . . . on such purchase and resale," which presumably refers to the price increase the dealer obtained by concealing the vehicle's history.[229] New York also offers a special private cause of action for treble damages or $100, whichever is greater, plus attorney fees, for failure to disclose the principal prior use of a vehicle or its history as a lemon buyback.[230] These statutory causes of action have the advantage of not requiring a showing of public impact, which New York's highest court has read into the state UDAP statute.[231]

Rhode Island broadly prohibits false or misleading advertisements by motor vehicle dealers.[232] It also prohibits actions that are arbitrary, in bad faith, or unconscionable, and that cause damage to any parties involved or to the public.[233] Any consumer who is injured by a violation may sue for an injunction against further violations and may seek actual damages, costs, and a reasonable attorney fee.[234] This private cause of action also applies to the state's new car damage disclosure law.[235] In addition, any contract or portion of a contract that violates these laws is void and

---

210 *See, e.g.*, Idaho Code § 49-1613 (Michie) (prohibiting, *inter alia*, misleading or inaccurate advertising, knowing sale of a stolen vehicle, violation of federal odometer laws).

211 Idaho Code § 49-1630 (Michie).

212 815 Ill. Comp. Stat. § 5/5-502.

213 815 Ill. Comp. Stat. §§ 5/5-101(i)(5) (new vehicle dealers), 5/5-102(i)(5) (used vehicle dealers), 5/5-104.3.

214 815 Ill. Comp. Stat. § 5/5-104.2.

215 Ky. Rev. Stat. Ann. § 190.062(1) (referring to violations of "this section"), (3) (incorporating Ky. Rev. Stat. Ann. §§ 190.010 to 190.080) (Michie).

216 Ky. Rev. Stat. Ann. § 190.0491 (Michie).

217 Ky. Rev. Stat. Ann. § 190.071(b) (Michie).

218 Ky. Rev. Stat. Ann. § 190.071(e) (Michie).

219 Ky. Rev. Stat. Ann. § 190.080(2) (Michie).

220 Ky. Rev. Stat. Ann. § 190.062(1) (Michie).

221 Neb. Rev. Stat. § 60-1440(1), (2).

222 Neb. Rev. Stat. § 60-1411.03.

223 N.H. Rev. Stat. Ann. § 357-C:12(IX).

224 N.H. Rev. Stat. Ann. § 357-C:3(I-b).

225 N.M. Stat. Ann. § 57-16-4 (Michie); *see* Salmeron v. Highlands Ford Sales, Inc., 271 F. Supp. 2d 1314 (D.N.M. 2003) (misrepresentation that car was demonstrator and failure to disclose its rental and collision history states claim for willfully defrauding retail buyer).

226 N.M. Stat. Ann. § 57-16-3(I) (Michie).

227 N.M. Stat. Ann. § 57-16-13 (Michie); *see* Salmeron v. Highlands Ford Sales, Inc., 271 F. Supp. 2d 1314 (D.N.M. 2003) (misrepresentation that car was demonstrator and failure to disclose its rental and collision history states claim); Anaya v. Gen. Motors Corp., 703 P.2d 169 (N.M. 1985) (consumer has right to sue manufacturer for breach of warranty under this statute).

228 N.M. Stat. Ann. § 57-16-13 (Michie).

229 N.Y. Veh. & Traf. Law § 471 (McKinney).

230 N.Y. Veh. & Traf. Law § 417-a (McKinney).

231 *See* National Consumer Law Center, Unfair and Deceptive Acts and Practices § 7.5.3.8 (6th ed. 2004 and Supp.).

232 R.I. Gen. Laws § 31-5.1-4(e)(3).

233 R.I. Gen. Laws § 31-5.1-4.

234 R.I. Gen. Laws § 31-5.1-13(a).

235 R.I. Gen. Laws § 31-5.1-18.

unenforceable.[236] This statutory cause of action has the advantage of avoiding state UDAP coverage questions created by the Rhode Island Supreme Court's broad construction of an exemption for transactions permitted under laws administered by a state or federal regulatory body.[237]

South Carolina prohibits any motor vehicle dealer or manufacturer from engaging in any action which is "arbitrary, in bad faith, or unconscionable and which causes damage to any of the parties or to the public."[238] Acts are arbitrary acts if they have no reasonable basis.[239] Judicial decisions define bad faith as the opposite of good faith, generally implying or involving actual or constructive fraud, or a design to deceive or mislead another, or a neglect or refusal to fulfill some duty or some contractual obligation, not prompted by an honest mistake as to one's rights or duties, but by some interested or sinister motive.[240] The same statute prohibits dealers from engaging in false or misleading advertising or representing and selling as new any motor vehicle that has been operated for demonstration purposes or is otherwise a used vehicle.[241]

Any contract in violation of these provisions is void and unenforceable.[242] In addition, any person injured "in his business or property" by a violation has a cause of action for double the actual damages plus costs and attorney fees, as well as, if the defendant acted maliciously, punitive damages up to three times actual damages.[243] These prohibitions and remedies are all found in a statute that deals primarily with the relationship between franchised dealers and manufacturers, but they are worded to protect consumers as well, and courts have applied them to consumers.[244] One possible

advantage of this statute is that it does not require any showing that the practice has been repeated or has the potential for repetition. By contrast, South Carolina courts have interpreted the state UDAP statute not to allow consumers to sue when the practice only affects the parties to the transaction.[245]

Texas provides that any person damaged by a violation of certain motor vehicle laws, including its general prohibition against false, deceptive, or misleading advertising,[246] may bring suit under the state UDAP statute.[247]

Utah allows a civil action to be maintained by a purchaser for violation of certain motor vehicle laws, including sale of a salvage vehicle without disclosure, making false statements on a damage disclosure statement, and fraudulent certification that a vehicle is entitled to an unbranded title.[248] The purchaser is entitled to $1000 or treble damages, whichever is greater, plus reasonable attorney fees and costs.

Washington extends a private cause of action for actual damages, costs, and attorney fees to any person who suffers an injury to their business or property by a violation of the statutes regulating motor vehicle dealers and manufacturers.[249] The substantive prohibitions to which this cause of action applies include odometer offenses and a general prohibition against dissemination of false or deceptive statements.[250] Any violation is also a UDAP violation.[251]

Wisconsin gives consumers a private cause of action for pecuniary loss caused by a licensed dealer's violation of certain provisions of the motor vehicle laws, including willful fraud; willful failure to perform any written agreement; fraudulent sales, leases, pre-lease agreements, repossessions, or transactions; fraudulent misrepresentation, circumvention, or concealment of certain material particulars of a transaction; unconscionable practices; and violation of various other motor vehicle laws.[252] The consumer may also recover costs and attorney fees.[253]

---

236 R.I. Gen. Laws § 31-5.1-14.

237 Chavers v. Fleet Bank, 844 A.2d 666 (R.I. 2004); *see* National Consumer Law Center, Unfair and Deceptive Acts and Practices § 2.3.3.3.2 (6th ed. 2004 and Supp.).

238 S.C. Code Ann. § 56-15-40(1) (Law. Co-op.).

239 Taylor v. Nix, 416 S.E.2d 619, 621 (S.C. 1992) (defining and upholding constitutionality of this prohibition); *see also* DeBondt v. Carlton Motorcars, Inc., 442 S.E.2d 611 (S.C. Ct. App. 2000) (defining arbitrary as "acts which are unreasonable, capricious or nonrational; not done according to reason or judgment; depending on will alone").

240 Taylor v. Nix, 416 S.E.2d 619, 621 (S.C. 1992); DeBondt v. Carlton Motorcars, Inc., 442 S.E.2d 611 (S.C. Ct. App. 2000).

241 S.C. Code Ann. § 56-15-40(4)(b), (c) (Law. Co-op.).

242 S.C. Code Ann. § 56-15-130 (Law. Co-op.).

243 S.C. Code Ann. § 56-15-110 (Law. Co-op.); *see* Toyota of Florence, Inc. v. Lynch, 442 S.E.2d 611, 616 (S.C. 1994) (both double damages and treble damages may be recovered under the statute); Taylor v. Nix, 416 S.E.2d 619 (S.C. 1992) (affirming award of both double and treble damages).

244 Taylor v. Nix, 416 S.E.2d 619 (S.C. 1992); DeBondt v. Carlton Motorcars, Inc., 442 S.E.2d 611 (S.C. Ct. App. 2000); Adams v. Grant, 358 S.E.2d 142 (S.C. Ct. App. 1986).

245 *See* National Consumer Law Center, Unfair and Deceptive Acts and Practices § 7.5.3.7 (6th ed. 2004 and Supp.).

246 Tex. Occ. Code Ann. § 2301.351 (Vernon).

247 Tex. Occ. Code Ann. § 2301.805 (Vernon).

248 Utah Code Ann. § 41-3-702(4).

249 Wash. Rev. Code § 46.70.190; *see also* Wash. Rev. Code § 46.70.070 (authorizing suit against dealer and surety by any retail purchaser who suffers loss or damage due to a dealer's violation).

250 Wash. Rev. Code § 46.70.180(1), (5).

251 Wash. Rev. Code § 46.70.310.

252 Wis. Stat. § 218.0163(2) (referring to various provisions of § 218.0116).

253 Wis. Stat. § 218.0163(2); *see* Kolupar v. Wilde Pontiac Cadillac, Inc., 683 N.W.2d 58 (Wis. 2004) (upholding fee award; trial court properly awarded less than consumer's attorney sought when fee request was inadequately documented).

Chapter 7

Common Law Fraud, Deceit, and Misrepresentation

7.1 Advantages and Disadvantages

Addition to note 9.

9   *Replace NCLC citation with*: National Consumer Law Center, Unfair and Deceptive Acts and Practices § 9.2.5.2 (6th ed. 2004 and Supp.).

7.2 Basic Elements of a Fraud Action

Add note 11.1 to end of first sentence of last bulleted item.

11.1   *See* Chavarria v. Fleetwood Retail Corp., 115 P.3d 799, 807 (N.M. Ct. App. 2005) (fact that consumer signed promissory note meets damage requirement even if consumer has not made any payments), *review granted*, 115 P.3d 230 (N.M. 2005).

Addition to note 12.

12   *See also* Century Sur. Co. v. Crosby Ins., Inc., 21 Cal. Rptr. 3d 115, 119 (2004).

7.3 Material Misrepresentations

7.3.1 Representation Must Have Been Misleading

Add note 14.1 at end of subsection's first sentence.

14.1   *See, e.g.*, Davis v. U.S. Bancorp, 383 F.3d 761, 769 (8th Cir. 2004) (affirming judgment for defendant when prospective borrower failed to show that prospective lender had made a false statement to her); Livingstone Flomeh-Mawutor v. Banknorth, 350 F. Supp. 2d 314 (D. Mass. 2004) (when loan officer's statements true, no action for fraud regardless of officer's ultimate motive).

7.3.2 Representation Must Have Been Material

Addition to notes 19, 21, 22, 24.

19   *Add at end of note: See also* Angel v. YFB Hemet, Inc., 2004 WL 1058180, at *4 (Cal. Ct. App. Apr. 30, 2004) (using dictionary's definition of "new," held that an issue of material fact existed as to whether car was new regardless of whether it was carried as new in state's vehicle title records).

21   *See, e.g.*, Werremeyer v. K.C. Auto Salvage Co., 2003 WL 21487311 (Mo. Ct. App. June 30, 2003) ("The fact that a car has or has not been wrecked is clearly a material factor in the decision to purchase."), *aff'd in relevant part*, 134 S.W.3d 633 (2004).

22   *See also* Griffith v. Byers Constr. Co. of Kan., Inc., 510 P.2d 198, 205 (Kan. 1973) (prospective purchaser of a residential building site would consider soil condition a material factor in purchase).

24   *See also* Sedgwick v. Bowers, 681 N.W.2d 607, 611 (Iowa 2004) (home sellers' failure to disclose previous water problems could be material even though their water problems arose in different area of house from later problems suffered by buyers, when both problems had same root cause); Chambers v. Kensington, 796 So. 2d 733 (La. Ct. App. 2001) (auctioneer's representation that tractor was being sold because of a repossession was material because in that case it was probable that there was nothing wrong with the tractor that made the owner want to sell it).

Add to text at end of subsection:

A salesperson's false explanation of a car's vehicle identification number, made to hide that the car had been pieced together, was sufficiently material although it was not the sole factor in the buyer's decision to buy the car.[24.1]

24.1   Werremeyer v. K.C. Auto Salvage Co., 134 S.W.3d 633, 635 (Mo. 2004) (en banc).

7.3.3 Fraud by Affirmative Statements

Page 154   ### 7.3.3.1 General

Addition to note 25.

25   *See, e.g.*, King v. O'Rielly Motor Co., 494 P.2d 718, 721 (Ariz. Ct. App. 1972) (representation that car was "like new," when it had been wrecked on the dealer's premises, supported action for fraud); Schemann v. Bill Scher Motors, Inc., 1980 WL 355241, at *4 (Ohio Ct. App. Oct. 9, 1980) (being told car was "ready" when repairs had not yet been made).

7.3.3.2 Fact Versus Opinion

Addition to notes 26, 29, 33, 34.

26   *See also* Rodi v. S. New England Sch. of Law, 389 F.3d 5, 14, 15 (1st Cir. 2004) (reversing dismissal in favor of defendant when defendant's assurances regarding school's impending accreditation could be reasonably understood by plaintiff as implying the existence of facts justifying the assurance); Tres-AAA Exxon v. City First Mortgage Inc., 870 So. 2d 905, 907, 908 (Fla. Dist. Ct. App. 2004) (reversing dismissal of claim arising from sale of property based on sellers' representations about the cost of improvements).

29   *Add to Nigh citation: rev'd on other grounds*, 125 S. Ct. 460 (2004) (Truth in Lending statutory damages calculation issue).

Page 155

33   *See also* Siegel v. Williams, 818 N.E.2d 510, 515, 516 (Ind. Ct. App. 2004) (oral promise as to future conduct may give rise to a claim for constructive fraud "if it induces one to place himself in a worse position than he would have been in had no promise been made and if the party making the promise derives a benefit as a result of the promise").

34   *See also* Gage Products Co. v. Henkel Corp., 393 F.3d 629, 646, 647 (6th Cir. 2004) (fraud claim could be based on promise of future conduct when circumstances yielded a reasonable inference that defendant did not intend to fulfill promise at the time made); Saia Food Distributors & Club, Inc. v. SecurityLink from Ameritech, Inc., 902 So. 2d 46 (Ala. 2004) (affirming summary judgment on grounds that plaintiff failed to show that, at the time of the misrepresentation, defendant did not intend to perform the act promised).

7.3.3.3 Examples of Actionable Statements

Addition to notes 40, 42.

40   *See also* King v. O'Rielly Motor Co., 494 P.2d 718, 721 (Ariz. Ct. App. 1972).

42   Werremeyer v. K.C. Auto Salvage Co., 2003 WL 21487311 (Mo. Ct. App. June 30, 2003) (salesman was recklessly indifferent to truth of statement; also fabricated explanation for scratched-out vehicle identification numbers), *aff'd in relevant part*, 134 S.W.3d 633 (2004).

Add to text after bulleted item containing note 42:

- That a car did not have frame damage;[42.1]

42.1   Johann, Inc. v. City Motors, Inc., 2002 WL 31684970 (Cal. Ct. App. Dec. 2, 2002) (unpublished).

Page 156

Add to text after bulleted item containing note 48:

- That a car's interior was clean and in good condition, that all major mechanical systems functioned normally, and that the car passed a smog test with zero emissions;[48.1]

48.1   Rudder v. Fedtrust Liquidations, 2004 WL 264260 (Cal. Ct. App. Feb. 13, 2004) (unpublished).

7.3.5 Fraud by Silence (Nondisclosure)

Page 157   ### 7.3.5.1 General

Add note 56.1 at end of first bulleted item.

56.1   Ensminger v. Terminix Int'l Co., 102 F.3d 1571, 1574, 1575 (10th Cir. 1996) (fiduciary relationship arose between termite inspector and prospective purchasers that created a duty to disclose termite damage to house).

Addition to notes 58, 61.

58   *See also* Lindberg Cadillac Co. v. Aron, 371 S.W.2d 651, 653 (Mo. Ct. App. 1963) (automobile owner's temporary patch of cracks in motor block).

61   *Cf.* Go For It v. Aircraft Sales Corp., 2003 WL 21504600 (N.D. Ill. June 27, 2003) (airplane seller's slightly dominant business position did not create duty of disclosure to commercial buyer).

7.3.5.2 Half-Truths

Replace note 63 with:

63   *Id.*; *see also* Alires v. McGehee, 85 P.3d 1191, 1196 (Kan. 2004) (home seller's disclosure of basement leakage caused by broken pipe but not other incidences of leakage amounted to affirmative misrepresentation); Rosas v. Hatz, 147 S.W.3d 560, 565, 566 (Tex. App. 2004) (buyers of house could maintain fraud action against seller, when seller's disclosure of some instances of leakage in home's basement, while literally true, suggested that there were no other instances of such leakage).

Addition to note 66.

66   *See also* Clark v. McDaniel, 546 N.W.2d 590, 592 (Iowa 1996) (salesman who indicated that car had suffered some damage had duty to disclose full extent of damage).

7.3.5.3 Seller's Superior Knowledge

Addition to notes 67, 70–73.

67   Salmeron v. Highlands Ford Sales, Inc., 271 F. Supp. 2d 1314 (D.N.M. 2003); Johnson v. Davis, 480 So. 2d 625, 628, 629 (Fla. 1985) (citing change in society's needs to support retreat from principles of *caveat emptor* and to find that sellers of home had duty to disclose its roof problems to purchasers); *see also* Lockhart v. Cmty. Auto Plaza, Inc., 695 N.W.2d 335 (Iowa Ct. App. 2004) (affirming punitive damages judgment against dealer based on dealer's failure to disclose "obvious risk" arising from previous damage to car); Walters v. Maloney, 758 S.W.2d 489, 497 (Mo. Ct. App. 1988) (even intelligent plaintiffs with business backgrounds were entitled to have their real estate broker disclose the existence of a third party's superior lien); Standish-Parkin v. Lorillard Tobacco Co., 786 N.Y.S.2d 13, 15 (App. Div. 2004) (sufficient evidence existed that defendant tobacco companies misrepresented the health risks of cigarette smoking); *cf.* Tietsworth v. Harley-Davidson, Inc., 677 N.W.2d 233 (Wis. 2004) (declining to decide whether superior knowledge creates duty to disclose in sale of consumer goods).

Page 158

70   *See also* Griffith v. Byers Constr. Co. of Kan., Inc., 510 P.2d 198, 205 (Kan. 1973) (lot owner had duty to disclose defect in soil condition to buyer).

71   *See, e.g.,* Streeks, Inc. v. Diamond Hill Farms, Inc., 605 N.W.2d 110 (Neb. 2000). *See also* Lindberg Cadillac Co. v. Aron, 371 S.W.2d 651, 653 (Mo. Ct. App. 1963) (automobile owner had duty to disclose cracks in motor block upon trading it in to dealership); Precision Enterprises, Inc. v. Duffack Enterprises, Inc., 710 N.W.2d 348, 356 (Neb. Ct. App. 2006); Schemann v. Bill Scher Motors, Inc., 1980 WL 355241, at *4 (Ohio Ct. App. Oct. 9, 1980) (regardless of label salesperson gave to car, he was required to disclose the fact that the automobile had been used as a demonstrator and had been damaged and repaired).

72   *Add at end of Wilson citation*: *aff'd on other grounds*, 2003 WL 21805618 (4th Cir. Aug. 7, 2003) (unpublished).

73   *Replace Smiley citation with*: 580 S.E.2d 283 (Ga. Ct. App. 2003); *add*: *See, e.g.,* Alejandre v. Bull, 98 P.3d 844, 848–851 (Wash. Ct. App. 2004) (reversing dismissal of fraud and negligent misrepresentation claims brought against house seller based on her failure to disclose plumbing problems).

Page 159

Add to text at end of subsection's sixth paragraph:

Another example is a disclosure that a vehicle "may" have suffered some damage. If the seller knows that it actually has suffered specific damage, the disclosure can be viewed as a half-truth that creates a duty of full disclosure.[76.1]

76.1   *See* § 7.8.3, *infra.*

Page 160

7.3.5.4 Statutory Duty to Disclose

Addition to notes 87, 91.

87   Johnson v. Ford Motor Co., 2003 WL 22794432 (Cal. Ct. App. Nov. 25, 2003) (unpublished), *rev'd in part on other grounds, remanded*, 113 P.3d 82 (Cal. 2005) (reversing reduction of punitive damages; remanding for further analysis); *see also* Lee v. Chrysler Corp., 2005 WL 449762, at *2 (Ohio Ct. App. Feb. 22, 2005) (finding that car buyer stated a claim for fraud based on seller's failure to disclose car's lemon history).

91   Conatzer v. Am. Mercury Ins. Co., 15 P.3d 1252, 1255, 1256 (Okla. Civ. App. 2000) (state title branding law imposed duty of disclosure on insurance company).

7.3.6 Automobile Fraud Precedent Listed by Type of Misrepresentation

Addition to notes 93–98.

93   Horne v. Claude Ray Ford Sales, Inc., 290 S.E.2d 497 (Ga. Ct. App. 1982) (jury question whether scienter established where defendant represented damaged vehicle as new); Honaker v. Ralph Pool's Albuquerque Auto Sales, Inc., 394 P.2d 978 (N.M. 1964) (misrepresentation of previously-owned vehicle as "new" may

be fraud even if buyer knows of mileage). *See, e.g.*, Hart v. Boehmer Chevrolet Sales, Inc., 337 Ill. App. 3d 742, 787 N.E.2d 350 (2003) (representing vehicle as new, when it had been damaged prior to sale).

Page 161
Page 162

94   *See, e.g.*, Salmeron v. Highlands Ford Sales, Inc., 271 F. Supp. 2d 1314 (D.N.M. 2003).

95   Chambers v. Kensington, 796 So. 2d 733 (La. Ct. App. 2001) (auctioneer's misrepresentation that Fed. Deposit Ins. Corp. was prior owner).

96   *See, e.g.*, Lewis v. Horace Mann Ins. Co., 2005 WL 3962818 (N.D. Ohio Aug. 23, 2005) (denying insurer's motion for summary judgment); Adkins v. Crown Auto, Inc., 2005 WL 1799728 (W.D. Va. July 27, 2005) (concealment that car consisted of two halves clipped together); Mobile Dodge, Inc. v. Alford, 487 So. 2d 866 (Ala. 1986) (misrepresentations that dealer would transfer good title and that car had never been wrecked, when it was actually assembled from parts of several wrecked and stolen cars); Werremeyer v. K.C. Auto Salvage Co., 134 S.W.3d 633, 635 (Mo. 2004) (en banc).

97   *See, e.g.*, Adkins v. Crown Auto, Inc., 2005 WL 1799728 (W.D. Va. July 27, 2005) (concealment that car consisted of two halves clipped together); Salmeron v. Highlands Ford Sales, Inc., 271 F. Supp. 2d 1314 (D.N.M. 2003) (failure to disclose that car had been in accident); Am. Honda Motor Co. v. Boyd, 475 So. 2d 835 (Ala. 1985) (representation that car was new when it had sustained pre-sale damage); Angel v. YFB Hemet, Inc., 2004 WL 1058180, at *4 (Cal. Ct. App. Apr. 30, 2004) (failure to disclose damage to car's undercarriage); Mitchell v. Backus Cadillac-Pontiac, Inc., 618 S.E.2d 87 (Ga. Ct. App. 2005) (misrepresentation that vehicle had been wrecked); Hart v. Boehmer Chevrolet Sales, Inc., 337 Ill. App. 3d 742, 787 N.E.2d 350 (2003) (representing vehicle as new, when it had been damaged prior to sale); Clark v. McDaniel, 546 N.W.2d 590, 592 (Iowa 1996) (failure to disclose full extent of repairs); Lockhart v. Cmty. Auto Plaza, Inc., 2004 WL 2952002 (Iowa Ct. App. Dec. 22, 2004) (dealer gave buyer a damage disclosure form that falsely indicated no damage to vehicle); Rhoads v. Signature Lincoln-Mercury, 866 So. 2d 1035 (La. Ct. App. 2004) (false statement that car had not been wrecked); Krysa v. Payne, 176 S.W.3d 150 (Mo. Ct. App. 2005) (vehicle was two halves welded together); Brown v. New Plaza Pontiac Co., 719 S.W.2d 468 (Mo. Ct. App. 1986); Lucia v. West Hills Auto & Truck Center, 2005 WL 3875895 (Ohio Ct. App. Aug. 22, 2005) (unpublished, citation limited) (nondisclosure of wreck history and salvage title); Turner v. Bob Ross Buick, 1993 WL 485256 (Ohio Ct. App. Nov. 22, 1993) (misrepresentation that car had not been damaged when in fact there had been a collision on the lot that caused a six-inch vertical crease in door); Sykes v. Brady-Bushey Ford, Inc., 2005 WL 2787517 (Va. Cir. Ct. Oct. 27, 2005) (denial of motion to dismiss; suit alleged constructive fraud, which requires showing of negligence or innocent misrepresentation); *see also* Commonwealth v. Pappas, 845 A.2d 829 (Pa. Super. Ct. 2004) (upholding theft by deception conviction when dealer misrepresented that cars had never been wrecked).

Page 163

98   *Add at end of Sandi citation*: *adopted, judgment entered by* 2001 U.S. Dist. LEXIS 876 (E.D.N.Y. Jan. 16, 2001). *Add:* Adkins v. Crown Auto, Inc., 2005 WL 1799728 (W.D. Va. July 27, 2005) (concealment of fact that rear half of clipped car had twice the mileage of front half).

Add to text after bulleted item containing note 98:

• Nondisclosure of a vehicle's history as a daily rental;[98.1]
• Sale of a stolen car;[98.2]

98.1   Salmeron v. Highlands Ford Sales, Inc., 271 F. Supp. 2d 1314 (D.N.M. 2003).

98.2   Neal v. Bavarian Motors, Inc., 882 A.2d 1022 (Pa. Super. Ct. 2005).

Addition to notes 99, 100.

99   *See, e.g.*, Chambers v. Kensington, 796 So. 2d 733 (La. Ct. App. 2001) (auctioneer's misrepresentation that tractor was being sold because of a repossession was material because in that case it was probable that there was nothing wrong with the tractor that made the owner want to sell it).

100 *See, e.g.*, Hummel v. Suglia, 2003 WL 22235370 (Ohio Ct. App. Sept. 30, 2003) (unpublished) (misrepresentation that engine was freshly rebuilt).

7.4 Scienter—the Seller's Knowledge That the Representation Is Misleading

Page 164

7.4.1 General

Addition to note 104.

104 *See also* Taylor v. Bennett Chevrolet/Buick, Inc., 609 S.E.2d 215 (Ga. Ct. App. 2005) (upholding jury instruction requiring knowledge and affirming verdict against plaintiffs, who had alleged that seller had held out car as new notwithstanding that it had been in a collision).

7.4.2 Whose Knowledge?

Addition to note 106.

106 Rhoads v. Signature Lincoln-Mercury, 866 So. 2d 1035 (La. Ct. App. 2004); Turner v. Bob Ross Buick, 1993 WL 485256 (Ohio Ct. App. Nov. 22, 1993) (dealer's efforts to keep sales staff uninformed about damage to cars is evidence of fraud); *see also* Rodi v. S. New Eng. Sch. of Law, 389 F.3d 5, 13 (1st Cir.

2004) (defendant, a law school, could be vicariously liable for the fraudulent misrepresentations made by high-ranking employees who were acting within the scope of their employment); Price v. Ford Motor Credit Co., 530 S.W.2d 249, 254 (Mo. Ct. App. 1975) (holding, on issue of punitive damages for conversion, that "corporate defendant is bound by the knowledge of all of its agents").

Page 165

Add note 107.1 to end of first sentence of subsection's third paragraph.

107.1   *See, e.g.,* Mitchell v. Backus Cadillac-Pontiac, Inc., 618 S.E.2d 87, 94 (Ga. Ct. App. 2005).

Addition to note 110.

110   *See, e.g.,* Adkins v. Crown Auto, Inc., 2005 WL 1799728 (W.D. Va. July 27, 2005) (seller's agent was culpable where he was involved in concealment of car's salvage status, even though he did not make the misrepresentations to the buyer).

7.4.3 Degree of Knowledge

7.4.3.1 General

Addition to note 114.

114   *Add to note after Keeton citation*: *See also* Francis v. Am. Bankers Life Assurance Co. of Fla., 861 A.2d 1040, 1046 (R.I. 2004) (allegation that telemarketer's agent misled plaintiff into incorrectly answering a question about her medical history did not sufficiently allege culpability necessary for negligent misrepresentation claim).

Page 166

7.4.3.2 Actual Knowledge

Addition to notes 115, 116, 119.

115   *See, e.g.,* Scott Imports v. Orton, 527 P.2d 513, 514 (Ariz. Ct. App. 1974) (imputing knowledge of falsity of odometer readings to dealership).

116   *See also* Angel v. YFB Hemet, Inc., 2004 WL 1058180, at *4 (Cal. Ct. App. Apr. 30, 2004) (when dealership mechanic made extensive repairs to vehicle, "inconceivable" that he would not have learned of damage to undercarriage); Brown v. New Plaza Pontiac Co., 719 S.W.2d 468, 472, 473 (Mo. Ct. App. 1986) (imputing agent's conduct to dealership in determining malice necessary for punitive damages arising from sale of wrecked car).

119   *See also* Crowder v. Bob Oberling Enterprises Inc., 499 N.E.2d 115, 118 (Ill. App. Ct. 1986) (car seller who had been told that car had had "paint and body work" was put on notice to inspect salvage car before selling it; his "attempt to hide behind a mask of ignorance merely illuminate[d] his culpability"); Lockhart v. Cmty. Auto Plaza, Inc., 2004 WL 2952002, at *3 (Iowa Ct. App. Dec. 22, 2004) (dealer's certification that vehicle had not been damaged was willful and wanton where damage was readily apparent upon a brief inspection, dealer admitted it inspected all vehicles when it purchased them, and an insurer was in chain of title).

Add note 120.1 to end of first sentence of subsection's last paragraph.

120.1   Horne v. Claude Ray Ford Sales, Inc., 290 S.E.2d 497, 498 (Ga. Ct. App. 1982); Bob Maddox Dodge, Inc. v. McKie, 270 S.E.2d 690 (Ga. Ct. App. 1980).

Addition to note 121.

121   Treadwell Ford, Inc. v. Campbell, 485 So. 2d 312 (Ala. 1986); Rudder v. Fedtrust Liquidations, 2004 WL 264260 (Cal. Ct. App. Feb. 13, 2004) (unpublished) (evidence of problems and that seller checked the car is sufficient to go to jury); Rhoads v. Signature Lincoln-Mercury, 866 So. 2d 1035 (La. Ct. App. 2004); *see also* Mobile Dodge, Inc. v. Alford, 487 So. 2d 866 (Ala. 1986) (circumstantial evidence sufficient to show that dealer knew it did not have good title to vehicle); Mitchell v. Backus Cadillac-Pontiac, Inc., 618 S.E.2d 87, 94 (Ga. Ct. App. 2005) (evidence that dealership had repaired the car supports finding that it knew of the damage); O'Brien v. B.L.C. Ins. Co., 768 S.W.2d 64, 67–69 (Mo. 1989) (en banc) (fact that buyer paid insurer more than double the salvage value of flood-damaged car in return for open title raised inference that insurer intended to deceive ultimate buyer of vehicle).

Add to text after sentence containing note 121:

Dealerships usually will admit that they made some inspection of the vehicle before buying it, even if just a "used car manager walkaround." This admission, coupled with expert testimony that the vehicle's history would be readily apparent to an experienced used car manager after such an inspection, is sufficient to prove scienter.

Addition to note 123.

123   *See also* Hudson v. Pollock, 598 S.E.2d 811, 814 (Ga. Ct. App. 2004) (finding fact issue regarding seller's knowledge of plumbing problems in home given evidence of previous repairs).

Page 169

7.4.3.4 Duty to Inspect As Aid to Finding of Recklessness

Add to text after third sentence of paragraph containing note 144:

Used car managers almost invariably make at least this sort of cursory inspection. If the defendant claims to have made no inspection at all, an expert witness may be able to rebut this claim by testifying about the practice in the used car industry.

Add to text at end of subsection:

The manufacturer may also have a database with information about the history of its cars which the manufacturer requires the dealer to check before certifying a car.

7.4.3.5 Negligent Misrepresentation

Addition to notes 153, 155, 157.

153   *See, e.g.*, Osterman v. Sears, Roebuck & Co., 80 P.3d 435 (Mont. 2003); Fresh Direct, L.L.C. v. Blue Martini Software, Inc., 776 N.Y.S.2d 301, 302, 303 (App. Div. 2004) (special relationship arose between software vendor and its client sufficient to sustain cause of action for negligent misrepresentation); *see also* Restatement (Second) of Torts § 552 (information negligently supplied for the guidance of others); H.C. Inv., L.L.C. v. Outboard Marine Co., 377 F.3d 645, 652, 653 (6th Cir. 2004) (Mich. law) (affirming liability of inspector under Restatement (Second) of Torts § 552); Presnell Constr. Managers, Inc. v. EH Constr., L.L.C., 134 S.W.3d 575, 582 (Ky. 2004) (adopting Restatement (Second) of Torts § 552). *But cf.* Lewis v. Horace Mann Ins. Co., 2005 WL 3962818 (N.D. Ohio Aug. 23, 2005) (Ohio recognizes negligent misrepresentation only for affirmative representations, not omissions).

Page 170

155   *Add at beginning of note*: Rose v. Ford, 2003 WL 21495081 (Cal. Ct. App. June 30, 2003) (unpublished) (allegation that defendant falsely stated that vehicle was in good working order and still under manufacturer's warranty stated claim for negligent misrepresentation); Laing v. Clair Car Connection, 2003 WL 1669624 (Me. Super. Ct. Jan. 29, 2003) (claim of negligent misrepresentation of condition of used car raises questions of fact that must be decided by jury); Don Smith Ford, Lincoln-Mercury, Inc. v. Bolinger, 2005 WL 711963, at *4 (Tenn. Ct. App. Mar. 29, 2005) (affirming judgment in favor of car buyer on negligent misrepresentation claim); *see also* Manon v. Tejas Toyota, Inc., 162 S.W.3d 743 (Tex. App. 2005) (affirming award in favor of minivan buyers that could have been based on either UDAP or negligent misrepresentation claim arising from dealer's misrepresentation regarding availability of trim).

157   *Add at end of note*: But see Smith v. Reinhart Ford, 68 Pa. D. & C.4th 432, 437, 438 (2004) (economic loss doctrine did not bar car buyer's fraud claim).

Page 171

7.4.3.6 Innocent Misrepresentation

Addition to note 162.

162   *See also* Sykes v. Brady-Bushey Ford, Inc., 2005 WL 2787517 (Va. Cir. Ct. Oct. 27, 2005) (denying motion to dismiss claim alleging negligent or innocent misrepresentation of vehicle's collision history and number of prior owners).

7.5 Intent to Induce

7.5.1 General

Addition to note 165.

165   *See also* In re Bozovic, 2004 WL 1905355 (Bankr. N.D. Ill. Aug. 24, 2004) (court must measure intent at time of representation); Hyler v. Garner, 548 N.W.2d 864, 871, 872 (Iowa 1996) (intent necessary in rescission action is that to act or refrain from acting; plaintiff need not show intent to deceive); Zapel v. Parker, 94 P.3d 766 (Mont. 2004) (table) (text available at 2004 WL 1053045, at *4) (affirming dismissal of property buyers' negligent misrepresentation claim when buyer failed to provide evidence that seller intended to induce reliance).

Page 172

7.5.2 *Remote Sellers and Others Not in Privity with Buyer*

Addition to note 167.

167   *Add to Varwig citation*: (quoting Restatement (Second) of Torts § 533); *add*: Grabinski v. Blue Springs Ford Sales, Inc., 136 F.3d 565, 569 (8th Cir. 1998) (fact that wholesaler's statements were not made directly to ultimate retail buyer no defense, because wholesaler expected representations to be extended to and relied on by retail buyer); *see also* Pelster v. Ray, 987 F.2d 514, 523 (8th Cir. 1993) (citing

Restatement (Second) of Torts § 533 in holding that car buyers could state a fraud claim against auctioneers); Learjet Corp. v. Spenlinhauer, 901 F.2d 198, 201 (1st Cir. 1990) (holding that plane purchaser had stated a claim based on representations made to the Federal Aviation Administration, which certified the plane before purchaser bought it); Lewis v. Horace Mann Ins. Co., 2005 WL 3962818 (N.D. Ohio Aug. 23, 2005) (insurer's concealment of vehicle's salvage status started chain of events that put dealer in position to misrepresent vehicle's history); W. Sunview Properties, Inc. v. Federman, 338 F. Supp. 2d 1106, 1120 (D. Haw. 2004) (question of fact existed as to whether defendants should have known that prospective buyers would rely on their misrepresentation of the price they paid for their property, made to a third party). *Cf.* Waller v. Avis Rent A Car System, Inc., 2005 WL 2660385 (Cal. Ct. App. Oct. 19, 2005) (unpublished, citation limited) (car rental company's misrepresentation of collision damage was indirect misrepresentation that would have been actionable if it had been material and had caused the damages of which the consumer complained).

Replace note 168 with:	168	Freeman v. Myers, 774 S.W.2d 892, 893 (Mo. Ct. App. 1989); *accord* Learjet Corp. v. Spenlinhauer, 901 F.2d 198 (1st Cir. 1990) (Kan. law); Harris v. Universal Ford, Inc., Clearinghouse No. 53,519 (E.D. Va. Feb. 5, 2001) (magistrate's report; case subsequently settled) (seller is liable to reasonably foreseeable subsequent buyers); Werremeyer v. K.C. Auto Salvage Co., 2003 WL 21487311 (Mo. Ct. App. June 30, 2003) (holding auctioneer liable for misrepresentation that dealer passed on to consumer), *aff'd in relevant part*, 134 S.W.3d 633 (2004); *see* § 2.6.3, *supra*; *see also* Brookings Mun. Utilities, Inc. v. Amoco Chem. Co., 103 F. Supp. 2d 1169, 1178, 1179 (D.S.D. 2000) (maker of statement can be liable for a statement made to a third person when maker expects that statement will be communicated to another who will be influenced by it); Bishop v. Mid-America Auto Auction, Inc., 772 F. Supp. 565 (D. Kan. 1991) (one who makes a fraudulent representation or concealment is liable to class of persons whom he intends or has reason to expect to act or refrain from acting in reliance); Shapiro v. Sutherland, 64 Cal. App. 4th 1534, 1547, 76 Cal. Rptr. 2d 101 (1998); Schnell v. Gustafson, 638 P.2d 850 (Colo. Ct. App. 1981) (sale of home). *But cf.* Don Smith Ford v. Bolinger, 2005 WL 711963 (Tenn. Ct. App. Mar. 29, 2005) (upstream sellers who made full disclosure of car's history and condition not liable).
Addition to note 169.	169	*See also* Hines v. Riverside Chevrolet-Olds, Inc., 655 So. 2d 909 (Ala. 1994); Carter v. Chrysler Corp., 743 So. 2d 456 (Ala. Civ. App. 1998).

Replace sentence containing note 170 with:

A seller should be liable to those that the seller intends or has reason to expect will rely on the representation or nondisclosure, regardless of whether they are in direct privity with each other.[170]

	170	*Retain as in main edition.*
Addition to notes 171, 173.	171	*See also* Werremeyer v. K.C. Auto Salvage Co., 2003 WL 21487311 (Mo. Ct. App. June 30, 2003) (auction had reason to expect that statements to long-time dealer would be repeated to a customer), *aff'd in relevant part*, 134 S.W.3d 633 (2004).
	173	*See also* Lewis v. Horace Mann Ins. Co., 2005 WL 3962818 (N.D. Ohio Aug. 23, 2005) (insurer's concealment of vehicle's salvage status started chain of events that put dealer in position to misrepresent vehicle's history).

Page 173

Add to text at end of subsection's third paragraph:		The original wrongdoer's nondisclosure enables the intervening owner to continue the fraud by passing off the vehicle to a new buyer.
Addition to note 177.	177	*Add at end of note*: *See also* Werremeyer v. K.C. Auto Salvage Co., 2003 WL 21487311 (Mo. Ct. App. June 30, 2003) (auctioneer misrepresented that vehicle had clean title), *aff'd in relevant part*, 134 S.W.3d 633 (2004).

7.6 Justifiable Reliance

7.6.2 Proving Reliance

Addition to notes 184, 186.	184	*See, e.g.*, Werremeyer v. K.C. Auto Salvage Co., 134 S.W.3d 633, 635 (Mo. 2004) (en banc) (affirming judgment against seller when buyer testified that he relied on seller's representation regarding obliterated vehicle identification number and seller did not dispute the reliance). *But see* Lacy v. Morrison, 906 S.W.2d 126 (Miss. Ct. App. 2004) (refusing to infer that truck buyer relied on seller's representation that a 1986 model truck was a 1989 model).

186   Werremeyer v. K.C. Auto Salvage Co., 2003 WL 21487311 (Mo. Ct. App. June 30, 2003), *aff'd in relevant part*, 134 S.W.3d 633 (2004).

Page 174

7.6.3 When Is Reliance Justifiable?

Addition to notes 196–199, 201, 202, 204.

196   *Replace "justifiably" in Krause citation parenthetical with "unjustifiably"*; *add*: *See also* Larsen v. Exclusive Cars, Inc., 97 P.3d 714, 716, 717 (Utah Ct. App. 2004) (reversing summary judgment for truck seller in fraud claim alleging that seller misrepresented truck's engine as new, when buyer drove truck twice before purchasing it and did not notice anything which would have led him to believe misrepresentation was not true; court noted that buyer was nineteen years old and was purchasing his first vehicle).

197   *See also* Baker v. Metro. Life Ins. Co., 907 So. 2d 419 (Ala. 2005) (insurance policy buyer's reliance on seller's statements regarding policy's self-sustaining qualities unreasonable given language of policy; court relied in part on buyer's age, education, and literacy); Rainey v. GAFVT Motors, Inc., 604 S.E.2d 840, 843 (Ga. Ct. App. 2004) (affirming summary judgment against car buyer who alleged that dealership had led him to believe that he was merely guaranteeing his son's loan to purchase car when in fact loan was in his name, financing documents identified him as the purchaser of the car, and son did not sign any of the sales documents).

198   *Add before Bud Clary Chevrolet citation in second paragraph of note*: *See, e.g.,* Precision Enterprises, Inc. v. Duffack Enterprises, Inc., 710 N.W.2d 348, 356 (Neb. Ct. App. 2006) (upholding trial court's conclusion that dealership did not reasonably rely on consumer's false statement that vehicle had not been damaged, where the vehicle was covered in mud and the hood was out of alignment). *Add*: *Accord* Doerr v. Henry, 806 P.2d 669 (Okla. Ct. App. 1990) (buyer has right to rely on veracity of seller without investigation); *see also* Jones v. W. Side Buick Auto Co., 93 S.W.2d 1083, 1087 (Mo. Ct. App. 1936) (plaintiff justifiably relied on mileage representation of odometer).

199   *See also* Horne v. Claude Ray Ford Sales, Inc., 290 S.E.2d 497 (Ga. Ct. App. 1982) (fraud is jury question where buyers would have discovered damage if they had opened trunk).

Page 175

201   *See, e.g.,* Kane v. Nxcess Motorcars, Inc., 2005 WL 497484, at *7 (Tex. App. Mar. 3, 2005) (given car seller's misrepresentation about car's paint, buyer's failure to inspect car did not preclude fraud claim); *see also* Alejandre v. Bull, 98 P.3d 844, 848, 849 (Wash. Ct. App. 2004) (rejecting home seller's argument that home buyers could not have justifiably relied on her failure to disclose septic system's problems because the property inspection they had performed should have alerted them to the defects), *review granted*, 113 P.3d 1039 (Wash. 2005); Kidd v. Mull, 595 S.E.2d 308, 316, 317 (W. Va. 2004) (neither independent investigation doctrine nor constructive notice doctrine undercut fraud claim of property purchaser based on seller's misrepresentation that parcel sold included riverfront property).

202   *Add to Wilson v. Dryvit citation*: *aff'd on other grounds*, 2003 WL 21805618 (4th Cir. Aug. 7, 2003); *add*: *See also* Alires v. McGehee, 85 P.3d 1191, 1199, 1200 (Kan. 2004) (real estate buyers could not show justifiable reliance on seller's misrepresentation as to basement leakage when they did not meet their obligation under the contract to have the property independently inspected); Calloway v. Wyatt, 97 S.E.2d 881, 886 (N.C. 1957) (property buyers could not show they justifiably relied on seller's statements regarding water supply when property seller's conduct in conjunction with plaintiffs' knowledge of the area should have raised suspicion of the statements, yet they nonetheless failed to investigate their truth); RD & J Properties v. Lauralea-Dilton Enterprises, L.L.C., 600 S.E.2d 492, 495, 496 (N.C. Ct. App. 2004) (real estate buyer must make an independent investigation of the property to meet reasonable reliance element unless buyer can show that it was denied the opportunity to investigate the property, could not have discovered the truth of the property's condition through reasonable diligence, or was induced to forego additional investigation by the seller's misrepresentation).

204   Johann, Inc. v. City Motors, Inc., 2002 WL 31684970 (Cal. Ct. App. Dec. 2, 2002) (unpublished); Werremeyer v. K.C. Auto Salvage Co., 2003 WL 21487311 (Mo. Ct. App. June 30, 2003) (buyer's comparison of vehicle identification numbers (VINs) on title to those on vehicle did not vitiate seller's fraud, when non-matching VINs were not visible and seller fabricated explanation for scratched-out VINs), *aff'd in relevant part*, 134 S.W.3d 633 (2004); *see also* Brown v. Bennett, 136 S.W.3d 552, 556 (Mo. Ct. App. 2004) (although property buyer had property inspected, buyer nonetheless could claim justifiable reliance on seller's misrepresentation about the property's flooding problems when misrepresentations were specific and distinct).

Page 176

7.6.4 Puffery

Addition to notes 209, 210.

209   *See also* Hicks v. Sumter Bank & Trust Co., 604 S.E.2d 594, 597 (Ga. Ct. App. 2004) (statement of vice president of bank to real estate developer that foreclosed property was ready for development and could support a residential project was mere sales puffing and could not support claim for fraud).

210   *See also* Kane v. Nxcess Motorcars, Inc., 2005 WL 497484, at *5 (Tex. App. Mar. 3, 2005) (statement that car is in "perfect condition" not puffery).

7.7 Proof of the Fraud Claim

7.7.1 Standard of Proof: Clear and Convincing Evidence Versus Preponderance of Evidence

Addition to note 217.

217   Add at end of Northwest Bank & Trust Co. citation: *aff'd in part, rev'd in part on other grounds*, 354 F.3d 721 (8th Cir. 2003); *replace Rogers citation with*: 68 P.3d 967 (Okla. 2003); *add at end of Williams citation*: *vacated, remanded for further consideration in light of State Farm Mut. Auto Ins. Co. v. Campbell*, 540 U.S. 801 (2003) (mem.).

7.7.2 Parol Evidence Rule

Page 177

Addition to note 224.

224   *See, e.g.*, Werremeyer v. K.C. Auto Salvage Co., 2003 WL 21487311 (Mo. Ct. App. June 30, 2003) ("it is for the jury to decide whether a party is entitled to rely on the verbal representations that conflicted with a written agreement"), *aff'd in relevant part*, 134 S.W.3d 633 (2004); Slack v. James, 614 S.E.2d 636 (S.C. 2005).

7.8 Defenses

7.8.1 Effect of Contract Disclaimer or Merger Clause

Addition to notes 226, 227.

226   *See also* Eicher v. Mid Am. Fin. Inv. Corp., 702 N.W.2d 792, 804 (Neb. 2005) (rule that one who fails to read a contract cannot avoid the effect of signing it applies only in absence of fraud); Van Der Stok v. Van Vorhees, 866 A.2d 972 (N.H. 2005) (disclaimer ineffective against claim for "positive fraud"); Slack v. James, 614 S.E.2d 636 (S.C. 2005) (real estate case; merger clause does not preclude negligent misrepresentation or fraud claim; a non-reliance clause might, but not if it is boilerplate); Union Bank v. Swenson, 707 P.2d 663, 665, 666 (Utah 1985) (summary judgment inappropriate when no specific factual determination made that writing was in fact an integration); Larsen v. Exclusive Cars, Inc, 97 P.3d 714, 716, 717 (Utah Ct. App. 2004) (given buyer's age and defendant's unequivocal statement that car had a new engine, buyer could have reasonably believed that the disclaimers in the sales contract all referred to the truck as described by the salesperson). *But see* Simpson v. Woodbridge Properties, L.L.C., 153 S.W.3d 682 (Tex. App. 2004) (upholding disclaimer clause in real estate contract); *but cf.* Dunn v. Northgate Ford, Inc., 16 A.D.3d 875, 794 N.Y.S.2d 449 (2005) (car buyer could not base fraud claim on salesperson's representation that her monthly car loan payments would be less than what they turned out to be when sales documents reflected correct number); Peabody v. Northgate Ford, Inc., 16 A.D.3d 879, 794 N.Y.S.2d 452 (2005) (car buyer could not base fraud claim on salesperson's misrepresentation as to price of car when sales documents reflected higher price); Evenson v. Quantum Indus., Inc., 687 N.W.2d 241, 245 (N.D. 2004) (affirming dismissal of fraud claim based on oral promise when contract contained contradicting language).

227   *See, e.g.*, Marrale v. Gwinnett Place Ford, 609 S.E.2d 659, 663 (Ga. Ct. App. 2005) (affirming summary judgment on fraud claim against buyer, who alleged that seller had failed to disclose that car had been in a collision, when contract included a merger clause and buyer had not acted to rescind the sale). *But cf.* Bob Maddox Dodge, Inc. v. McKie, 270 S.E.2d 690 (Ga. Ct. App. 1980) (warranty disclaimer had no effect where buyer rescinded due to fraud).

Add to text after sentence containing note 227:

But many courts hold that such merger clauses have no effect on fraud claims.[227.1]

227.1   J.C. Whitney & Co. v. Renaissance Software Corp., 2000 U.S. Dist. LEXIS 6180 (N.D. Ill. Apr. 19, 2000) (mag.) (integration clause does not preclude showing of reliance for fraudulent inducement claim, even in commercial case), *adopted in relevant part, reversed in part on other grounds*, 98 F. Supp. 2d 981 (N.D. Ill. 2000); Boydstun Metal Works v. Parametric Tech. Corp., 1999 U.S. Dist. LEXIS 10226 (D. Or. May 19, 1999) (integration clause did not bar claim for intentional misrepresentation), *adopted by* 1999 U.S. Dist. LEXIS 10227 (D. Or. June 21, 1999); Braund, Inc. v. White, 486 P.2d 50, 9 U.C.C. Rep. Serv. 183 (Alaska 1971); Wagner v. Rao, 180 Ariz. 486, 885 P.2d 174 (Ct. App. 1994) (when auto seller represented car as a "ground up restoration," integration clause did not preclude buyer's misrepresentation suit; it was for jury to decide whether reliance was reasonable given the integration clause); Bill Dreiling Motor Co. v. Shultz, 168 Colo. 59, 450 P.2d 70 (1969) (parol evidence rule inapplicable to fraud, so car buyers could testify to fraudulent inducement despite integration clause); Martinez v. Zovich, 867 A.2d 149 (Conn. App. Ct. 2005) (fraud in sale of home); Ed Fine Oldsmobile, Inc. v. Knisley, 319 A.2d 33, 14 U.C.C. Rep. Serv. 700 (Del. Super. Ct. 1974) (integration clause does not bar fraud claim for misrepresentation of prior use of vehicle); City Dodge, Inc. v. Gardner, 232 Ga. 766, 208 S.E.2d 794, 15 U.C.C. Rep. Serv. 598 (1974) (seller misrepresented vehicle's wreck history; merger clause does not bar fraud claim; reliance is question of fact for jury); Potomac Leasing Co. v. Thrasher, 181 Ga. App. 883, 354 S.E.2d 210 (1987); Hanks v. Hubbard Broad., Inc., 493 N.W.2d 302, 310 (Minn. Ct. App. 1992) (employment contract); Beshears v. S-H-S Motor Sales Corp., 433 S.W.2d 66 (Mo. Ct. App. 1968) (clause disclaiming any oral statements ineffective as to fraud claim concerning misrepresentation of vehicle as demonstrator); Fecik v. Capindale, 54 Pa. D. & C.2d 701 (C.P. Montgomery County 1971) (provision that contract is entire agreement of parties does not prevent testimony concerning fraud in odometer misrepresentation case); First Nat'l Bank v. Brooks Farms, 821 S.W.2d 925 (Tenn. 1991) (disclaimer of reliance in contract did not preclude plaintiff's claim that contract was induced by fraud); George Robberecht Seafood, Inc. v. Maitland Bros., 220 Va. 109, 255 S.E.2d 682, 26 U.C.C. Rep. Serv. 669 (1979) (misrepresentation of condition of airplane; clause that contract could not be extended altered, or varied except by written instrument did not prevent evidence of fraudulent inducement); *cf.* Starr v. Fordham, 420 Mass. 178, 648 N.E.2d 1261 (1995) (integration clause in attorneys' partnership agreement does not insulate party from fraud, but if contract was fully negotiated and voluntarily signed, plaintiff may not raise oral assertions that are inconsistent with specific contract clauses); Galmish v. Cicchini, 90 Ohio St. 3d 22, 734 N.E.2d 782 (2000) (integration clause does not bar parol evidence of fraud unless the fraud claim is based on prior statements or agreements that differ from those in final contract). *But see* Peerless Wall & Window Covering, Inc. v. Synchronics, Inc., 85 F. Supp. 2d 519 (W.D. Pa. 2000) (commercial case) (parol evidence that contradicts terms of contract that contains integration clause only permitted to show fraud in the execution, not fraud in the inducement), *aff'd,* 234 F.3d 1265 (3d Cir. 2000) (table); Sunquest Info. Sys. v. Dean Witter Reynolds, Inc., 40 F. Supp. 2d 644 (W.D. Pa. 1999) (integration clause barred fraud in the inducement claim in commercial case; court acknowledges that Pennsylvania cases are conflicting); Goodyear Tire & Rubber Co. v. Chiles Power Supply, Inc., 7 F. Supp. 2d 954 (N.D. Ohio 1998) (commercial case) (disclaimer of reliance in contract precluded action for fraudulent inducement based on any representation made prior to entering into the contract); Kidd v. Spector, 1998 U.S. Dist. LEXIS 19558 (S.D.N.Y. Dec. 15, 1998) (plaintiff could not maintain claim of fraudulent inducement based on representations specifically disclaimed in the contract); Menaldi v. Pay-Per-View Network, 1998 U.S. Dist. LEXIS 6378 (S.D.N.Y. May 5, 1998) (commercial case) (while general integration clause will not bar a claim of fraud in the inducement, when contract explicitly addressed matter underlying alleged misrepresentation, no claim as a matter of law), *aff'd,* 182 F.3d 900 (2d Cir. 1999); Whittenburg v. L.J. Holding Co., 830 F. Supp. 557 (D. Kan. 1993) (purchase of business jet; plaintiff could not maintain negligent misrepresentation claim when contract contained an integration clause and disclaimed all other remedies for negligence); UAW-GM Human Res. Ctr. v. KSL Recreation Corp., 228 Mich. App. 486, 579 N.W.2d 411 (1998) (merger clause barred fraud claim when alleged fraud did not relate to merger clause or invalidate the entire contract for union's rental of convention hall).

7.8.2 Effect of "As Is" Clauses

Page 178

Addition to notes 230, 232, 233.

230   *See, e.g.,* Werremeyer v. K.C. Auto Salvage Co., 2003 WL 21487311 (Mo. Ct. App. June 30, 2003), *aff'd in relevant part,* 134 S.W.3d 633 (2004); Perkins v. Land Rover, 2003 WL 22939452 (Ohio Ct. App. Dec. 5, 2003) (unpublished); *see also* Northwest Bank & Trust Co. v. First Ill. Nat'l Bank, 354 F.3d 721 (8th Cir. 2003) (Iowa law) (disclaimer does not bar fraud claim even by sophisticated lending institution); Martinez v. Zovich, 867 A.2d 149 (Conn. App. Ct. 2005) (fraud in sale of home); Bauer v. Giannis, 2005 WL 2045771 (Ill. App. Ct. Aug. 16, 2005) (real estate case; "as is" clause ineffective as to fraud claim that was based on written misrepresentations); Morningstar v. Hallett, 858 A.2d 125, 129–131 (Pa. Super. Ct. 2004) ("as is" clause only pertained to implied warranties about the horse being sold and condition in which buyer found the horse, and thus did not preclude fraud action based on seller's misrepresentation about the horse's age); Dixon v. Ford, 608 S.E.2d 879 (S.C. Ct. App. 2005) (fraud in sale of home); Kane v. Nxcess Motorcars, Inc., 2005 WL 497484, at *6, *7 (Tex. App. Mar. 3, 2005) (applying three-pronged test to hold that "as is" clause did not necessarily preclude car buyer's fraud suit against dealership). *But see* Bynum v. Prudential Residential Services, Ltd. P'ship, 129 S.W.3d 781, 789, 790 (Tex. App. 2004) (home buyers not entitled to have "as is" clause and disclaimers set aside on the grounds that they were boilerplate and that buyers lacked sufficient sophistication); *cf.* Sunset Pointe at Silver Lakes Associates, Ltd. v. Vargas, 881 So. 2d 12, 14 n.1 (Fla. Dist. Ct. App. 2004) (real estate case relying on fifty-year old decision, Faulk v. Weller K-F Cars, Inc., 70 So. 2d 578 (Fla. 1954), to find no fraud claim when oral representations contradicted written contract; *Faulk* is distinguishable from most consumer cases because the consumer was seeking the costs she had to pay under a thirty-day 50-50 warranty, and such a warranty presupposes that the car might need repairs).

232   *See also* Savage v. Doyle, 153 S.W.3d 231 (Tex. App. 2004) ("as is" clause did not bar deceptive trade practices act claim arising out of house purchase, based on seller's failure to disclose roof repair).

233   *See also* Werremeyer v. K.C. Auto Salvage Co., 2003 WL 21487311 (Mo. Ct. App. June 30, 2003) (upholding trial court's discretion in excluding disclaimer documents and signs), *aff'd in relevant part,* 134 S.W.3d 633 (2004).

Page 179

7.8.4 *Custom of Trade*

Addition to note 242.

242 *See also* Bauer v. Giannis, 2005 WL 2045771 (Ill. App. Ct. Aug. 16, 2005) ("as is" clause inadmissible in real estate fraud case); Jones v. W. Side Buick Auto Co., 93 S.W.2d 1083, 1086 (Mo. Ct. App. 1936) (rejecting defendant's argument that rolling back odometer was a custom of the trade that excused the misrepresentation).

Page 180

7.8.5 *Preemption by Other Statutes and Election of Remedies*

Add note 243.1 to end of subsection's first sentence.

243.1 *See* Whittom v. Alexander-Richardson P'ship, 851 S.W.2d 504, 506, 507 (Mo. 1993) (en banc) (discussing distinction between election of remedies and election of inconsistent theories of recovery).

Addition to note 245.

245 Scott v. Blue Springs Ford Sales, Inc., 176 S.W.3d 140 (Mo. 2005) (fraud and UDAP claims are not inconsistent, so both can be submitted to the jury; after the verdict the court should determine the extent to which the awards merge); Wilkins v. Peninsula Motor Cars, Inc., 587 S.E.2d 581 (Va. 2003); *see also* Popp Telcom v. Am. Sharecom, Inc., 210 F.3d 928, 936, 937 (8th Cir. 2000) (no prejudice to defendant from shareholders' assertion of common law fraud claims even though they had already received an award pursuant to a separate appraisal judgment); MidAmerica Fed. Sav. & Loan Ass'n v. Shearson/American Express, Inc., 962 F.2d 1470, 1473, 1474 (10th Cir. 1992) (plaintiff may recover attorney fees pursuant to statute even though underlying judgment awarded pursuant to other claims); Majcher v. Laurel Motors, Inc., 680 N.E.2d 416, 422 (Ill. App. Ct. 1997) (election of remedies doctrine does not apply when plaintiff did not pursue an inconsistent action in suit against dealer arising from odometer fraud); United Laboratories, Inc. v. Kuykendall, 437 S.E.2d 374, 380, 381 (N.C. 1993) (plaintiff need not elect between attorney fees and punitive damages when rights to them arise from different courses of conduct).

Replace "the consumer does not have to elect" in sentence containing note 246 with:

in most jurisdictions the consumer does not have to elect

Addition to note 246.

246 *See, e.g.,* Equitable Life Leasing Corp. v. Abbick, 757 P.2d 304, 306 (Kan. 1988) (UDAP remedies not inconsistent with common law fraud remedies, therefore plaintiff need not elect between them); Freeman v. A & J Auto MN, Inc., 2003 WL 22136807 (Minn. Ct. App. Sept. 16, 2003) (unpublished) (may litigate inconsistent remedies but judge must ensure that verdicts are consistent); Wilkins v. Peninsula Motor Cars, Inc., 587 S.E.2d 581, 583, 584 (Va. 2003) (trial court erred by requiring car buyer to elect among different causes of action when awarded UDAP damages, punitive damages arising from fraud claim, and fees and costs ancillary to UDAP claim); *see also* Brown v. King, 601 S.E.2d 296 (N.C. Ct. App. 2004) (non-auto case); Miller v. United Automax, 2005 WL 1490977 (Tenn. June 24, 2005) (consumer has right to elect jury's award of actual damages and punitive damages on fraud count and also seek attorney fees on UDAP count); Concrete Spaces, Inc. v. Sender, 2 S.W.3d 901, 908, 909 (Tenn. 1999) (allowing plaintiff to elect award after verdict prevents double recovery while realizing goal of deterrence, and preserves for review all findings on liability and damages).

Add to text after sentence containing note 246:

A plaintiff who recovers actual damages and punitive damages on a fraud claim and attorney fees on a UDAP claim need not choose between these two awards, because the two recoveries are not duplicative and their purposes are different.[246.1]

246.1 Miller v. United Automax, 2005 WL 1490977 (Tenn. June 24, 2005) (sale of car with undisclosed damage); Wilkins v. Peninsula Motor Cars, Inc., 587 S.E.2d 581 (Va. 2003).

7.9 Actual Damages

7.9.1 *General*

Addition to notes 249, 253, 261, 263.

249 *See also* Chavarria v. Fleetwood Retail Corp., 115 P.3d 799, 807 (N.M. Ct. App. 2005) (fact that consumer signed promissory note meets damage requirement even if consumer has not made any payments), *review granted*, 115 P.3d 230 (N.M. 2005); Rainey v. GAFVT Motors, Inc., 604 S.E.2d 840, 844 (Ga. Ct. App. 2004) (car buyer who alleged he was led to believe he was merely guaranteeing his son's loan and not executing the loan himself could not maintain fraud claim because the losses he suffered did not differ from those he would have suffered as guarantor).

253 *See also* Arthur v. Bill Swad Chrysler Plymouth Co., 1975 WL 181405, at *4 (Ohio Ct. App. June 10,

1975) (when plaintiffs failed to submit proof of any value for loss of use, they could not recover damages based on that loss).

261   Tietsworth v. Harley-Davidson, Inc., 677 N.W.2d 233 (Wis. 2004).

263   *Delete Tietsworth citation.*

Add to text at end of subsection's fourth paragraph:

The effect of a misrepresentation on the consumer's warranty or lemon law rights should always be considered in assessing damages. For example, if prior wreck damage means that the warranty on the vehicle is void, the value of the warranty may be an element of the consumer's damages. If the state lemon law covers demonstrators but not previously-titled used vehicles, or covers new vehicles but not used vehicles, the loss of lemon law rights, if quantifiable, might be an element of damages when the seller misrepresented the prior use of the vehicle.[264.1]

264.1   Tuckish v. Pompano Motor Co., 337 F. Supp. 2d 1313 (S.D. Fla. 2004) (noting that, by selling consumer a used vehicle represented as new, the dealer eliminated consumer's lemon law rights).

7.9.2 Causation

Addition to notes 267, 269.

267   *See, e.g.,* Taylor v. Bennett Chevrolet/Buick, Inc., 609 S.E.2d 215 (Ga. Ct. App. 2005) (upholding jury instruction requiring proximate cause and affirming verdict against plaintiffs, who had alleged that seller had held out car as new notwithstanding that it had been in a collision).

269   *See also* O'Brien v. B.L.C. Ins. Co., 768 S.W.2d 64, 68 (Mo. 1989) (en banc) (rejecting insurer's argument that dealer's fraud was an intervening cause between ultimate buyer's damages and insurer's violation of salvage titling statute which should insulate insurer from liability).

7.9.3 Measure of Actual Damages: Benefit-of-Bargain Versus Out-of-Pocket Damages

Add note 275.1 after "Utah" in subsection's first sentence.

275.1   Lamb v. Bangart, 525 P.2d 602, 609 (Utah 1974).

7.10 Punitive or Exemplary Damages

7.10.1 Actual Damages As Precondition to Punitive Damages

Addition to notes 288, 289.

288   *Add at end of note*: *See also* Mobile Infirmary Med. Ctr. v. Hodgen, 884 So. 2d 801 (Ala. 2003) (requirement of actual damages satisfied by medical expenses paid by insurer, even though jury could not award such damages because of abolition of collateral source rule; jury should be given special interrogatory about amount); *cf.* Asa-Brandt, Inc. v. ADM Investor Services, Inc., 344 F.3d 738, 746 n.14 (8th Cir. 2003) (Iowa law) (punitive damages may be based on nominal damages).

289   *See* Home Pride Foods v. Martin, 2003 WL 23005185 (Iowa Ct. App. Dec. 24, 2003) (actual damages must be shown but need not be awarded); Roberie v. VonBokern, 2003 WL 22976126 (Ky. Ct. App. Dec. 19, 2003) (unpublished) (punitive damages may be awarded even without actual damages; remanding to trial court for analysis of *State Farm* factors).

7.10.2 Relationship to Rescission Remedy

Addition to note 293.

293   *See also* Bickerstaff Automotive, Inc. v. Tsepas, 574 S.E.2d 322 (Ga. Ct. App. 2002) (affirming award of punitive damages after buyer rescinded sale due to fraud).

Replace subsection's second paragraph with:

The modern trend is to acknowledge that certain consumer fraud cases, even when framed as equitable actions, simply call out for punitive damages. In fact, equity may at times demand the award of punitive damages in order to provide complete relief and "to deter clearly unacceptable behavior."[295] The underlying rationale of the older rule, prohibiting the award of punitive damages in equitable actions, was to shield those who may have caused damage without any kind of legal injury from having to pay punitive damages.[296] Some courts construed this rule as requiring an award of actual damages as a basis for punitive damages. However, when the action for equitable relief requires the plaintiff to show that the defendant has invaded a legally protected interest, the award of that relief can satisfy this traditional concern.[297] Accordingly, modern courts should reject the formalistic argument that punitive damages can not be recovered without recovery of compensatory or at least nominal damages.[297.1] To hold otherwise leads to the illogical rule that punitive damages are available for the tort of fraud in a law action, but not in an equitable action, allowing the remedy, not the conduct, to drive the result.[297.2]

Even where courts retain the formalistic rule, the requirement of "actual damages" should be construed broadly to encompass other types of harm that can support an award of punitive damages.[297.3] Thus, the requirement of actual damages can be satisfied by a jury's finding that the plaintiff has suffered actual damages, even if no award for actual damages is made. For example, in a replevin action, even though actual damages were not an element of the action, punitive damages were upheld when the trial judge specifically instructed the jury that it could not return a verdict for punitive damages unless it was satisfied that actual damages had been shown.[297.4] Likewise, if the cause of action would permit a plaintiff to recover compensatory or nominal damages, the judgment in the plaintiff's favor should be sufficient to support punitive damages.[297.5]

Defendants also argue that punitive damages suggest vengeance, a motive considered to be inconsistent with the aims of courts sitting in equity.[297.6] However, notwithstanding the name, punitive—perhaps better labeled as exemplary—damages seek to deter fraud; to fail to award them could in fact invite others to defraud "secure in the conviction that they will not be punished," at least when the plaintiff seeks an equitable remedy.[297.7] Accordingly, punitive damages are perfectly consistent with rescission.[297.8]

Another justification for excluding punitive damages from equitable actions arises from the traditional division between courts at law and courts in equity in England. In states that have eliminated this distinction between courts, or between such causes of action, the justification dissolves.[297.9] Even when states retain the English division, courts of equity should have the jurisdiction and power to award punitive damages as part of their duty to award complete relief.[297.10]

295   *See* Madrid v. Marquez, 33 P.3d 683, 686 (N.M. Ct. App. 2001).

296   Vill. of Peck v. Denison, 450 P.2d 310, 313–315 (Idaho 1969) (affirming award of punitive damages in conjunction with an injunction; rejecting argument that award of actual damages was a "talismanic necessity" for the award of punitive damages).

297   Vill. of Peck v. Denison, 450 P.2d 310, 315 (Idaho 1969); Madrid v. Marquez, 33 P.3d 683, 686 (N.M. Ct. App. 2001) ("justice is better served by allowing the award of punitive damages in those equity cases where the conduct of the wrongdoer warrants punitive damages in order to deter clearly unacceptable behavior"; affirming award of punitive damages against defendant who had fraudulently induced elderly homeowners to transfer their house to defendant and then tried to force them from the property).

297.1   *See, e.g.*, Madrid v. Marquez, 33 P.3d 683, 686 (N.M. Ct. App. 2001).

297.2   *See* Black v. Gardner, 320 N.W.2d 153, 160, 161 (S.D. 1982) (commenting on inconsistency and affirming award of punitive damages in guardianship action); Gill v. Godwin, 442 S.W.2d 661, 663 (Tenn. Ct. App. 1967) (affirming award of punitive damages in fraud case).

297.3   Medasys Acquisition Corp. v. SDMS, Prof'l Corp., 55 P.3d 763, 766, 767 (Ariz. 2002) (en banc) (holding that damages for rescission can satisfy actual damages requirement for purposes of punitive damages award); *see also* Hutchison v. Pyburn, 567 S.W.2d 762, 766 (Tenn. Ct. App. 1977) (plaintiffs' proof of their entitlement to rescission of the deed, refund of the purchase price, and incidental damages such as moving expenses, satisfied the "actual damages" prerequisite to recovery of punitive damages in Tennessee).

297.4   Haskins v. Shelden, 558 P.2d 487, 493 (Alaska 1976) (approving jury instruction that provided "[i]n order to recover exemplary damages, there must be actual damages shown").

297.5   Fousel v. Ted Walker Mobile Homes, Inc., 602 P.2d 507, 510 (Ariz. Ct. App. 1979) (affirming award of punitive damages in fraud suit to rescind contract for purchase of mobile home when plaintiff recovered consequential damages); Mehovic v. Mehovic, 514 S.E.2d 730, 733–735 (N.C. Ct. App. 1999) (affirming award of $24,500 in rescission action based on fraud when plaintiff awarded just one dollar in compensatory damages); Hutchison v. Pyburn, 567 S.W.2d 762, 765, 766 (Tenn. Ct. App. 1977) (plaintiff could seek punitive damages in suit to rescind deed of real property on grounds of fraud when plaintiff recovered refund of purchase price and incidental damages for moving expenses).

297.6   *See, e.g.*, Madrid v. Marquez, 33 P.3d 683, 685, 686 (N.M. Ct. App. 2001) (rejecting argument).

297.7   Charles v. Epperson & Co., 137 N.W.2d 605, 618, 619 (Iowa 1965) (affirming award of punitive damages in shareholder derivative action arising from fraud); *see also* Hutchison v. Pyburn, 567 S.W.2d 762, 764

(Tenn. Ct. App. 1977) (punitive damages serve to deter fraudulent conduct and relate to the defendant's actions in causing the injury rather than to the extent of the injury itself).

297.8 Hutchison v. Pyburn, 567 S.W.2d 762, 765 (Tenn. Ct. App. 1977) (rejecting argument that doctrine of election of remedies precluded award of punitive damages in a rescission action).

297.9 *See, e.g.,* Starkovich v. Noye, 529 P.2d 698, 701–703 (Ariz. 1974) (affirming award of punitive damages in declaratory judgment action that sought reformation of a joint venture agreement due to fraud; noting that distinction between actions at law and in equity had been eliminated in Arizona); Charles v. Epperson & Co., 137 N.W.2d 605, 618, 619 (Iowa 1965) (affirming award when single court system); I.H.P. Corp. v. 210 Cent. Park S. Corp., 239 N.Y.S.2d 547, 548 (N.Y. 1963) (affirming award of punitive damages in action for injunction, noting that state courts have general jurisdiction).

297.10 *See, e.g.,* Tideway Oil Programs, Inc. v. Serio, 431 So. 2d 454, 459–464 (Miss. 1983) (holding that state chancery courts had subject matter jurisdiction to assess punitive damages); *see also* Gould v. Starr, 558 S.W.2d 755, 770, 771 (Mo. Ct. App. 1977) (rejecting lack of jurisdiction argument and affirming award of punitive damages in equitable action for an accounting against trustees); Jones v. Morrison, 458 S.W.2d 434, 438 (Tenn. Ct. App. 1970) (chancery courts had jurisdiction to award exemplary damages, upholding award of such damages awarded in conjunction with an injunction); Kneeland v. Bruce, 336 S.W.2d 319, 325 (Tenn. Ct. App. 1960) (upholding award of punitive damages to plaintiff who was defrauded out of her land).

7.10.3 Elements of Punitive Damages Claim

Addition to notes 298, 302, 306, 308, 311.

298 *See, e.g.,* Tanguay v. Seacoast Tractor Sales, Inc., 494 A.2d 1364 (Me. 1985) (must be clear and convincing evidence that tortfeasor acted with malice; no error in award of $1500 punitive damages against dealer who misrepresented history of car that had been immersed in salt water); Darcars Motors v. Borzym, 841 A.2d 828 (Md. 2004) (must show actual malice, in other words, actual knowledge of falsity and intent to deceive; proof of ability to pay unnecessary).

Page 185

302 Lewis v. Horace Mann Ins. Co., 2005 WL 3962818 (N.D. Ohio Aug. 23, 2005) (insurer's conscious disregard of salvage title law would justify punitive damages); Werremeyer v. K.C. Auto Salvage Co., 2003 WL 21487311 (Mo. Ct. App. June 30, 2003) (reckless indifference sufficient; shown by salesman's fabrication of explanations for vehicle's discrepancies), *aff'd in relevant part*, 134 S.W.3d 633 (2004); *see also* Chong v. Parker, 361 F.3d 455 (8th Cir. 2004) (evil motive or reckless indifference required for punitive damages on Missouri UDAP claim).

306 *See* Johnson v. Ford Motor Co., 2003 WL 22794432 (Cal. Ct. App. Nov. 25, 2003) (unpublished) (intentional fraud is sufficient to support punitive damages without any further finding that conduct was despicable), *rev'd, remanded on other grounds*, 35 Cal. 4th 1191, 29 Cal. Rptr. 3d 401 (2005) (disagreeing with court of appeals' reduction of punitive damage award; remanding for new analysis of *State Farm* factors). *But cf.* Darcars Motors v. Borzym, 841 A.2d 828 (Md. 2004) (fraud can be based on reckless disregard, but actual malice required for punitive damages).

308 *See, e.g.,* Darcars Motors v. Borzym, 841 A.2d 828 (Md. 2004).

Page 186

311 *Delete Darcars Motors citation.*

7.10.4 State Statute May Limit Size of Punitive Damages Award

Add note 312.1 at end of sentence containing note 312.

312.1 *LOUISIANA:* Gray v. State, through the Dep't of Highways, 202 So. 2d 24, 30 (La. 1967) (punitive damages not permitted under civil law system); Ricard v. State, 382 So. 2d 190, 193 (La. Ct. App. 1980) (punitive damages not allowed unless specifically provided for), *aff'd*, 390 So. 2d 882 (La. 1980).
MASSACHUSETTS: Flesner v. Technical Communications Corp., 575 N.E.2d 1107, 1112 (Mass. 1991) (punitive damages not allowed unless expressly authorized by statute); Santana v. Registrar of Voters, 502 N.E.2d 132, 135 (Mass. 1986).
NEBRASKA: Distinctive Printing & Packaging Co. v. Cox, 443 N.W.2d 566 (Neb. 1989) (interpreting Neb. Const. art. VII, § 5 to bar punitive damages); Miller v. Kingsley, 230 N.W.2d 472 (Neb. 1975) (interpreting Nebraska Constitution to bar punitive damages).
NEW HAMPSHIRE: N.H. Rev. Stat. Ann. § 507:16 (no punitive damages may be awarded in any action unless otherwise authorized by statute).
WASHINGTON: Steele v. Johnson, 458 P.2d 889, 890 (Wash. 1969) (punitive damages not allowed unless expressly authorized by legislature).

Addition to note 313.

313 *See also* Mobile Infirmary Med. Ctr. v. Hodgen, 884 So. 2d 801 (Ala. 2003) (declining to revisit question of constitutionality of prior statute, as legislature has replaced it).

Replace note 315 with:

315 Reust v. Alaska Petroleum Contractors, Inc., 127 P.3d 807 (Alaska 2005) (reaffirming previous decision that caps do not violate equal protection or right to jury trial; payment of one-half of award to state does not violate takings clause); Anderson v. State *ex rel.* Cent. Bering Sea Fishermen's Ass'n, 78 P.3d 710

(Alaska 2003) (affirmance by equally divided court) (statute requiring fifty percent of punitive damages to be paid to state is not unconstitutional taking and does not violate equal protection or substantive due process); Evans *ex rel.* Kutch v. State, 56 P.3d 1046 (Alaska 2002) (affirmance by equally divided court) (caps on punitive and non-economic damages not facially unconstitutional).

Add to text after sentence containing note 315:

It has also interpreted it to apply to all causes of action in which punitive damages are claimed, not just to torts.[315.1]

315.1   Reust v. Alaska Petroleum Contractors, Inc., 127 P.3d 807 (Alaska 2005).

Add to text at end of Arkansas entry:

Ark. Code Ann. § 16-55-208 limits the punitive damage award per plaintiff to the greater of the following: $250,000; or three times the amount of compensatory damages awarded in the action, not to exceed one million dollars ($1,000,000). These limits do not apply if, at the time of the injury, the defendant intentionally pursued a course of conduct for the purpose of causing injury or damage, and the defendant's conduct did, in fact, harm the plaintiff. Limitation amounts are to be adjusted every three years in accordance with the Consumer Price Index rate.

Add to text at end of Colorado entry:

The intermediate appellate court has upheld caps on non-economic damages, using reasoning that would apply to punitive damages as well.[316.1]

316.1   Stewart v. Rice, 25 P.3d 1233 (Colo. Ct. App. 2000) (upholding statute capping non-economic damages), *rev'd on other grounds*, 47 P.3d 316 (Colo. 2002); Scharrel v. Wal-Mart Stores, Inc., 949 P.2d 89 (Colo. Ct. App. 1997) (statute capping non-economic damages upheld against due process, equal protection, and state open court challenges); *see also* Scholz v. Metro. Pathologists, Prof'l Corp., 851 P.2d 901 (Colo. 1993) (statute capping non-economic damages in healthcare malpractice cases upheld against equal protection, due process, and state right to jury trial challenges).

Page 187

Add note 316.2 at end of Florida entry.

316.2   *See* Coral Cadillac, Inc. v. Stephens, 867 So. 2d 556 (Fla. Dist. Ct. App. 2004) (interpreting pre-1999 version of cap not to apply to consumer transactions; certifying this question to state supreme court).

Add note 317.1 at end of sentence following sentence containing note 317.

317.1   This provision's constitutionality was upheld in State v. Mosely, 436 S.E.2d 632 (Ga. 1993) (no violation of takings, jury trial, or access to courts constitutional provisions).

Add to text after Georgia entry:

Idaho: Idaho Code § 6-1604 (Michie) caps punitive damages at the greater of $250,000 or three times compensatory damages, raises the standard of proof to clear and convincing evidence, and eliminates wanton behavior (but not fraudulent behavior) as grounds for punitive damages.

Add to text after first sentence of Illinois entry:

735 Ill. Comp. Stat. § 5/2-1207 requires the court, after trial of a civil action, to determine the reasonableness of any punitive damages award and to apportion the award among the plaintiff, the plaintiff's attorney, and the Illinois Department of Human Services.

Replace sentence containing note 320 and last sentence of Indiana entry with:

The state supreme court has held that the seventy-five percent rule does not amount to a taking of property or services without just compensation and is not an unconstitutional tax.[320]

320   Cheatham v. Pohle, 789 N.E.2d 467 (Ind. 2003).

Add note 320.1 at end of first sentence of Kansas entry.

320.1   *See* Smith v. Printup, 866 P.2d 985 (Kan. 1993) (statute allowing court, rather than jury, to determine amount of punitive damages did not deny due process, equal protection, or right to jury trial; no right to punitive damages, so legislature may cap or abolish them).

Add to text after Kansas entry:

Mississippi: Miss. Code Ann. § 11-1-65 allows punitive damages only if actual damages are awarded. The amount allowed is limited based on the net worth of defendant, calculated using generally accepted accounting principles: $20 million if net worth of defendant is more than $1 billion; $15 million if net worth is more than $750 million but less than $1 billion; $5 million if net worth is more than $500 million but less than $750 million; $3.75 million if net worth is more than $100 million but less than $500 million; $2.5 million if net worth is more than $50 million but less than $100 million; 2% of net worth if net worth is less than

$50 million. The statute sets criteria for punitive damages, and requires the court to review the jury award for reasonableness. The limits do not apply if the act causing injury resulted in a felony conviction, or if the tortfeasor was under the influence of alcohol or drugs.

Missouri: Mo. Rev. Stat. § 537.675 provides that half of an award of punitive damages, after deducting attorney fees and expenses, goes to the state, into a fund that provides compensation to certain uncompensated tort victims and funding for civil legal services.[320.2] This provision does not apply to health care malpractice actions under Mo. Rev. Stat. § 538.300. Mo. Rev. Stat. § 510.265 limits punitive damage awards to the greater of $500,000 or five times the net amount of the judgment awarded to the plaintiff against the defendant. These limitations do not apply if the State of Missouri is the plaintiff requesting punitive damages or the defendant pleads guilty to or is convicted of a felony arising out of the acts or omissions pleaded by the plaintiff. They also are inapplicable to civil actions as to discrimination.

Montana: Mont. Code Ann. § 27-1-220 bars punitive damages in actions arising from contract or breach of contract, except for product liability cases and as otherwise provided by statute. For other causes of action, punitive damages are limited to the lesser of $10 million or 3% of defendant's net worth.[320.3] This section does not limit damages in class actions.

> 320.2   The statute's constitutionality was upheld in Hoskins v. Bus. Men's Assurance, 79 S.W.3d 901 (Mo. 2002) and Fust v. Att'y Gen., 947 S.W.2d 424 (Mo. 1997).
>
> 320.3   *See also* Mont. Code Ann. § 27-1-710 (limit of $250,000 for liquor liability).

Add to text at end of New Jersey entry:

These caps do not apply to cases involving impaired driving, certain civil rights violations, sexual abuse of a minor, and the confidentiality of HIV/AIDS records.

Replace sentence containing note 324 with:

The cap applies per plaintiff, so if two plaintiffs sue the same defendant each can be awarded punitive damages up to the cap.[324] The state supreme court has upheld the statute against a variety of constitutional challenges.[324.1]

> 324   Rhyne v. K-Mart Corp., 594 S.E.2d 1 (N.C. 2004).
>
> 324.1   *Id.*

Replace "manufactured" in sentence containing note 325 with:

manufactured, unless approval was secured by knowingly withholding or misrepresenting material information, or by bribing a federal official.[325]

> 325   *Retain as in main edition.*

Add to text at end of North Dakota entry:

Caps do not apply to certain accidents involving impaired driving, if defendant has been convicted of operating under the influence within the previous five years.

Replace final sentence of Ohio entry with:

In 2001, the legislature amended the statute to specify criteria for awarding punitive damages without setting a cap. Two years later, it amended the statute again, this time setting a cap in tort actions (as defined by the statute) of two times the amount of compensatory damages. The new statute includes special protections for individuals and small employers, and also restricts multiple awards of punitive damages against the same defendant.

Page 188

Add to text after Oklahoma entry:

Oregon: Or. Rev. Stat. § 31.735 provides that sixty percent of any punitive damages award will go to the state, to be added to the Crime Victims Compensation fund. Or. Rev. Stat. § 31.740 bars punitive damages against licensed health care practitioners acting within the scope of their licenses and without malice.

Add note 327.1 at end of first sentence of Texas entry.

> 327.1   *See* Signal Peak Enterprises v. Bettina Investments, Inc., 138 S.W.3d 915 (Tex. App. 2004) (only damages awarded on fraud claim, not those awarded on contract claim, can be included in the calculation of economic damages).

Add note 327.2 at end of second sentence of Texas entry.

> 327.2   *See* Mission Res., Inc. v. Garza Energy Trust, 166 S.W.3d 301 (Tex. App. 2005) (cap did not apply when plaintiffs proved felony theft beyond a reasonable doubt and jury so found); Signal Peak Enterprises v. Bettina Investments, Inc., 138 S.W.3d 915 (Tex. App. 2004) (trier of fact must make specific finding that defendant's conduct constitutes one of the enumerated felonies).

Addition to note 328.

328   *Add at end of Hall citation*: *review granted*, 2003 Tex. LEXIS 46 (Tex. Apr. 17, 2003).

Add to text after Texas entry:

Utah: Utah Code Ann. § 78-18-1 allows punitive damages only if compensatory or general damages are awarded (this provision does not apply in the case of operating a vehicle or boat under the influence of alcohol or drugs). Fifty percent of all punitive damages awards of $20,000 or more must, after payment of attorney fees and costs, go to the state's general fund. The Utah Supreme Court struck down an earlier version of the 50% requirement,[328.1] but it did not express an opinion about the currently significantly different statutory language.[328.2] A separate statute, Utah Code Ann. § 78-14-7.1, caps non-economic damages in medical malpractice actions and has been held constitutional by the state supreme court.[328.3]

328.1   Smith v. Price Dev. Co. 125 P.3d 945 (Utah 2005).

328.2   *Id.* at 951 n.5.

328.3   Judd v. Drezga, 103 P.3d 135 (Utah 2004) (rejecting challenges based on open courts, uniform operation of laws, due process, jury trial, and separation of powers provisions of state constitution).

Addition to note 329.

329   *Add at beginning of note*: *See also* Al-Abood *ex rel.* Al-Abood v. El Shamari, 217 F.3d 225 (4th Cir. 2000) (cap applies to entire lawsuit, not to each defendant separately; court expresses no opinion concerning multiple plaintiffs); Transition, Inc. v. Austin, 2002 WL 1050240 (E.D. Va. Mar. 15, 2002) (application to multiple plaintiffs an open question); Advanced Marine Enterprises, Inc. v. PRC, Inc., 501 S.E.2d 148 (Va. 1998) (statutory cap on "punitive damages" does not apply to "treble damages" permitted by another statute, in this case criminal statute forbidding conspiracy to injure another's business).

Page 189

Replace § 7.10.6 with:

7.10.6 Constitutional and Judicial Limits

7.10.6.1 Overview of Supreme Court Rulings

The constitutional boundaries of punitive damages awards are set out in four Supreme Court cases: *Pacific Mutual Life Ins. Co. v. Haslip*,[336] *TXO Production Corp. v. Alliance Resources Corp.*,[337] *BMW of North America, Inc. v. Gore*,[338] and *State Farm Mutual Automobile Insurance Co. v. Campbell*.[339] All four of these cases concerned fraud.

Taken together, these cases establish that states may impose punitive damages that are reasonably necessary to further the legitimate interests of punishing unlawful conduct and deterring its repetition, so long as those interests relate to the state's protection of its own citizens and its own economy.[340] However, the Due Process Clause of the Fourteenth Amendment, which protects against the deprivation of property without due process of law, prohibits a state from imposing a grossly excessive punishment on a tortfeasor.[341] The four cases outline both procedural and substantive protections against "grossly excessive" punitive damages awards.

Haslip emphasizes the importance of the process through which a court and jury consider and award punitive damages. To meet the procedural safeguards approved by *Haslip*, a judge should direct the jury to exercise its discretion within reasonable constraints. The court should instruct the jury on the nature and purpose of punitive damages, identifying the damages as punishment, and explaining that they are not compulsory.[342] Additionally, the trial court, post-verdict, should conduct a "meaningful and adequate review" of the award.[343] Finally, an appellate court should review both the verdict and the post-trial review, a review that should "make certain that the punitive damages are

336   499 U.S. 1, 111 S. Ct. 1032, 113 L. Ed. 2d 1 (1991).

337   509 U.S. 443, 113 S. Ct. 2711, 125 L. Ed. 2d 366 (1993).

338   517 U.S. 559, 116 S. Ct. 1589, 134 L. Ed. 2d 809 (1996).

339   538 U.S. 408, 123 S. Ct. 1513, 155 L. Ed. 2d 585 (2003).

340   BMW of N. Am., Inc. v. Gore, 517 U.S. 559, 567–571, 116 S. Ct. 1589, 134 L. Ed. 2d 809 (1996) (holding that a state may not base a punitive damages award on a defendant's conduct in other states if such conduct is legal in those states).

341   State Farm Mut. Auto. Ins. Co. v. Campbell, 538 U.S. 408, 416,

417 (2003); *Gore*, 517 U.S. at 568; TXO Production Corp. v. Alliance Resources Corp., 509 U.S. 443, 454, 113 S. Ct. 2711, 125 L. Ed. 2d 366 (1993).

342   Pac. Mut. Life Ins. Co. v. Haslip, 499 U.S. 1, 19, 111 S. Ct. 1032, 113 L. Ed. 2d 1 (1991).

343   *Id.* at 20 (approving post-trial procedure that required trial court to reflect in the record reasons for interfering or not interfering with award on grounds of excessiveness after considering the culpability of the defendant's conduct, the desirability of discouraging others from similar conduct and the impact of the award on the parties and third parties); *see also* Grabinski v. Blue Springs Ford Sales, Inc., 136 F.3d 565 (8th Cir. 1998) (remanding case for review of jury's award of punitive damages in used car fraud case when trial court failed to review the award post-verdict). On remand in *Grabinski*, the district court upheld the $210,000 award after going through the excessiveness analysis. Grabinski v. Blue Springs Ford Sales, 1998 U.S. Dist. LEXIS 17015 (W.D. Mo. Oct. 27, 1998), *aff'd in relevant part, rev'd in part on other grounds*, 203 F.3d 1024 (8th Cir. 2000) (affirming award of punitive damages and reversing denial of attorney fees).

reasonable in their amount and rational in light of their purpose to punish what has occurred and deter its repetition."[344] The appellate court's review is de novo, although it must defer to the trial court's findings of fact unless they are clearly erroneous.[345]

Procedural safeguards are not all that is required by the Fourteenth Amendment, however. Even with such safeguards the amount of an award may be so grossly excessive as to violate the Fourteenth Amendment. In *Gore* the Supreme Court set forth three "guideposts" by which to judge whether the amount of a punitive damages verdict exceeds constitutional limits. Six years later, in *State Farm*, the Court further interpreted these guideposts, assigning to each an appropriate weight and discussing the various considerations which make up the components of each guidepost.

7.10.6.2 The Three Guideposts: Reprehensibility, Ratio, and Relationship to Civil and Criminal Penalties

7.10.6.2.1 Overview of Gore and State Farm

In *Gore* the Supreme Court overturned a $2,000,000 award of punitive damages against an automobile distributor who had not disclosed to the plaintiff, a buyer of a new BMW, that it had repainted the car after it had been damaged by acid rain in transport.[346] The Court identified three guideposts that indicated that this award was so grossly excessive that it violated the Fourteenth Amendment: "[T]he degree of reprehensibility of the nondisclosure; the disparity between the harm or potential harm suffered by Dr. Gore and his punitive damages award; and the difference between this remedy and the civil penalties authorized or imposed in comparable cases."[347]

In *State Farm*,[348] an automobile policyholder and his wife brought suit against his insurance company because of the company's treatment of a third party's car accident claim against them. After hearing evidence that the company had failed to properly investigate the claim, had misrepresented the evaluation of the claim and the corresponding risk of the policyholder's exposure to an excess judgment, and had altered and destroyed records on the matter, a jury found the company liable for bad faith, fraud, and intentional infliction of emotional distress. The jury then awarded $2.5 million in compensatory damages and $145 million in punitive damages. The trial court reduced the awards to $1 million and $25 million, respectively, but the Utah Supreme Court reinstated the original punitive damages award.[349] The United States Supreme Court then reversed the reinstatement of the award, striking the punitive damages award after evaluating it under the three *Gore* guideposts.

7.10.6.2.2 Reprehensibility

The first guidepost by which to evaluate a jury's punitive damages verdict is the degree of reprehensibility of the defendant's conduct.[350] The Court stated in both in *State Farm* and *Gore* that it is the primary factor, "the most important indicium of the reasonableness of a punitive damages award."[351] The Court in *State Farm* pulled from *Gore*'s discussion of this guidepost a list of five factors to be considered in evaluating an act's reprehensibility:

- Whether the harm is physical as opposed to economic;
- Whether the tortious conduct shows an indifference to or reckless disregard of the health or safety of others;
- Whether the target of the conduct had financial vulnerability;
- Whether the conduct involved repeated actions or was only an isolated incident; and
- Whether the harm resulted from intentional malice, trickery, or deceit, or mere accident.[352]

Most of *State Farm*'s analysis of the reprehensibility guidepost focuses on the evidence of repetition. The Court's primary concern was that the jury might have based its award on evidence of what the Court characterized as dissimilar, out-of-state acts by the defendant.[353] Expert witnesses had given extensive testimony about a nationwide scheme of State Farm's to deceive and cheat customers in order to limit payouts on claims to meet fiscal targets.[354] The Court was offended by what it viewed as the use of the case

---

344 *Haslip*, 499 U.S. at 21.

345 Cooper Indus., Inc. v. Leatherman Tool Group, 532 U.S. 424, 121 S. Ct. 1678, 149 L. Ed. 2d 674 (2001).

346 BMW had adopted a nationwide policy of not disclosing damage to cars in the course of transportation if the cost of repairing the damage did not exceed three percent of the car's suggested retail price. 517 U.S. at 562, 563. In this case the evidence showed that while the cost of repair was only $601.37, less than one and one-half percent of the car's price, the repair reduced the car's value by about $4000, the amount of actual damages awarded to the buyer. *Id.*

The jury had awarded the buyer $4000 in actual damages and $4,000,000 in punitive damages, a figure apparently reached by multiplying the actual damages by the number of cars estimated to have been similarly repainted. *Id.* Upon review, the Alabama Supreme Court cut the punitive damages award in half. *Id.* Nonetheless, the award did not pass constitutional scrutiny.

347 *Gore*, 517 U.S. at 575.

348 538 U.S. 408, 123 S. Ct. 1513, 155 L. Ed. 2d 585 (2003).

349 Campbell v. State Farm Mut. Auto. Ins. Co., 65 P.3d 1134 (Utah 2001), *rev'd*, 538 U.S. 408 (2003).

350 *Gore*, 517 U.S. at 575, 576.

351 *Gore*, 517 U.S. at 575; *accord State Farm*, 538 U.S. at 419.

352 *State Farm*, 538 U.S. at 419.

353 *Id.* at 420–423.

354 Campbell v. State Farm Mut. Auto. Ins. Co., 2001 WL 1246676, at *9 (Utah Oct. 19, 2001), *rev'd*, 538 U.S. 408 (2003).

"as a platform to expose, and punish, the perceived deficiencies of State Farm's operations throughout the country."[355]

According to *State Farm*, a jury may not use punitive damages to punish a defendant for out-of-state conduct that was lawful when it occurred, and ordinarily a state has no right to punish a defendant even for out-of-state conduct that was unlawful when it occurred. Evidence of lawful or unlawful out-of-state conduct can, however, be admitted to show the deliberateness or culpability of a defendant with respect to the tort committed in the state.[356] It can also be introduced to show recidivism, another factor in the reprehensibility guidepost.[357] But the court must instruct the jury that it may not use such evidence to punish a defendant for acts that were lawful where they occurred.[358]

Any out-of-state conduct that is admitted into evidence must "have a nexus to the specific harm suffered by the plaintiff."[359] Nexus is an issue for evidence of in-state conduct as well. A state may not use punitive damages to punish a defendant for behavior that is dissimilar to that at issue in the case, regardless of how "unsavory" such behavior might be.[360]

In *Gore*, the Court emphasized that the harm—the failure to disclose the repainting—was purely economic, with no effect on safety, performance or even appearance for at least the nine months it took the plaintiff to discover it. The Court pointed out, however, that "infliction of economic injury, when done intentionally through affirmative acts of misconduct [as in *TXO*], or when the target is financially vulnerable, can warrant a substantial penalty."[361] These two factors, which were not present in *Gore*, could support a punitive damages award in an automobile fraud case involving more egregious conduct or a poor consumer, even if the

consumer suffered only economic damage.[362] A court may also be willing to treat stress and trauma as non-economic harm that shows greater reprehensibility, even in the absence of any physical injury.[363]

7.10.6.2.3 Ratio to compensatory damages

The second guidepost, the ratio of punitive damages to compensatory damages, was at issue in both *Gore* and *State Farm*. In developing the guidepost, the *Gore* decision quoted earlier precedent, asking whether there was "a reasonable relationship between the punitive damages award and the *harm likely to result* from the defendant's conduct as well as the harm that actually has occurred."[364] Thus, the basis of comparison is not just the actual damages award, but what it might have been had the conduct led to more dire results.[365] Potential harm was not a factor in *Gore*, however, given that "there [was] no suggestion that Dr. Gore or any other BMW purchaser was threatened with any additional potential harm by BMW's nondisclosure policy." Thus, the ratio of punitive damages to actual damages, five hundred to one, was held unreasonable.[366] In contrast, a higher award might be justified when a car seller's fraud relates to a safety defect that could cause serious bodily harm.

In *State Farm*, the Court proposed boundaries driven far more by arithmetic than by conduct. While purporting to reject a "bright-line ratio," the Court warned that "in practice, few awards exceeding a single-digit ratio between punitive and compensatory damages, to a significant degree, will satisfy due process."[367] The Court did acknowledge that a higher ratio could be consistent with due process if an egregious act causes only a small amount of economic harm or if the amount of harm is difficult to determine.[368] None-

---

355 *State Farm*, 538 U.S. at 420.

356 *Id.* at 422; *In re Exxon Valdez*, 296 F. Supp. 2d 1071, 1093 (D. Alaska 2004) (lawful out-of-state conduct is admissible to show recklessness); Bocci v. Key Pharm., Inc., 76 P.3d 669 (Or. Ct. App.), *as amended by* 79 P.3d 908 (Or. Ct. App. 2003); *see also* Eden Elec., Ltd. v. Amana Co., 370 F.3d 824 (8th Cir. 2004) (no error for jury to consider out-of-state conduct that furthered in-state fraudulent scheme); Boyd v. Goffoli, 608 S.E.2d 169 (W. Va. 2004) (punitive damages can be based on out-of-state conduct that is part of defendant's scheme that directly injures plaintiffs in forum state, as long as forum state has significant contact with plaintiffs' claims).

357 *State Farm*, 538 U.S. at 423.

358 *Id.* at 422.

359 *Id.* at 422.

360 *Id.* at 422, 423.

361 *Gore*, 517 U.S. at 576 (citation omitted); *see also* Eden Elec., Ltd. v. Amana Co., 370 F.3d 824 (8th Cir. 2004) (affirming $10 million punitive damages award in light of defendant's egregious fraud even though compensatory damages of $2.1 million represented solely economic harm); Bardis v. Oates, 119 Cal. App. 4th 1, 14 Cal. Rptr. 3d 89 (2004) (allowing $1.5 million punitive damages on compensatory award of $165,527.63 even though harm was entirely economic, when defendant's misconduct was egregious).

362 *See* Watson v. Johnson Mobile Homes, 284 F.3d 568, 572 (5th Cir. 2002) (in affirming fraud verdict, court noted that "taking advantage of someone who is relatively unsophisticated or financially vulnerable is particularly deserving of rebuke").

363 Campbell v. State Farm Mut. Auto. Ins. Co., 98 P.3d 409, 415, 416 (Utah 2004).

364 517 U.S. at 581; *see TXO*, 509 U.S. at 460; *Haslip*, 499 U.S. at 21.

365 *See TXO*, 509 U.S. at 462 (affirming punitive damages award of $10,000,000 even though actual damages were only $19,000, award not grossly excessive "in light of the amount of money potentially at stake").

366 *Gore*, 517 U.S. at 582; *see also* Watson v. Johnson Mobile Homes, 284 F.3d 568, 572 (5th Cir. 2002) (in affirming reduction of punitive damages award from $700,000 to $150,000 in case in which mobile home seller had wrongfully withheld a $4000 deposit, court noted that even if figure included amounts forfeited by other injured applicants—*Gore* suggests including harm suffered by individuals similarly situated—ratio would still have been 50:1).

367 *State Farm*, 538 U.S. 408, 425.

368 *Id.* at 425 (quoting *Gore*, 517 U.S. at 582) (but note that the *State Farm* Court rejected the argument that punitive damages could be supported by evidence of the unlikelihood of detection, coupled with evidence of defendant's wealth; 538 U.S. at 426);

theless, the Court insisted that the converse is also true: that when compensatory damages are "substantial," a lesser ratio—maybe even one to one—will reach the upper limit of due process.[369]

State Farm also reiterates the principle stated in *Gore* and *TXO* that the relevant ratio is between punitive damages and not just actual harm but also potential harm from the defendant's conduct.[370] In *State Farm* and *Gore* there appears to have been no claim that the potential harm was greater than the actual harm that had already occurred, but in *TXO* the Court, in approving a ten million dollar punitive damages award, cited evidence that the defendant's scheme, if it had succeeded, would have defrauded the plaintiff of one to four million dollars, not just the $19,000 awarded as actual damages.

7.10.6.2.4 Relationship to civil and criminal penalties

The third guidepost by which to assess a punitive damages award's consistency with due process is to compare the damages to comparable civil and criminal penalties that could have been imposed for the conduct.[371] This guidepost serves the purpose of ensuring that "a person receives fair notice not only of the conduct that will subject him to punishment, but also of the severity of the penalty that a state may impose."[372] Because in *Gore* the maximum civil penalty under Alabama's unfair and deceptive acts and practices (UDAP) statute was $2000,[373] one-tenth of one percent of the award, this guidepost weighed against the award.

In *State Farm*, the Court claimed that the "most relevant civil sanction" under Utah state law for the kind of conduct committed by State Farm was only $10,000, a tiny fraction (less than 1/100 of a percent) of the $145 million dollar award. The Court dismissed as speculative the Utah Supreme Court's conclusion that the defendant was also at risk of loss of its business license, disgorgement of profits, and imprisonment, because these conclusions were based on the evidence of out-of-state and dissimilar conduct that the Court had already decided was inappropriate to the review.[374] This aspect of the opinion suggests that plaintiffs should treat the availability of other civil penalties as a question of fact, and should present evidence that the very conduct that harmed the plaintiffs is subject to specific

penalties. The penalties need not be likely or common, however. *State Farm* reaffirms the statement in *Gore* that the relevant penalties are those that are either authorized *or* imposed in comparable cases.[375]

State Farm holds that the existence of a criminal penalty has a bearing on the seriousness with which the State views a wrongful action, but it cautions against over-reliance on criminal penalties to support punitive damages. The Court states that great care must be taken to avoid use of the civil process to assess criminal penalties that can be imposed only after the heightened protections of a criminal trial.[376]

7.10.6.3 Winning and Protecting Punitive Damages Awards After *Gore* and *State Farm*

7.10.6.3.1 Introduction

Gore and *State Farm* create obstacles to large punitive damages awards in automobile fraud cases, but they are not insurmountable obstacles. The consumer's attorney should take care to address each of the elements of each of the guideposts identified by these two cases, plus any elements that state law requires.

In nearly all automobile fraud cases, the proof will have shown that the defendant's acts involved intentional malice, trickery, or deceit rather than mere accident, thus satisfying one of the five elements of the reprehensibility guidepost. The following subsections focus on ways to deal with other standards imposed by *Gore* and *State Farm*.

7.10.6.3.2 Showing risk of serious or physical harm

One of the guideposts for determining reprehensibility is whether the plaintiff suffered physical as opposed to economic harm.[377] Neither *Gore* nor *State Farm* involved misconduct that put others at risk of serious harm, which is a crucial distinction from many car fraud cases.[378] Many automobile fraud cases involve nondisclosure of excessive mileage or serious structural defects, problems that may render the car unsafe and risk grave physical injury or even death, in addition to substantial economic loss. Accordingly, in auto fraud cases the plaintiff should present evidence of any safety risks created by the defendant's fraud, including

---

        see Werremeyer v. K.C. Auto Salvage Co., 2003 WL 21487311 (Mo. Ct. App. June 30, 2003) (unlikelihood that fraud would be detected is factor favoring higher ratio), *aff'd in relevant part, rev'd in part on other grounds,* 134 S.W.3d 633 (Mo. 2004) (reversing denial of prejudgment interest but affirming award in all other respects).

369 *State Farm*, 538 U.S. at 425.
370 *Id.* at 418, 425.
371 *Gore*, 517 U.S. at 583, 584.
372 *Gore*, 517 U.S. at 574.
373 *Id.*
374 *State Farm*, 538 U.S. 408, 428.

375 *Id.*
376 *Id.*
377 *See* § 7.10.6.2.2, *supra.*
378 Several courts have pointed out that *Gore* and *State Farm* did not involve any potential harm, so their failure to consider potential harm when calculating the ratio does not have any bearing on the continuing validity of the rule that potential harm should be considered when it has been established by the evidence. *See In re* Exxon Valdez, 296 F. Supp. 2d 1071, 1098 (D. Alaska 2004).

the risk to not just the plaintiff but to friends and family members who have ridden in the defective car and to those who have shared the road with it.[379] This evidence will show that the potential harm is physical rather than purely economic, and that the tortious conduct showed an indifference to or reckless disregard of the health and safety of others, two factors cited by *State Farm* for determining reprehensibility.[380] While *State Farm* cautions against consideration of "dissimilar acts" and "other parties' hypothetical claims" against a defendant as part of the reprehensibility analysis,[381] it in no way prohibits consideration of similar, non-hypothetical acts toward others.[382]

Grabinski v. Blue Springs Ford Sales, Inc.,[383] illustrates how the *Gore* factors can be applied successfully when such risks, and indifference to them, are present. In that case a dealer had misrepresented a poorly repaired prior wreck as "very nice" and "driving fine." The Eighth Circuit Court of Appeals characterized the defendants' concealment of the prior wreck damage as "egregious," with respect to both the plaintiff's physical safety and her economic interests.[384] Noting that the reprehensibility of the defendant's conduct is to be given the greatest weight in the *Gore* analysis, the court affirmed an award of $210,000 in punitive damages and $7835 in actual damages. Likewise, in *Parrott v. Carr*

Chevrolet, Inc.,[385] the Oregon Supreme Court stressed that the defendant's failure to disclose prior wreck damage implicated the vehicle's overall safety and evidenced an indifference to the consumer's health and safety and that of the public who would share the road with the vehicle. The risk of physical injury makes it likely that the punitive damages awards would have been upheld in these cases even if they had been decided after *State Farm*.

A threat may also be physical even if physical force is never actually used. For example, the Sixth Circuit considered the plaintiff's injuries to be primarily physical rather than economic where she was detained by security guards who surrounded her in a show of force and had handcuffs at their disposal.[386] It is not uncommon for an auto dealer to detain consumers, whether by taking their car keys or parking their cars in.

7.10.6.3.3 Including all actual and potential harm in the ratio

The risk of serious harm caused by an auto fraud defendant's conduct aids the constitutional analysis in a second way, by minimizing the ratio between compensatory and punitive damages. *Gore* and *TXO* make it clear that courts are to evaluate the ratio between punitive damages and actual *or* potential damages caused by the defendant's conduct. A major factor the Court cited in *TXO* when upholding a punitive damages award 526 times greater than the $19,000 compensatory damages award was that the plaintiff's loss if the defendant's fraud had succeeded could have amounted to one to four million dollars.[387] By contrast, in *Gore* the car's undisclosed defect was purely cosmetic, one with no potential to cause additional harm, and in *State Farm* the defendant's misconduct, while it inflicted emotional distress, did not put the plaintiffs at risk of further calamity.

---

379   *See* Action Marine, Inc. v. Cont'l Carbon, Inc., 2006 WL 173653 (M.D. Ala. Jan. 23, 2006) (taking risk of physician harm from defendant's environmental pollution into account even though plaintiffs did not claim personal injury); Grefer v. Alpha Technical, 901 So. 2d 1117, 1148–49 (La. Ct. App. 2005) (taking risk of harm to plaintiff company's employees into account in upholding $112 million of $1 billion punitive damage award, even though actual damages were solely economic); Krysa v. Payne, 176 S.W.3d 150 (Mo. Ct. App. 2005) (upholding $500,000 punitive damage award, a ratio of 27-to-1, where expert testified that concealed wreck damage made vehicle dangerous); Bocci v. Key Pharm., 76 P.3d 669, 674 (Or. Ct. App.), *as amended by* 79 P.3d 908 (Or. Ct. App. 2003) (severe irreparable brain damage that defendant's act caused second plaintiff can be considered in reprehensibility analysis for this plaintiff).

380   538 U.S. 408, 419.

381   *Id.* at 422, 423.

382   Romo v. Ford Motor Co., 113 Cal. App. 4th 738, 6 Cal. Rptr. 3d 793, 806 (2003) (citing manufacturer's reckless disregard for other consumers' safety); Diamond Woodworks, Inc. v. Argonaut Ins. Co., 109 Cal. App. 4th 1020, 135 Cal. Rptr. 2d 736 (2003) (considering physical harm to plaintiff company's worker even though harm to plaintiff was purely economic); Bocci v. Key Pharm., Inc., 76 P.3d 669, 674 (Or. Ct. App.), *as amended by* 79 P.3d 908 (Or. Ct. App. 2003) (taking into account physical harm caused to plaintiff doctor's patient by defendant's promotion of dangerous drug).

383   203 F.3d 1024 (8th Cir. 2000).

384   *Id.* The court also pointed out that the jury instructions themselves required the jury to evaluate the reprehensibility of the defendants' conduct by requiring them to find the conduct outrageous or recklessly indifferent; accordingly, the language of the jury instruction itself can reinforce the verdict under this *Gore* factor.

385   331 Or. 537, 17 P.3d 473 (2001); *see also* Werremeyer v. K.C. Auto Salvage Co., 2003 WL 21487311 (Mo. Ct. App. June 30, 2003) (upholding punitive damages award when sale of wrecked and reassembled car without disclosure posed danger to buyers and public), *aff'd in relevant part, rev'd in part on other grounds*, 134 S.W.3d 633 (Mo. 2004) (reversing denial of prejudgment interest but affirming award in all other respects). *But see* Johnson v. Ford Motor Co., 2003 WL 22794432 (Cal. Ct. App. Nov. 25, 2003) (unpublished) (failure to disclose lemon history did not create risk of physical harm because car could have been sold even with disclosure; opinion fails to recognize that disclosure would have allowed buyers to take precautions to avoid injury), *rev'd, remanded on other grounds*, 35 Cal. 4th 1191, 29 Cal. Rptr. 3d 401 (2005) (disagreeing with Court of Appeals' reduction of punitive damage award; remanding for new analysis of *State Farm* factors).

386   Romanski v. Detroit Entertainment, L.L.C., 428 F.3d 629, 643–44 (6th Cir. 2005). *See also* Russo v. Hartford, 2006 WL 516747 (D. Conn. Mar. 2, 2006).

387   *TXO*, 509 U.S. at 462.

In many auto fraud cases the potential harm will dwarf the compensatory damages, so what appears to be a large ratio will actually be small for purposes of the *Gore* analysis. For example, in *Grabinski v. Blue Springs Ford Sales, Inc.*,[388] a jury awarded a total of $7835 in actual damages and $210,000 in punitive damages against a dealer who had misrepresented an improperly repaired, dangerous, previously wrecked vehicle as being "very nice" and "driving fine." In upholding the verdict, the district court held that the denominator of the ratio should be expanded to include not only the actual damages awarded, but also the potential harms faced by the plaintiff and her passengers not measured by that award.[389] In addition, the denominator should reflect the emotional distress suffered by the plaintiff while coping with the numerous serious mechanical problems suffered by her car.[390] As adjusted, the ratio, though not quantified by the court, fell within constitutional boundaries.[391] The Eighth Circuit affirmed the punitive damages award without finding it necessary to decide what components should be included in the amount to which the punitive damage award should be compared.[392]

Another case followed a similar analysis. A dealer fraudulently misrepresented the history of a vehicle that had actually been wrecked and then repaired by welding two half-vehicles together. As a result, the vehicle was unsafe to drive, and the buyers could have suffered serious injury. The court upheld an award of $18,449.53 in compensatory damages and $500,000 in punitive damages. While the court did not attempt to quantify the potential harm, it held that the potential harm had to be considered in evaluating the punitive damage award.[393]

It is also important to make sure that the jury awards all appropriate compensatory damages on the claims for which punitive damages are available. If the law of the jurisdiction requires the jury to be instructed not to award duplicative compensatory damages on multiple counts, the consumer's attorney should still ask the jury to reveal its analysis of the compensatory damages on each claim. For example, the verdict form could ask the jury to itemize for the fraud count the amount of compensatory damages caused by the fraud that is already reflected in the award on another count, and the amount of compensatory damages that is awarded solely for the fraud. Otherwise the court will be unable to determine the amount of compensatory damages to compare to the punitive damages award.[394] Even without this level of precision in the jury award, though, some courts have taken a common sense approach in determining the award to which the punitive damages should be compared. The Ninth Circuit, for example, considered both the nominal damages awarded for a § 1981 discrimination claim and the $50,000 damages awarded for breach of contract, when the conduct was intertwined.[395] In another case, even though a jury did not identify a certain portion of its award as compensatory, a district court treated it as compensatory in computing the ratio.[396] And the Third Circuit used the attorney fee award in a bad faith insurance claim denial case as the basis for calculating the ratio, following state decisions that treated such an award as compensatory.[397]

Even if the jury is not permitted to include certain types of harm in its compensatory damages award, that harm should be included in calculating the ratio. Including all damage suffered in the calculation of the ratio, whether or not it is compensable under the law of the jurisdiction, will allow a higher punitive damages award.[398] For example, state law capped one portion of the plaintiff's damages at $500,000, but the court used the jury's full award of $800,000 in discussing the ratio.[399] In another case, a court

---

388 203 F.3d 1024 (8th Cir. 2000), *aff'g* 1998 U.S. Dist. LEXIS 17015 (W.D. Mo. Oct. 27, 1998).

389 1998 U.S. Dist. LEXIS 17015, at *11, *12.

390 *Id.* at *12.

391 See Chrysler Corp. v. Schiffer, 736 So. 2d 538 (Ala. 1999), in which the Alabama Supreme Court ordered the plaintiff, who had won a punitive damages award of $325,000, to accept a reduction to $150,000 or face a new trial. The court characterized the damage to the truck—a poorly fitted door, bent oil pan and bent drive shaft—as "fundamentally economic" in nature, noting that the drive shaft, while causing vibration, did not affect safety.

392 Grabinski v. Blue Springs Ford Sales, Inc., 203 F.3d 1024, 1027 (8th Cir. 2000).

393 Krysa v. Payne, 176 S.W.3d 150, 160 (Mo. Ct. App. 2005).

394 *See* McClain v. Metabolife Int'l, Inc., 259 F. Supp. 2d 1225, 1235 (N.D. Ala. 2003) (describing difficulty of calculating ratio when jury was instructed not to award duplicate damages on multiple counts); *see also* Textron Fin. Corp. v. Nat'l Union Fire Ins. Co., 118 Cal. App. 4th 1061, 13 Cal. Rptr. 3d 586 (2004) (ratio is to be based solely on compensatory damages awarded on claims for which punitive damages are available); Atkinson v. Orkin Exterminating Co., 604 S.E.2d 385 (S.C. 2004) (same).

395 Bains L.L.C. v. Arco Products Co., 405 F.3d 764 (9th Cir. 2005).

396 Sheedy v. City of Philadelphia, 2005 WL 375657 (E.D. Pa. Feb. 15, 2005) (fair compensatory award would be up to $100,000, even though jury awarded only $3075, so $200,000 in punitive damages is appropriate). *See also* CGB Occupational Therapy, Inc. v. RHA Pa. Nursing Homes, 2005 WL 1595428 (E.D. Pa. July 5, 2005) (concluding that Third Circuit allows at least some latitude in determining the actual damages to which the punitive damage award is to be compared; 19-to-1 ratio is probably closer to 3-to-1 if all harm is considered).

397 Willow Inn, Inc. v. Pub. Serv. Mut. Ins. Co., 399 F.3d 224, 235–237 (3d Cir. 2005).

398 *See also* In re Exxon Valdez, 296 F. Supp. 2d 1071, 1101, 1102 (D. Alaska Jan. 28, 2004) (expressing view that amount voluntarily paid by defendant before trial should be included as compensatory damages when calculating ratio, but noting contrary Ninth Circuit authority); Simon v. San Paolo U.S. Holding Co., 35 Cal. 4th 1159, 29 Cal. Rptr. 3d 379, 388–93, 113 P.3d 63 (2005) (all harm, and potential harm, caused by defendant's acts may be considered, but causation not shown here); Romo v. Ford Motor Co., 113 Cal. App. 4th 738, 6 Cal. Rptr. 3d 793 (2003) (approving 3-to-1 and 5-to-1 ratios in wrongful death case even though actual damages were about $5 million; court takes into account that loss of life is undercompensated).

399 Williams v. Philip Morris, Inc., 92 P.3d 126, 144 (Or. Ct. App. 2004), *aff'd on other grounds*, 127 P.3d 1165, 1181 (Or. 2006) (finding punitive damage award proper regardless of calculation

based punitive damages on the actual damages that the plaintiff suffered, even though she could not recover them from the defendant in question because another defendant had already paid them.[400] In a Sixth Circuit opinion, however, one judge held that where the court reduced the jury's compensatory damage award by 50% because of the plaintiff's comparative fault, only the reduced award could be considered in computing the ratio. Otherwise, the punitive damage award would punish the defendant for conduct that was the fault of the plaintiff.[401] The second judge on the panel disagreed with this conclusion, and the third judge, dissenting, considered it irrelevant.[402]

Likewise, emotional distress damages should be included in the denominator even if they are not compensable in a fraud claim.[403] If harm caused by emotional distress is included in the denominator, however, the advocate should be prepared for arguments that a smaller multiplier is appropriate. In *State Farm*, the jury's compensatory damages award included compensation for emotional distress. The Supreme Court worried that the jury may have used the punitive damages award to compensate the plaintiffs for the distress they suffered due to the outrageous acts of their insurer, thus duplicating that component of the compensatory damages award.[404] It may be possible to avoid this issue by instructing the jury that emotional distress damages are not to be punitive and punitive damages are not to include any compensation for emotional distress. However, if the consumer's attorney has a choice between pressing for

emotional distress damages or punitive damages, the former may be preferable because of their greater insulation from review under *Gore* standards. One court has held that if prejudgment interest is part of compensatory damages, it should be included in the denominator also,[405] but attorney fees and costs should not.[406]

While the Supreme Court cautioned that a compensatory damages award that includes damages for emotional distress may already have a punitive component that the punitive damages award should not duplicate,[407] the Court also approved a higher ratio when the harm is difficult to quantify.[408] Accordingly, a number of courts have upheld higher ratios when the harm the plaintiff suffered is largely emotional distress or some other intangible.[409]

In calculating the ratio, many courts after *State Farm* have compared punitive damages not just to the plaintiff's actual damages award, but also to the potential damages that the defendant's actions could have caused[410] or to the future

---

of compensatory award); *see also* Lowe Excavating Co. v. Int'l Union of Operating Engineers, 832 N.E.2d 495, 506 (Ill. App. Ct. 2005) (taking attorney fees that plaintiff incurred into account in approving punitive damage award that would otherwise bear 75-to-1 ratio to actual damages), *appeal allowed*, 844 N.E.2d 38 (Ill. 2005).

400   Turner v. Firstar Bank, 2006 WL 539448 (Ill. App. Ct. Mar. 6, 2006).

401   Clark v. Chrysler Corp., 436 F.3d 594, 607 n.16 (6th Cir. 2006).

402   *Id.*, at 613–14 (Kennedy, J., concurring in part and concurring in the judgment), 620 n.3 (Moore, J., concurring in part and dissenting in part).

403   *See* § 9.9.3.2, *infra*.

404   *State Farm*, 538 U.S. 408, 426; *see* Bach v. First Union Nat'l Bank, 149 Fed. Appx. 354, 365 (6th Cir. 2005) (punitive damage award must be reduced because it duplicates compensatory award for pain and suffering), *on remand*, 2006 WL 840381 (S.D. Ohio Mar. 30, 2006) (reducing punitive damage award by subtracting compensatory damage award from it to eliminate duplication; result is 5.5-to-1 ratio); Johnson v. Ford Motor Co., 2003 WL 22794432 (Cal. Ct. App. Nov. 25, 2003) (unpublished) (higher ratio can be allowed in auto fraud case when actual damages are purely economic and do not include any award for personal outrage), *rev'd, remanded on other grounds*, 35 Cal. 4th 1191, 29 Cal. Rptr. 3d 401 (2005) (disagreeing with court of appeals' failure to consider recidivism and deterrence when it reduced punitive damage award; remanding for new analysis of *State Farm* factors); *see also* Boyd v. Goffoli, 608 S.E.2d 169 (W. Va. 2004) (rejecting argument that emotional distress damages must be excluded when calculating ratio).

405   Bardis v. Oates, 119 Cal. App. 4th 1, 14 Cal. Rptr. 3d 89 (2004). *See also* Goddard v. Farmers Ins. Co., 126 P.3d 682 (Or. Ct. App. 2006) (prejudgment interest is part of compensatory component of award, and should be included in sum to which punitive damage award is compared).

406   Bardis v. Oates, 119 Cal. App. 4th 1, 14 Cal. Rptr. 3d 89 (2004). *But cf.* Lowe Excavating Co. v. Int'l Union of Operating Engineers, 832 N.E.2d 495, 506 (Ill. App. Ct. 2005) (taking attorney fees that plaintiff incurred into account in approving punitive damage award that would otherwise bear 75-to-1 ratio to actual damages), *appeal allowed*, 844 N.E.2d 38 (Ill. 2005).

407   *State Farm*, 538 U.S. at 426; *see also* Casumpang v. Int'l Longshore & Warehouse Union, 411 F. Supp. 2d 1201, 1220 (D. Hawaii 2005) (citing probable duplication as reason for remittur).

408   *Id.* at 425 (quoting *Gore*).

409   Planned Parenthood v. Am. Coalition of Life Activists, 422 F.3d 949, 963 (9th Cir. 2005) (citing fact that some actual damage was not quantifiable as reason to approve 9-to-1 ratio); Romanski v. Detroit Entertainment, L.L.C., 428 F.3d 629, 645 (6th Cir. 2005); Mathias v. Accor Econ. Lodging, Inc., 347 F.3d 672, 677 (7th Cir. 2003); Sherman v. Kasotakis, 314 F. Supp. 2d 843, 875 (N.D. Iowa 2004) (harm for racial slur and segregated seating in restaurant hard to quantify; upholding $12,500 punitive damages when jury awarded $1 nominal compensatory damages).

410   Asa-Brandt, Inc. v. ADM Investor Services, Inc., 344 F.3d 738 (8th Cir. 2003) ($1.25 million punitive damages award not excessive in light of potential harm of $3.9 million, even though jury awarded only nominal damages); *In re* Exxon Valdez, 296 F. Supp. 2d 1071, 1098, 1103, 1104 (D. Alaska 2004) (upholding $4.5 billion punitive damages award in environmental tort class action when compensatory damages were about $513 million but harm would have been much greater if pilot's boneheaded maneuver after crash had ripped larger hole in hull); Craig v. Holsey, 590 S.E.2d 742 (Ga. Ct. App. 2003); Krysa v. Payne, 176 S.W.3d 150, 160 (Mo. Ct. App. 2005); Williams v. Philip Morris Inc., 127 P.3d 1165, 1180 (Or. 2006); *see also* Willow Inn, Inc. v. Pub. Serv. Mut. Ins. Co., 399 F.3d 224, 234 (3d Cir. 2005) (potential harm from an unsuccessful attempt at fraud may be considered, but not shown here); Bains L.L.C. v. Arco Products Co., 405 F.3d 764 (9th Cir. 2005) (same); Romo v. Ford Motor Co., 113 Cal. App. 4th 738, 6 Cal. Rptr. 3d 793 (2003) (approving ratios of 3-to-1 and 5-to-1 in wrongful death

harm that could occur.[411] One particularly clear-cut example involved a drunk driver who crashed into the plaintiff's vehicle, pushing her into the lane of oncoming traffic. The plaintiff luckily escaped serious injury and was awarded only $8801.40 in compensatory damages. The court noted that the plaintiff could have died as a result of the defendant's misconduct and upheld a $200,000 punitive damages award—a 22.7-to-1 ratio to the actual damages award.[412] As another court pointed out, if the purpose of the due process analysis is to make sure that the defendant was on notice of the potential severity of the penalty it would face, potential harm is relevant because "a reasonable person analyzing the consequences of his conduct would naturally look to not only what is sure to happen but also to what could possibly happen."[413]

It appears that the potential harm to others in the state may also be considered in calculating the ratio. In *Parrott v. Carr Chevrolet, Inc.*,[414] for example, the Oregon Supreme Court considered not only the actual injury to the plaintiff, but also the potential injury that the misconduct may have caused to past, present, and future customers. While in *State Farm* the United States Supreme Court referred twice to the ratio between the punitive damages and the harm *to the plaintiff*,[415] a later portion of the opinion seems to acknowledge that harm to others in the state, if proven, could have been

considered in calculating the ratio.[415.1] The Court in *Gore* also recognized this possibility, twice suggesting that the punitive damages award could be legitimately measured against the harm that the defendant's practice caused to all consumers in the state.[415.2] Courts since *State Farm* have differed as to whether harm to others can be considered in the ratio.[415.3]

State Farm appears to reject a Seventh Circuit Court of Appeals view that the amount necessary to achieve deterrence, and therefore an appropriate measure for punitive damages, is "the harm done by the wrong, divided by the probability of detecting the injury and prosecuting the claim."[415.4] The Supreme Court held that the infrequency of punishment could not support the large punitive damages award in *State Farm*.[415.5] In any event, the Seventh Circuit's formula understates the amount necessary for deterrence, as a wrongdoer would have nothing to lose by trying the illegal act if the total penalty was merely the amount of the illegal gains. The Seventh Circuit's opinion is also marred by erroneous factual assumptions about the frequency with which odometer fraud is discovered and prosecuted, which led it to minimize the appropriate punitive damages award.[415.6] Nevertheless, *State Farm* reiterates that punitive

---

case even though actual damages were about $5 million; court takes into account that loss of life is undercompensated); Roberie v. VonBokern, 2003 WL 22976126 (Ky. Ct. App. Dec. 19, 2003) (unpublished) (punitive damages may be awarded even without actual damages; potential harm may be considered in ratio; remanding to trial court for *State Farm* analysis); Trinity Evangelical Lutheran Church v. Tower Ins. Co., 661 N.W.2d 789 (Wis. 2003) (upholding $3.5 million punitive damages award in insurance bad faith case even though no actual damages were awarded, when ratio was 7-to-1 to harm that would have occurred if defendant's misconduct had succeeded).

411 Planned Parenthood v. Am. Coalition of Life Activists, 422 F.3d 949, 963 (9th Cir. 2005) (citing fact that emotional distress and other costs will likely continue in future as reason to approve 9-to-1 ratio); Planned Parenthood v. Am. Coalition of Life Activists, 300 F. Supp. 2d 1055 (D. Or. 2004) (taking potential of future harm into account in upholding ratios ranging from 31.8-to-1 to 6.7-to-1 against defendants who blockaded abortion clinics and threatened physical harm against providers); In re Exxon Valdez, 296 F. Supp. 2d 1071, 1104, 1105 (D. Alaska 2004) (accommodating potential future harm by allowing higher ratio; upholding $4.5 billion punitive damages award on $513 million compensatory damages in environmental tort class action).

412 Craig v. Holsey, 590 S.E.2d 742 (Ga. Ct. App. 2003); *accord* Strenke v. Hogner, 704 N.W.2d 309, 316–17 (Wis. Ct. App. 2005) (upholding $225,000 punitive damage award even though compensatory damages were only $2000 where drunk driver's reckless actions could have seriously injured or killed the plaintiff).

413 *In re* Exxon Valdez, 296 F. Supp. 2d 1071, 1090 (D. Alaska 2004).

414 331 Or. 537, 17 P.3d 473, 489 (2001).

415 *State Farm*, 538 U.S. 408, 418, 424.

415.1 *Id.* at 427 ("With respect to the Utah Supreme Court's second justification [that State Farm's policies affected numerous Utah consumers], the Campbells' inability to direct us to testimony demonstrating harm to the people of Utah (other than those directly involved in this case) indicates that the adverse effect on the State's general population was in fact minor.").

415.2 *Gore*, 517 U.S. at 582.

415.3 *Harm to others can be considered*: In re Exxon Valdez, 296 F. Supp. 2d 1071, 1103 (D. Alaska 2004) (potential harm to others can be included in ratio, but not necessary here); *see also* Roth v. Farner-Bocken Co., 667 N.W.2d 651 (S.D. 2003) (accepting that harm to others can be included in ratio, but not shown here); *cf.* S. Union Co. v. Southwest Gas Corp., 415 F.3d 1001, 1011 (9th Cir. 2005), *as amended by* 423 F.3d 1117 (9th Cir. 2005) (appropriate to take non-economic damage to the judicial process and exploitation of high public office into account). *Harm to others can not be considered*: Bardis v. Oates, 119 Cal. App. 4th 1, 14 Cal. Rptr. 3d 89, 101 (2004); Textron Fin. Corp. v. Nat'l Union Fire Ins. Co., 118 Cal. App. 4th 1061, 13 Cal. Rptr. 3d 586, 603 (2004) (refusing to consider harm defendant caused to others); Williams v. Philip Morris Inc., 127 P.3d 1165 (Or. 2006) (jury may consider harm to others in determining punitive damages, but court cannot include it in calculating ratio); Bocci v. Key Pharm., Inc., 76 P.3d 669, 674 (Or. Ct. App.), *as amended by* 79 P.3d 908 (Or. Ct. App. 2003).

415.4 Perez v. Z Frank Oldsmobile, Inc., 223 F.3d 617, 621 (7th Cir. 2000). Thus, if a $5000 injury were redressed one time in five, optimal damages would be $25,000 according to the Seventh Circuit.

415.5 *State Farm*, 538 U.S. 408, 427. *But see* Mathias v. Accor Econ. Lodging, Inc., 347 F.3d 672 (7th Cir. 2003) (reiterating relevance of likelihood of detection even after *State Farm*).

415.6 The Seventh Circuit suggested that odometer fraud is frequently discovered and prosecuted, so a multiplier of three is appropriate. In fact, studies show that odometer rollbacks probably number in the hundreds of thousands, and prosecutions probably are on the order of several thousand. If one were to adopt

damages should be imposed to deter unlawful conduct, so the question whether a particular award is within the range to achieve deterrence should still be a legitimate inquiry.

7.10.6.3.4 Using the right ratio for the right defendant

Many auto fraud cases will involve several defendants, each of whom participated in the fraud at some stage in the vehicle's history. Because a punitive damages award is the individual liability of the defendant to whom it relates,[415.7] it would be wrong to add up all the punitive damages awards against all the defendants and compare that to the compensatory damages award. Instead, as the Eighth Circuit Court of Appeals recognized in *Grabinski*, the appropriate way of calculating the ratios is to divide each individual punitive damages award by that individual's liability for actual damages.[415.8] This arithmetic, applied to the respective defendants in that case, produced ratios that ranged from a low of 5-to-1 for one of the individual defendants, to a high of 99-to-1 for the wholesaler.[415.9] The Ninth Circuit has also adopted this method of calculation.[415.10]

In using this method of calculation, how should an actual damages award be treated when each of several defendants is jointly and severally liable for it? For example, if a defendant is found jointly and severally liable, along with three others, for a compensatory damages award of $40,000, should a punitive damages award of $200,000 against that defendant be compared to $40,000, for a 5-to-1 ratio, or to that defendant's *pro rata* share of $40,000 (that is $10,000), for a 20-to-1 ratio? The Eighth Circuit used each defendant's *pro rata* share of the actual damage award, on the theory that the constitutionality of the punitive damages award depends on the amount of actual damages *payable* by that defendant.[415.11] Arguably, however, the punitive damages award

should be compared to the full amount of damages for which the defendant is liable, not just that defendant's *pro rata* share. Using the full compensatory damages award is more consistent with *State Farm* and *Gore*, which instruct courts to compare punitive damages to the "harm to the plaintiff,"[415.12] not the amount a particular defendant pays. Also, any of a group of defendants who are jointly and severally liable for an award can be required to pay the full amount, so using a defendant's *pro rata* share of the award does not necessarily even reflect the amount that defendant will pay.

The Ninth Circuit has adopted a sounder approach, basing the ratio on the full compensatory damage award for which the defendant is liable, even if others are jointly and severally liable for that award.[415.13] The Seventh Circuit similarly dealt with a case in which a $29 million compensatory damages award had been entered against two defendants. In reviewing the $15 million punitive damages award against one of the defendants, and the $12.5 million award against the other, the court calculated the ratio by comparing each defendant's punitive damages award to the entire $29 million compensatory damages award.[415.14]

Additional complexities arise if there are multiple plaintiffs as well as multiple defendants. The Ninth Circuit has held that the ratios should be analyzed on a defendant-by-defendant, plaintiff-by-plaintiff basis. Thus, if two defendants are jointly and severally liable for $40,000 in compensatory damages to each of two plaintiffs, but each defendant is liable to each plaintiff for differing amounts of punitive damages, the Ninth Circuit compares the punitive damages awarded against a particular defendant in favor of a particular plaintiff to the $40,000 compensatory damage award.[415.15] The court rejected the suggestion that compensatory or punitive damage awards in favor of multiple plaintiffs or against multiple defendants should be aggregated before the comparison is made. The court reasoned that looking at the aggregate punitive damage award against all defendants failed to allow for the possibility that the reprehensibility of individual defendants may differ, and would impermissibly shift the focus away from a particular defendant's conduct to the defendants' conduct *en grosse*. In addition, the court's task should be to determine whether any or all of the *defendants* had their due process rights violated. Unfortunately, however, when the court calculated a remittur, it failed to use its own formula, but reverted to a calculation that used the aggregate amount of the punitive damage awards against all defendants.

---

    the Seventh Circuit's logic, but not its faulty factual assumptions, then for a dealer that is caught for the first time in a $5000 odometer rollback case but evidence suggests has made a hundred other rollbacks, then punitive damages should be $500,000.

415.7   *See* § 9.11.1.4, *infra*.

415.8   Grabinski v. Blue Springs Ford Sales, Inc., 203 F.3d 1024, 1026 (8th Cir. 2000); *see also* Kaufman v. Monte (*In re* Kaufman), 315 B.R. 858, 869 (Bankr. N.D. Cal. 2004).

415.9   Grabinski v. Blue Springs Ford Sales, Inc., 203 F.3d 1024, 1026 (8th Cir. 2000).

415.10   Planned Parenthood v. Am. Coalition of Life Activists, 422 F.3d 929 (9th Cir. 2005). *But see* Bardis v. Oates, 119 Cal. App. 4th 1, 14 Cal. Rptr. 3d 89, 104 n.7 (2004) (comparing total of all punitive damages awards to the compensatory damages for which defendants were jointly liable, when individual defendant was owner and manager of corporate defendant).

415.11   *Grabinski*, 203 F.3d at 1026; *see also* Advocat, Inc. v. Sauer, 111 S.W.3d 346 (Ark. 2003) (using full joint and several liability of each defendant, but comparing it to aggregate total of punitive damages awards against all defendants, with same result as in *Grabinski*; court uses this method of calculation without analysis).

415.12   *State Farm*, 538 U.S. 408, 424; *Gore*, 517 U.S. 559, 580 (ratio is between punitive damages and "harm inflicted on the plaintiff").

415.13   Planned Parenthood v. Am. Coalition of Life Activists, 422 F.3d 949, 960–62 (9th Cir. 2005).

415.14   Estate of Moreland v. Dieter, 395 F.3d 747, 757 (7th Cir. 2005).

415.15   Planned Parenthood v. Am. Coalition of Life Activists, 422 F.3d 949, 961–62 (9th Cir. 2005).

7.10.6.3.5 *Justifying a high ratio*

Another factor that may favor large punitive damages awards in auto fraud cases is that compensatory damages awards are often relatively small. While *State Farm* states that punitive damages awards that significantly exceed a single-digit ratio to compensatory damages will rarely satisfy due process, it acknowledges that a higher ratio may be appropriate when a particularly egregious act causes only a small amount of economic harm.[415.16]

A number of courts have taken this statement seriously and have approved punitive damages awards more than nine times compensatory damages when the amount of actual damages is small.[415.17] The most striking cases have in-

---

415.16 *State Farm*, 538 U.S. 408, 425; *see* Johnson v. Ford Motor Co., 2003 WL 22794432 (Cal. Ct. App. Nov. 25, 2003) (unpublished) (higher ratio can be allowed in auto fraud case when actual damages are purely economic), *rev'd, remanded on other grounds*, 35 Cal. 4th 1191, 29 Cal. Rptr. 3d 401 (2005) (disagreeing with court of appeals' reduction of punitive damage award; remanding for new analysis of *State Farm* factors).

415.17 Romanski v. Detroit Entertainment, L.L.C., 428 F.3d 629 (6th Cir. 2005) (upholding $600,000 of jury's $875,000 punitive damage award on compensatory damages of $279.05, a 2750-to-1 ratio); Williams v. Kaufman County, 352 F.3d 994 (5th Cir. 2004) (affirming $15,000 punitive damages award when jury awarded $100 nominal damages, a 150-to-1 ratio, in § 1983 strip search case); Mathias v. Accor Econ. Lodging, Inc., 347 F.3d 672 (7th Cir. 2003) (upholding 37.2-to-1 ratio when compensatory damages to hotel guest bitten by bedbugs was $5000); Asa-Brandt, Inc. v. ADM Investor Services, Inc., 344 F.3d 738 (8th Cir. 2003) ($1.25 million punitive damages award not excessive in light of potential harm of $3.9 million, even though jury awarded only nominal damages); Lincoln v. Case, 340 F.3d 283 (5th Cir. 2003) (ordering *remittur* of $100,000 punitive damages award to $55,000 on $500 compensatory damages, an 110-to-1 ratio, in housing discrimination case); Dunn v. Vill. of Put-in-Bay, 2004 WL 169788 (N.D. Ohio Jan. 26, 2004) (upholding $23,422.50 punitive damages award on $1577.50 compensatory damages, a 14.8-to-1 ratio, in light of small compensatory award in § 1983 excessive force case and difficulty of placing value on constitutional violation not accompanied by lasting physical consequences); Jones v. Rent-A-Center, Inc., 281 F. Supp. 2d 1277 (D. Kan. 2003) (upholding $290,000 punitive damages award on $10,000 compensatory damages in Title VII case because Title VII $300,000 damages cap gives defendants fair warning of potential liability); S. Union Co. v. Southwest Gas Corp., 281 F. Supp. 2d 1090 (D. Ariz. 2003) (upholding $60 million punitive damages award on $390,072.58 compensatory damages, a ratio of 153-to-1, when potential harm was high, some damage was unquantifiable, and defendant breached public trust); Craig v. Holsey, 590 S.E.2d 742 (Ga. Ct. App. 2003) (upholding 22.7-to-1 ratio when drunk driver crashed into plaintiff's car, pushing her into oncoming traffic, but caused only $8801.40 actual damages); Lowe Excavating Co. v. Int'l Union of Operating Engineers, 832 N.E.2d 495 (Ill. App. Ct. 2005) (approving punitive damages of $325,000 on compensatory damages of $4280, a 75-to-1 ratio; court takes into account that plaintiff incurred attorney fees of at least $325,000), *appeal allowed*, 844 N.E.2d 38 (Ill. 2005); Phelps v. Louisville Water Co., 103 S.W.3d 46 (Ky. 2003) (affirming $2 million punitive damages award, an 11.3-to-1 ratio, because of

low compensatory damages award of $176,361.64 for wrongful death); Krysa v. Payne, 176 S.W.3d 150, 160 (Mo. Ct. App. 2005) (upholding $500,000 punitive damages on $18,449,53 actual damages, a 27-to-1 ratio, where concealed wreck damage made vehicle dangerous); Werremeyer v. K.C. Auto Salvage Co., 2003 WL 21487311 (Mo. Ct. App. June 30, 2003) (approving a 13.9-to-1 ratio in consumer automobile fraud case when the fraud was difficult to detect), *aff'd in relevant part, rev'd in part on other grounds*, 134 S.W.3d 633 (Mo. 2004) (reversing denial of prejudgment interest but affirming award in all other respects); Madeja v. MPB Corp., 821 A.2d 1034 (N.H. 2003) (upholding 35-to-1 punitive damages award in sexual harassment case; opinion does not state dollar amounts of compensatory or punitive damages awards); Hollock v. Erie Ins. Exch., 842 A.2d 409 (Pa. Super. Ct. 2004) (affirming 10-to-1 ratio, with compensatory damages of $278,825 and punitive damages of $2,800,000, in insurance bad faith case), *appeal granted in part*, 2005 WL 3692710 (Pa. June 28, 2005); Smith v. Fairfax Realty, Inc., 82 P.3d 1064 (Utah 2003) (affirming $5,500,000 punitive damages award on compensatory damages of $1,007,221, a 5.5-to-1 ratio, in commercial case involving solely economic loss); Strenke v. Hogner, 704 N.W.2d 309, 316–17 (Wis. Ct. App. 2005) (upholding $225,000 punitive damages on $2000 compensatory damages, a 112.5-to-1 ratio, against drunk driver whose reckless actions could have killed the plaintiff); Gibson v. Overnite Transp. Co., 671 N.W.2d 388, 394 n.3 (Wis. Ct. App. 2003) (affirming $250,000 punitive damages award, an 8-to-1 ratio, when employee's $33,000 compensatory award in defamation claim against former employer did not include any emotional distress damages); *see also* Casciola v. F.S. Air Service, Inc., 120 P.3d 1059 (Alaska 2005) (upholding $300,000 punitive damages on $30,000 compensatory damages; higher ratio also meets Alaska standards where compensatory damages are small relative to the cost of litigating); Trinity Evangelical Lutheran Church v. Tower Ins. Co., 661 N.W.2d 789 (Wis. 2003) (upholding $3.5 million punitive damages award in insurance bad faith case, even though no actual damages were awarded, when ratio was 7-to-1 to harm that would have occurred if defendant's misconduct had succeeded); *cf.* Munro v. Golden Rule Ins. Co., 393 F.3d 720 (7th Cir. 2004) (interpreting Mathias v. Accor Lodging, Inc., 347 F.3d 672 (7th Cir. 2003), as allowing larger ratio when defendant's acts inflict small losses on hundreds of people); Super. Fed. Bank v. Mackey, 129 S.W.3d 324 (Ark. Ct. App. 2003) (remanding 28.5-to-1 punitive damages award to trial court for evaluation in light of Supreme Court's intervening decision in *State Farm*). *But see* Jones v. Sheahan, 2003 WL 22508171 (N.D. Ill. Nov. 4, 2003) ($25,000 compensatory damages award not so low for excessive force claim as to justify 10-to-1 and 20-to-1 ratios); Simon v. San Paolo U.S. Holding Co., 35 Cal. 4th 1159, 29 Cal. Rptr. 3d 379, 396, 113 P.3d 63 (2005) ($1.7 million punitive damage award on $5000 compensatory damages, a 340-to-1 ratio, is grossly excessive where $5000 was accurate measure of actual harm); Roth v. Farner-Bocken Co., 667 N.W.2d 651 (S.D. 2003) (vacating $500,000 punitive damages award, a 20-to-1 ratio, when compensatory award of $25,000 was large for minor invasion of privacy and included emotional distress, reprehensibility was minimal, and there was no repetition); *cf.* Daka v. McCrae, 839 A.2d 682 (D.C. 2003) (26-to-1 ratio excessive in sexual harassment case when compensatory damages were $187,500 and included primarily emotional distress, even though defendant's actions were repeated, and defendant's liability was based on negligent supervision; remanded with instructions to allow punitive damages award no

volved awards of nominal damages.[415.18] Courts in these cases have reasoned that strict proportionality would defeat the ability to make an award that was punitive, and have approved ratios as high as 2172-to-1.[415.19] Nonetheless, courts have by no means confined this treatment to nominal damages cases, but have approved higher ratios because of small compensatory damages awards even when the award was as high as $278,825, especially when the award was small for the type of injury suffered.[415.20] One factor a

number of courts have cited in approving higher ratios is the difficulty of quantifying certain types of injuries, such as fear, emotional distress, and violations of individual constitutional rights.[415.21] Many courts have also approved puni-

---

larger than five times actual damages).

[415.18] Kemp v. Am. Tel. & Tel. Co., 393 F.3d 1354 (11th Cir. 2004) (approving punitive damages of $250,000 when actual damages were $115.05, a 2172-to-1 ratio); Fabri v. United Technologies Int'l, Inc., 387 F.3d 109 (2d Cir. 2004) (ratio analysis not fully applicable when damages are nominal, but $500,000 punitive damages excessive when jury awarded $1 nominal damages and evidence of reprehensibility was unexceptional); Williams v. Kaufman County, 352 F.3d 994 (5th Cir. 2004) (affirming $15,000 punitive damages award when jury awarded $100 nominal damages, a 150-to-1 ratio, in § 1983 strip search case); Sherman v. Kasotakis, 314 F. Supp. 2d 843 (N.D. Iowa 2004) (affirming punitive damages of $12,500 when jury awarded nominal compensatory damages of $1 for racial slur and segregated seating in restaurant; if punitive damages were based on single-digit formula they would not be punitive when nominal damages are awarded); Myers v. Workmen's Auto Ins. Co., 95 P.3d 977 (Idaho 2004) (affirming $300,000 punitive damages when jury awarded nominal damages of $735, a 408-to-1 ratio); *see also* Local Union No. 38, Sheet Metal Workers' Int'l Ass'n v. Pelella, 350 F.3d 73 (2d Cir. 2003) (affirming $25,000 punitive damages award on nominal award of $1 compensatory damages in union member's breach of contract case, when union did not preserve error; court states that *State Farm* ratios may not apply with equal force when nominal damages are awarded); Asa-Brandt, Inc. v. ADM Investor Services, Inc., 344 F.3d 738 (8th Cir. 2003) ($1.25 million punitive damages award not excessive in light of potential harm of $3.9 million, even though jury awarded only nominal damages). *But see* Pestco, Inc. v. Associated Prods., Inc., 880 A.2d 700, 710 (Pa. Super. Ct. 2005) ($25,000 punitive damage award was unconstitutionally disproportionate to compensatory damage award of $1.00; court also concludes on state law grounds that there was no basis for any punitive damage award); *but cf.* Home Pride Foods v. Martin, 2003 WL 23005185 (Iowa Ct. App. Dec. 24, 2003) (punitive damages can be awarded when jury finds liability but awards no damages, but court "cannot reconcile" $82,228.20 punitive damages award with *State Farm*).

[415.19] Kemp v. Am. Tel. & Tel. Co., 393 F.3d 1354 (11th Cir. 2004) (approving punitive damages of $250,000 when actual damages were $115.05; confining punitive damages to single-digit ratio would fail to deter and punish large multinational corporation).

[415.20] CGB Occupational Therapy, Inc. v. RHA Pa. Nursing Homes, 2005 WL 1595428 (E.D. Pa. July 5, 2005) (upholding $2 million of jury's $30 million punitive damages on compensatory damages of $109,000, a 19-to-1 ratio; court notes that plaintiff probably suffered damages that are not reflected in the compensatory award); Superior Fed. Bank v. Jones & Mackey Constr. Co., 2005 WL 3307074 (Ark. Ct. App. Dec. 7, 2005) (upholding $3,080,000 punitive damages where compensatory damages on tort claim were $175,000, a 17.6-to-1 ratio; compensatory damages would be $385,000 if contract and tort awards were aggregated); Williams v. Philip Morris Inc., 127 P.3d 1165 (Or. 2006) (reinstating $79.5 million punitive damage award in

smoker's wrongful death case, a 97-to-1 or 152-to-1 ratio depending on calculation of compensatory damage award); Hollock v. Erie Ins. Exch., 842 A.2d 409 (Pa. Super. Ct. 2004) (affirming 10-to-1 ratio because of "limited" compensatory damages award of $278,825 in insurance bad faith case), *appeal granted in part*, 2005 WL 3692710 (Pa. June 28, 2005); Mission Res., Inc. v. Garza Energy Trust, 166 S.W.3d 301 (Tex. App. 2005) (affirming $10 million punitive damages when compensatory damages were $543,776, a 20-to-1 ratio, and defendant acted with malice and its conduct amounted to felony theft); Schwigel v. Kohlmann, 694 N.W.2d 467 (Wis. Ct. App. 2005) (affirming punitive damages of $375,000 when compensatory damages were $12,000, a 30-to-1 ratio, even though just one incident and no physical injury, threat to health or safety, or vulnerable victim involved); *see also* Clark v. Chrysler Corp., 436 F.3d 594, 607 (6th Cir. 2006) (taking relatively small compensatory award into account in approving punitive damages of two times compensatory damages); Willow Inn, Inc. v. Pub. Serv. Mut. Ins. Co., 399 F.3d 224 (3d Cir. 2005) (upholding $150,000 punitive damages award when compensatory damages were $2000; by treating a $135,000 award for attorney fees and costs as compensatory damages, court views ratio as only slightly more than 1-to-1); *In re* Exxon Valdez, 296 F. Supp. 2d 1071, 1104 (D. Alaska 2004) ($513,147,740 compensatory damages award is small because it is only $15,704 per class member); Bardis v. Oates, 119 Cal. App. 4th 1, 14 Cal. Rptr. 3d 89, 106 (2004) (higher ratio justified when compensatory damages of $165,527.63 were relatively small in comparison to defendants' misconduct); Phelps v. Louisville Water Co., 103 S.W.3d 46 (Ky. 2003) (affirming $2 million punitive damages award, an 11.3-to-1 ratio, because of low compensatory damages award of $176,361.64 for wrongful death). S. Union Co. v. Southwest Gas Corp., 415 F.3d 1001 (9th Cir. 2005), *as amended by* 423 F.3d 1117 (9th Cir. 2005) (remanding for determination of amount of remittur; $60 million in punitive damages too high where compensatory damages were $390,072); *But see* Bains L.L.C. v. Arco Products Co., 405 F.3d 764 (9th Cir. 2005) ($50,000 not small; district court must reduce punitive damages from $5 million to somewhere between $300,000 and $450,000); Harris v. Archer, 134 S.W.3d 411 (Tex. App. 2004) (actual damages of $101,000 are substantial; ordering *remittur* of $750,000 punitive damages award in business fraud case to $407,790, to achieve 4-to-1 ratio).

[415.21] Mathias v. Accor Econ. Lodging, Inc., 347 F.3d 672, 676 (7th Cir. 2003) (emotional distress); Lincoln v. Case, 340 F.3d 283 (5th Cir. 2003) (higher ratio justified in housing discrimination case because of inherently low or hard-to-determine actual injuries); Sherman v. Kasotakis, 314 F. Supp. 2d 843 (N.D. Iowa 2004) (racial slur and segregated seating in restaurant); Planned Parenthood v. Am. Coalition of Life Activists, 2004 WL 144204 (D. Or. Jan. 28, 2004) (fear); Dunn v. Vill. of Put-in-Bay, 2004 WL 169788 (N.D. Ohio Jan. 26, 2004) (constitutional violation not accompanied by lasting physical consequences); Jones v. Rent-A-Center, Inc., 281 F. Supp. 2d 1277, 1290 (D. Kan. 2003) (injuries in sexual harassment cases are primarily personal and therefore difficult to quantify); *see also* Planned Parenthood v. Am. Coalition of Life Activists, 422 F.3d 949 (9th Cir. 2005) (citing fact that some actual damage was not quantifiable as reason to approve 9-to-1 ratio); Romanski v. Detroit Entertainment, L.L.C., 428 F.3d 629, 645 (6th Cir. 2005); Day v. Ingle's

tive damages ratios at the high end of the "single digit" range, sometimes even when compensatory damages were substantial.[415.22] On the other hand, some courts have im-

posed smaller ratios when compensatory damages were

Market, 2006 WL 239290 (E.D. Tenn. Jan. 25, 2006); Romanski v. Detroit Entertainment, L.L.C., 428 F.3d 629, 643–44 (6th Cir. 2005); Russo v. Hartford, 2006 WL 516747 (D. Conn. Mar. 2, 2006) (violation of First Amendment rights); Lowry's Reports, Inc. v. Legg Mason, Inc., 302 F. Supp. 2d 455 (D. Md. 2004) (*Gore* and *State Farm* do not apply to statutory damages claims under federal copyright law because of difficulties of proving and providing compensation for actual harm); Lowe Excavating Co. v. Int'l Union of Operating Engineers, 832 N.E.2d 495, 505 (Ill. App. Ct. 2005), *appeal allowed*, 844 N.E.2d 38 (Ill. 2005).

415.22 Planned Parenthood v. Am. Coalition of Life Activists, 422 F.3d 949 (9th Cir. 2005) (approving punitive damages of nine times compensatory damages against anti-abortion activists who threatened physicians with violence); Zhang v. Am. Gem Seafoods, Inc., 339 F.3d 1020 (9th Cir. 2003) (affirming $2,600,000 million punitive damages award, a 7-to-1 ratio, in § 1981 employment discrimination case, even though $360,000 compensatory damages award included emotional distress); Action Marine, Inc. v. Cont'l Carbon, Inc., 2006 WL 173653 (M.D. Ala. Jan. 23, 2006) (upholding punitive damages of $17.5 million on compensatory damages of $1.9 million, a ratio greater than 9-to-1); *In re* Exxon Valdez, 296 F. Supp. 2d 1071 (D. Alaska 2004) (upholding $4.5 billion punitive damages award in environmental tort class action when compensatory damages were about $513 million, an approximately 9-to-1 ratio); Millazzo v. Universal Traffic Serv., Inc., 289 F. Supp. 2d 1251 (D. Colo. 2003) (reducing punitive damages awards in Title VII case to a 2.25-to-1 ratio for one plaintiff and a 9-to-1 ratio for another, when their injuries were psychological and difficult to quantify); McClain v. Metabolife Int'l, Inc., 259 F. Supp. 2d 1225 (N.D. Ala. 2003) (allowing punitive damages award of nine to one, reduced from twenty to one, on compensatory award of $50,000 in fraud/products liability case); Advocat, Inc. v. Sauer, 111 S.W.3d 346 (Ark. 2003) (affirming, after *remitturs*, $21 million punitive damages award on $5 million compensatory damages for nursing home's neglect of decedent); Johnson v. Ford Motor Co., 135 Cal. App. 4th 137, 37 Cal. Rptr. 3d 283, 292 (2005) (upholding $175,000 of jury's multi-million dollar punitive damage award in lemon laundering case where compensatory damages were $17,811.60, a ratio just under 10-to-1); Boeken v. Philip Morris Inc., 127 Cal. App. 4th 1640, 26 Cal. Rptr. 3d 638 (2005) (affirming $50 million in punitive damages on compensatory award of $5,539,127, a 9-to-1 ratio, when defendant's conduct was extraordinarily reprehensible; court might have approved higher ratio except that other deterrents had been adopted); Bardis v. Oates, 119 Cal. App. 4th 1, 14 Cal. Rptr. 3d 89 (2004) (allowing $1.5 million punitive damages on compensatory award of $165,527.63, a 9-to-1 ratio, even though harm was entirely economic, when defendant's misconduct was egregious); Hensley v. Philip Morris, Inc., 114 Cal. App. 4th 1429, 9 Cal. Rptr. 3d 29 (2004) (allowing 6-to-1 ratio, reduced from a 17-to-1 ratio, even though compensatory damages were $1.5 million, in light of defendant's extraordinarily reprehensible conduct); Turner v. Firstar Bank, 2006 WL 539448 (Ill. App. Ct. Mar. 6, 2006) (upholding $225,000 of a $500,000 punitive damage award on compensatory damages of $25,000, a 9-to-1 ratio, for wrongful repossession); Bocci v. Key Pharm., Inc., 76 P.3d 669 (Or. Ct. App. 2003), *as amended by* 79 P.3d 908 (Or. Ct. App. 2003) (allowing $3.5 million punitive damages award, remitted from $22.5

million, on compensatory award of $500,000, a 7-to-1 ratio, in favor of doctor whose patient suffered physical harm due to drug company's suppression of dangers of medication); Boyd v. Goffoli, 608 S.E.2d 169 (W. Va. 2004) (upholding punitive damages that were 3.3 times compensatory damages of $300,000, or 8.4 times the non-emotional distress component); *see also* Eden Elec., Ltd. v. Amana Co., 370 F.3d 824 (8th Cir. 2004) (affirming $10 million punitive damage award in fraud case when compensatory damages were $2.1 million, a 4.5-to-1 ratio); Rhone-Poulenc Agro, S.A. v. DeKalb Genetics Corp., 345 F.3d 1366 (Fed. Cir. 2003) (affirming $50 million punitive damages award, a 3.3-to-1 ratio, in commercial fraud case even though $15 million compensatory award was large and damages were economic only); Jurinko v. Med. Protective Co., 2006 WL 785234 (E.D. Pa. Mar. 29, 2006) (upholding punitive damages of $6.25 million on compensatory damages of $1.66 million, a 3.76-to-1 ratio); Bach v. First Union Nat'l Bank, 2006 WL 840381 (S.D. Ohio Mar. 30, 2006) (reducing punitive damage award in FCRA case from $2.6 million to $2.2 million where compensatory damages were $400,000, a 5.5-to-1 ratio); Chicago Title Ins. Corp. v. Magnuson, 2005 WL 2373430 (S.D. Ohio Sept. 26, 2005) (upholding $32.4 million punitive damage award on $10.8 million compensatory damages, a 3-to-1 ratio); Harrelson v. R.J., 882 So. 2d 317 (Ala. 2003) (approving jury's 5-to-1 ratio for sexual assault); Union Pac. R.R. Co. v. Barber, 149 S.W.3d 325 (Ark. 2004) (upholding $25 million punitive damages award on $5.1 million compensatory damages in wrongful death case); Simon v. San Paolo U.S. Holding Co., 35 Cal. 4th 1159, 29 Cal. Rptr. 3d 379, 113 P.3d 63 (2005) (upholding $50,000 of $1.5 million punitive damage award where compensatory damages were $5000 and reprehensibility was not great); Romo v. Ford Motor Co., 113 Cal. App. 4th 738, 6 Cal. Rptr. 3d 793 (2003) (approving ratios of 3-to-1 and 5-to-1 in wrongful death case even though actual damages were about $5 million; court takes into account that loss of life is undercompensated); Diamond Woodworks, Inc. v. Argonaut Ins. Co., 109 Cal. App. 4th 1020, 135 Cal. Rptr. 2d 736 (2003) (allowing $1 million punitive damages award on $258,570 compensatory damages in insurance bad faith/fraud case, a ratio of 3.8-to-1 after *remitturs* of both punitive and compensatory damages awards); Benham v. Wallingford Auto Park, Inc., 2003 WL 22905163 (Conn. Super. Ct. Nov. 26, 2003) (awarding $35,000 in punitive damages on $5000 compensatory damages, a 7-to-1 ratio, on UDAP claim against dealer who reneged on offer to exchange vehicle if consumer was dissatisfied); Campbell v. State Farm Mut. Auto. Ins. Co., 98 P.3d 409 (Utah 2004) (on remand, approving punitive damages of nine times compensatory damages of $1,002,086.75 in bad faith insurance case); *cf.* Bogle v. McClure, 332 F.3d 1347 (11th Cir. 2003) (affirming 4-to-1 ratio in § 1983 employment discrimination case, with compensatory damages of $500,000 and punitive damages of $2,000,000, even though compensatory damages represented just emotional distress); Borne v. Haverhill Golf & Country Club, 791 N.E.2d 903 (Mass. App. Ct. 2003) (upholding ratios ranging from almost 4-to-1 to 1.37-to-1 in country club sex discrimination case even though actual damages were mostly emotional distress); Harris v. Archer, 134 S.W.3d 411 (Tex. App. 2004) (4-to-1 ratio is close to line, but allows 4-to-1 ratio in business fraud case when actual damages were substantial, harm was only economic, victims were not vulnerable, and acts were intentional but not repeated). *But see* Gallatin Fuels, Inc. v. Westchester Fire Ins. Co., 2006 WL 840341 (W.D. Pa. Mar. 28, 2006) (reducing punitive damage award from $20 million to

substantial or the evidence of reprehensibility was weaker.[415.23] Some courts have treated single-digit ratios, or ratios of 4-to-1 or less, as presumptively reasonable.[415.24] This approach is consistent with the Seventh Circuit's observation that the "judicial function is to police a range, not a point."[415.25]

[415.23] Clark v. Chrysler Corp., 436 F.3d 594, 606–07 (6th Cir. 2006) (reducing punitive damages from $3 million, a 13-to-1 ratio, to $471,258, a 2-to-1 ratio, where evidence of reprehensibility was weak); Boerner v. Brown & Williamson Tobacco Co., 394 F.3d 594 (8th Cir. 2005) (reducing $15 million punitive damages award to $5 million when compensatory damages were $4,025,000); Eden Elec., Ltd. v. Amana Co., Ltd. P'ship, 370 F.3d 824 (8th Cir. 2004) (when harm was only economic, victim was not financially vulnerable, and there was no repetition, 8.5-to-1 ratio reduced to 4.76-to-1); Conseco Fin. Servicing Corp. v. N. Am. Mortgage Co., 381 F.3d 811 (8th Cir. 2004) (reducing punitive damages from $18 million to $7 million when compensatory damages were $3.5 million); Motorola Credit Corp. v. Uzan, 388 F.3d 39 (2d Cir. 2004) (vacating and remanding $2 billion award when compensatory damages were same amount; compensatory damages alone exceeded defendant's net worth); Stogsdill v. Healthmark Partners, L.L.C., 377 F.3d 827 (8th Cir. 2004) (reducing $5 million punitive damages to $2 million when compensatory damages were $500,000 and defendant neglected nursing home patient but was not malicious); Williams v. Conagra Poultry Co., 378 F.3d 790 (8th Cir. 2004) (reducing punitive damages award from $6,063,750 to $600,000, the same amount as compensatory damages); Disorbo v. Hoy, 343 F.3d 172 (2d Cir. 2003) (allowing only $75,000 punitive damages award on $25,000 compensatory damages in § 1983 excessive force case); Casumpang v. Int'l Longshore & Warehouse Union, 411 F. Supp. 2d 1201 (D. Hawaii 2005) (reducing $1 million punitive damage award to $240,000 where compensatory damages were also $240,000; court notes Supreme Court's special caution against large punitive damage awards against unions); Richardson v. Tricom Pictures & Productions, Inc., 334 F. Supp. 2d 1303 (S.D. Fla. 2004) (reducing punitive damages from $50,000 to $20,000 in Title VII case when back pay award was $20,000 and evidence of reprehensibility was weak); Textron Fin. Corp. v. Nat'l Union Fire Ins. Co., 118 Cal. App. 4th 1061, 13 Cal. Rptr. 3d 586 (2004) (reducing punitive damages to four times compensatory damages awarded on bad faith and fraud claims; when compensatory damages are neither exceptionally high nor low and defendant's conduct neither exceptionally extreme nor trivial, outer constitutional limit is approximately 4-to-1 ratio); Daka v. McCrae, 839 A.2d 682 (D.C. 2003) (26-to-1 ratio excessive in sexual harassment case when compensatory damages were $187,500, and included primarily emotional distress, and defendant's liability was based on negligent supervision, even though defendant's actions were repeated; remanded with instructions to allow punitive damages no larger than five times actual damages); Park v. Mobil Oil Guam, Inc., 2004 WL 2595897 (Guam Nov. 16, 2004) (reducing punitive damages from 56-to-1 ratio to 3-to-1 when compensatory damages were $150,000, plaintiff was not vulnerable, harm was only economic, and defendant's conduct was isolated); Grefer v. Alpha Technical, 901 So. 2d 1117, 1150–52 (La. Ct. App. 2005) (reducing punitive damage award to $112 million (twice actual damages) where compensatory award was generous and not well supported); Blust v. Lamar Adver. Co., 157 Ohio App. 3d 787, 813 N.E.2d 902 (2004) ($32,000 compensatory damages substantial for trespass, so 70-to-1 punitive damages ratio is excessive); Goddard v. Farmers Ins. Co., 120 P.3d 1260, 1282–84 (Or. Ct. App. 2005) (reducing punitive damages from

---

$4.5 million where compensatory damages were $1.325 million, a 3.4-to-1 ratio).

16-to-1 to 3-to-1 where compensatory damages were $1.2 million; court attempts to achieve rough equality with punitive damage awards in other cases involving similar level of reprehensibility), *modified on other grounds, adhered to*, 126 P.3d 682 (Or. Ct. App. 2006); Waddill v. Anchor Hocking, Inc., 78 P.3d 570 (Or. Ct. App. 2003) (reducing punitive damages from $1 million on $100,854 compensatory damages to a 4-to-1 ratio, when defendant recklessly disregarded plaintiff's health and safety, but did not act intentionally); SAS & Assocs., Inc. v. Home Mktg. Servicing, Inc., 168 S.W.3d 296 (Tex. App. 2005) (affirming trial court's reduction of punitive damages from 18 to 3 times compensatory damages of $7574 for fraud, where defendant acted with malice but there were no other aggravating circumstances).

[415.24] Diesel Machinery, Inc. v. B.R. Lee Indus., Inc., 418 F.3d 820, 840 (8th Cir. 2005) ($2.66 million punitive damage award on $665,000 compensatory damages, a 4-to-1 ratio, not unconstitutional); Estate of Moreland v. Dieter, 395 F.3d 747 (7th Cir. 2005) (affirming $27 million punitive damages when compensatory damages were $29 million); Kapelanski v. Johnson, 390 F.3d 525 (7th Cir. 2004) (3.3-to-1 ratio "easily permissible"); Hangarter v. Provident Life & Accident Ins. Co., 373 F.3d 998, 1015 (9th Cir. 2004) (2.6-to-1 ratio); Rhone-Poulenc Agro, S.A. v. DeKalb Genetics Corp., 345 F.3d 1366, 1372 (Fed. Cir. 2003) (4-to-1 ratio is "threshold where the punitive award may become suspect"); Zhang v. Am. Gem Seafoods, Inc., 339 F.3d 1020, 1044 (9th Cir. 2003); Morales v. Jones, 2006 WL 268770 (E.D. Wis. Feb. 1, 2006) (upholding $65,000 punitive damages on $20,000 compensatory damages, a 3.5-to-1 ratio); Day v. Ingle's Market, 2006 WL 239290 (E.D. Tenn. Jan. 25, 2006); Gibson v. Total Car Franchising Corp., 223 F.R.D. 265 (M.D.N.C. 2004) (upholding 3.12-to-1 ratio as well within single-digit range); Marmer•v. Unicco Serv. Co., 2003 WL 22462053 (E.D. Pa. Oct. 2, 2003) (2-to-1 ratio is well within the bounds of constitutional propriety); Bowen & Bowen Constr. Co. v. Fowler, 593 S.E.2d 668 (Ga. Ct. App. 2004) (finding 2.5-to-1 ratio acceptable without extended discussion); Reading Radio, Inc. v. Fink, 833 A.2d 199, 215 n.3 (Pa. Super. Ct. 2003) (2-to-1 ratio not suspect); Bunton v. Bentley, 176 S.W.3d 21 (Tex. App. 2005) (finding $1 million punitive damages on $300,000 compensatory damages, a 3.33-to-1 ratio, reasonable without extended analysis); *see also* MacGregor v. Mallinckrodt, Inc., 373 F.3d 923 (8th Cir. 2004) (finding 2-to-1 ratio acceptable). *But see* Williams v. Conagra Poultry Co., 378 F.3d 790 (8th Cir. 2004) (ratio only slightly more than ten to one requires special justification; reducing punitive damages from $6,063,750 to $600,000, the same amount as compensatory damages); Disorbo v. Hoy, 343 F.3d 172 (2d Cir. 2003); Bogle v. McClure, 332 F.3d 1347, 1362 (11th Cir. 2003); Simon v. San Paolo U.S. Holding Co., 35 Cal. 4th 1159, 29 Cal. Rptr. 3d 379, 395, 113 P.3d 63 (2005) (single digit multipliers are not presumptively valid); Bunton v. Bentley, 153 S.W.2d 50 (Tex. 2004) (fact that ratio is just three to one is insufficient to uphold punitive damages award).

[415.25] Mathias v. Accor Econ. Lodging, Inc., 347 F.3d 672, 678 (7th Cir. 2003); *see also* Williams v. Kaufman County, 352 F.3d 994, 1016 n.78 (5th Cir. 2003) (punitive damages award is higher than awards in similar cases, but court's balancing of factors is "necessarily unscientific"). *But see* Disorbo v. Hoy, 343 F.3d 172 (2d Cir. 2003).

The *State Farm* Court's approval of higher ratios in cases involving small compensatory damages is especially suitable to automobile fraud cases, in which the seller's behavior, though scandalous, may not cause the plaintiff to suffer high out-of-pocket damages. Most of the automobile fraud cases that have resulted in large punitive damages awards have involved compensatory damages of less than $10,000,[415.26] an entirely different scale of magnitude from the one million dollar compensatory damages award in *State Farm*.

7.10.6.3.6 Avoiding rigid arithmetical ratios

Although it focused on ratios, *State Farm* reiterated the Supreme Court's earlier disavowal of "rigid benchmarks."[415.27] Many courts have taken the Supreme Court at its word.[415.28] The Fifth Circuit has stressed that the ratio analysis only embodies a general evaluation of reasonableness.[415.29] The Seventh Circuit commented that a rule limiting punitive damages to a 4-to-1 or single-digit ratio would be unreasonable because it would undermine the goals of punitive damages awards.[415.30] Both the Supreme Court[415.31] and many other courts[415.32] have recognized that deterrence

is one of the two goals of punitive damages. This principle necessarily implies that, when the defendants are obdurate, the award should be increased until it actually achieves deterrence.[415.33] As the Court stated in *Gore*, "strong medicine is required to cure [a recidivist's] disrespect for the law."[415.34]

7.10.6.3.7 Presenting evidence of the plaintiff's vulnerability

Because of their lower cost, used cars are often bought by those who can least afford to be defrauded. *State Farm* named the financial vulnerability of the target of the defendant's deceit as a factor to be considered when evaluating the reprehensibility of the conduct.[415.35] The plaintiff's age, so-

---

415.26 *See* § 7.10.8, *infra*.

415.27 *State Farm*, 538 U.S. at 424, 425 (" '[W]e have consistently rejected the notion that the constitutional line is marked by a simple mathematical formula. . . .' We decline again to impose a bright-line ratio which a punitive damages award cannot exceed." (citation omitted)).

415.28 Kemp v. Am. Tel. & Tel. Co., 393 F.3d 1354 (11th Cir. 2004) (approving punitive damages of $250,000 when actual damages were $115.05; confining punitive damages to single-digit multiplier would fail to deter and punish large multinational corporation). See Jones v. Rent-A-Center, 281 F. Supp. 2d 1277 (D. Kan. 2003) and cases cited in § 7.10.6.3.5, *supra*. See also Simon v. San Paolo U.S. Holding Co., 35 Cal. 4th 1159, 29 Cal. Rptr. 3d 379, 395, 113 P.3d 63 (2005). *But cf.* Williams v. Conagra Poultry Co., 378 F.3d 790 (8th Cir. 2004) (ratio only slightly more than ten to one requires special justification; reducing punitive damages from $6,063,750 to $600,000, the same amount as compensatory damages); Bardis v. Oates, 119 Cal. App. 4th 1, 14 Cal. Rptr. 3d 89 (2004) (42-to-1 ratio can not stand in absence of extraordinary factors); Atkinson v. Orkin Exterminating Co., 604 S.E.2d 385, 392 (S.C. 2004) (127-to-1 ratio is presumptively excessive).

415.29 Williams v. Kaufman County, 352 F.3d 994, 1016 (5th Cir. 2003); *accord* Lincoln v. Case, 340 F.3d 283, 293 (5th Cir. 2003) (ratio merely gives the court an idea whether the size of the award is suspect).

415.30 Mathias v. Accor Econ. Lodging, Inc., 347 F.3d 672, 676, 677 (7th Cir. 2003).

415.31 *State Farm*, 538 U.S. 408, 416; *accord* BMW of N. Am., Inc. v. Gore, 517 U.S. 559, 568, 116 S. Ct. 1589, 134 L. Ed. 2d 809 (1996) ("Punitive damages may properly be imposed to further a state's legitimate interest in punishing unlawful conduct and deterring its repetition.").

415.32 Johnson v. Ford Motor Co., 35 Cal. 4th 1191, 29 Cal. Rptr. 3d 401, 413–14 (2005). *See*, *e.g.*, Kemp v. Am. Tel. & Tel. Co., 393 F.3d 1354, 1363–1365 (11th Cir. 2004) (upholding award of $115.05 actual damages and $250,000 punitive damages, a

172-to-1 ratio, for billing fraud, because a lesser punitive damages award "would utterly fail to serve the traditional purposes underlying an award of punitive damages, which are to punish and deter"); Mathias v. Accor Econ. Lodging, Inc., 347 F.3d 672 (7th Cir. 2003) (suit in negligence against motel franchise for renting rooms known to be infested with bedbugs; upholding $5000 in actual damages and $186,000 in punitive damages, a 37-to-1 ratio, with an extensive analysis of *State Farm* emphasizing deterrence as well as other factors); Johansen v. Combustion Eng'g, Inc., 170 F.3d 1320, 1339 (11th Cir. 1999) (upholding a punitive damages award of $4.35 million, which was approximately one-hundred times the amount of actual damages awarded by the jury, as "justified by the need to deter this and other large organizations from a 'pollute and pay' environmental policy").

415.33 *See* Eden Elec., Ltd. v. Amana Co., Ltd. P'ship, 258 F. Supp. 2d 958 (N.D. Iowa 2003) (punitive damages must be set at an amount that will achieve deterrence), *aff'd*, 370 F.3d 824 (8th Cir. 2004). But see Romo v. Ford Motor Co., 113 Cal. App. 4th 738, 6 Cal. Rptr. 3d 793, 799–804 (2003) (construing *State Farm* to abandon criterion of actual deterrence), *disapproved on this issue by* Johnson v. Ford Motor Co., 35 Cal. 4th 1191, 29 Cal. Rptr. 3d 401 (2005); Krysa v. Payne, 176 S.W.3d 150, 155 (Mo. Ct. App. 2005).

415.34 *Gore*, 517 U.S. at 577.

415.35 *State Farm*, 538 U.S. 408, 419; *see also* Planned Parenthood v. Am. Coalition of Life Activists, 422 F.3d 949, 958–59 (9th Cir. 2005) (physicians were financially vulnerable since their livelihoods were threatened by anti-abortion activists' threats); Jurinko v. Med. Protective Co., 2006 WL 785234 (E.D. Pa. Mar. 29, 2006) (physician was vulnerable where insurer's refusal to tender policy limits exposed him to liability that would have cost him his life savings; Krysa v. Payne, 176 S.W.3d 150, 160 (Mo. Ct. App. 2005) (vehicle buyers were financially vulnerable where vehicle's price was at upper limit of what they could afford and its dangerous condition meant they had to risk driving it with its safety problems, borrow vehicles from others, or alter their schedules to drive each other around in their other car); Goddard v. Farmers Ins. Co., 120 P.3d 1260, 1282 (Or. Ct. App. 2005) (taking plaintiff's financial vulnerability into account), *modified on other grounds, adhered to*, 126 P.3d 682 (Or. Ct. App. 2006); Boyd v. Goffoli, 608 S.E.2d 169 (W. Va. 2004) (fact that defendants fraudulently induced plaintiffs to quit their jobs made them financially vulnerable); *cf.* Clark v. Chrysler Corp., 436 F.3d 594, 604 (6th Cir. 2006) (plaintiff's financial vulnerability is relevant if case involves economic damage, not physi-

phistication, and ability to understand business transactions are also relevant to this factor.[415.36] Any evidence that the defendant selected the plaintiff as a target for the fraud scheme because of such characteristics is also relevant to liability for punitive damages.[415.37] Presenting strong evidence on these issues may help support a punitive damages award. Almost any individual consumer is vulnerable to some extent because of the difficulty and expense of mounting a suit to redress a fraudulent sale.[415.38] Even a business may be considered financially vulnerable, for example, if it is a small family-owned business that lacks financial reserves.[415.39]

7.10.6.3.8 *Presenting evidence of other penalties for the specific conduct at issue*

The severe criminal and administrative penalties for dealer misconduct that exist in many states will also support a substantial punitive damages award in automobile fraud cases. The fact that some types of misconduct by the dealership can result in the "corporate death penalty"—revocation of the company's charter—shows the high degree of reprehensibility of the dealer's conduct.[415.40] Though the *State Farm* opinion dismissed the Utah Supreme Court's use of such factors to justify the large verdict, its opposition arose from the state court's references to the out-of-state conduct evidence that should not have been considered. So long as counsel can show that the misconduct toward the plaintiff alone would justify severe criminal and administrative penalties, the third guidepost will be satisfied.

In determining whether a punitive damages award is excessive under the third guidepost, it is appropriate to compare it to the amount of money that the defendant would lose if its license to do business were revoked.[415.41] In a decision issued after *State Farm*, the Seventh Circuit reiterated that possible license revocation may be considered.[415.42] The plaintiff should take care to establish that this penalty is authorized for the specific acts the defendant committed toward the plaintiff. The Federal Trade Commission Act may also be a useful comparison, as it authorizes fines of up to $10,000 per day for failing to comply with a rule relating to unfair and deceptive practices.[415.43] Because misrepresentation of the mechanical condition of a used vehicle and making oral or written statements that contradict the window sticker are violations of the FTC Used Car Rule,[415.44] it will often be possible to show a violation of this rule. Many state deceptive practices (UDAP) statutes also include substantial civil penalties.[415.45]

In *Parrott*, the Oregon Supreme Court held that the penalties for UDAP violations, including loss of a business license and civil penalties up to $25,000 per violation, provided sufficient notice to the dealership that its acts could have serious economic consequences.[415.46] Likewise, in *Grabinski*, the Eighth Circuit agreed that Missouri's sanctions for comparable conduct—civil penalties of up to

---

cal injury; defendant's wealth is irrelevant to plaintiff's vulnerability).

415.36 *See, e.g.,* Kemp v. Am. Tel. & Tel. Co., 393 F.3d 1354 (11th Cir. 2004) (defendant's misrepresentations were designed to exploit unsophisticated and economically vulnerable customers).

415.37 *Cf.* Bach v. First Union Nat'l Bank, 149 Fed. Appx. 354, 365 (6th Cir. Aug. 22, 2005) (unpublished, citation limited) (need only show that victim was vulnerable, not that defendant targeted her because of vulnerability).

415.38 Werremeyer v. K.C. Auto Salvage Co., 2003 WL 21487311 (Mo. Ct. App. June 30, 2003), *aff'd in relevant part, rev'd in part on other grounds,* 134 S.W.3d 633 (Mo. 2004) (reversing denial of prejudgment interest but affirming award in all other respects).

415.39 Willow Inn, Inc. v. Pub. Serv. Mut. Ins. Co., 399 F.3d 224, 232 (3d Cir. 2005); *see also* Bains L.L.C. v. Arco Products Co., 405 F.3d 764 (9th Cir. 2005) (characterizing corporation as "highly vulnerable financially"); Grefer v. Alpha Technical, 901 So. 2d 1117, 1149 (La. Ct. App. 2005); *see also* Lowe Excavating Co. v. Int'l Union of Operating Engineers, 832 N.E.2d 495, 503–04 (Ill. App. Ct. 2005), *appeal allowed,* 844 N.E.2d 38 (Ill. 2005).

415.40 Grabinski v. Blue Springs Ford Sales, 1998 U.S. Dist. LEXIS 17015 (W.D. Mo. Oct. 27, 1998), *aff'd in relevant part, rev'd in part on other grounds,* 203 F.3d 1024 (8th Cir. 2000); Krysa v. Payne, 176 S.W.3d 150 (Mo. Ct. App. 2005); *see also* Hollock v. Erie Ins. Exch., 842 A.2d 409 (Pa. Super. Ct. 2004) (upholding punitive damages award in light of potential fines and revocation of business license), *appeal granted in part,* 2005 WL 3692710 (Pa. June 28, 2005).

415.41 United Technologies Corp. v. Am. Home Assurance Co., 118 F. Supp. 2d 174 (D. Conn. 2000); *see also* Parrott v. Carr Chevrolet, Inc., 331 Or. 537, 17 P.3d 473, 489 (2001) (citing potential license revocation as factor in reinstating full one million dollar punitive damages award).

415.42 Mathias v. Accor Econ. Lodging, Inc., 347 F.3d 672, 678 (7th Cir. 2003); *see also* Willow Inn, Inc. v. Pub. Serv. Mut. Ins. Co., 399 F.3d 224, 237, 238 (3d Cir. 2005) (citing potential loss of business license in upholding punitive damages award).

415.43 15 U.S.C. § 45(m)(1)(A), (C); *see* Bristol Tech., Inc. v. Microsoft Corp., 114 F. Supp. 2d 59 (D. Conn. 2000) (citing possibility of FTC fines in support of $1 million punitive damages award), *vacated,* 250 F.3d 152 (2d Cir. 2001) (vacating judgment pursuant to settlement agreement; expressing doubt about whether district court had jurisdiction to consider punitive damages issues); Union Pac. R.R. Co. v. Barber, 149 S.W.3d 325 (Ark. 2004) (comparing punitive damages award to fines imposed for each day of non-compliance; *see also* Stogsdill v. Healthmark Partners, L.L.C., 377 F.3d 827 (8th Cir. 2004) ($10,000 civil penalty per violation of adult neglect law relevant to punitive damage award against nursing home, but insufficient to justify $5 million award, which court reduces to $2 million).

415.44 16 C.F.R. §§ 455.1(a)(1), 455.4.

415.45 *See* § 8.4, *infra*; National Consumer Law Center, Unfair and Deceptive Acts and Practices (6th ed. 2004 and Supp.); *see also* Boeken v. Philip Morris Inc., 127 Cal. App. 4th 1640, 26 Cal. Rptr. 3d 638 (2005) (taking cumulative UDAP penalties for repetitive conduct into account). Note that in Cooper Indus., Inc. v. Leatherman Tool Group, 532 U.S. 424, 121 S. Ct. 1678, 149 L. Ed. 2d 674 (2001), the Court expressed some doubt about whether a UDAP violation should be treated as a single violation or as multiple violations for purposes of the *Gore* analysis, but it did not dispute that UDAP civil penalties are an appropriate analogy.

415.46 Parrott v. Carr Chevrolet, Inc., 331 Or. 537, 17 P.3d 473 (2001).

$1000 per violation, felony criminal penalties, and loss of the license to do business—were "legislative judgments [that] weigh heavily in favor of an award of punitive damages."[415.47] Many other statutes allow civil penalties to be imposed per violation, creating a large potential liability.[415.48] The focus of the comparison should be the outer limits of the prospective sanctions, because the purpose of the analysis is to determine whether the defendant was on notice of its potential liability.[415.49]

Even if a civil penalty is not large, it may be the same as the fine imposed for serious felonies, showing that the jurisdiction considers the miscondut to be extremely serious.[415.50]

A number of states and a few federal statutes cap punitive damages at a certain amount. The existence of such a law can demonstrate that the defendant had fair notice that the penalties could be as high as the cap.[415.51] Even the exclusion of the defendant's tort from the provisions of the state cap is probative, because it places the defendant on notice that society considers the conduct in question worthy of punishment greater than the cap.[415.52] Punitive damage awards in similar cases also place the defendant on notice of the potential penalties.[415.53]

In presenting evidence of the other penalties applicable to the defendant's conduct, the plaintiff should be careful not to focus too heavily on criminal penalties. In *State Farm* the Supreme Court held that criminal penalties have less utility than civil and administrative remedies in determining the amount of a punitive damages award.[415.54] Nonetheless,

criminal penalties give the defendants notice of the potential magnitude of the punishment—the outer limit—that might be imposed for certain conduct,[415.55] and courts have continued to find them a useful part of their analysis since *State Farm*.[415.56]

A punitive damages award can be upheld even though comparable civil and criminal penalties are substantially lower. In *State Farm*, for example, the most relevant civil sanction was a $10,000 fine, yet the Supreme Court approved punitive damages of $1 million.[415.57] Courts have also upheld punitive damages awards without evidence of comparable civil or criminal penalties, holding that this evidence is not essential to the analysis.[415.58]

415.47 Grabinski v. Blue Springs Ford Sales, 203 F.3d 1024, 1025, 1026 (8th Cir. 2000).

415.48 *See, e.g.,* Jurinko v. Med. Protective Co., 2006 WL 785234 (E.D. Pa. Mar. 29, 2006) (insurance laws); Goddard v. Farmers Ins. Co., 120 P.3d 1260, 1283 (Or. Ct. App. 2005) (state insurance laws), *modified on other grounds, adhered to,* 126 P.3d 682 (Or. Ct. App. 2006).

415.49 *In re* Exxon Valdez, 296 F. Supp. 2d 1071, 1107 (D. Alaska 2004).

415.50 Campbell v. State Farm Mut. Auto. Ins. Co., 98 P.3d 409, 419 (Utah 2004).

415.51 *See* Jones v. Rent-A-Center, 281 F. Supp. 2d 1277 (D. Kan. 2003) (existence of $300,000 Title VII damages cap for employers supports award of $10,000 actual and $290,000 punitive damages).

415.52 Craig v. Holsey, 590 S.E.2d 742 (Ga. Ct. App. 2003).

415.53 Romanski v. Detroit Entertainment, L.L.C., 428 F.3d 629, 646–49 (6th Cir. 2005); Casumpang v. Int'l Longshore & Warehouse Union, 411 F. Supp. 2d 1201, 1221 (D. Hawaii 2005); Gibson v. Total Car Franchising Corp., 223 F.R.D. 265, 275 (M.D.N.C. 2004); Sherman v. Kasotakis, 314 F. Supp. 2d 843 (N.D. Iowa 2004); *see also* Goddard v. Farmers Ins. Co., 120 P.3d 1260, 1282–83 (Or. Ct. App. 2005) (comparing punitive damage award to those in similar cases as part of ratio analysis), *modified on other grounds, adhered to,* 126 P.3d 682 (Or. Ct. App. 2006). *But cf.* Clark v. Chrysler Corp., 436 F.3d 594, 607 (6th Cir. 2006) (suggesting that this guidepost should focus on civil penalties rather than other punitive damage awards).

415.54 *State Farm*, 538 U.S. 408, 428; *see* § 7.10.6.2.4, *supra.*

415.55 *In re* Exxon Valdez, 296 F. Supp. 2d 1071, 1107 (D. Alaska 2004).

415.56 *Id.*; Rhone-Poulenc Agro, S.A. v. DeKalb Genetics Corp., 345 F.3d 1366, 1372 (Fed. Cir. 2003); Williams v. Philip Morris Inc., 127 P.3d 1165, 1179–80 (Or. 2006); Strenke v. Hogner, 704 N.W.2d 309, 317 (Wis. Ct. App. 2005) (appropriate to consider criminal penalties drunk driver would have faced if he had caused more serious injury). *But see* Romo v. Ford Motor Co., 113 Cal. App. 4th 738, 6 Cal. Rptr. 3d 793, 804 (2003) (construing *State Farm* as fundamentally changing role of criminal penalties in the analysis), *disapproved by* Johnson v. Ford Motor Co., 35 Cal. 4th 1191, 29 Cal. Rptr. 3d 401 (2005) (disapproving other aspects of *Romo* court's analysis of constitutional criteria).

415.57 *State Farm*, 538 U.S. at 428; *see also* Action Marine, Inc. v. Cont'l Carbon, Inc., 2006 WL 173653 (M.D. Ala. Jan. 23, 2006) (this guidepost is afforded less weight than others; maximum civil penalty of $250,000 gives defendant adequate notice of potential $17.5 million punitive damage award).

415.58 Willow Inn, Inc. v. Pub. Serv. Mut. Ins. Co., 399 F.3d 224 (3d Cir. 2005) (affirming punitive damages award despite disparity to other penalties; third guidepost not very helpful); Sherman v. Kasotakis, 314 F. Supp. 2d 843 (N.D. Iowa 2004); Shiv-Ram, Inc. v. McCaleb, 892 So. 2d 299 (Ala. 2003); Craig v. Holsey, 590 S.E.2d 742 (Ga. Ct. App. 2003) (modest penalties not conclusive when other laws put defendant on notice of potential size of punitive damages award); Phelps v. Louisville Water Co., 103 S.W.3d 46 (Ky. 2003) (absence of significant criminal penalties not conclusive when defendant had other reasons to be aware of potential consequences of its conduct); Mission Res., Inc. v. Garza Energy Trust, 166 S.W.3d 301 (Tex. App. 2005) (upholding punitive damages even though they were ten times greater than criminal fine for similar conduct; court characterizes this guidepost as the least helpful); Boyd v. Goffoli, 608 S.E.2d 169 (W. Va. 2004); Schwigel v. Kohlmann, 694 N.W.2d 467 (Wis. Ct. App. 2005); *see also* Mathias v. Accor Econ. Lodging, Inc., 347 F.3d 672 (7th Cir. 2003) (taking judicial notice of sanctions that could be imposed for defendant's conduct; parties' failure to submit evidence on this issue is not fatal to punitive damages award); Boeken v. Philip Morris Inc., 127 Cal. App. 4th 1640, 26 Cal. Rptr. 3d 638 (2005) (when there are no comparable civil penalties, this guidepost is neutral). *But cf.* Clark v. Chrysler Corp., 436 F.3d 594, 608 (6th Cir. 2006) (significantly lower potential civil penalties may indicate that punitive damage award is excessive).

7.10.6.3.9 *Finding and presenting evidence of repetition*

The fourth factor under the reprehensibility guidepost is whether the conduct involved repeated actions or was only an isolated incident. Auto fraud cases, particularly those involving odometer fraud, often involve conduct that the defendant engages in as a matter of business practice, and when caught it should be punished accordingly. Such evidence helped support large punitive damages awards in *Krysa*,[415.59] *Grabinski*,[415.60] and *Parrott*.[415.61] Courts applying *State Farm* have considered both similar acts toward others[415.62] and repeated instances of misconduct toward the plaintiff during the dispute at issue.[415.63] Courts have also treated misconduct in the litigation itself, such as attempts to falsify evidence, as evidence of repetition or reprehensibility.[415.64]

Counsel should maximize discovery of similar conduct, regardless of where it occurred, and connect it carefully to the wrongs committed in the client's case. A major lesson of *State Farm* is that a defendant may not be punished for conduct committed in other jurisdictions that was lawful there, or for conduct unrelated to the acts that hurt the plaintiff.[415.65] Evidence of other acts need not be identical, but it must be closely related.[415.66] Nor, as a general rule, does a state have a legitimate basis to impose punishment for unlawful out-of-state conduct.[415.67] Nonetheless, out-of-state conduct, whether lawful or unlawful, *is* admissible to show the defendant's deliberateness or culpability in committing the in-state tort.[415.68] This evidence must have a "nexus" to the immediate claim, and the jury must be instructed that it may not use the evidence to punish the defendant for out-of-state acts that were lawful where they occurred.[415.69] It may also help protect a punitive damages award if the court instructs the jury that it can only consider this evidence to determine the defendant's deliberateness or culpability in committing the in-state acts.

Evidence of repetition is particularly potent if the defendant has been punished in the past for similar acts. If a goal

---

415.59 Krysa v. Payne, 176 S.W.3d 150, 155 (Mo. Ct. App. 2005).

415.60 203 F.3d at 1026.

415.61 17 P.3d at 487 (citing "evidence from which the jury could have concluded that defendant's treatment of plaintiff was not an isolated incident in that it had established business procedures that it could employ to cover any failure to disclose").

415.62 Diesel Machinery, Inc. v. B.R. Lee Indus., Inc., 418 F.3d 820 (8th Cir. 2005); Lincoln v. Case, 340 F.3d 283, 293 (5th Cir. 2003) (defendant discriminated against testers as well as against plaintiff); Union Pac. R.R. Co. v. Barber, 149 S.W.3d 325 (Ark. 2004) (railroad ignored dangerous crossing despite near misses involving others); Rose Care, Inc. v. Ross, 2005 WL 1283679 (Ark. Ct. App. June 1, 2005); Johnson v. Ford Motor Co., 135 Cal. App. 4th 137, 37 Cal. Rptr. 3d 283, 292 (2005) (design and implementation by large national corporation of company-wide program that permitted and encouraged efforts to circumvent lemon law demonstrates high degree of reprehensibility); Trinity Evangelical Lutheran Church v. Tower Ins. Co., 661 N.W.2d 789 (Wis. 2003) (similar case thirty years earlier); *see also* Planned Parenthood v. Am. Coalition of Life Activists, 422 F.3d 949, 959 (9th Cir. 2005) (prior threats and violence against others may be considered where threats made against these plaintiffs more intimidating).

415.63 Gallatin Fuels, Inc. v. Westchester Fire Ins. Co., 2006 WL 840341 (W.D. Pa. Mar. 28, 2006) (evidence of repeated acts toward the plaintiff is relevant but carries less force than similar acts toward third parties); Jurinko v. Med. Protective Co., 2006 WL 785234 (E.D. Pa. Mar. 29, 2006); Superior Fed. Bank v. Jones & Mackey Constr. Co., 2005 WL 3307074 (Ark. Ct. App. Dec. 7, 2005); Lowe Excavating Co. v. Int'l Union of Operating Engineers, 832 N.E.2d 495, 504 (Ill. App. Ct. 2005), *appeal allowed*, 844 N.E.2d 38 (Ill. 2005); Trinity Evangelical Lutheran Church v. Tower Ins. Co., 661 N.W.2d 789 (Wis. 2003). *But see* Willow Inn, Inc. v. Pub. Serv. Mut. Ins. Co., 399 F.3d 224 (3d Cir. 2005) (repeated conduct toward this plaintiff does not satisfy recidivism factor, but does show defendant's improper motive).

415.64 Union Pac. R.R. Co. v. Barber, 149 S.W.3d 325, 348 (Ark. 2004) (destruction of evidence).

415.65 *State Farm*, 538 U.S. 408, 418–424; Clark v. Chrysler Corp., 436 F.3d 594, 609–10 (6th Cir. 2006) (urging jury to send defendant a message was not a request to punish defendant for extraterritorial conduct).

415.66 Clark v. Chrysler Corp., 436 F.3d 594, 610 (6th Cir. 2006) (evidence of substantially similar accident was properly admitted); Williams v. Conagra Poultry Co., 378 F.3d 790, 797 (8th Cir. 2004) (some racist incidents at place of employment sufficiently similar to those against plaintiff, others not); Webb v. CSX Transportation, Inc., 615 S.E.2d 440 (S.C. 2005) (improper to admit evidence of acts in other jurisdictions and acts not related to railroad crossing safety); Atkinson v. Orkin Exterminating Co., 604 S.E.2d 385 (S.C. 2004) (extermination company's attempts fifteen years earlier to increase rates on long-term contracts not similar enough to its refusal to allow contract to be transferred from original home owner to this plaintiff).

415.67 The court's reasoning is that proper adjudication of such acts would require the court to include other parties and apply the laws of other jurisdictions. *State Farm*, 538 U.S. at 421, 422. This reasoning suggests that a jury may punish a defendant for out-of-state torts for which the defendant has already been judged liable.

415.68 *State Farm*, 538 U.S. 408, 422; *accord* BMW of N. Am., Inc. v. Gore, 517 U.S. 559, 574 n.21, 116 S. Ct. 1589, 134 L. Ed. 2d 809 (1996) ("Of course, [the Alabama Supreme Court's decision] does not mean that evidence of out-of-state transactions is irrelevant in a case of this kind. To the contrary, . . . such evidence may be relevant to the determination of the degree of reprehensibility of the defendant's conduct."); *see* Eden Elec., Ltd. v. Amana Co., 370 F.3d 824 (8th Cir. 2004) (jury may consider out-of-state conduct that was part of fraudulent scheme), *aff'd*, 370 F.3d 824 (8th Cir. 2004); Boeken v. Philip Morris Inc., 127 Cal. App. 4th 1640, 26 Cal. Rptr. 3d 638 (2005); *see also* Markham v. Nat'l States Ins. Co., 2004 WL 3019309 (W.D. Okla. Dec. 27, 2004) (relevant to reprehensibility); Henley v. Philip Morris, Inc., 114 Cal. App. 4th 1429, 9 Cal. Rptr. 3d 29, 71, 72 (2004); Bocci v. Key Pharm., Inc., 76 P.3d 669, 674 (Or. Ct. App.), *as amended by* 79 P.3d 908 (Or. Ct. App. 2003). *But see* FMC Corp. v. Helton, 2005 WL 256475 (Ark. Feb. 3, 2005) (excluding evidence of out-of-state conduct without considering its relevance to prove intent and absence of mistake or the possible use of a limiting instruction).

415.69 *State Farm*, 538 U.S. at 422.

of punitive damages is deterrence,[415.70] and if prior punitive measures have not accomplished this goal, then it should be clear that a more substantial award—in other words, a higher ratio—is necessary. For example, a $500,000 punitive damage award, bearing a 27-to-1 ratio to compensatory damages, was justified against an auto dealer who sold a rebuilt wreck to the plaintiffs despite having lost two previous suits for similar actions, one of which had resulted in a $170,000 verdict. The defendant had also, in his testimony, expressed an unwillingness to alter his business practices. The court held that "it was reasonable for the jury to conclude that a significantly larger award would be necessary to deter [the dealer] from similar behavior in the future."[415.71]

7.10.6.3.10 Stressing reprehensibility

The defendant's reprehensibility is the most important factor in determining whether a punitive damage award meets constitutional standards.[415.72] While the Supreme Court identified five guideposts to evaluate reprehensibility, not all need be shown to uphold a punitive damages award.[415.73] A strong showing of egregious conduct militates powerfully in favor of upholding a punitive damage award.[415.74]

7.10.6.3.11 Presenting evidence of defendant's wealth when appropriate

In the section of its opinion discussing the ratio of punitive damages to compensatory damages, the *State Farm* Court stated:

> The remaining premises for the Utah Supreme Court's decision bear no relation to the award's reasonableness or proportionality to the harm. . . . Here the argument that State Farm will be punished in only the rare case, coupled with reference to its assets . . . had little to do with the actual harm sustained by the Campbells. The wealth of a defendant can not justify an otherwise unconstitutional punitive damages award. *Gore*, 517 U.S., at 585, 116 S. Ct. 1589 ("The fact that BMW is a large corporation rather than an impecunious individual does not diminish its entitlement to fair notice of the demands that the several States impose on the conduct of its business."); see also

id., at 591, 116 S. Ct. 1589 (Breyer, J., concurring) ("[Wealth] provides an open-ended basis for inflating awards when the defendant is wealthy. . . . That does not make its use unlawful or inappropriate; it simply means that this factor cannot make up for the failure of other factors, such as 'reprehensibility,' to constrain significantly an award that purports to punish a defendant's conduct.").[415.75]

The implications of this passage are not entirely clear.[415.76] The Court's quotation of Justice Breyer's concurrence in *Gore* indicates that it agrees that the use of the defendant's wealth is not per se unlawful or inappropriate. The Court is also clear that the defendant's wealth can not justify an otherwise unconstitutional award, in other words, it is not a sufficient basis in and of itself to uphold a punitive damage award.[415.77] The opinion does not, however, give any indication as to what role the defendant's wealth may play in determining punitive damages.[415.78] One possible interpretation is that the defendant's wealth is relevant to determine where within a range of constitutionally permissible ratios a punitive damages award should fall. Another possible interpretation is that the defendant's wealth is relevant to determining the appropriate ratio only if the plaintiff introduces evidence that a smaller award would not have a deterrent effect. Yet another view is that the defendant's wealth may be admissible on state law grounds, but that whatever award the jury makes must meet the *State Farm* standards without consideration of the defendant's wealth.

Since *State Farm* was decided, a number of courts have continued to consider the defendant's wealth as a factor in figuring punitive damages awards.[415.79] In addition, the

---

415.70 *Id.* at 416; Simon v. San Paolo U.S. Holding Co., 35 Cal. 4th 1159, 29 Cal. Rptr. 3d 379, 397–98, 113 P.3d 63 (2005).

415.71 Krysa v. Payne, 176 S.W.3d 150, 161 (Mo. Ct. App. 2005).

415.72 State Farm Mut. Auto. Ins. Co. v. Campbell, 538 U.S. 408, 419, 123 S. Ct. 1513, 155 L. Ed. 2d 585 (2003).

415.73 Diesel Machinery, Inc. v. B.R. Lee Indus., Inc., 418 F.3d 820, 839 (8th Cir. 2005).

415.74 Goddard v. Farmers Ins. Co., 120 P.3d 1260, 1282 (Or. Ct. App. 2005).

415.75 *Id.* at 427, 428.

415.76 *See* McClain v. Metabolife Int'l, Inc., 259 F. Supp. 2d 1225, 1229 (N.D. Ala. 2003) ("[t]his court is not helped by" *State Farm's* discussion of the role of defendant's wealth; court finds it unnecessary to address the question); Henley v. Philip Morris, 114 Cal. App. 4th 1429, 9 Cal. Rptr. 3d 29, 74 (2004) (characterizing the constitutional soundness of the use of defendant's wealth as "uncertain" after *State Farm*, but finding it unnecessary to decide the question).

415.77 *See* Bains L.L.C. v. Arco Products Co., 405 F.3d 764 (9th Cir. 2005) (juries have traditionally been permitted to consider defendant's assets in determining an award that will carry "the right degree of sting," but defendant's wealth can not make up for absence of other factors); Mathias v. Accor Econ. Lodging, Inc., 347 F.3d 672, 677 (7th Cir. 2003) (citing *State Farm* for proposition that defendant's wealth is not sufficient basis for awarding punitive damages).

415.78 *See* Williams v. Philip Morris Inc., 127 P.3d 1165, 1181 (Or. 2006) (jury may levy higher punitive damage award against wealthy defendant as long as final award does not exceed limits established by *Gore* guideposts).

415.79 Romanski v. Detroit Entertainment, L.L.C., 428 F.3d 629, 647–50 (6th Cir. 2005) (must take defendant's wealth into account to make sure that punitive damage award achieves deterrence, but must also ensure that award is not significantly higher than necessary); Motorola Credit Corp. v. Uzan, 388 F.3d

Seventh Circuit has held that a defendant's wealth is relevant to the *State Farm* analysis because wealth may enable a defendant to mount an aggressive defense that makes it uneconomical for small claimants to win suits unless substantial punitive damages are awarded.[415.80] The Seventh Circuit also held that one of the purposes of punitive damages is to limit the defendant's ability to profit from its wrongdoing,[415.81] which would justify consideration of the income the defendant realized from the activities involved in the case. Some courts have also considered the defendant's wealth as an additional factor after making the *Gore/State Farm* analysis, that is, after determining that the punitive damages award met the three guideposts. This further analysis evaluates whether the size of the award would accomplish the goal of deterrence in light of the defendant's wealth but without destroying the defendant financially.[415.82]

7.10.6.3.12 Framing jury instructions

Carefully drafted jury instructions may help avoid *State Farm* issues.[415.83] Referring in the jury instructions to the guideposts and to the purposes of punitive damages as set forth in to *State Farm* may give the trial court and reviewing courts greater confidence that the jury's award reflects a measured weighing of the appropriate factors. If evidence of out-of-state conduct is admitted,[415.84] *State Farm* requires that the jury be instructed that it may not use this evidence to punish a defendant for action that was lawful in the jurisdiction where it occurred.[415.85] It may also be helpful to instruct the jury that, as *State Farm* holds,[415.86] this evidence *can* be used to determine the deliberateness or culpability of the defendant in committing the in-state acts.

In *State Farm* the Supreme Court expressed concern that the punitive damages award duplicated the emotional distress portion of the plaintiffs' compensatory damages. An instruction to the jury that it should give full compensation for emotional distress in the compensatory damages award, and that the purpose of any punitive damages award is different, may help avoid this problem. In an appropriate case the consumer's attorney might also want to ask the jury to itemize emotional distress damages and other damages, so that the court does not wrongly assume that a large

---

39 (2d Cir. 2004) (defendant's inability to pay should have been considered under Illinois law); Eden Elec., Ltd. v. Amana Co., Ltd. P'ship, 370 F.3d 824 (8th Cir. 2004) (defendant's wealth must be considered if deterrence is to be achieved); Bach v. First Union Nat'l Bank, 2006 WL 840381 (S.D. Ohio Mar. 30, 2006) (defendant's wealth is relevant to amount necessary for deterrence); Dewick v. Maytag Corp., 324 F. Supp. 2d 889 (N.D. Ill. 2004) (evidence of net worth is admissible on state law grounds); Shiv-Ram, Inc. v. McCaleb, 892 So. 2d 299 (Ala. 2003); Union Pac. R.R. Co. v. Barber, 149 S.W.3d 325 (Ark. 2004); Simon v. San Paolo U.S. Holding Co., 35 Cal. 4th 1159, 29 Cal. Rptr. 3d 379, 397–98, 113 P.3d 63 (2005) (defendant's wealth is relevant to determine the level of punishment necessary to achieve deterrence); Boeken v. Philip Morris Inc., 127 Cal. App. 4th 1640, 26 Cal. Rptr. 3d 638 (2005); Smith v. Fairfax Realty, 82 P.3d 1064, 1072 (Utah 2003) (considering defendant's wealth because punitive damages should be tailored to what is necessary to deter the particular defendant from repeating the prohibited conduct); Trinity Evangelical Lutheran Church v. Tower Ins. Co., 661 N.W.2d 789, 804 (Wis. 2003); Gibson v. Overnite Transp. Co., 671 N.W.2d 388, 395 (Wis. Ct. App. 2003) (wealth is an appropriate factor); *see also* Kemp v. Am. Tel. & Tel. Co., 393 F.3d 1354 (11th Cir. 2004) (small award would not serve goals of punishment and deterrence when defendant is large multinational corporation); Roth v. Farner-Bocken Co., 667 N.W.2d 651, 670 (S.D. 2003) (defendant's financial resources are relevant, but need not be considered when the reprehensibility and harm guideposts require the award to be reduced). *But cf.* Clark v. Chrysler Corp., 436 F.3d 594, 604 (6th Cir. 2006) (to serve as justification for punitive damages, defendant's wealth must bear some relation to the harm sustained by plaintiff); Textron Fin. Corp. v. Nat'l Union Fire Ins. Co., 118 Cal. App. 4th 1061, 13 Cal. Rptr. 3d 586 (2004) (rejecting argument that punitive damages award of $360,000 would be laughable in light of defendant's wealth).

415.80 Mathias v. Accor Econ. Lodging, Inc., 347 F.3d 672, 677 (7th Cir. 2003); *accord* Hollock v. Erie Ins. Exch., 842 A.2d 409 (Pa. Super. Ct. 2004), *appeal granted in part*, 2005 WL 3692710 (Pa. June 28, 2005).

415.81 Mathias v. Accor Econ. Lodging, Inc., 347 F.3d 672, 677 (7th Cir. 2003).

415.82 *In re* Exxon Valdez, 296 F. Supp. 2d 1071, 1105, 1106 (D. Alaska 2004); *see also* Jones v. Sheahan, 2003 WL 22508171 (N.D. Ill. Nov. 4, 2003) (defendants can not avoid punitive

---

damages award on grounds of poverty when they did not submit evidence of their finances).

415.83 Jury instructions that have been scrutinized under the *State Farm* guideposts are recited in *In re* Exxon Valdez, 296 F. Supp. 2d 1071, 1080–1083 (D. Alaska 2004). *See also* Synergetics, Inc. v. Hurst, 2005 WL 3358298 (E.D. Mo. Dec. 9, 2005) (reciting and upholding jury instructions); Romo v. Ford Motor Co., 113 Cal. App. 4th 738, 6 Cal. Rptr. 3d 793, 804, 805 (2003) (quoting selections from jury instructions that court finds did not comport with *State Farm*); *cf.* Pac. Mut. Life Ins. Co. v. Haslip, 499 U.S. 1, 19, 111 S. Ct. 1032, 113 L. Ed. 2d 1 (1991) (decision includes language that the Supreme Court found acceptable for jury instructions on punitive damages, but *Haslip* predates the court's elaboration of the constitutional principles in *Gore* and *State Farm*).

415.84 *See* §§ 7.10.6.2.2, 7.10.6.3.8, *supra*.

415.85 *State Farm*, 538 U.S. 408, 422; *see* Clark v. Chrysler Corp., 436 F.3d 594, 611–12 (6th Cir. 2006) (limiting instruction unnecessary where plaintiff did not introduce evidence of out-of-state conduct); Diesel Machinery, Inc. v. B.R. Lee Indus., Inc., 418 F.3d 820, 838–39 (8th Cir. 2005) (punitive damages instruction should have limited jury's consideration of out-of-state conduct, but defendants did not object to it and it was not plain error); Sand Hill Energy, Inc. v. Smith, 142 S.W.3d 153 (Ky. 2004) (reversing and remanding punitive damages award because of failure to give instruction concerning out-of-state conduct; setting forth instructions for trial court to use on remand); Sandoz Pharmaceuticals Corp. v. Gunderson, 2005 WL 2694816 (Ky. Ct. App. Feb. 3, 2006) (vacating punitive damage award because trial court failed to give limiting instruction regarding evidence of out-of-state conduct).

415.86 *State Farm*, 538 U.S. at 422.

percentage of the compensatory damages award represents emotional distress.[415.87]

The jury instructions should make sure that the jury identifies all damage the plaintiff suffered on each count for which punitive damages are sought. If those damages duplicate damages awarded on other counts, the jury should still identify them so that the court knows what compensatory damages figure to compare to the punitive damages award.

415.87 *But cf.* McClain v. Metabolife Int'l, Inc., 259 F. Supp. 2d 1225, 1230 (N.D. Ala. 2003) (presuming that compensatory damages did not include emotional distress when jury interrogatories allowed it to lump physical pain and suffering with mental anguish).

Page 195

7.10.7 Liability of Principals for Punitive Damages Due to the Conduct of Their Agents

Addition to note 416.

416 *See* Werdann v. Mel Hambelton Ford, Inc., 79 P.3d 1081 (Kan. Ct. App. 2003) (selling wrongfully repossessed vehicle, keeping the proceeds, and failing to discipline employee established ratification); *see also* Greenpoint Credit Corp. v. Perez, 75 S.W.3d 40 (Tex. App. 2002) (identifying factors, but finding plaintiff's proof insufficient), *vacated pursuant to settlement agreement*, 2003 Tex. LEXIS 50 (Tex. Apr. 24, 2003).

Page 196

7.10.8 Examples of Punitive Damages Awards Against Car Dealers

Add to text after bulleted Bishop v. Mid-America entry:

• *Krysa v. Payne*, 176 S.W.3d 150 (Mo. Ct. App. 2005): intermediate appellate court upholds $18,449.53 in compensatory damages and $500,000 in punitive damages against owners of used car dealership who misrepresented number of vehicle's prior owners and concealed fact that vehicle was actually two halves welded together.

Add to text after Douglas v. Ostermeier bulleted entry:

• *Johnson v. Ford Motor Co.*, 135 Cal. App. 4th 137, 37 Cal. Rptr. 3d 283 (2005): $17,811.60 actual damages and $175,000 punitive damages (reduced from $10 million on constitutional grounds) against manufacturer that had practice of laundering lemons.

Add to text after bulleted Chrysler Corp. v. Schiffer entry:

• *Werremeyer v. K.C. Auto Salvage Co.*, 134 S.W.3d 633 (2004): $9000 in compensatory damages and $125,000 in punitive damages (after a $75,000 *remittur*) against auctioneer, and $20,000 punitive damages against dealer, when auctioneer misrepresented title as clean when car was actually reassembled from two cars, one wrecked and the other stolen, and dealer fabricated explanations for scratched-out vehicle identification numbers.

• *Coral Cadillac, Inc. v. Stephens*, 867 So. 2d 556 (Fla. Dist. Ct. App. 2004): affirming award of $12,500 actual damages and $133,050 punitive damages for misrepresentation of car's repair and collision history; court certifies to state supreme court a question regarding interpretation of the former version of the state's cap on punitive damages.

• *Turner v. Bob Ross Buick*, 1993 WL 485256 (Ohio Ct. App. Nov. 22, 1993): $4,500 compensatory damages and $120,000 punitive damages for concealment of collision damage.

• *Wilkins v. Peninsula Motor Cars, Inc.*, 587 S.E.2d 581 (Va. 2003): actual damages of $1,862.86 and punitive damages of $100,000 on fraud count, plus $34,183 in attorney fees on UDAP count when dealer represented previously-titled car as new despite 972 miles on odometer.

7.11 The Rescission Remedy

7.11.1 Advantages and Disadvantages

Addition to notes 418–421, 424.

418 *Add to beginning of note: See also* Bill Dreiling Motor Co. v. Shultz, 168 Colo. 59, 450 P.2d 70 (1969) (affirming rescission of car sale when seller misrepresented its mechanical condition); Brown v. Garrett,

261 Ga. App. 823, 584 S.E.2d 48 (2003); Bickerstaff Automotive, Inc. v. Tsepas, 574 S.E.2d 322 (Ga. Ct. App. 2002).

Page 197

419   *See* Brown v. Garrett, 261 Ga. App. 823, 584 S.E.2d 48 (2003) (error to allow jury to return verdict for less than purchase price if buyer rescinded).

420   *See also* Marrale v. Gwinnett Place Ford, 609 S.E.2d 659, 663 (Ga. Ct. App. 2005) (holding that buyer's failure to act to restore the car to the seller upon discovering the alleged fraud, as required by Ga. Code Ann. § 13-4-60, barred his rescission claim).

421   *See also* Majcher v. Laurel Motors, Inc., 680 N.E.2d 416, 423 (Ill. App. Ct. 1997) (holding that trial court did not err in refusing to award dealer set-off when plaintiff had testified that car ran terribly, was unsafe, and needed frequent repairs); Neal v. Bavarian Motors, Inc., 882 A.2d 1022 (Pa. Super. Ct. 2005) (trial court had discretion to disbelieve dealer's testimony regarding value of consumer's use of stolen car before it was impounded by police).

424   *See, e.g.*, Urquhart v. Philbor Motors, Inc., 780 N.Y.S.2d 176, 177, 178 (App. Div. 2004) (reversing dismissal of plaintiff's action to rescind the sale of a car alleged to have been designated as salvage; action for rescission on grounds of fraud does not require plaintiff to establish actual pecuniary loss).

Page 198

7.11.2 Consumer's Slowness in Responding, Other Conduct May Preclude Rescission

Addition to notes 428, 429.

428   *See also* Mitchell v. Backus Cadillac-Pontiac, Inc., 618 S.E.2d 87, 93 (Ga. Ct. App. 2005) (attempting to return car was sufficient where dealer refused to accept it); Bob Maddox Dodge, Inc. v. McKie, 270 S.E.2d 690 (Ga. Ct. App. 1980) (renouncing title to vehicle at trial was sufficient tender where seller had already taken possession of it from repair shop).

429   *But cf.* Scott v. Team Toyota, 622 S.E.2d 925 (Ga. Ct. App. 2005) (tender inadequate where it was conditioned on seller's payment of treble damages).

7.11.3 Election of Damages Versus Rescission Remedy After Case Is Filed

Addition to note 436.

436   *See, e.g.*, Honaker v. Ralph Pool's Albuquerque Auto Sales, Inc., 394 P.2d 978 (N.M. 1964).

Add to text at end of subsection:

In Missouri, the election of remedies doctrine does not bar a defrauded consumer whose judgment for rescission is reversed from seeking damages on remand.[439]

439   Davis v. Cleary Bldg. Corp., 143 S.W.3d 659 (Mo. Ct. App. 2004).

8.1 Introduction

Page 199

Addition to note 1.

1   *Replace NCLC UDAP citation with*: National Consumer Law Center, Unfair and Deceptive Acts and Practices (6th ed. 2004 and Supp.).

8.2 Warranty Claims

8.2.1 Advantages and Disadvantages in Automobile Fraud Cases

Addition to note 2.

2   *See also* Krack v. Action Motors Corp., 867 A.2d 86 (Conn. Ct. App. 2005) (dealer's unknowing sale of rebuilt salvage vehicle without disclosure is breach of implied warranty of merchantability; no showing of fault on seller's part is required).

Page 200

Add to text before sentence containing note 6:

There may also be a state law basis for a fee award.[5.1]

5.1   *See* § 8.2.10, *infra*.

Add to text at end of subsection's eleventh paragraph:

While revocation of acceptance may be inconsistent with a fraud claim, in many jurisdictions a consumer can litigate inconsistent claims and then make an election after the jury returns a verdict.[10.1]

10.1   *See* Freeman v. A & J Auto MN, Inc., 2003 WL 22136807 (Minn. Ct. App. Sept. 16, 2003) (unpublished).

Add to text at end of subsection:

In 2003, the National Conference of Commissioners on Uniform State Laws (NCCUSL) and the American Law Institute (ALI) finalized a revised version of Articles 2 and 2A of the Uniform Commercial Code for consideration by state legislatures. As of early 2005, no state legislature had adopted the revised articles, and because the revision process was highly controversial it is likely that they will face considerable opposition. Some of the more significant changes that these revisions would make in warranty law are to:

- Exclude "information," an undefined term, from Article 2, and leave it up to the courts to determine whether Article 2 applies to a product that contains a computer chip;[11.1]
- Provide for electronic signatures, documents, and notices, with even fewer consumer protections than provided by the Uniform Electronic Transactions Act;[11.2]
- Separate out obligations created by 1) a remote seller's advertisements, or 2) when a remote seller furnishes, along with the goods, a description of the goods, an affirmation of fact about the goods, or a promise of repair, replacement or refund: these obligations would not be warranties, but would run directly from the remote seller to the buyer, and would apply only to new goods;[11.3]
- Treat "remedial promises"—promises to repair or replace goods, or to refund the purchase price—separately from warranties, and measure the statute of limitations from the date of breach of the promise rather than from the date of delivery of the goods;[11.4]

- Require certain language to be used in some circumstances for disclaimers of implied warranties;[11.5]
- Allow post-revocation or post-rejection use of a product if reasonable under the circumstances, but obligate the buyer to pay the seller for the value of the use in appropriate circumstances;[11.6]
- Provide that failure to give notice of breach bars the buyer from a remedy only to the extent that the seller is prejudiced thereby;[11.7]
- Adopt a discovery rule, with some significant limits, even for warranties that do not extend to future performance.[11.8]

11.1   Revised U.C.C. § 2-103(1)(k).

11.2   Revised U.C.C. §§ 2-103(a), (b), (f), (g), (h), (m), (p), 2-203, 2-211, 2-213.

11.3   Revised U.C.C. §§ 2-313A, 2-313B.

11.4   Revised U.C.C. §§ 2-103(1)(h), 2-725(2)(c).

11.5   Revised U.C.C. § 2-316.

11.6   Revised U.C.C. § 2-608(4).

11.7   Revised U.C.C. § 2-607(3)(a).

11.8   Revised U.C.C. § 2-725.

8.2.2 Dealer's Breach of Warranty of Title

Page 201

8.2.2.1 Nature of Warranty of Title

Addition to note 15.

15   *Replace Saber citation with*: Saber v. Dan Angelone Chevrolet, Inc., 811 A.2d 644 (R.I. 2002); *add*: Am. Container Corp. v. Hanley Trucking Corp., 111 N.J. Super. 322, 268 A.2d 313 (Super. Ct. Ch. Div. 1970).

8.2.2.2 Application of Warranty of Title to Automobile Fraud Cases

Addition to notes 16, 17.

16   *Replace Moore citation with*: 786 N.E.2d 903 (Ohio Ct. App. 2002). *Add:* Neal v. Bavarian Motors, Inc., 882 A.2d 1022 (Pa. Super. Ct. 2005).

17   *See also* Bradley v. K & E Investments, Inc., 847 S.W.2d 915 (Mo. Ct. App. 1993) (affirming order requiring seller's floor plan financer to convey certificate of title to consumer buyer; neither floor plan agreement nor financer's possession of title certificate creates security interest).

Add note 18.1 at end of subsection's first paragraph.

18.1   *See, e.g.*, Freeman v. A & J Auto MN, Inc., 2003 WL 22136807 (Minn. Ct. App. Sept. 16, 2003) (unpublished).

Add to text after first sentence of subsection's second paragraph:

A state statute may prohibit titling or registration of a gray market vehicle because of its noncompliance with these standards.[18.2]

18.2   *See, e.g.*, Tex. Trans. Code § 501.030; Ky. Rev. Stat. Ann. § 186A.097 (West); Utah Code Ann. § 41-1a-225; Va. Code Ann. § 46.2-602; W. Va. Code § 17A-3A-3.

Add to text after sentence containing note 19:

Several federal decisions hold that such statutes are preempted by the Clean Air Act,[19.1] but the warranty of title is breached whenever there is a colorable challenge to title, even if title is ultimately found to be good.[19.2]

19.1   Sims v. Fla. Dep't of Highway Safety & Motor Vehicles, 862 F.2d 1449 (11th Cir. 1989); Direct Auto. Imports Ass'n, Inc. v. Townsley, 804 F.2d 1408 (5th Cir. 1986); Ga. Auto. Importers Compliance Ass'n, Inc. v. Bowers, 639 F. Supp. 352 (N.D. Ga. 1986) (state statute requiring compliance with federal emissions standards before vehicle could be titled or registered is preempted).

19.2   *See* § 8.2.2.1, *supra*.

Addition to note 21.

21   *But cf.* Freeman v. A & J Auto MN, Inc., 2003 WL 22136807 (Minn. Ct. App. Sept. 16, 2003) (unpublished) (when parties' contract only obliged seller to transfer a salvage title to buyer, transfer of such a title would comply with warranty of title even though vehicle would have to be inspected before registration could be renewed).

Replace note 23 with:

23   Mobile Dodge, Inc. v. Alford, 487 So. 2d 866 (Ala. 1986); Am. Container Corp. v. Hanley Trucking Corp., 111 N.J. Super. 322, 268 A.2d 313 (Super. Ct. Ch. Div. 1970) (buyer can assert breach of warranty of title claim because of cloud on title when vehicle was seized by police due to obliterated vehicle identification number and other discrepancies); Saber v. Dan Angelone Chevrolet, Inc., 811 A.2d 644 (R.I. 2002); Colton v. Decker, 540 N.W.2d 172, 30 U.C.C. Rep. Serv. 2d 206 (S.D. 1995).

Addition to notes 24–26.	24 Mobile Dodge, Inc. v. Alford, 487 So. 2d 866 (Ala. 1986); Loudon Motors, Inc. v. United Fire & Cas. Co., 2004 WL 943860 (Ohio Ct. App. May 3, 2004) (unpublished) (vehicle is stolen when seller transfers possession in exchange for counterfeit check); Butler v. Buick Motor Co., 813 S.W.2d 454 (Tenn. Ct. App. 1991).
Page 202	25 Whittenberger v. Tom O'Brien Nissan, 1995 WL 809835 (Mass. Super. Ct. Jan. 27, 1995), *as amended by* 1995 WL 809484 (Mass. Super. Ct. Mar. 16, 1995).
	26 Kubota Credit Corp. v. Tillman, 49 U.C.C. Rep. Serv. 2d 926 (Tenn. Ct. App. 2004) (unpublished).

Add to text at end of subsection:

Furthermore, when someone entrusts possession of a vehicle to a car dealer, the dealer has the power to transfer all the rights of the entruster to a buyer in the ordinary course of business.[26.1]

26.1   U.C.C. § 2-403; *see* Bank One v. Amercani, 610 S.E.2d 103 (Ga. Ct. App. 2005).

8.2.2.3 Disclaimer of Warranty of Title

Addition to notes 28, 29.

28   *Replace Moore citation with*: 786 N.E.2d 903 (Ohio Ct. App. 2002).

29   *See* Werremeyer v. K.C. Auto Salvage Co., 2003 WL 21487311 (Mo. Ct. App. June 30, 2003) ("as is, where is" insufficient to disclaim warranty of title), *aff'd in part, rev'd in part on other grounds,* 134 S.W.3d 633 (Mo. 2004) (reversing denial of prejudgment interest but affirming award in all other respects).

8.2.2.4 Remedies for Breach of Warranty of Title

Replace note 34 with:

34   *Id.*; Murdock v. Godwin, 154 Ga. App. 824, 269 S.E.2d 905 (1980); Page One Auto Sales, Inc. v. Annechino, 2003 WL 21313291 (N.Y. Sup. Ct. Mar. 12, 2003) (in special circumstances court may use value at time of dispossession instead of time of sale, but such circumstances not shown here).

Add to text after sentence containing note 35:

The buyer is also entitled to incidental and consequential damages.[35.1]

35.1   Page One Auto Sales, Inc. v. Annechino, 2003 WL 21313291 (N.Y. Sup. Ct. Mar. 12, 2003) (awarding dealer incidental damages for cost of car rentals, attorney fees incurred in replevin actions, registration fees, reimbursements to end-users, and so forth, but finding proof of consequential damages insufficient).

Add to text at end of subsection's second paragraph:

In fact the expenses of any litigation with third parties, whether successful or not, should be recoverable.[36.1]

36.1   Page One Auto Sales, Inc. v. Annechino, 2003 WL 21313291 (N.Y. Sup. Ct. Mar. 12, 2003).

Add to text after subsection's third paragraph:

Warranty of title problems often arise because a dealer sells the car to a consumer without paying the former owner of the car or without paying a floor plan financer who has a security interest in the vehicle. The dealer then is unable to deliver good title to the new buyer. Dealers who stoop to such fraud are usually on their way out of business. If the dealership is closed and insolvent, the entity that financed the new buyer's purchase should be considered a potential defendant. If the dealer referred the consumer to the financing entity, assigned the new buyer's retail installment contract to the entity, or had a business relationship with the entity, then the financing entity will be liable for the consumer's losses, up to a cap, under the FTC Holder Rule.[37.1] The buyer's rights to the car may override those of a floor plan financer in any event.[37.2]

37.1   *See* § 9.4.4, *infra.*

37.2   *See, e.g.*, First Nat'l Bank v. Buss, 143 S.W.3d 915 (Tex. App. 2004).

8.2.3 Express Warranties

8.2.3.2 Express Warranties in Automobile Fraud Cases

Page 203

8.2.3.2.1 Odometer reading and statements as express warranties

Addition to notes 47, 50, 51.

47   *But cf.* T.T. Exclusive Cars, Inc. v. Christie's, Inc., 1996 WL 737204 (S.D.N.Y. Dec. 24, 1996) (seller's statement of vehicle's mileage, placed in auction catalog, is not warranty when catalog expressly disclaimed all warranties; court should have ruled that express warranties can not be disclaimed).

50   *Delete Wantagh Auto Sales Inc. citation.*

51   *Delete Wantagh Auto Sales Inc. citation.*

Page 204

8.2.3.2.2 Other express warranties

Addition to notes 55–57.

55   *See, e.g.*, Terrell v. R & A Mfg. Partners, Ltd., 835 So. 2d 216 (Ala. Civ. App. 2002).
56   *See also* Peabody v. P.J.'s Auto Vill., Inc., 153 Vt. 55, 569 A.2d 460, 462 (1989) (describing vehicle as a "1974 Saab" was UDAP violation when it was actually half of a 1974 Saab clipped to half of a 1972 Saab).
57   *See, e.g.*, Mitchell v. Backus Cadillac-Pontiac, Inc., 618 S.E.2d 87, 95 (Ga. Ct. App. 2005) (statement that vehicle had never been wrecked created express warranty, but buyer failed to prove damages).

Add to text after sentence containing note 57:

A description of a car as "new" is an express warranty.[57.1]

57.1   Horne v. Claude Ray Ford Sales, Inc., 290 S.E.2d 497 (Ga. Ct. App. 1982).

Delete second sentence of subsection's third paragraph.

Add to text after subsection's third paragraph:

Some used car dealers sell "certified" used cars, which are represented to have passed a multi-point safety inspection. Such a certification would lead the average consumer to believe that the vehicle had not suffered major damage, yet many certification programs allow vehicles with major damage to be certified. Because express warranties are to be construed against the drafter,[59.1] such a certification should be interpreted as including an assurance that the vehicle has not suffered major wreck damage. The details of the certification program may also bolster a fraud claim, as a dealer who performed such a detailed inspection is unlikely to have failed to notice signs of wreck damage. The dealer may also have misrepresented that the car was a certified used car when in fact it did not meet the standards for certification, thereby creating additional warranty claims, as well as UDAP and fraud claims.

59.1   *See* National Consumer Law Center, Consumer Warranty Law § 7.3.4.3 (2d ed. 2001 and Supp.).

8.2.3.3 Disclaimers and Parol Evidence

Addition to note 60.

60   *See, e.g.*, Perkins v. Land Rover, 2003 WL 22939452 (Ohio Ct. App. Dec. 5, 2003) (unpublished) ("as is" clause can not preclude express warranty claim).

8.2.4 Implied Warranties

Page 206

8.2.4.2 Implied Warranties in Automobile Fraud Cases

Addition to notes 80, 81.

80   Lockhart v. Cmty. Auto Plaza, Inc., 695 N.W.2d 335 (Iowa Ct. App. 2004) (concealed wreck damage, poorly repaired, breaches implied warranty of merchantability).
81   *See* Terrell v. R & A Mfg. Partners, Ltd., 835 So. 2d 216 (Ala. Civ. App. 2002) (model year discrepancy breaches implied warranty of merchantability because car would not pass without objection in the trade); Krack v. Action Motors Corp., 867 A.2d 86 (Conn. App. Ct. 2005) (salvaged vehicle cannot pass without objection in the trade). *But cf.* Mitchell v. Backus Cadillac-Pontiac, Inc., 618 S.E.2d 87, 96 (Ga. Ct. App. 2005) (denying claim that car with collision history would not pass without objection in the trade because of buyer's failure to cite authority).

Add to text after sentence containing note 81:

A "gray market" vehicle that is sold in the United States but does not conform to federal standards also does not pass without objection in the trade so is not merchantable.[81.1]

81.1   Geo. Byers Sons, Inc. v. East Europe Import Export, Inc. 488 F. Supp. 574, 580 (D. Md. 1980) (distributor's sale of gray market motorcycles to dealer).

Add to text after subsection's second paragraph:

Government safety standards are another benchmark for the implied warranty of merchantability. Goods that do not meet government safety standards will not pass without objection in the trade and are not fit for ordinary purposes.[83.1] Inability to pass a mandatory state inspection makes a vehicle unmerchantable.[83.2] A number of states have laws that require proper repair of airbags after deployment.[83.3] Rebuilt salvage vehicles that do not meet these standards should be considered unmerchantable.

83.1   Geo. Byers Sons v. E. Europe Imp. Exp., Inc., 488 F. Supp. 574, 580 (D. Md. 1980) (motorcycles sold without certificate of compliance with federal motor vehicle safety standards are unmerchantable).

83.2   Kimpel v. Delaware Pub. Auto Auction, 2001 WL 1555932 (Del. Ct. Com. Pl. Mar. 6, 2001).

83.3   *See* § 6.3bS, *supra.*

8.2.4.3 Disclaimers

<table>
<tr><td>Page 207</td><td></td></tr>
</table>

8.2.4.3.3 State law restrictions on disclaimers

Addition to note 93.

93   N.M. Stat. Ann. § 57-16A-3.1 (Michie) (requiring fifteen-day, 500-mile implied warranty on used cars).

Add to text after "New Jersey" in subsection's final sentence:

New Mexico,

Page 209

Add new subsection to text after § 8.2.6:

8.2.6a Privity

Historically the notion of privity of contract limited warranty rights so that only the immediate buyer could enforce a warranty, and only against the direct seller. Thus a buyer could not sue the manufacturer and a subsequent owner could not sue the dealer. The privity doctrine has come under increasing attack, especially in consumer transactions. There are now many exceptions to it and many jurisdictions have abolished it.

The privity doctrine and the exceptions to it are discussed in detail in another manual.[123.1] The most important exceptions are:

- The federal Magnuson-Moss Warranty Act makes manufacturers who issue "written warranties" directly liable to consumers even when the consumer is in privity only with the dealer.[123.2]

- Almost all states[123.3] recognize that a buyer can enforce an *express* warranty against a remote seller without regard to privity. Thus, for example, if a remote seller's odometer statement qualifies as an express warranty, the fact that the buyer did not contract directly with that seller should not stand in the way of a warranty claim.

- More than half the states have abolished privity as a requirement for implied warranty claims, at least in consumer cases, either by statute or by judicial decision. In these states the buyer of a rebuilt wreck or other unmerchantable vehicle should be able to bring warranty claims against remote sellers as well as the immediate seller. A number of other states have not yet definitively decided the issue, while a minority still cling to the privity requirement.

- Even when privity is required in some circumstances the buyer qualifies as a third-party beneficiary of the warranty or can show that the direct seller was the agent of the remote seller.

123.1   National Consumer Law Center, Consumer Warranty Law Ch. 6 (2d ed. 2001 and Supp.).

123.2   15 U.S.C. § 2310(d)(1).

123.3   The only exceptions are Arizona, Idaho, and possibly Illinois and Wisconsin, but Arizona allows a non-U.C.C. warranty claim to be asserted without privity.

8.2.7 Revocation of Acceptance As a UCC Remedy

8.2.7.1 Introduction

Replace note 125 with:

125   *See* National Consumer Law Center, Unfair and Deceptive Acts and Practices §§ 5.1.2.2.6, 5.1.2.2.7 (6th ed. 2004 and Supp.).

Page 210

8.2.7.2 When May a Consumer Revoke Acceptance?

Add to text at end of subsection:

The fact that a vehicle can only be titled as a salvage vehicle can be a substantial impairment in and of itself that allows the buyer to revoke acceptance.[127.1]

> 127.1   Urquhart v. Philbor Motors, Inc., 9 A.D.3d 458, 780 N.Y.S.2d 176 (2004).

8.2.9 *The Damage Remedy and Limitations on Remedies Clauses*

Page 213

8.2.9.2 Punitive Damages

Addition to notes 148, 149, 154.

> 148   *See, e.g.*, Poindexter v. Morse Chevrolet, Inc., 270 F. Supp. 2d 1286 (D. Kan. 2003) (punitive damages not allowed on warranty claim itself, but only on the tort claim); Salter v. Al-Hallaz, 2003 WL 1872991 (D. Kan. Apr. 10, 2003); *see also* Carvel Corp. v. Noonan, 350 F.3d 6, 24, 25 (2d Cir. 2003) (for punitive damages claims arising out of contract, New York requires that egregious conduct be directed at the public generally; certifying to state supreme court a question concerning application of this rule).

Page 214

> 149   *See, e.g.*, Asa-Brandt, Inc. v. ADM Investor Services, Inc., 344 F.3d 738, 746 (8th Cir. 2003) (Iowa law) (affirming punitive damages award on contract claim); Myers v. Workmen's Auto Ins. Co., 95 P.3d 977 (Idaho 2004) (punitive damages available in contract action if party's acts and state of mind are sufficiently wrongful); Dold v. Sherow, 552 P.2d 945 (Kan. 1976) (affirming punitive damages on warranty claim when there was sufficient evidence of fraud); *see also* Zurn Contractors, Inc. v. B.F. Goodrich Co., 746 F. Supp. 1051 (D. Kan. 1990) (no punitive damages under breach of contract claim unless plaintiff pleads and proves an independent tort causing additional injury; note that the later case Equitable Life Leasing Corp. v. Abbick, 757 P.2d 304 (Kan. 1988), disavows the requirement of additional damages).

> 154   *See also* Myers v. Workmen's Auto Ins. Co., 95 P.3d 977 (Idaho 2004) (punitive damages available in contract action if party's acts and state of mind are sufficiently wrongful).

Page 216

8.2.10 *Attorney Fees*

Addition to notes 169, 170.

> 169   *See* Lockhart v. Cmty. Auto Plaza, Inc., 695 N.W.2d 335 (Iowa Ct. App. 2004) (affirming Magnuson-Moss fee award when dealer's sale of car with undisclosed, poorly-repaired wreck damage breached implied warranty of merchantability).

> 170   *Replace JHC Ventures, Ltd. P'ship citation with*: 94 S.W.3d 762 (Tex. App. 2002) (commercial case) (warranty is not a contract claim, so provision of Tex. Civ. Prac. & Rem. Code Ann. § 38.001(8) (Vernon) allowing fees for contract claims inapplicable).

Add note 170.1 at end of sentence containing note 170.

> 170.1   Ark. Code Ann. § 16-22-308 (Michie); Cal. Civ. Code § 1717 (West); Conn. Gen. Stat. § 42-150bb; Fla. Stat. Ann. § 57.105(7) (West); Haw. Rev. Stat. § 607-14; Mont. Code Ann. § 28-3-704; N.H. Rev. Stat. Ann. § 361:C-2; N.Y. Gen. Oblig. Law § 5-327 (McKinney); Or. Rev. Stat. § 20.096; Utah Code Ann. § 78-27-56.5; Wash. Rev. Code § 4.84.330; *see* Mo. Rev. Stat. § 408.092 (fees to enforce credit agreement); *see also* Schulz v. Honsador, Inc., 690 P.2d 279 (Haw. 1984) (breach of warranty is in nature of *assumpsit* so fees are allowable under Haw. Rev. Stat. § 607-14).

Add to text at end of subsection:

A state may also have other statutes or procedural rules that provide for fee shifting in some circumstances.[175.1]

> 175.1   *See* Krack v. Action Motors Corp., 867 A.2d 86 (Conn. Ct. App. 2005) (affirming award of $38,626 in fees when consumer recovered $9715.10 in damages on warranty claim under statute applicable when defendant removes small claims case to higher court).

Page 217

8.3 Mistake

Addition to notes 183, 187.

> 183   *See In re* Invenux, Inc., 298 B.R. 442, 51 U.C.C. Rep. Serv. 2d 563 (Bankr. D. Colo. 2003); *see also* Morningstar v. Hallett, 858 A.2d 125, 54 U.C.C. Rep. Serv. 2d 716 (Pa. Super. Ct. 2004) ("as is" disclaimer no bar to claim of mistake).

> 187   *Replace Bernal citation with*: 836 So. 2d 516 (La. Ct. App. 2002).

Replace note 189 with:

> 189   National Consumer Law Center, Unfair and Deceptive Acts and Practices § 9.5.10 (6th ed. 2004 and Supp.).

Replace note 191 with:

> 191   *See* § 8.4.10, *infra*; National Consumer Law Center, Unfair and Deceptive Acts and Practices § 8.8 (6th ed. 2004 and Supp.).

8.4 UDAP Claims

8.4.1 Advantages and Disadvantages in Automobile Fraud Cases

8.4.1.1 Strengths and Benefits of UDAP Claims

Addition to note 193.   193   *Replace first NCLC UDAP citation with*: National Consumer Law Center, Unfair and Deceptive Acts and Practices (6th ed. 2004 and Supp.).

Page 218

Replace note 194 with: 194   *See* National Consumer Law Center, Unfair and Deceptive Acts and Practices § 4.2.17.1 (6th ed. 2004 and Supp.).

8.4.1.4 Disadvantages of UDAP Claims

Replace note 200 with: 200   *See* § 8.4.9, *infra. See generally* National Consumer Law Center, Unfair and Deceptive Acts and Practices § 7.5.3 (6th ed. 2004 and Supp.).

Page 219

Add note 202.1 at end of subsection.   202.1   Wilkins v. Peninsula Motor Cars, Inc., 587 S.E.2d 581 (Va. 2003) (plaintiff may recover actual damages and punitive damages on fraud claim and attorney fees on UDAP claim).

8.4.2 Scope Issues

Replace note 205 with: 205   *See* National Consumer Law Center, Unfair and Deceptive Acts and Practices §§ 2.3.1., 2.3.3 (6th ed. 2004 and Supp.).

Replace note 207 with: 207   National Consumer Law Center, Unfair and Deceptive Acts and Practices § 2.2.1 (6th ed. 2004 and Supp.).

Addition to notes 208, 209.   208   *Replace NCLC citation with*: National Consumer Law Center, Unfair and Deceptive Acts and Practices §§ 2.3.8, 4.2.15.3 (6th ed. 2004 and Supp.); *add: See, e.g.*, Freeman v. A & J Auto MN, Inc., 2003 WL 22136807 (Minn. Ct. App. Sept. 16, 2003) (unpublished).

209   Roberts v. Shawnee Mission Ford, 2003 WL 22143727 (D. Kan. Aug. 20, 2003) (consumer's trade-in of vehicle to dealer not covered by Kansas UDAP statute because it was for purposes of resale). *But see* Chong v. Parker, 361 F.3d 455 (8th Cir. 2004) (Missouri UDAP statute covers non-merchant seller of undisclosed salvage car).

8.4.3 Deception Standard

Addition to note 210.   210   *Replace NCLC citation with*: National Consumer Law Center, Unfair and Deceptive Acts and Practices § 4.2.4 (6th ed. 2004 and Supp.).

Replace note 211 with: 211   National Consumer Law Center, Unfair and Deceptive Acts and Practices § 4.2.5 (6th ed. 2004 and Supp.); *see* Freeman v. A & J Auto MN, Inc., 2003 WL 22136807 (Minn. Ct. App. Sept. 16, 2003) (unpublished) (negligent misrepresentation of car's salvage history can be UDAP violation).

Page 220

Addition to note 218.   218   Morningstar v. Hallett, 858 A.2d 125, 54 U.C.C. Rep. Serv. 2d 716 (Pa. Super. Ct. 2004) ("as is" disclaimer no bar to UDAP claim); Padgett's Used Cars and Leasing, Inc. v. Preston, 2005 WL 2290249 (Tex. App. Sept. 21, 2005) (unpublished, citation limited); Kane v. Nxcess Motorcars, Inc., 2005 WL 497484 (Tex. App. Mar. 3, 2005) (unpublished) ("as is" clause does not preclude UDAP claim based on knowing misrepresentation).

Replace note 219 with: 219   *See* § 8.4.2, *supra. See generally* National Consumer Law Center, Unfair and Deceptive Acts and Practices §§ 2.3.8, 4.2.15.3 (6th ed. 2004 and Supp.).

Replace note 220 with:

220   National Consumer Law Center, Unfair and Deceptive Acts and Practices § 4.2.16 (6th ed. 2004 and Supp.).

8.4.4 Failure to Disclose As Deceptive

Addition to note 223.

223   *Replace NCLC citation with*: National Consumer Law Center, Unfair and Deceptive Acts and Practices Appx. A (6th ed. 2004 and Supp.).

Add to text after sentence containing note 223:

Or the UDAP statute or regulation may require disclosure when goods are defective, blemished, deteriorated, or reconditioned.

Addition to notes 224, 225, 228, 233.

224   *Replace Kenny citation parenthetical with*: (no violation of UDAP regulation requiring disclosures in advertisements when there was no evidence of any advertisement and when consumers would have bought car on same terms if collision and rental history had been disclosed; distinguished in Emmanuelli v. Merriam Motors, Inc., 2003 WL 22080496 (Conn. Super. Ct. Aug. 25, 2003), which notes that UDAP duty to disclose may also arise by virtue of common law or otherwise).

Page 221

225   *Replace NCLC citation with*: National Consumer Law Center, Unfair and Deceptive Acts and Practices § 4.2.14 (6th ed. 2004 and Supp.); *add*: *See, e.g.*, Go For It v. Aircraft Sales Corp., 2003 WL 21504600 (N.D. Ill. June 27, 2003) (failure to disclose airplane's crash history to commercial buyer may be UDAP violation even though not fraudulent suppression); Freeman v. A & J Auto MN, Inc., 2003 WL 22136807 (Minn. Ct. App. Sept. 16, 2003) (unpublished) (remote prior owners can be held liable under UDAP statute for placing wrecked car in stream of commerce without obtaining salvage title as required by law). *But see* Tietsworth v. Harley-Davidson, Inc., 677 N.W.2d 233 (Wis. 2004) (one of Wisconsin's UDAP statutes, which prohibits any deceptive "advertisement, announcement, statement or representation," does not impose duty to disclose).

228   *Replace NCLC citation with*: National Consumer Law Center, Unfair and Deceptive Acts and Practices § 4.2.13 (6th ed. 2004 and Supp.).

233   *Replace NCLC citation with*: National Consumer Law Center, Unfair and Deceptive Acts and Practices §§ 4.2.14.3.5, 4.2.14.3.6, 4.2.14.3.7 (6th ed. 2004 and Supp.).

8.4.5 Unfairness and Unconscionability

8.4.5.1 Unfairness

Page 222

Replace note 235 with:

235   National Consumer Law Center, Unfair and Deceptive Acts and Practices Appx. A (6th ed. 2004 and Supp.).

Replace note 238 with:

238   National Consumer Law Center, Unfair and Deceptive Acts and Practices § 4.3.3.5 (6th ed. 2004 and Supp.).

8.4.5.2 Unconscionability

Addition to note 240.

240   *Replace NCLC citation with*: National Consumer Law Center, Unfair and Deceptive Acts and Practices (6th ed. 2004 and Supp.).

8.4.6 Violation of Another Statute

Page 223

8.4.6.1 Introduction

Add to text at end of subsection's first paragraph:

Many cases have found violations of state motor vehicle statutes to be UDAP violations.[243.1]

243.1   *See* Diaz v. Paragon Motors of Woodside, Inc., 2006 WL 802289 (E.D.N.Y. Mar. 29, 2006); §§ 6.2.1.9, 6.3, *supra*.

8.4.6.2 Precedent Finding Statutory Violations to Be Automatic UDAP Violations

Replace note 258 with:

258 National Consumer Law Center, Unfair and Deceptive Acts and Practices § 5.2.7.1 (6th ed. 2004 and Supp.).

Page 224

Addition to notes 260, 262.

260 Locascio v. Imports Unlimited, Inc., 309 F. Supp. 2d 267 (D. Conn. 2004) (violation of statute requiring buyer to be given certificate of title, which would have revealed rebuilt brand, is UDAP violation).

262 *Add to Nigh citation*: , *rev'd on other grounds*, 125 S. Ct. 460 (2004) (Truth in Lending statutory damages calculation issue).

8.4.8 Application of UDAP Standards to Automobile Fraud Cases

Page 225

8.4.8.1 Odometer Rollbacks and Mileage Misrepresentations

Addition to notes 267, 268.

267 Barrett v. Brian Bemis Auto World, 408 F. Supp. 2d 539 (N.D. Ill. 2005) (dealer's failure to disclose that title was marked "not actual mileage" was UDAP violation); Padgett's Used Cars and Leasing, Inc. v. Preston, 2005 WL 2290249 (Tex. App. Sept. 21, 2005) (unpublished, citation limited) (misrepresentation that odometer showed actual mileage).

268 *Add to Sandi citation*: *adopted, judgment entered by* 2001 U.S. Dist. LEXIS 876 (E.D.N.Y. Jan. 16, 2001).

Page 226

8.4.8.2 Salvage and Collision History

Addition to notes 270–272.

270 Chong v. Parker, 361 F.3d 455 (8th Cir. 2004) (Mo. law) (remanding for consideration of UDAP punitive damages); Coral Cadillac, Inc. v. Stephens, 867 So. 2d 556 (Fla. Dist. Ct. App. 2004) (affirming award of $12,500 actual damages and $133,050 punitive damages when jury found both fraud and deceptive practices in misrepresentation of car's collision and repair history; court certified question of interpretation of former version of state punitive damages cap to state supreme court); Byers v. Santiam Ford, Inc., 574 P.2d 1122 (Or. 1978) (affirming award of punitive damages on UDAP claim where dealer misrepresented car's collision history); Padgett's Used Cars and Leasing, Inc. v. Preston, 2005 WL 2290249 (Tex. App. Sept. 21, 2005) (unpublished, citation limited); Kane v. Nxcess Motorcars, Inc., 2005 WL 497484 (Tex. App. Mar. 3, 2005) (unpublished) (misrepresentation that car sold over Internet had not been repainted); Peabody v. P.J.'s Auto Vill., Inc., 153 Vt. 55, 569 A.2d 460, 462 (1989) (describing vehicle as a "1974 Saab" was deceptive when it was actually half of a 1974 Saab clipped to half of a 1972 Saab); *see also* Marrale v. Gwinnett Place Ford, 609 S.E.2d 659 (Ga. Ct. App. 2005) (even if salesman did not know that car had been in wreck, he knew that he did not know its real condition); Laing v. Clair Car Connection, 2003 WL 1669624 (Me. Super. Ct. Jan. 29, 2003) (dismissing claim under one of Maine's UDAP statutes because dealer complied with damage disclosure law, but allowing claim under other UDAP statute to go to jury); *see also* York v. Conway Ford, Inc., 480 S.E.2d 726 (S.C. 1997) (trial court erred in directing verdict for defendant on UDAP claim involving concealment of prior collision history; transaction had impact on public interest as required by state UDAP statute).

271 Freeman v. A & J Auto MN, Inc., 2003 WL 22136807 (Minn. Ct. App. Sept. 16, 2003) (unpublished) (negligent misrepresentation of car's salvage history can be UDAP violation).

272 *See, e.g.*, Locascio v. Imports Unlimited, Inc., 309 F. Supp. 2d 267 (D. Conn. 2004) (violation of statute requiring buyer to be given certificate of title, which would have revealed rebuilt brand, is UDAP violation); Salmeron v. Highlands Ford Sales, Inc., 271 F. Supp. 2d 1314 (D.N.M. 2003); Szwebel v. Pap's Auto Sales, Inc., 2003 WL 21750841 (N.D. Ill. July 29, 2003) (mag.); Go For It v. Aircraft Sales Corp., 2003 WL 21504600 (N.D. Ill. June 27, 2003) (failure to disclose airplane's crash history to commercial buyer); Hart v. Boehmer Chevrolet Sales, Inc., 337 Ill. App. 3d 742, 787 N.E.2d 350 (2003) (failure to disclose pre-sale damage to new car is UDAP violation when damage exceeds statutory six percent threshold); Freeman v. A & J Auto MN, Inc., 2003 WL 22136807 (Minn. Ct. App. Sept. 16, 2003) (unpublished) (remote prior owners can be held liable under UDAP statute for placing wrecked car in stream of commerce without obtaining salvage title as required by law); Cohen v. Express Fin. Services, Inc., 145 S.W.3d 857 (Mo. Ct. App. 2004) (affirming UDAP punitive damages award against dealership and salesman who failed to disclose that vehicle had been extensively damaged and improperly repaired); Blankenship v. Town & Country Ford, Inc., 622 S.E.2d 638 (N.C. Ct. App. 2005); Lucia v. West Hills Auto & Truck Center, 2005 WL 3875895 (Ohio Ct. App. Aug. 22, 2005) (unpublished, citation limited); Smith v. Reinhart Ford, 2004 WL 3092495 (Pa. C.P. Sept. 29, 2004) (upholding consumer's right to seek damages and attorney fees under UDAP statute when dealer concealed vehicle's wreck history; economic

loss doctrine does not bar UDAP claim). *But cf.* Don Smith Ford, Lincoln-Mercury v. Bolinger, 2005 WL 711963 (Tenn. Ct. App. 2005) (unpublished) (no UDAP violation when dealer sold vehicle "as is" with full disclosure of all damage and repairs; dealer did not know that vehicle title would be branded rebuilt so did not have to disclose this fact).

Page 227

Replace note 276 with:

276　Locascio v. Imports Unlimited, Inc., 309 F. Supp. 2d 267 (D. Conn. 2004); *see* § 8.4.6, *supra.*

8.4.8.3　Lemon Laundering and Nondisclosure of History of Mechanical Problems

Addition to note 278.

278　*See* Alexander v. DaimlerChrysler Corp., 2004 WL 179369 (N.C. Super. Ct. Jan. 30, 2004) (both manufacturer and dealer may be liable, but here manufacturer made required disclosure).

Replace note 280 with:

280　National Consumer Law Center, Unfair and Deceptive Acts and Practices § 4.2.15 (6th ed. 2004 and Supp.).

Addition to notes 285, 286, 288.

285　*Add to Nigh citation: rev'd on other grounds,* 125 S. Ct. 460 (2004) (Truth in Lending statutory damages calculation issue); *add:* Rose v. Ford, 2003 WL 21495081 (Cal. Ct. App. June 30, 2003) (unpublished) (UDAP violation to misrepresent that vehicle was in good working order).

Page 228

286　*See also* Check v. Clifford Chrysler-Plymouth, 342 Ill. App. 3d 150, 794 N.E.2d 829 (2003) (selling repaired car as new without inspecting the repair work is UDAP violation).

288　*See also* Rose v. Ford, 2003 WL 21495081 (Cal. Ct. App. June 30, 2003) (unpublished) (UDAP violation to misrepresent that vehicle was in good working order).

8.4.8.4　Nature of Prior Use

Addition to notes 292–294.

292　Diaz v. Paragon Motors of Woodside, Inc., 2006 WL 802289 (E.D.N.Y. Mar. 29, 2006) (violation of state motor vehicle statute requiring disclosure is UDAP violation); Salmeron v. Highlands Ford Sales, Inc., 271 F. Supp. 2d 1314 (D.N.M. 2003) (history as a rental vehicle); Me. Rev. Stat. Ann. tit. 10, § 1475(2-A)(B) (West); 29-250-104 Me. Code R. § 1 (dealer has duty to disclose prior owner's principal use); Md. Regs. Code tit. 11, § 11.12.01.14(M) (requires vehicles used for purposes other than a consumer good to be clearly and conspicuously identified; for example: when used for public or governmental purposes and normally driven by multiple drivers, or when used for driver training, as executive driven vehicles, as demonstrators, as taxicabs, or as short-term rentals); Fay v. O'Connell, 12 U.C.C. Rep. Serv. 2d 987 (Mass. App. Ct. 1990) (failure to disclose prior use in truck pulling contests). *But cf.* Locascio v. Imports Unlimited, Inc., 309 F. Supp. 2d 267 (D. Conn. 2004) (no violation when plaintiff proved only that vehicle had been titled to "Golden Key Lease, Inc." but not that that company had used it as a daily rental).

Page 229

293　Padgett's Used Cars and Leasing, Inc. v. Preston, 2005 WL 2290249 (Tex. App. Sept. 21, 2005) (unpublished, citation limited). *But cf.* Hamilton v. O'Connor Chevrolet, Inc., 399 F. Supp. 2d 860 (N.D. Ill. 2005) (statement that car was "privately owned" cannot be construed as representation that it had only one owner); Sykes v. Brady-Bushey Ford, Inc., 2005 WL 2787517 (Va. Cir. Ct. Oct. 27, 2005) (denial of motion to dismiss).

294　Salmeron v. Highlands Ford Sales, Inc., 271 F. Supp. 2d 1314 (D.N.M. 2003).

Replace sentence containing note 296 with:

It is similarly deceptive to represent that a damaged rental car sold at auction was driven only by the dealer's general manager[296] or that the dealership obtained a car from a friend of the salesman when in fact it was a poorly repaired wrecked vehicle that came from another used car dealer.[296.1]

296　State *ex rel.* Danforth v. Independence Dodge, Inc., 494 S.W.2d 362 (Mo. Ct. App. 1973).

296.1　Cohen v. Express Fin. Services, Inc., 145 S.W.3d 857 (Mo. Ct. App. 2004) (affirming punitive damages award under UDAP statute).

Add to text at end of subsection's second paragraph:

Discovering the records of all repairs that the rental company performed on the vehicle can be helpful in showing the judge why prior use as a rental vehicle is a material fact that the seller should have disclosed. Typically the records will show considerably more dents, scrapes, and collisions than non-rental cars suffer.

Page 230

8.4.8.5 Sale of Used Cars As New

Addition to notes 301, 305, 309, 311.

301   *See* Tuckish v. Pompano Motor Co., 337 F. Supp. 2d 1313 (S.D. Fla. 2004); Scott v. Team Toyota, 622 S.E.2d 925 (Ga. Ct. App. 2005) (plaintiff may pursue UDAP claim where car represented as new actually had been previously titled, even though buyer knew it had been driven 1200 miles, where previous titling reduced its value); Bennett v. D.L. Claborn Buick, Inc., 414 S.E.2d 12 (Ga. Ct. App. 1991) (whether dealer misrepresented car's intrinsic quality by describing it as new when it had been used as demonstrator is jury question).

305   *See also* Scott v. Team Toyota, 622 S.E.2d 925 (Ga. Ct. App. 2005) (plaintiff may pursue UDAP claim where car represented as new actually had been previously titled, even though buyer knew it had been driven 1200 miles, where previous titling reduced its value).

309   Hart v. Boehmer Chevrolet Sales, Inc., 337 Ill. App. 3d 742, 787 N.E.2d 350 (2003) (allegation of representation that vehicle was new, when it had been damaged prior to sale, creates issue of fact).

311   *See also* Bennett v. D.L. Claborn Buick, Inc., 414 S.E.2d 12 (Ga. Ct. App. 1991) (whether dealer misrepresented car's intrinsic quality by describing it as new when it had been used as demonstrator is jury question, even though it had never been titled).

Add to text at end of subsection's fourth paragraph:

The FTC's Used Car Rule requires dealers to display a Buyers Guide as a window sticker in all used vehicles offered for sale.[314.1] "Used vehicle" is defined as one driven more than the limited use necessary in moving or road testing the vehicle prior to delivery to a consumer.[314.2] A dealer who misrepresents a used car as new is highly likely to violate this rule, because the window sticker could easily alert the buyer that the vehicle is used. A number of cases hold that a violation of the FTC's Used Car Rule is a UDAP violation.[314.3] The seller's failure to comply with the rule may also be evidence of fraud.

The effect on the consumer's lemon law rights of a misrepresentation that a used car is new should always be considered in assessing damages. If the state lemon law only covers new vehicles, the loss of lemon law rights, if quantifiable, might be an element of damages.[314.4]

314.1   16 C.F.R. § 455.2.

314.2   16 C.F.R. § 455.1(d)(2).

314.3   *See, e.g.*, Tuckish v. Pompano Motor Co., 337 F. Supp. 2d 1313 (S.D. Fla. 2004) (failure to post Buyers Guide, which deceived consumer into believing that car was new, states UDAP claim). *See generally* National Consumer Law Center, Consumer Warranty Law § 14.7.8 (2d ed. 2001 and Supp.).

314.4   *See, e.g.*, Tuckish v. Pompano Motor Co., 337 F. Supp. 2d 1313 (S.D. Fla. 2004) (noting that, by selling consumer a used vehicle represented as new, the dealer eliminated consumer's lemon law rights).

Page 231

8.4.8.6 Misrepresentations Concerning Clear Title

Addition to note 316.

316   *See also* Neal v. Bavarian Motors, Inc., 882 A.2d 1022 (Pa. Super. Ct. 2005) (upholding treble damages award on UDAP count where seller knew or should have known that vehicle was stolen).

8.4.8.7 Gray Market Vehicle Sales

Addition to note 322.

322   N.H. Rev. Stat. Ann. §§ 357-C:3(I-b)(a), 357-C:3(I-b)(e); *see also* Alaska Stat. §§ 45.25.465 (non-UDAP statute requiring window sticker disclosure if used motor vehicle was manufactured for sale in another country), 45.25.470 (requiring dealer to disclose in writing if motor vehicle was originally manufactured for sale in another country).

Add to text at end of subsection's second paragraph:

Other states have statutes that do not refer specifically to gray market sales, but require a special disclosure if a new vehicle is sold without a manufacturer's warranty, which is a common feature of a gray market sale.[322.1] The state's motor vehicle titling laws may also require a notation on the title that the vehicle was originally manufactured for a foreign market.[322.2] Violation of such a statute may be a UDAP violation.[322.3]

322.1   *See, e.g.*, Ky. Rev. Stat. Ann. § 190.0491 (West) (prohibiting sale of a new vehicle without a warranty unless the lack of a warranty is prominently displayed).

322.2   *See, e.g.*, 75 Pa. Con. Stat. § 1106(b)(9).

322.3   *See* § 3.9.4, *supra*.

8.4.9 Limitations on UDAP Litigation

Replace note 324 with:

324   *See* National Consumer Law Center, Unfair and Deceptive Acts and Practices § 7.5.2 (6th ed. 2004 and Supp.).

Replace note 325 with:

325   The Illinois notice requirement, applicable only to car dealers and financers, was struck down as a special law by Allen v. Woodfield Chevrolet, Inc., 208 Ill. 2d 12, 280 Ill. Dec. 501, 802 N.E.2d 752 (2003).

Replace note 327 with:

327   *See* National Consumer Law Center, Unfair and Deceptive Acts and Practices § 7.5.4 (6th ed. 2004 and Supp.).

Addition to notes 328, 329.

328   *Replace Allen citation with*: 208 Ill. 2d 12, 280 Ill. Dec. 501, 802 N.E.2d 752 (2003).

329   Marrale v. Gwinnett Place Ford, 609 S.E.2d 659 (Ga. Ct. App. 2005) (when car is offered for sale to the public by a dealer, UDAP claim may be based on individual salesman's misrepresentation); Nelson v. Lusterstone Surfacing Co., 605 N.W.2d 136 (Neb. 2000) (UDAP statute does not cover sale of undisclosed wreck by non-dealer).

Add note 329.1 after "interest" in sentence following sentence containing note 329.

329.1   *See, e.g.,* Diaz v. Paragon Motors of Woodside, Inc., 2006 WL 802289 (E.D.N.Y. Mar. 29, 2006); Marrale v. Gwinnett Place Ford, 609 S.E.2d 659 (Ga. Ct. App. 2005) (offering a product for sale by opening one's door to the general public is sufficient); Catrett v. Landmark Dodge, Inc., 253 Ga. App. 639, 560 S.E.2d 101, 105 (2002) (car sale met public interest requirement where dealer opened its doors to general public and misrepresented car's condition to buyer); York v. Conway Ford, Inc., 480 S.E.2d 726 (S.C. 1997) (impact on public interest established since car dealer was in business of selling cars and concealment of prior wreck damage had potential for repetition).

Page 232

8.4.10 UDAP Remedies

Addition to note 338.

338   *See, e.g.,* Neal v. Bavarian Motors, Inc., 882 A.2d 1022 (Pa. Super. Ct. 2005) (upholding treble damages award on UDAP count where seller knew or should have known that vehicle was stolen).

Replace note 339 with:

339   *See* National Consumer Law Center, Unfair and Deceptive Acts and Practices § 8.4.1 (6th ed. 2004 and Supp.).

Addition to notes 340, 341.

340   *See* Chong v. Parker, 361 F.3d 455 (8th Cir. 2004) (Mo. law) (remanding for new trial on UDAP punitive damages when seller misrepresented car's collision history); Crowder v. Bob Oberling Enters., Inc., 499 N.E.2d 115, (Ill. Ct. App. 1986) (affirming award of $5540 in compensatory damages and $9000 in punitive damages on UDAP claim against dealer that failed to disclose car's salvage history); Cohen v. Express Fin. Services, Inc., 145 S.W.3d 857 (Mo. Ct. App. 2004) (affirming UDAP punitive damages award against dealership and salesman who failed to disclose that vehicle had been extensively damaged and improperly repaired); Byers v. Santiam Ford, Inc., 574 P.2d 1122 (Or. 1978) (affirming award of punitive damages on UDAP claim where dealer misrepresented car's collision history); *cf.* Check v. Clifford Chrysler-Plymouth, 342 Ill. App. 3d 150, 794 N.E.2d 829 (2003) (evidence insufficient for punitive damages in case involving faulty pre-sale repair of new car's scratched paint). *But cf.* Locascio v. Imports Unlimited, Inc., 309 F. Supp. 2d 267 (D. Conn. 2004) (evidence insufficient for punitive damages on UDAP claim against seller who concealed branded title from buyer).

341   *Replace NCLC citation with*: National Consumer Law Center, Unfair and Deceptive Acts and Practices § 8.7 (6th ed. 2004 and Supp.); *add*: *See, e.g.,* Vineyard v. Varner, 2003 WL 22794467 (Tenn. Ct. App. Nov. 25, 2003) (unpublished) (affirming trial court's decision to award rescission in odometer misrepresentation case).

Replace note 342 with:

342   *See* National Consumer Law Center, Unfair and Deceptive Acts and Practices § 8.4.1.5 (6th ed. 2004 and Supp.).

Add to text after subsection's second paragraph:

One decision, however, refuses to award treble damages for the same acts under both the state UDAP statute and a state motor vehicle law.[343.1] Many UDAP statutes also authorize injunctive relief, either by referring to it specifically or by authorizing equitable remedies in general.[343.2]

343.1   Blankenship v. Town & Country Ford, Inc., 622 S.E.2d 638, 642 (N.C. Ct. App. 2005).

343.2   National Consumer Law Center, Unfair and Deceptive Acts and Practices § 8.6.2 (6th ed. 2004 and Supp.).

Replace note 344 with:

344   *See* National Consumer Law Center, Unfair and Deceptive Acts and Practices § 8.8 (6th ed. 2004 and Supp.).

8.5 Federal RICO Claims

8.5.1 Advantages and Disadvantages

Page 233

Replace note 350 with:	350	*See* National Consumer Law Center, Unfair and Deceptive Acts and Practices § 9.2.5.1 (6th ed. 2004 and Supp.).
Addition to note 351.	351	*Replace NCLC citation with*: National Consumer Law Center, Unfair and Deceptive Acts and Practices § 9.2 (6th ed. 2004 and Supp.).

8.5.2 Elements of a RICO Claim

Replace NCLC citation in subsection's second sentence with:

Unfair and Deceptive Acts and Practices § 9.2 (6th ed. 2004 and Supp.)

Page 234

Replace note 357 with:	357	*See* National Consumer Law Center, Unfair and Deceptive Acts and Practices §§ 9.2.3.7.3 (pattern of racketeering activity), 9.2.4 (predicate mail fraud and wire fraud offenses) (6th ed. 2004 and Supp.).
Addition to notes 360, 361.	360	*Replace NCLC citation with*: National Consumer Law Center, Unfair and Deceptive Acts and Practices § 9.2.3.2.3 (6th ed. 2004 and Supp.).
	361	*Replace NCLC citation with*: National Consumer Law Center, Unfair and Deceptive Acts and Practices § 9.2.3.3 (6th ed. 2004 and Supp.).
Replace note 363 with:	363	*See* National Consumer Law Center, Unfair and Deceptive Acts and Practices §§ 9.2.3.7.3 (pattern of racketeering activity), 9.2.4 (predicate mail fraud and wire fraud offenses) (6th ed. 2004 and Supp.).
Replace note 365 with:	365	*See* National Consumer Law Center, Unfair and Deceptive Acts and Practices § 9.2.5.4 (6th ed. 2004 and Supp.).
Addition to note 366.	366	*Replace NCLC citation with*: National Consumer Law Center, Unfair and Deceptive Acts and Practices § 9.2.3.6 (6th ed. 2004 and Supp.).
Replace note 368 with:	368	*See* National Consumer Law Center, Unfair and Deceptive Acts and Practices § 9.2.6.4 (6th ed. 2004 and Supp.).

8.5.3 Application to Automobile Fraud Cases

Page 235

Replace note 370 with:	370	*See* National Consumer Law Center, Unfair and Deceptive Acts and Practices § 9.2.4 (6th ed. 2004 and Supp.).
Addition to notes 371, 380.	371	*But cf.* United States v. Strong, 371 F.3d 225 (5th Cir. 2004) (mailing too remote from fraud when state office mailed documents to headquarters for microfilming after defendant had already accomplished the fraud).
	380	*Add at end of note's first paragraph*: *But see* Krupps v. Tustin Nissan, 2003 WL 1984479, at *1, *2 (Cal. Ct. App. Apr. 30, 2003) (sustaining *demurrer* to RICO claim based on car dealer's misrepresentation of used car as new; plaintiff's unspecific and "conclusory" statements that car dealer had made similar misrepresentations to other customers did not satisfy pattern pleading requirement).
Replace note 381 with:	381	*See* National Consumer Law Center, Unfair and Deceptive Acts and Practices § 9.2.3.2.3 (6th ed. 2004 and Supp.).

8.6 State RICO Claims

Page 236

8.6.1 Overview

Addition to note 386.

386　*Replace NCLC citation with*: National Consumer Law Center, Unfair and Deceptive Acts and Practices Appx. C (6th ed. 2004 and Supp.).

Page 237

8.6.2 Advantages of State RICO Claims over UDAP and Federal RICO Claims

Replace note 391 with:

391　*See generally* National Consumer Law Center, Unfair and Deceptive Acts and Practices § 9.3.9 (6th ed. 2004 and Supp.).

Chapter 9

Litigating Automobile Fraud Cases

9.2 Advising the Automobile Fraud Client

Page 240

9.2.3 How to Return the Vehicle

Add to text after subsection's second paragraph:

When the dealer is likely to attempt to thwart the consumer's attempt to return the vehicle, some attorneys advise their clients to follow a twelve-step procedure:[4.1]

1. Write a note to the dealership's president, stating: "Dear President of [dealership], As stated in my attorney's letter, I am returning your car to you."
2. Date and sign the note.
3. Make two copies of the signed note, one for your attorney, and one for you to keep.
4. Prepare an envelope addressed to: "President of [dealership]" and put the original of the note in the envelope, without sealing the envelope.
5. Remove all personal belongings, paperwork, and other items from the car. Ask a friend to help and to bring a "getaway" car.
6. Drive the getaway car while your friend drives your car and holds the envelope with the note. Early morning may be best if the service department, but not the sales department, is open.
7. Have your friend drive the car onto the dealership's lot, stopping near the front door, *not* on the street.
8. Have your friend take the license plates off the car and hold on to them.
9. Have your friend put the car keys in the envelope with the note and seal it.
10. Have your friend go to the dealership and ask the receptionist or whomever is there to give the envelope to the dealership president. You do not go in—stay in the getaway car.
11. If anyone objects or says things like "you can't do this," or refuses to take the envelope, have the friend just drop the envelope on the floor, turn, and leave. Your friend is not to argue or even talk, other than to ask that the envelope be given to the president. Your friend should *not sign anything*.
12. Drive away in the getaway car.

4.1 This list was developed by Wisconsin attorney Dani Joy and Chicago attorney Dmitry Feofanov, both of whom have extensive consumer law practices.

9.2.5 Asking the Client to Perform the Preliminary Investigation

Add to text at end of subsection's second paragraph:

Obtaining a copy of the client's credit report may provide important details about how the defendant arranged financing and will show if the defendant has made a negative report about the transaction. The attorney may also want the client to visit the defendant's websites and print all screens, and obtain corporate records from the secretary of state and the Securities and Exchange Commission.[6.1]

6.1 *See* § 2.5.1.3, *supra.*

9.2.6 Placing the Attorney-Client Relationship on a Sound Footing

Page 241

Add to text at end of subsection:

Being without a reliable car means that clients who have automobile fraud problems may be more likely than others to change residences or jobs. It is important at the initial interview to secure multiple ways to contact the client, including an e-mail address and the address and telephone number of at least one person outside the client's household who will always be able to reach the client.

9.3 Pleading and Jurisdiction

9.3.1 Selecting Claims to Plead

Add to text after sentence containing note 11:

Most jurisdictions allow any number of claims to be joined in a single case as long as they arise out of the same transaction.[11.1]

> 11.1 *See, e.g.,* Sykes v. Brady-Bushey Ford, Inc., 2005 WL 2787517 (Va. Cir. Ct. Oct. 27, 2005) (contract and tort claims arising from sale of salvage car without disclosure).

Add note 11.2 at end of second sentence of subsection's fifth paragraph.

> 11.2 *See* Wilkins v. Peninsula Motor Cars, Inc., 587 S.E.2d 581 (Va. 2003) (plaintiff may recover actual damages and punitive damages on fraud claim and attorney fees on UDAP claim).

Add to text before sentence containing note 12:

Selecting a fee-shifting claim that will not involve significant factual disputes and can be decided on summary judgment is especially helpful.

Page 242

Add to text before subsection's last paragraph:

Whatever claims are pleaded, many attorneys find it helpful to chart the consumer's claims at an early stage of the case. The chart should show the elements for each cause of action and the law applicable to each defense and each special legal issue.

9.3.3 Federal Jurisdiction

9.3.3.2 Supplemental Jurisdiction over State Law Claims

Page 243

Addition to note 28.

> 28 *See* Robertson v. Crown Auto, Inc., 2006 WL 681000 (W.D. Va. Mar. 14, 2006) (exercising supplemental jurisdiction over claims of state odometer law violations, consumer fraud, and common law fraud).

9.3.4 Personal Jurisdiction over Out-of-State Defendants

Page 244

Add to text at end of subsection's sixth paragraph:

Utah courts had jurisdiction over a Virginia seller who advertised nationally, made misrepresentations to the Utah buyer by telephone, and shipped a car to Utah.[46.1] But Texas did not have jurisdiction over a suit against an Indiana RV dealer that made misrepresentations by telephone to a Texas buyer, where the buyer initiated the transaction, the dealer did not advertise in Texas or on the Internet, the dealer had no physical presence in Texas, and the RV was shipped to the buyer in Texas only because the buyer so requested.[46.2]

A Virginia case held that an out-of-state seller who sold a vehicle to a Virginia resident through an Internet auction was subject to Virginia's long-arm jurisdiction.[46.3] The court held that, because the auction was without reserve, the contract was formed at the time and place of the buyer's winning bid. The court also stressed that the seller was a nationwide commercial seller who had made many previous sales, foresaw out-of-state sales, and delivered the car to Virginia. A Maine court reached a similar conclusion, holding that it had jurisdiction over a Florida seller who advertised a vehicle on an Internet auction without disclosing its collision history, communicated with a Maine consumer about the vehicle, answered his inquiries, prepared the sale paperwork, arranged to ship the vehicle to Maine, complied with Maine's tax and pollution regulations, and negotiated the truck's return when the consumer discovered its defects.[46.4] On the other hand, a New York court had no jurisdiction over a seller when the car was sold through an Internet auction and delivered in Florida.[46.5]

46.1	Lee v. Frank's Garage & Used Cars, Inc., 97 P.3d 717 (Utah Ct. App. 2004).
46.2	Michiana Easy Livin' Country, Inc. v. Holten, 168 S.W.3d 777 (Tex. 2005).
46.3	Malcolm v. Esposito, 2003 WL 23272406 (Va. Cir. Ct. Dec. 12, 2003); *see also* McGuire v. Lavoie, 2003 WL 23174753 (N.D. Tex. Aug. 9, 2003) (finding jurisdiction in Texas when Wisconsin resident offered tractors for sale through Internet auction, then terminated the auction and sold them directly to Texas resident, when seller knew identity and location of buyer). *But cf.* Metcalf v. Lawson, 802 A.2d 1221 (N.H. 2002) (New Hampshire has no jurisdiction over non-commercial E-Bay seller who had no control over who would bid, could not exclude buyers from particular jurisdictions, and may not have learned that buyer was located in New Hampshire until after the sale was final).
46.4	Montalvo v. First Interstate Fin. Corp., 2005 WL 380727 (Me. Super. Ct. Jan. 3, 2005).
46.5	Jones v. Munroe, 773 N.Y.S.2d 498 (N.Y. App. Term 2003).

Addition to notes 49, 51.

49   *Accord Ex parte* Trancalli Chrysler Plymouth Dodge, Inc., 876 So. 2d 459 (Ala. 2003) (Alabama has no jurisdiction over Georgia dealer that Alabama dealer located for Alabama buyer through computerized database locator, when buyer then traveled to Georgia to buy car); Lewis v. Horace Mann Ins. Co., 2003 WL 22251577 (Ohio Ct. App. Oct. 2, 2003) (unpublished) (Ohio does not have jurisdiction over Michigan seller who sold car at Michigan auction to Michigan dealer, who sold it to Ohio company).

51   *See also* Rabiroads v. DFK Leasing Co., 68 F. Supp. 2d 850 (N.D. Ohio 1999) (Ohio does not have jurisdiction over Florida corporation that leased truck in Florida to Ohio resident).

Page 245

Add note 51.1 to end of first sentence of subsection's last paragraph.

51.1   *See* Lewis v. Horace Mann Ins. Co., 2005 WL 3692818 (N.D. Ohio Aug. 23, 2005) (applying Ohio law to consumer's fraud and negligent misrepresentation claims where Illinois-based insurer insured car in Michigan and arranged for car to be sold to there after it was involved in an accident, after which it was auctioned in Michigan and ultimately sold to an Ohio dealer, who sold it to consumer).

Replace note 52 with:

52   *See* National Consumer Law Center, Unfair and Deceptive Acts and Practices § 7.6.3 (6th ed. 2004 and Supp.).

9.3.5 Mandatory Arbitration Clauses

9.3.5.1 General

Replace note 53 with:

53   (4th ed. 2004 and Supp.).

Replace note 54 with:

54   *See* National Consumer Law Center, Consumer Arbitration Agreements § 2.2.1.2 (4th ed. 2004 and Supp.).

Replace the third bulleted item with:

• The consumer never knowingly signed the arbitration agreement (for example, forgery or fraud in the factum).[58] The United States Supreme Court has recently ruled that, where an agreement that includes an arbitration clause is allegedly void, that determination is for the arbitrator, not the court, as long as the reason the contract is alleged to be void does not relate to the arbitration agreement.[58.1]

58   National Consumer Law Center, Consumer Arbitration Agreements § 4.5.2 (4th ed. 2004 and Supp.).

58.1   Buckeye Check Cashing, Inc v. Cardegna, 2006 WL 386362 (U.S. Feb. 21, 2006).

Page 246

Replace note 71 with:

71   *Id.* § 9.3.1.

9.3.5.2 Odometer Act and RICO Claims When Arbitration Agreement Restricts Punitive Damages

Addition to note 76.

76   *Add to PacifiCare Health Sys., Inc. citation*: 538 U.S. 401.

9.3.5.3 Punitive Damages Claims and Arbitration

Addition to note 80.

80   *Add parenthetical to Pinedo citation*: (arbitration clause held to be unconscionable, in part because it barred employee from recovering damages that were provided under employment statutes); *add: See* Hadnot v. Bay, Ltd., 344 F.3d 474 (5th Cir. 2003) (Title VII case); Alexander v. Anthony Int'l, Ltd. P'ship, 341 F.3d 256 (3d Cir. 2003) (employment case); Hausmaninger Benoe Lang Alford & Geselowitz, Certified Public Accountants, Inc. v. Paychex, Inc., 2002 WL 1839273, at *3 (Cal. Ct. App. Aug. 12, 2002) ("the limitations on remedies in the contract are against public policy and render the arbitration clause unenforceable"); Carll v. Terminix Int'l Co., 793 A.2d 921 (Pa. Super. Ct. 2002) (arbitration clause prohibiting direct, indirect, special, incidental, consequential, exemplary, or punitive damages is unconscionable); West Virginia *ex rel.* Dunlap v. Berger, 567 S.E.2d 265 (W. Va. 2002) (arbitration clause prohibiting award of punitive damages is unconscionable). *But see* Brennan v. Bally Total Fitness, 198 F. Supp. 2d 377 (S.D.N.Y. 2002) (not unconscionable for arbitration clause to bar employee from pursuing certain damage remedies, capping certain damage awards, and shortening the limitations period); Veal v. Orkin Exterminating Co., 2001 U.S. Dist. LEXIS 4846 (W.D. Mich. Apr. 9, 2001) ("The fact that the arbitration provision prohibits the recovery of exemplary, treble, liquidated, or punitive damage does not of itself render the contract substantively unreasonable.").

Page 247

Add to text at end of subsection's fifth paragraph:

Of course, if the clause does not explicitly limit punitive damages, the consumer must provide some evidence that arbitration does in fact limit those damages.[83.1]

83.1   *See, e.g.*, Palm Beach Motor Cars Ltd. v. Jeffries, 885 So. 2d 990 (Fla. Dist. Ct. App. 2004).

9.3.5.4 Does the Arbitration Clause Apply to Tort Claims?

Addition to note 85.

85   *See also* King Motor Co. of Ft. Lauderdale v. Jones, 901 So. 2d 1017 (Fla. Dist. Ct. App. 2005); Stacy David, Inc. v. Consuegra, 845 So. 2d 303 (Fla. Dist. Ct. App. 2003); Simpson v. Grimes, 849 So. 2d 740 (La. Ct. App. 2003) (claim of forgery on separate document not covered by broad arbitration clause); Northwest Chrysler Plymouth v. DaimlerChrysler Corp., 2005 WL 1432352 (Mo. Ct. App. June 21, 2005); Scaglione v. Kraftmaid Cabinetry, Inc., 2002 WL 31812941 (Ohio Ct. App. Dec. 13, 2002) (holding that the tortfeasor/victim relationship is inherently separate from the employer/employee relationship).

9.3.5.5 Bringing Punitive Damages Claim Against Deep Pocket That Participated in Fraud, But Was Not Signatory to Arbitration Clause

Replace note 88 with:

88   *See* National Consumer Law Center, Consumer Arbitration Agreements § 6.3 (4th ed. 2004 and Supp.).

9.4 Liability of Potential Defendants

Page 248

9.4.1 Strategic Considerations

Replace note 91 with:

91   *See id.* § 6.3.

9.4.2 Potential Defendants

Replace second bulleted item with:

• The manufacturer, if the case involves lemon laundering or other misdeeds by the manufacturer, or if the dealer who defrauded the consumer was acting as the manufacturer's agent.

Replace note 93 with:

93   National Consumer Law Center, Unfair and Deceptive Acts and Practices § 6.4 (6th ed. 2004 and Supp.).

Add to text after sentence containing note 94:

Adding the entity that financed the sale can complicate the case, but it has some advantages. If the consumer needs to withhold payment in order to pay for alternative transportation and wants to seek a preliminary injunction against negative credit reporting, the financing entity is a necessary party. The financing agency may also be more willing to allow the consumer to substitute a replacement car as collateral for the loan if it is a party. It may place effective pressure on the dealer to resolve the case. Sometimes the financing entity will stipulate that it need not participate in discovery or trial and will be bound by the outcome against the dealer.

Page 249

Replace "Theories" in subsection's last sentence with:

A dealer that treats an individual as its agent, for example, by letting the individual use the dealer's license, can be held liable for fraud perpetrated by the individual even if the dealer is unaware of it.[101.1] Theories

101.1   Westside Investments, Inc. v. Rabizadeh, 2004 WL 1045923 (Cal. Ct. App. May 10, 2004) (unpublished).

9.4.3 Ratification, Acceptance of Benefits, and Civil Conspiracy

Addition to note 106.

106   *See also* Werdann v. Mel Hambelton Ford, Inc., 79 P.3d 1081 (Kan. Ct. App. 2003) (dealer ratified employee's fraud by failing to discipline him and by selling vehicle without applying proceeds to consumer's balance).

Add to text at end of subsection's third paragraph:

Failure to discipline the employee who defrauded the consumer is also evidence of ratification.[106.1]

106.1   Werdann v. Mel Hambelton Ford, Inc., 79 P.3d 1081 (Kan. Ct. App. 2003).

Addition to note 110.

110   *But cf.* Chong v. Parker, 361 F.3d 455 (8th Cir. 2004) (Mo. law) (lender not liable because did not have knowledge of the fraud).

Page 250

Replace note 114 with:

114   *See* National Consumer Law Center, Unfair and Deceptive Acts and Practices § 6.5.2.3 (6th ed. 2004 and Supp.); *see also* Restatement (Second) of Torts § 876 (liability of persons acting in concert).

9.4.4 Recovering from the Creditor for the Dealer's Misconduct

Addition to note 126.

126   *See, e.g.,* Bennett v. D.L. Claborn Buick, Inc., 414 S.E.2d 12 (Ga. Ct. App. 1991) (by virtue of FTC Holder Rule, creditor is liable for auto fraud claims that buyer could have asserted against dealer).

Page 251

Replace note 127 with:

127   *See* National Consumer Law Center, Unfair and Deceptive Acts and Practices § 6.6 (6th ed. 2004 and Supp.).

Addition to notes 129, 130.

129   *Cf.* Eromon v. Grand Auto Sales, Inc., 333 F. Supp. 2d 702 (N.D. Ill. Aug. 4, 2004) (holder is liable for seller's state and federal odometer violations, up to amount paid, but opinion misconstrues holder liability for UDAP violations).

130   *Replace NCLC citation with*: National Consumer Law Center, Unfair and Deceptive Acts and Practices § 6.6.3.4.1 (6th ed. 2004 and Supp.).

Replace note 131 with:

131   *See* National Consumer Law Center, Unfair and Deceptive Acts and Practices § 6.6.4 (6th ed. 2004 and Supp.).

9.4.5 Liability of Car Auction for Acts of Undisclosed Principal

Addition to notes 134, 136.

134   Chambers v. Kensington, 796 So. 2d 733 (La. Ct. App. 2001).

136   *See also* § 6.6.4, *supra* (private remedies for violation of auction statutes).

Page 252

Add to text at end of subsection:

In addition, the Federal Odometer Act prohibits any person from conspiring to violate the disclosure requirements.[143.1] Consequently even those not responsible for making disclosures are still liable under the Act if they assist in the making of improper disclosures. Thus, if an auction fills out the title transfer information for the seller and improperly discloses the mileage, then the auction can be held liable under the Act for statutory and treble damages.

143.1   49 U.S.C. § 32703(4); *see also* § 4.7, *supra*.

Add new subsection to text after § 9.4.5:

9.4.5a On-Line Auctions

Sometimes consumers purchase vehicles through on-line auctions. If the seller posted a false description of the vehicle on the auction's website, the consumer certainly has a claim against the seller. However, a number of courts have held that a federal statute, 15 U.S.C. § 230, protects the auction itself from liability. That statute provides that no provider or user of an interactive computer service shall be treated as the publisher or speaker of any information provided by another content provider. It further provides that no cause of action may be brought and no liability may be imposed under any state or local law that is inconsistent with it.[143.2] A California appellate decision applied this statute to immunize eBay from claims arising from the sale of forged autographed sports memorabilia through its on-line auction.[143.3]

143.2   15 U.S.C. § 230(c)(1), (e)(3).
143.3   Gentry v. eBay, 99 Cal. App. 4th 816, 121 Cal. Rptr. 2d 703 (2002); *cf.* Grace v. eBay, Inc., 16 Cal. Rptr. 3d 192 (Ct. App. 2004) (15 U.S.C. § 230 applies to on-line auction, but does not protect it from common law liability as distributor (as opposed to speaker or publisher) of defamatory statement).

Add new subsection to text after § 9.4.6:

9.4.7 Joint and Several Liability

9.4.7.1 Overview

If the wrongful acts or omissions of more than one entity combine to produce a single injury, it is necessary to determine whether—and how—to allocate liability among the wrongdoers.[148.1] If two tortfeasors are jointly and severally liable, the plaintiff may sue either of them or both of them, and, if the plaintiff recovers a judgment against both of them, may recover partly from one and partly from the other or in full from either.[148.2]

Historically, there were two situations in which each wrongdoer could be held liable for the entire amount of the damages:[148.3]

(1) Concerted action—an agreement, which may be tacit or explicit, to act together to commit a wrongful act, or to use wrongful means to commit a lawful act.

(2) Concurring or consecutive independent acts that result in one indivisible injury.

This subsection will discuss these theories of joint and several liability, their historical scope, and the extensive changes made by state law in the past thirty years. Note that state law today varies widely as to the scope of joint and several liability.[148.4] Most states have replaced it, in at least some situations, with comparative fault, where each wrongdoer, including the plaintiff, if his or her fault contributes to the damage, is assigned a percentage of fault, and is liable for that percentage of the damages.[148.5] Advocates should look closely at their state's statutes, and the cases interpreting them.

9.4.7.2 Concerted Action

The strongest case for joint and several liability is concerted action.[148.6] If persons combine to do wrong, "the act

148.1   This subsection deals only with cases in which each defendant's actions are alleged to be tortious. Vicarious liability, imposed because of a legal relationship to the hands-on wrongdoer—i.e., assignee, principal—is discussed in §§ 9.4.4, 9.4.5, *supra*.
148.2   Dan B. Dobbs, The Law of Torts § 170, at 413 (2002).
148.3   Consumer Prot. Div. v. Morgan, 874 A.2d 919 (Md. 2005) (applying tort concepts to UDAP case; concerted tortfeasors jointly and severally liable; damages to be apportioned among concurrent tortfeasors if possible); 3 Fowler Harper, Fleming James & Oscar Gray, The Law of Torts § 10.1 (2d ed. 1986).

148.4   *See generally* Restatement (Third) of Torts: Apportionment of Liability (2000). Section 17 notes that there is "no majority rule," describes the basic types of state statute, and lists the states having each type.
148.5   Dan B. Dobbs, The Law of Torts §§ 385, 389 (2002); *see, e.g.,* Ariz. Rev. Stat. Ann. § 12-2506; Cal. Civ. Code § 1431.2 (West); Colo. Rev. Stat. § 13-21-111.5; Conn. Gen. Stat. § 52-572h(g), (h), (o); Fla. Stat. § 768.81; 735 Ill. Comp. Stat. § 5/2-1117; Kan. Stat. Ann. § 60-258a; Ky. Rev. Stat. Ann. § 411.182 (West); Mich. Comp. Laws § 600.6304(6)(b); Neb. Rev. Stat. § 25-21,185.10; N.Y. C.P.L.R. 1600–1603 (McKinney); Or. Rev. Stat. § 31.600 to 31.610; Vt. Stat. Ann. tit. 12, § 1036; Wash. Rev. Code § 4.22.070; Wyo. Stat. Ann. § 1-1-109.
148.6   Woods v. Cole, 693 N.E.2d 333 (Ill. 1998) (comparative fault statute inapplicable to tortfeasors who act in concert; legal relationship among them makes "the act of one the act of all"); Dan B. Dobbs, The Law of Torts § 385 (2000); Restatement (Third) of Torts: Apportionment of Liability § 15 (2000).

of one is the act of all" and each wrongdoer is liable for the entire damages.[148.7] A formal agreement need not be shown, unless a state statute so requires; "tacit agreement" may be implied from a course of conduct.[148.8]

Some comparative fault statutes explicitly do not apply to concerted action cases, although the exception may be narrow.[148.9] Courts in other states have construed the statute to exclude concerted action.[148.10]

Courts have reached varying results on the question whether there can be concerted action in a negligence case. One court held that there can, where the officers and directors of a defunct savings and loan had formally agreed to unacceptably risky lending practices.[148.11] Other cases, and at least one statute, allow concerted action liability only for intentional torts.[148.12] Most states explicitly recognize causes of action for civil conspiracy or aiding and abetting tortious conduct.[148.13]

9.4.7.3 Concurring or Consecutive Individual Acts

Historically, if several independent acts resulted in one indivisible wrong, each wrongdoer was liable for the full amount of damages.[148.14] The burden was on the defendants to show that damages could be apportioned to one or another wrongdoer.[148.15] This is still the rule in about fourteen states.[148.16]

Comparative fault statutes,[148.17] which focus on percentage of fault rather than percentage of damages, are a response to the perceived injustice of requiring a minimally faulty, but solvent, defendant to pay for the more serious

---

148.7 Woods v. Cole, 693 N.E.2d 333 (Ill. 1998) (comparative fault statute inapplicable to tortfeasors who act in concert; legal relationship among them makes "the act of one the act of all"); Sieben v. Sieben, 646 P.2d 1036 (Kan. 1982) ("comparative fault statute" does not change common law rule that defendants found liable in intentional tort actions are jointly and severally liable); Consumer Prot. Div. v. Morgan, 874 A.2d 919 (Md. 2005) (applying tort concepts to UDAP case; concerted tortfeasors jointly and severally liable; damages to be apportioned among concurrent tortfeasors if possible); Neal v. Bavarian Motors, Inc., 882 A.2d 1022 (Pa. Super. Ct. 2005) (car dealer and finance company who "acted in concert" to sell stolen car jointly and severally liable to innocent purchaser); Restatement (Second) of Torts § 876 (1979); Restatement (Third) of Torts: Apportionment of Liability § 15 (2000).

148.8 Resolution Trust Co. v. Heiserman, 898 P.2d 1049 (Colo. 1995); Neal v. Bavarian Motors, Inc., 882 A.2d 1022 (Pa. Super. Ct. 2005) (car dealer and finance company who "acted in concert" to sell stolen car jointly and severally liable to innocent purchaser; dealer who "knew or should have known" of theft was more culpable, but finance company's failure to comply with required procedures was "inexcusable").

148.9 Ariz. Rev. Stat. Ann. § 12-2506 (conscious agreement to common plan to engage in intentional tort and substantial participation in the tort; substantial assistance to intentional tortfeasor insufficient in absence of conscious agreement); Colo. Rev. Stat. § 13-21-111.5 (tortfeasors consciously conspire and deliberately pursue common plan); Neb. Rev. Stat. § 25-21,185.10 (acting in concert as part of a common enterprise or plan); N.Y. C.P.L.R. 1602(10) (McKinney) (acting knowingly or intentionally and in concert to produce the act or failure upon which liability is based); Wash. Rev. Code § 4.22.070(1)(a) ("acting in concert").

148.10 Woods v. Cole, 693 N.E.2d 333 (Ill. 1998) (legal relationship among concerted tortfeasors makes act of one the act of all; comparative fault statute inapplicable); Sieben v. Sieben, 646 P.2d 1036 (Kan. 1982) ("comparative fault statute" does not change common law rule that defendants found liable in intentional tort actions are jointly and severally liable); *see also* Restatement (Third) of Torts: Apportionment of Liability § 15 (2000).

148.11 Resolution Trust Co. v. Heiserman, 898 P.2d 1049 (Colo. 1995).

148.12 Ariz. Rev. Stat. Ann. § 12-2506.

148.13 *See, e.g.*, Aetna Cas. & Sur. Co. v. Leahey Constr. Co., 219 F.3d 519 (6th Cir. 2000) (prediction of Ohio law; elements include

actual knowledge and substantial assistance); Rice v. Paladin Entrs., Inc., 128 F.3d 233 (4th Cir. 1997) (Md. law) (civil cause of action for aiding and abetting tortious conduct); Banks v. Consumer Home Mortgage Inc., 2003 WL 21251584 (E.D.N.Y 2003) (elements of claim for aiding and abetting fraud are fraud (with usual elements), actor's knowledge, and "substantial assistance" by the aider and abettor); Lewis v. Lead Indus. Ass'n, 793 N.W.2d 869 (Ill. 2003) (defining civil conspiracy as the combination of two or more persons or entities for the purpose of accomplishing by concerted action, either an unlawful purpose, or a lawful purpose by unlawful means; must show that one party to the agreement has committed a tortious act in furtherance of the agreement). *See generally* § 9.4.3, *supra*; National Consumer Law Center, Unfair and Deceptive Acts and Practices § 6.5.2.3 (6th ed. 2004 and Supp.); Restatement (Second) of Torts § 876(b) (1979).

148.14 Dan B. Dobbs, The Law of Torts §§ 171, 174, 385 (2000); Fowler Harper, Fleming James & Oscar Gray, The Law of Torts § 10.1 (1986 and Supp.); Restatement (Second) of Torts § 879 (1979).

148.15 Consumer Prot. Div. v. Morgan, 874 A.2d 919 (Md. 2005) (compares concerted and concurrent tortfeasors; concurrent tortfeasors jointly and severally liable only for "single indivisible injury," that is, if allocation impractical); Restatement (Second) of Torts § 433B (1979).

148.16 Nance v. Miami Sand & Gravel, 825 N.E.2d 826 (Ind. Ct. App. 2005) (for joint and several liability, in absence of agency relationship, must show either concerted action to accomplish a wrong or independent acts that combine to produce a single injury); Paine v. Spottiswoode, 612 A.2d 235 (Me. 1992) (where separate and independent acts of negligence result in single indivisible injury, all are liable); Consumer Prot. Div. v. Morgan, 874 A.2d 919 (Md. 2005) (applying tort concepts to UDAP case; allocation is possible because UDAP damages are amount of each wrongdoer's own ill-gotten gain); Strahin v. Cleavenger, 603 S.E.2d 197 (W. Va. 2004) (West Virginia "committed to the concept of joint and several liability;" persons whose "wrongful acts or omissions, whether committed intentionally or negligently, concur to cause injury are . . . jointly and severally liable").

The comments to *Restatement (Third) of Torts: Apportionment of Liability* § 17 (2000) list the following "pure joint and several liability" states: Alabama, Arkansas, Delaware, District of Columbia, Maine, Maryland, Massachusetts, Minnesota, North Carolina, Pennsylvania, Rhode Island, South Carolina, South Dakota, Virginia, West Virginia.

148.17 *Restatement (Third) of Torts: Apportionment of Damages* § 17 (2000) describes the basic types of state statutes, and lists the states having each type.

misconduct of a judgment-proof co-defendant. When the result is to shift the burden of an uncollectible judgment to an even less faulty plaintiff, one may question whether this approach is any fairer. Some state statutes provide that if a judgment against one defendant is uncollectible, that share of the damages may be reallocated among the other defendants, still in proportion to their share of fault.[148.18] Some comparative fault statutes establish a threshold percentage, below which a defendant will not be jointly liable,[148.19] others provide different rules for different types of damages,[148.20] and some eliminate joint and several liability altogether.[148.21] Many apply only to negligence claims or to certain specified causes of action.

One difficult problem, as to which state legislatures and courts have reached varying results, is whether to allocate liability where one defendant acted negligently and another acted intentionally.[148.22] Allocation in such cases may be

especially harsh if the intentional wrongdoer, to whom a large share of fault must be allocated, is missing, incarcerated, or simply judgment-proof. The *Restatement (Third) of Torts* takes the position that one who is liable for failure to protect another from "the specific risk of an intentional tort" is jointly liable for the intentional wrongdoer's share of comparative responsibility.[148.23] Courts following this rule hold that "[n]egligent tortfeasors should not be allowed to reduce their fault by the intentional fault of another that they had a duty to prevent."[148.24] This rule applies only where the other tortfeasor acted intentionally,[148.25] and the risk must be specific.[148.26]

148.18 *See, e.g.,* Conn. Gen. Stat.§ 52-572h; Mich. Comp. Laws § 600.6304(6)(b); Or. Rev. Stat. § 31.610.

148.19 735 Ill. Comp. Stat. § 5/2-1117 (25%); N.Y. C.P.L.R. 1600–1603 (McKinney) (50%).

148.20 Cal. Civ. Code § 1431.2 (West) (non-economic damages allocated by percentage of fault); 735 Ill. Comp. Stat. § 5/2-1117 (defendant less than 25% at fault is only severally liable for non-medical damages; note that all defendants are jointly and severally liable for medical expenses); Neb. Rev. Stat. § 25-21,185.10 (in absence of concerted action, liability is joint and several for economic damages, comparative fault for non-economic).

148.21 The comments to *Restatement (Third) of Torts: Apportionment of Liability* § 17 (2000) list the following purely several liability states: Alaska Stat. § 09.17.080; Ariz. Rev. Stat. Ann. § 12-2506; Colo. Rev. Stat. § 13-22-111.5; Idaho Code Ann. § 6-803; Ind. Code § 34-4-33-5; Kan. Stat. Ann. § 60-258(a); Ky. Rev. Stat. Ann. § 411.182 (West); La. Civ. Code Ann. art. 2323; Mich. Comp. Laws § 600.6304; Nev. Rev. Stat. § 41.141; N.M. Stat. § 41-3A-1; N.D. Cent. Code § 32.03.2; Tennessee ("judicially adopted"); Vt. Stat. Ann. tit. 12, § 1036; Wyo. Stat. Ann. § 1-1-109.

148.22 *Slack v. Farmers Ins. Exch.,* 5 P.3d 280 (Colo. 2000) (apportionment required regardless of kind of fault); *Bhinder v. Sun Co.,* 819 A.2d 822 (Conn. 2003) (Connecticut statute, Conn. Gen. Stat. § 52-572h(o), allows apportionment only for negligence; franchisor of gas station which negligently failed to protect employees from crime not entitled to have its share of fault reduced by that of robber who killed cashier); *Blazovic v. Andrich,* 590 A.2d 222 (N.J. 1991) (collection of cases on both sides of issue; defendant entitled to have fault apportioned among all defendants, whether their conduct was negligent, reckless or intentional); *Shin v. Sunriver Preparatory Sch., Inc.,* 111 P.3d 762 (Or. Ct. App. 2005) (negligence different in kind

from intentional fault; boarding school that negligently failed to supervise student's visit with abusive father not entitled to apportionment); *Tegman v. Accident & Med. Investigations, Inc.,* 75 P.3d 497 (Wash. 2003) (lawyer who negligently enabled non-lawyer's unauthorized practice and theft not liable for share of fault attributed to non-lawyer's intentional torts); *Teton County Sheriff's Dep't v. Bassett,* 8 P.3d 1079 (Wyo. 2000) (apportionment required regardless of kind of fault); Allen L. Schwarz, Annotation, *Application of Comparative Negligence Principles to Intentional Torts,* 18 A.L.R.5th 525 (1994).

148.23 *Restatement (Third) of Torts: Apportionment of Liability* § 14 (2000).

148.24 *Kan. State Bank & Trust Co. v. Specialized Transp. Services, Inc.,* 819 P.2d 587 (Kan. 1991); *see also Merrill Crossings Assocs. v. McDonald,* 705 So. 2d 560 (Fla. 1998) (negligent tortfeasor may not reduce fault by shifting it to another tortfeasor whose intentional criminal conduct was a foreseeable result of its negligence); *Veazey v. Elmwood Plantation Associates, Ltd.,* 650 So. 2d 712 (La. 1994) (La. law allows apportionment among negligent and intentional tortfeasors, but public policy requires that negligent tortfeasors not be allowed to reduce liability by share of intentional tortfeasor whose actions they had duty to prevent; negligent landlord jointly liable for share of fault assigned to unidentified rapist). *But see Netseway v. City of Tempe,* 909 P.2d 441 (Ariz. Ct. App. 1995) (comparative fault even where duty to prevent intentional tort; here, municipal police who failed to block intersection when high-speed chase approaching); *Blazovic v. Andrich,* 590 A.2d 222 (N.J. 1991) (apportionment allowed, even though defendant bar had duty to protect plaintiff customer against attack by co-defendant fellow customer); *Barth v. Coleman,* 878 P.2d 319 (N.M. 1994) (same).

148.25 *Wood v. Groh,* 7 P.3d 1163 (Kan. 2000) (comparative fault applied if defendant negligently allowed gun to fall into hands of teenager who negligently shot plaintiff); *Marceaux v. Gibbs,* 699 So. 2d 1065 (La. 1997) (comparative fault applied where escaping prisoner drove negligently when fleeing from negligently supervised work crew).

148.26 *Restatement (Third) of Torts: Apportionment of Liability* § 14, illus. 2, 3, 5 (2000).

9.5 Discovery

9.5.1 Discovery Should Begin Before Suit Is Filed

Page 253

Add note 148.1 at end of first sentence of subsection's second paragraph.

148.1 *See* §§ 2.2, 2.5, 9.2.5, *supra* (investigating auto fraud cases).

Add note 148.2 at end of second sentence of subsection's third paragraph.

148.2   *See, e.g.*, Lang v. Super. Ct., 826 P.2d 1228 (Ariz. Ct. App. 1992) (discussing ethical rules and split among states).

9.5.2 Items to Seek in Formal Discovery

Add to text after subsection's first paragraph:

Whether documents are obtained by document request or subpoena, it is important to ask for the originals rather than copies. It is easier to detect alterations and forgeries on originals than on copies. In addition, handwritten notes can often be found on the backs of the original documents.

Add to text after subsection's second paragraph:

If forgery is an issue, it is useful to send interrogatories asking the dealer to identify all persons, whether employees or others, who either saw or claim to have seen the consumer sign the document in question. A second interrogatory can ask for the identities of everyone who saw or claims to have seen the consumer on or about the dealership property during the time the documents were purportedly signed. Getting the original rather than a copy of the document with the forged signature may be essential if a handwriting expert is to examine the document. Suggestions about using handwriting experts may be found in § 9.8.6.4, *infra*.

Addition to note 152.

152   *Replace cross-reference at end of note with: See also* § 9.8.1.1, *infra. Add: Accord* Iosello v. Lawrence, 2004 WL 1194741 (N.D. Ill. May 26, 2004) (identities of credit repair organization's other clients discoverable in class action; not protected as confidential proprietary information or by attorney-client privilege); Salmeron v. Highlands Ford Sales, Inc., 220 F.R.D. 667 (D.N.M. 2003); Marks v. Global Mortgage Group Inc., 218 F.R.D. 492 (S.D. W. Va. 2003) (Gramm-Leach-Bliley Act does not prevent disclosure of identifying information about other customers in response to discovery); *Ex parte* Nat'l W. Life Ins. Co., 899 So. 2d 218 (Ala. 2004) (Gramm-Leach-Bliley Act does not prevent financial institution from being compelled by court order to produce customers' non-public personal information; court should issue protective orders to protect customers' privacy); *Ex parte* Mut. Sav. Life Ins. Co., 899 So. 2d 986 (Ala. 2004) (judicial process exception in Gramm-Leach-Bliley Act allows court to order insurance company to produce other customers' applications without providing opt-out notice to those customers; court should issue protective orders to protect other customers' information); Colonial Life & Accident Ins. Co. v. Super. Ct., 31 Cal. 3d 785, 183 Cal. Rptr. 810, 647 P.2d 86 (1982) (names, addresses, and files of other claimants discoverable through trial court's procedure of sending letters to claimants; relevant for punitive damages and to meet Unfair Insurance Practices statute requirement that insurer's unfair claims settlement practices be a general business practice); Flores v. Super. Ct., 2002 WL 1613845 (Cal. Ct. App. July 19, 2002) (unpublished) (identities of other customers discoverable, subject to appropriate orders to protect privacy and trade secrets); Fla. First Fin. Group v. De Castro, 815 So. 2d 789 (Fla. Dist. Ct. App. 2002) (ordering debt collector to produce records of correspondence and telephone calls to other debtors does not violate privacy protections of state and federal debt collection laws); Martino v. Barnett, 595 S.E.2d 65 (W. Va. 2004) (neither state insurance law nor Gramm-Leach-Bliley Act precludes party from obtaining information about other customers through discovery); *see also* Grange Mut. Ins. Co. v. Trude, 151 S.W.3d 803 (Ky. 2004) (discovery regarding similar claims is relevant in bad faith insurance suit); *In re* Lexington Ins. Co., 2004 WL 210576 (Tex. App. Feb. 2, 2004) (unpublished) (Gramm-Leach-Bliley Act does not prevent court from ordering insurance company to produce denial letters with identifying information redacted).

Add to text at end of subsection's third paragraph:

Tips for successfully compelling this discovery are discussed in § 9.5.4, *infra*. Regardless of what discovery produces the consumer's attorney should also conduct an independent investigation to uncover pattern evidence.

Add to text at end of subsection's fourth paragraph:

Another approach is to have a neutral person mail a notice to each customer, advising them of the issue in litigation and instructing them to lodge an objection if they want to maintain their privacy.

Page 254

Replace "a relevant factor" in sentence containing note 156 with:

a relevant factor in many states

Addition to note 156.

156   *But see* Utah Code Ann. § 78-18-1 (prima facie case must be made that award of punitive damages is reasonably probably before discovery of a party's wealth may be conducted; exceptions for cases involving operating boat or vehicle while intoxicated).

Add to text at end of subsection:

Most courts hold that a litigant may discover financial information without first having to make out a prima facie case of entitlement to punitive damages.[156.1]

Another item to seek in discovery is the dealer's correspondence, if any, with its bonding company about the claim. Dealers often make important admissions in this correspondence.

156.1   Krenning v. Hunter Health Clinic, Inc., 166 F.R.D. 33 (D. Kan. 1996); Caruso v. Coleman Co., 157 F.R.D. 344 (E.D. Pa. 1994).

9.5.3 *Making the Most of Available Discovery Techniques*

Add to text after subsection's second paragraph:

Another consideration is whether the jurisdiction places limits on certain types of discovery requests. The number of interrogatories may be limited, for example, but not the number of document requests or requests for admission. Requests for admission can be very effective in establishing facts, especially when the proponent has a good idea of what the true facts are.

Add note 158.1 to end of second sentence of subsection's third paragraph.

158.1   A sample notice of a 30(b)(6) deposition may be found on the CD-Rom accompanying this volume.

Add to text at end of subsection's third paragraph:

It is important to schedule the deposition of the defendant so that there is time to follow up with additional discovery to deal with any defenses or issues that the deposition reveals.

9.5.4 *Preparing for Discovery Battles*

Page 255

Add to text after fourth sentence of subsection's fourth paragraph:

To rebut the defendant's claim that production would be too burdensome, the consumer's attorney should offer to do the clerical work such as pulling files and making copies.

Addition to note 159.

159   *Replace first NCLC Consumer Law Pleadings citation with*: National Consumer Law Center, Consumer Law Pleadings No. 1, § 3.2 (Cumulative CD-Rom and Index Guide); *replace second NCLC Consumer Law Pleadings citation with*: National Consumer Law Center, Consumer Law Pleadings No. 2, § 6.2.2 (Cumulative CD-Rom and Index Guide).

9.5.5 *The Defendant's Deposition of the Consumer Plaintiff*

Add to text after subsection's first paragraph:

In preparation for the deposition, the client should be advised to listen carefully to the questions, and not to answer unless the meaning of the question is clear; to answer only what is asked, without elaboration or rambling; and not to get upset or argue with the opposing attorney. Clients should be instructed not to bring anything to the deposition—correspondence, documents, receipts, even a purse or wallet—that they would mind showing to the opposing attorney. It may be appropriate to instruct the client to prepare and bring a list of certain specific facts that are likely to come up in the deposition, such as the vehicle's mileage or a list of all the things that are wrong with the car.

Page 256

Add to text at end of subsection:

With respect to emotional distress damages or punitive damages it is usually best for the plaintiff not to name a specific figure, but instead to refer to "whatever the jury feels is appropriate," or some similar phrase.

9.5.6 *Videotaping the Deposition*

9.5.6.1 Right to Videotape the Deposition

Replace subsection's second and third sentences with:

Federal Rule of Civil Procedure 30(b)(2) states that the deposition may be recorded by sound-and-visual means, and the party taking the deposition shall bear the cost of the recording. Rule 30(b)(3) states that with prior notice, any party may designate another method to record the deponent's testimony in addition to that specified by the person taking the deposition.

9.7 Class Actions

Page 257

9.7.1 *General*

Addition to note 173.

173 *Replace Gridley v. State Farm citation with*: *But cf.* Gridley v. State Farm Mut. Auto. Ins. Co., 840 N.E.2d 269 (Ill. 2005) (Louisiana resident cannot bring Louisiana class action for title laundering against Illinois-based insurer under Illinois UDAP statute, because claim arose in Louisiana; unjust enrichment claim must also be litigated in Louisiana).

Page 259

9.7.3 *Claims to Assert in Automobile Fraud Class Actions*

Replace note 186 with:

186 *See* National Consumer Law Center, Unfair and Deceptive Acts and Practices §§ 8.5, 9.2.7.3 (6th ed. 2004 and Supp.).

Addition to note 190.

190 *Replace NCLC UDAP citation with*: National Consumer Law Center, Unfair and Deceptive Acts and Practices §§ 8.5.4.2.2, 8.5.4.2.9 (6th ed. 2004 and Supp.).

Page 260

9.7.4 *Naming Appropriate Defendants*

Replace note 194 with:

194 *See* § 9.4.4, *supra*; National Consumer Law Center, Unfair and Deceptive Acts and Practices § 6.6.3 (6th ed. 2004 and Supp.).

9.7.5 *Class Pleadings and Certification*

Add note 196.1 at end of first sentence of subsection's last paragraph.

196.1 Fed. R. Civ. P. 23(c)(1)(C) was revised, effective Dec. 1, 2003, to delete the provision for conditional class certification but to provide that an order granting or denying class certification can be amended at any time up until final judgment.

9.8 Evidentiary Issues

9.8.1 *Evidence of Other Bad Acts*

Page 261

9.8.1.1 General

Add to text after sentence containing note 201:

These are not "other" acts.[201.1]

201.1 Elliot v. Turner Constr. Co., 381 F.3d 995 (10th Cir. 2004) (acts that are part of the same tortious event are not "other" acts, so Rule 404(b) analysis is unnecessary).

Add to text after sentence containing note 203:

If the case involves a claim of conspiracy, other conspirators' acts in furtherance of the conspiracy are not "other" acts but are central to the conspiracy, so the restrictions on admissibility of evidence of other acts are inapplicable.[203.1]

203.1 U.S. v. Gibbs, 190 F.3d 188, 217–18 (3d Cir. 1999).

Addition to note 205.

205   *See* Taylor v. Bennett Chevrolet/Buick, Inc., 609 S.E.2d 215 (Ga. Ct. App. 2005) (nondisclosure of extent of damage to a used car not similar enough to sale of wrecked car as new). *But see* Lee v. Hodge, 882 P.2d 408, 411 (Ariz. 1994) (other acts need not always be substantially similar to those alleged by plaintiff, although they must be similar if introduced to show intent or absence of mistake; when plaintiff alleged that repair shop intentionally damaged car, prior incidents of damaging customer's car are admissible, but not bribery and overcharges).

Add to text at end of subsection's fourth paragraph:

The list of permissible purposes in the federal rule is illustrative rather than exhaustive.[207.1]

207.1   Fed. R. Evid. 404(b) (using term "such as").

Addition to note 208.

208   Lee v. Hodge, 882 P.2d 408, 412, 413 (Ariz. 1994) (prior acts evidence is critical for proving intent; while it may be harmful to defendant, there is no unfair prejudice).

Page 262

Add to text at end of subsection's eighth paragraph:

Proof might also be simplified by using requests for admission or stipulations once discovery has uncovered the other acts. A chart or summary of the similar transactions, admissible under Federal Rule of Evidence 1006, is another good way to simplify the evidence and also keeps the other acts prominent in the jury's mind.

If the admissibility of other acts evidence is not completely resolved prior to trial, it may be helpful to prepare a short brief on the question to give to the court when the opponent objects to the evidence. The consumer's attorney might even bring two briefs, one arguing for admissibility as part of the consumer's affirmative case, and one for admissibility as rebuttal evidence if the defendant opens the door by claiming that the actions toward the consumer were an innocent mistake or that the dealer always follows proper procedures. If the trial court refuses to admit the evidence, the consumer's attorney should make sure to follow the jurisdictional requirements for preserving the error, such as making a proffer of the evidence.

Addition to note 217.

217   Cory v. Aztec Steel Building, Inc., 225 F.R.D. 667 (D. Kan. 2005) (ordering discovery of other buyers' identities for UDAP and RICO claims despite seller's privacy objections); Salmeron v. Highlands Ford Sales, Inc., 220 F.R.D. 667 (D.N.M. 2003) (ordering defendant auto dealer to produce names and contact information for other consumers who bought former daily rental vehicles, when court-supervised questionnaire to those buyers had produced only fourteen percent response rate); Colonial Life & Accident Ins. Co. v. Super. Ct., 31 Cal. 3d 785, 183 Cal. Rptr. 810, 647 P.2d 86 (1982) (names, addresses, and files of other claimants discoverable through trial court's procedure of sending letters to claimants; relevant for punitive damages and to meet Unfair Insurance Practices statute requirement that insurer's unfair claims settlement practices be a general business practice); Fla. First Fin. Group v. De Castro, 815 So. 2d 789 (Fla. Dist. Ct. App. 2002) (ordering debt collector to produce records of correspondence and telephone calls to other debtors does not violate privacy protections of state and federal debt collection laws); Stokes v. Nat'l Presto Indus., Inc., 2005 WL 831363 (Mo. Ct. App. Apr. 12, 2005) (other accidents involving same type of product were relevant to product liability and negligence claims, and trial court erred in denying discovery); *see also In re* Ocwen Fed. Bank, 872 So. 2d 810 (Ala. 2003) (requiring lender to produce customer lists and list of complaints against it); Grange Mut. Ins. Co. v. Trude, 151 S.W.3d 803 (Ky. 2004) (discovery regarding similar claims is relevant in bad faith insurance suit); Schmitt v. Lalancette, 830 A.2d 16 (Vt. 2003) (trial court abused discretion in ordering plaintiff not to contact other customers of defendant and was unjustified in denying discovery of other customers' identities). *But cf.* Roberts v. Shawnee Mission Ford, Inc., 352 F.3d 358 (8th Cir. 2003) (denying discovery of vehicle sales made by dealer not involved in sale to plaintiff, even though an employee of that dealership was allegedly involved in rolling back odometer of plaintiff's car).

Add to text after sentence containing note 217:

The Gramm-Leach-Bliley Act does not prevent disclosure of the identities of other customers.[217.1]

217.1   Marks v. Global Mortgage Group Inc., 218 F.R.D. 492 (S.D. W. Va. 2003); Martino v. Barnett, 595 S.E.2d 65 (W. Va. 2004) (neither state insurance law nor Gramm-Leach-Bliley Act precludes party from obtaining information about other customers through discovery).

9.8.1.2 To Show Intent or Motive

Addition to note 219.

219   Jannotta v. Subway Sandwich Shops, Inc., 125 F.3d 503, 517 (7th Cir. 1997) (other incidents of fraud "highly probative" of intent); Salmeron v. Highlands Ford Sales, Inc., 220 F.R.D. 667 (D.N.M. 2003)

(other incidents are "highly relevant" to prove intent); Lee v. Hodge, 882 P.2d 408, 411–413 (Ariz. 1994); Murdock v. Godwin, 154 Ga. App. 824, 826, 269 S.E.2d 905 (1980); Medina v. Town & Country Ford, Inc., 355 S.E.2d 831 (N.C. Ct. App. 1987), *aff'd without opinion*, 364 S.E.2d 140 (N.C. 1988).

Page 263

Replace note 221 with:

221   *See* National Consumer Law Center, Unfair and Deceptive Acts and Practices §§ 4.2.4, 8.4.2.3.1 (6th ed. 2004 and Supp.).

Addition to note 222.

222   Carter v. Mueller, 120 Ill. App. 3d 314, 457 N.E.2d 1335, 1340–41 (1983) (misrepresentation regarding condition of apartment). *See also* United States v. Verduzco, 373 F.3d 1022 (9th Cir. 2004) (admissible to prove intent as rebuttal of defendant's duress defense).

9.8.1.3 To Show Preparation or Plan

Addition to notes 224, 225.

224   United States v. DeCicco, 370 F.3d 206 (1st Cir. 2004) (evidence of defendant's prior attempts to burn down warehouse admissible to show plan to commit arson).

225   *See also* United States v. Tse, 375 F.3d 148 (1st Cir. 2004).

Add to text after sentence containing note 225:

In fact, the acts of co-conspirators are not "other acts" at all, but are an essential part of plaintiff's proof of the conspiracy claim.[225.1]

225.1   United States v. Gibbs, 190 F.3d 188, 217, 218 (3d Cir. 1999).

Addition to note 226.

226   *See* § 9.4.3, *supra*; National Consumer Law Center, Unfair and Deceptive Acts and Practices § 6.4.2 (6th ed. 2004 and Supp.).

Page 264

9.8.1.4 To Show Knowledge

Addition to notes 228, 229, 233.

228   *Add to White citation: as amended by* 335 F.3d 833 (9th Cir. 2003).

229   *Replace NCLC citation with*: National Consumer Law Center, Unfair and Deceptive Acts and Practices §§ 6.4, 6.5 (6th ed. 2004 and Supp.).

233   *See also* Vista Resorts, Inc. v. Goodyear Tire & Rubber Co., 2004 WL 2609563 (Colo. Ct. App. Nov. 18, 2004) (evidence of other customers' complaints admissible to show manufacturer's knowledge of defect).

9.8.1.5 To Show Absence of Mistake or Accident

Addition to note 234.

234   Marks v. Global Mortgage Group Inc., 218 F.R.D. 492 (S.D. W. Va. 2003) (admissible to show pattern or practice); Lee v. Hodge, 882 P.2d 408, 411–413 (Ariz. 1994) (prior instances when repair shop damaged customer's car shows it was not a mistake; laws of probability make it unlikely all three occasions were accidents); Medina v. Town & Country Ford, Inc., 355 S.E.2d 831 (N.C. Ct. App. 1987), *aff'd without opinion*, 364 S.E.2d 140 (N.C. 1988); *see also* Andrews v. City & County of San Francisco, 205 Cal. App. 3d 938, 252 Cal. Rptr. 716 (1988) (evidence of prior assaults by police officer admissible to show that arrestee's injuries were not accidental).

Add to text at end of subsection:

Similarly, it should also be admissible to rebut any bona fide error defense under a consumer protection statute. Even if the trial court has refused to admit evidence of other acts as part of the consumer's affirmative case, it may admit the evidence to rebut a claim by the dealer that the actions that harmed the plaintiff were just an accident or mistake.

9.8.1.6 To Show Habit or Routine Practice

Addition to notes 235, 236.

235   *See* Carter v. Mueller, 120 Ill. App. 3d 314, 457 N.E.2d 1335, 1340–41 (1983) (admissible to show modus operandi).

236   *See* Marks v. Global Mortgage Group Inc., 218 F.R.D. 492 (S.D. W. Va. 2003) (admissible to show pattern or practice).

9.8.1.7 To Support Punitive Damages Claims

Replace "BMW" in sentence containing note 237 with:

BMW of North America, Inc.

Addition to note 238.

238   Salmeron v. Highlands Ford Sales, Inc., 220 F.R.D. 667 (D.N.M. 2003); Brockman v. Regency Fin. Corp., 124 S.W.3d 43 (Mo. Ct. App. 2004) (malicious prosecution action arising from vehicle deficiency judgment suit); *see also* Jannotta v. Subway Sandwich Shops, Inc., 125 F.3d 503, 517 (7th Cir. 1997); Colonial Life & Accident Ins. Co. v. Super. Ct., 31 Cal. 3d 785, 183 Cal. Rptr. 810, 647 P.2d 86 (1982).

Replace note 239 with:

239   State Farm Mut. Auto. Ins. Co. v. Campbell, 538 U.S. 408, 123 S. Ct. 1513, 155 L. Ed. 2d 585 (2003).

9.8.1.8 Admissibility Under RICO and UDAP Statutes

Replace note 241 with:

241   *See* National Consumer Law Center, Unfair and Deceptive Acts and Practices §§ 9.2, 9.3 (6th ed. 2004 and Supp.).

Addition to note 242.

242   *See also* Colonial Life & Accident Ins. Co. v. Super. Ct., 31 Cal. 3d 785, 183 Cal. Rptr. 810, 647 P.2d 86 (1982) (relevant to meet Unfair Insurance Practices statute requirement that insurer's unfair claims settlement practices be a general business practice); Cisneros v. U.D. Registry, Inc., 39 Cal. App. 4th 548, 564, 46 Cal. Rptr. 2d 233 (1995) (plaintiffs who seek injunction against unfair business practice are entitled to present evidence of similar practices involving other consumers).

Add to text at end of subsection:

Some UDAP statutes apply only to entities that are engaged in the business of entering into consumer transactions.[242.1] Evidence of other transactions is relevant to show that a seller meets this standard.[242.2]

242.1   *See* National Consumer Law Center, Unfair and Deceptive Acts and Practices § 2.3.4 (6th ed. 2004 and Supp.).

242.2   Black v. Iovino, 219 Ill. App. 3d 378, 580 N.E.2d 139 (1991).

9.8.1.9 Impeachment

Addition to note 243.

243   *See also* Andrews v. City & County of San Francisco, 205 Cal. App. 3d 938, 252 Cal. Rptr. 716 (1988) (evidence of prior assaults by police officer admissible to impeach his testimony that he was a patient man who exercised restraint when booking arrestees; error to exclude this evidence because of possible prejudice, because it would leave officer's testimony unrebutted); Gingerich v. Kline, 75 S.W.3d 776 (Mo. Ct. App. 2002) (where physician testified that a particular negative outcome was exceedingly rare, evidence of previous occurrences by his medical practice group was admissible).

Add to text after sentence containing note 243:

The evidence is admissible even if the trial court has refused to admit it for other purposes. The consumer's attorney might want to start by cross-examining the defendant about the particular transactions that show the other bad acts, and then call those witnesses in rebuttal.

9.8.2 Evidence of Other Consumer Complaints

Addition to note 246.

246   *Add to White citation*: *as amended by* 335 F.3d 833 (9th Cir. 2003); *add*: *See* Vista Resorts, Inc. v. Goodyear Tire & Rubber Co., 2004 WL 2609563 (Colo. Ct. App. Nov. 18, 2004); Noah v. Gen. Motors Corp., 882 So. 2d 235 (Miss. Ct. App. 2004) (abstract of other complaints not hearsay when introduced to show that manufacturer had notice of defect, but excluded here on other grounds).

Replace note 249 with:

249   Fed. R. Evid. 807.

9.8.4 Evidence of Other Settlements with the Defendant

Addition to note 257.

257   *See also* Appx. I.7, *infra* (sample motion in limine seeking exclusion of evidence of settlement offers).

Add to text after sentence containing note 257:

Nor may a defendant introduce a settlement offer to negate fraudulent intent, show a lack of damages, or defend against punitive damages.[257.1]

257.1   Clevenger v. Bolingbrook Chevrolet, Inc., 401 F. Supp. 2d 878 (N.D. Ill. 2005) (odometer fraud); Byers v. Santiam Ford, Inc., 574 P.2d 1122 (Or. 1978) (dealer that misrepresented car's collision history may not introduce evidence of offer to replace it after suit filed as defense to punitive damages, since this subsequent conduct does not bear on state of mind at time of wrongdoing); Ward v. Dick Dyer and Assocs., Inc., 403 S.E.2d 310, 313 (S.C. 1991) (evidence of post-sale offer to repurchase or replace car with concealed wreck damage does not negate wrongdoing at time of sale so is inadmissible as defense to punitive damage claim). *See also* Goodyear Tire & Rubber Co. v. Chiles Power Supply, Inc., 332 F.3d 976, 980 (6th Cir. 2003) (citing strong public policy reasons favoring confidentiality of settlement offers). *But cf.* Gunn Infiniti v. O'Byrne, 996 S.W.2d 854 (Tex. 1999) (offer by defendant that would ameliorate consumer's injury but does not require consumer to release claims is relevant to affirmative defense of failure to mitigate damages, but not relevant here because seller required release of claims).

Addition to note 258.

258   *Accord* United States v. Serian, 895 F.2d 432, 434 (8th Cir. 1990) (prior consent decrees admissible to show motive, intent, plan, and knowledge).

Replace sentence containing note 259 with:

Prior consent decrees can be admitted to show intent and knowledge.[259]

259   Bradbury v. Phillips Petroleum Co., 815 F.2d 1356, 1363 (10th Cir. 1987); Wegerer v. First Commodity Corp., 744 F.2d 719 (10th Cir. 1984) (prior consent decree admissible to show intent and knowledge); Kerr v. First Commodity Corp., 735 F.2d 281, 286 (8th Cir. 1984).

Add to text after sentence containing note 261:

In addition, evidence of the defendant's *refusal* to resolve the consumer's complaint should not be barred. First, it bears on the defendant's original intent, as it is a continuation of that intent; second, it is relevant to any Magnuson-Moss or warranty claim that requires the consumer to give notice of a defect or afford the defendant an opportunity to cure; and third, since it is not a settlement offer, it simply does not fall within the scope of rules of evidence that bar settlement offers.

9.8.5 *Parol Evidence Rule and Merger Clauses*

Replace note 265 with:

265   *See* National Consumer Law Center, Unfair and Deceptive Acts and Practices § 4.2.15 (6th ed. 2004 and Supp.).

9.8.6 *Witness Testimony*

Page 268

9.8.6.2 Testimony and Statements of Adverse Parties and Persons Associated with Adverse Parties

Add to text at end of subsection's first paragraph:

The consumer's attorney should call adverse parties as witnesses only if they have been deposed, however. Otherwise their testimony is difficult or impossible to control. The consumer's attorney should subpoena any adverse parties rather than assuming that they will appear at the trial. A good time to subpoena an adverse witness is at the conclusion of that witness's deposition. If the trial date is not yet known, the consumer's attorney should get detailed contact information for the witness, including home address and date of birth.

9.8.6.3 Mechanic Testimony

Add to text after subsection's first sentence:

Selecting a mechanic and arranging for an inspection are discussed in § 2.2.9, *supra*.

Page 269

Addition to note 275.

275   *But cf.* Lewis v. Horace Mann Ins. Co., 2005 WL 3692818 (N.D. Ohio Aug. 23, 2005) (striking expert's affidavit because of failure to list his qualifications).

Add to text after subsection's second paragraph:

Careful preparation of the expert's testimony is essential. The expert should have firm, well-analyzed opinions and be able to justify them and the techniques used to reach them.[275.1]

275.1   *See* § 9.8.6.5, *infra*.

Addition to note 277.

277   *See also* Fed. R. Evid. 902(11) (allowing admission of certified copies of business records upon advance notice to the opposing party).

Page 270

9.8.6.4 Other Expert Witnesses

Add note 286.1 at end of subsection's seventh paragraph.

286.1   *See* Deputy v. Lehman Bros., Inc., 345 F.3d 494 (7th Cir. 2003) (discussing qualifications of document examiners; vacating exclusion of testimony and remanding for further evaluation).

Add to text at end of subsection's third-to-last paragraph:

Helpful guidelines for evaluating forgeries may be found at an FBI website.[286.2]
286.2   www.fbi.gov/hq/lab/handbook/intro12.htm.

Add to text after first sentence of subsection's last paragraph:

It is important to make sure that the consumer's expert does not have a record of citations or warnings from government agencies regarding business practices.

Page 271

9.8.6.7 Defendants' Assertion of Fifth Amendment Privilege

Addition to note 299.

299   *See also* Curcio v. United States, 354 U.S. 118, 124, 77 S. Ct. 1145, 1149, 1 L. Ed. 2d 1225 (1957) (corporation has no privilege against self-incrimination; individual can be required to produce corporation's documents but can refuse to testify about them if testimony would be personally incriminating).

Replace sentence containing note 300 and following sentence with:

In contrast to criminal cases, however, in a civil case there is no constitutional bar against drawing an adverse inference from a witness's invocation of the privilege against self-incrimination.[300]

There are limits though when drawing an adverse inference from a witness's assertion of the privilege. First, state law or rules of court may limit or prohibit the drawing of an adverse inference.[300.1] In addition a claim of privilege can not, without more, prove a fact, even in situations in which failure to deny is treated as an admission.[300.2] If, however, a party asserts the privilege in the face of probative evidence silence may corroborate that evidence.[300.3]

A non-party's claim of privilege may allow a negative inference to be drawn against a party, if justified by the non-party's relationship to the party and role in the litigation. If the non-party is an employee of the party, or involved with the party in some kind of conspiracy or joint venture, the inference will probably be permissible.[300.4] Whether the witness is a party or a non-party courts have discretion in deciding whether to draw an adverse inference from a claim of privilege, considering, among other things, whether the probative value of the inference outweighs its potential for prejudice.[300.5] Courts also have broad discretion to deal with parties' abuse of the privilege to gain tactical advantage. For example, a party might claim privilege during discovery but waive the privilege at trial so as to surprise its adversary, or a party seeking relief from the court might claim privilege as to matters essential to the other party's defense.[300.6]

When faced with a witness who is asserting the Fifth Amendment privilege, the plaintiff should not focus solely on the facts surrounding the plaintiff's case, but should also ask the witness such questions as whether the witness rolled back odometers on other vehicles and whether the witness is still rolling back odometers.

300   Baxter v. Palmigiano, 425 U.S. 308, 96 S. Ct. 1551, 47 L. Ed. 2d 810 (1976).
300.1   *See, e.g.*, Cal. Evid. Code § 913 (West) (forbidding adverse inference; applicable to both criminal and civil cases).
300.2   Doe v. Glanzer, 232 F.3d 1258 (9th Cir. 2000) (plaintiff could not introduce evidence of defendant's claim of privilege in response to discovery question when there was no other evidence on that subject); LaSalle Bank Lake View v. Seguban, 54 F.3d 387 (7th Cir. 1995) (when non-movant claims privilege in response to motion for summary judgment, movant must produce evidence; silence is "a relevant factor to be considered in light of the proffered evidence"); Nat'l Acceptance Co. v. Bathalter, 705 F.2d 924 (7th Cir. 1983) (claim of privilege in response to allegation in complaint not an admission).
300.3   Baxter v. Palmigiano, 425 U.S. 308, 96 S. Ct. 1551, 47 L. Ed. 2d 810 (1976); Peiffer v. Lebanon Sch. Dist., 848 F.2d 44 (3d Cir. 1988); Nat'l Acceptance Co. v. Bathalter, 705 F.2d 924 (7th Cir. 1983); *In re* Santaella, 298 B.R. 793 (Bankr. S.D. Fla. 2002) (claim of privilege served to support conclusion, based on other evidence, that debtor had concealed assets; silence when one would be expected to speak is "a powerful

persuader"); Johnson v. Missouri Bd. of Nursing Home Administrators, 130 S.W.3d 619 (Mo. Ct. App. 2004) (license revocation case, but summary judgment process same as in civil action; once prima facie case made out, party's silence supported inference that she was unable to deny the allegations).

300.4   LiButti v. United States, 178 F.3d 114 (2d Cir. 1999) (Internal Revenue Service was suing transferee of allegedly fraudulent transfer; court gave "heavy weight" to claim of privilege by transferor, who was transferee's father); Parker v. Olympus Health Care, 264 F. Supp. 2d 998 (D. Utah 2003) (adverse inference against employer on question whether employer knew employee was rapist could be drawn from employee's claim of privilege when other compelling evidence was present); Lentz v. Metro. Prop. & Cas. Co., 768 N.E.2d 538 (Mass. 2002) (alleged conspiracy to defraud insurer; claim of privilege by non-party adjustors and body shop owners, who would be key players in conspiracy if it existed, permitted inference against party).

300.5   Doe v. Glanzer, 232 F.3d 1258 (9th Cir. 2000) (evidence that defendant invoked privilege during deposition as to whether he had ever taken certain test was inadmissible when results of test would have been inadmissible under *Daubert*); In re Handy & Harman Ref. Group, Inc., 266 B.R. 32 (Bankr. D. Conn. 2001) (even when there is no constitutional bar to drawing adverse inference, court must determine whether probative value outweighed by prejudice); *see also In re* Carp, 340 F.3d 15 (1st Cir. 2003) (negative inference permitted but not required; bankruptcy court did not abuse discretion); Sampson v. City of Schenectady, 160 F. Supp. 2d 336 (N.D.N.Y. 2001) (permitted but not required; court properly denied summary judgment when party who was facing criminal charges claimed privilege in response to summary judgment evidence, but expressed willingness to testify after criminal matters were disposed of); *In re* Santaella, 298 B.R. 793 (Bankr. S.D. Fla. 2002) (courts have discretion in deciding whether to draw adverse inference from invocation of privilege); Johnson v. Missouri Bd. of Nursing Home Administrators, 130 S.W.3d 619 (Mo. Ct. App. 2004) (adverse inference "permitted but not required"; inference proper here, when party remained silent in face of strong evidence).

300.6   McMullen v. Bay Ship Mgmt., 335 F.3d 215 (3d Cir. 2003) (dismissal of case for plaintiff's claim of privilege during discovery was improper; less drastic remedies would have been sufficient); Sec. & Exch. Comm'n v. Colello, 139 F.3d 674 (9th Cir. 1998) (court properly shifted burden of proof concerning origin of funds to party claiming privilege, and granted summary judgment when he failed to produce evidence); Serafino v. Hasbro, Inc., 82 F.3d 515 (1st Cir. 1996) (dismissal was proper when plaintiff alleged retaliatory termination of contract but claimed privilege as to non-retaliatory reasons for termination—in other words, that defendant had learned of kickbacks and overcharging); Sec. & Exch. Comm'n v. Greystone Nash, Inc., 25 F.3d 187 (3d Cir. 1994) (careful case-by-case balancing required; defendants who claimed privilege during discovery should not have been barred from testifying at trial because plaintiffs not unfairly surprised); United States v. Parcels of Land, 903 F.2d 36 (1st Cir. 1990) (drug forfeiture; landowner's affidavit properly stricken, resulting in summary judgment, because he repeatedly invoked privilege during deposition); Gutierrez-Rodriguez v. Cartagena, 882 F.2d 553, 577 (1st Cir. 1989) (Fifth Amendment does not guarantee right to surprise adversary at trial; defendant properly barred from testifying after he claimed privilege as to all questions during discovery); Jackson v. Microsoft, 211 F.R.D. 423 (W.D. Wash. 2002) (dismissal proper when plaintiff claimed privilege as to certain questions in discovery, other evidence was present, information was critical, and there was no other reasonable way to obtain it), aff'd, 2003 WL 22359615 (9th Cir. Oct. 16, 2003) (table); Griffith v. Griffith, 506 S.E.2d 526 (S.C. Ct. App. 1998) (denial of alimony proper when wife claimed privilege when questioned about adultery; one who seeks relief in a civil case may not invoke privilege as to proper questions related to the subject matter in issue; plaintiff may be forced to choose between waiving privilege and being barred from going forward; note that other evidence was introduced).

Add to text at end of subsection's first paragraph:

Asking the witness numerous questions allows the trier of fact to draw adverse inferences on more issues.[301.1] Note, however, that courts have discretion to control the questioning of a witness who is expected to claim privilege, so as to avoid abuse.[301.2]

301.1   *See* Doe v. Glanzer, 232 F.3d 1258 (9th Cir. 2000).

301.2   Lentz v. Metro. Prop. & Cas. Co., 768 N.E.2d 538 (Mass. 2002).

Page 272

Addition to note 302.

302   McMullen v. Bay Ship Mgmt., 335 F.3d 215 (3d Cir. 2003) (dismissal too severe a sanction when less drastic remedies available, such as continuing case until criminal case disposed of); Peiffer v. Lebanon Sch. Dist., 848 F.2d 44 (3d Cir. 1988) (school board not required to continue hearing concerning firing of employee until after completion of criminal case against employee); Sampson v. City of Schenectady, 160 F. Supp. 2d 336 (N.D.N.Y. 2001) (summary judgment properly denied when defendant, who was facing criminal charges, claimed privilege in face of summary judgment evidence, but stated he would be willing to answer after criminal matters disposed of).

9.8.7 Documentary Evidence

9.8.7.1 Title and Registration Documents

Addition to note 305.

305　*See also* Fed. R. Evid. 902(11) (allowing admission of certified copies of business records upon advance notice to the opposing party).

Add to text at end of subsection's fourth paragraph:

The consumer will also have to establish the authenticity of the report. If the dealer will not stipulate to the authenticity of the report, and a request for admissions is unsuccessful, authenticity can be established by a telephone deposition of an employee of the summary title service.[307.1] It is important to establish exactly what was on the report when the dealer accessed it.[307.2]

Another possible basis for admitting a summary title history is to explain why the consumer took a particular course of action. For example, the consumer may have tried to return the car after learning of a problem through a summary title report.

307.1　*See* § 2.5.11, *supra.*
307.2　*Id.*

Page 273

9.8.7.2 Records of Dealer, Manufacturer, Auction House, Repair Shop, and Other Business Entities

Addition to note 323.

323　*See also* Fed. R. Evid. 902(11) (allowing admission of certified copies of business records upon advance notice to the opposing party).

9.9 Trial of Automobile Fraud Cases

Page 274

9.9.1 Preparing for Jury Trial

Add to text at end of subsection's second paragraph:

After a case is over, whether successful or unsuccessful, it is valuable to ask the trial judge or the bailiff for suggestions about how to improve.

9.9.2 Voir Dire

Add to text after third sentence of subsection's first paragraph:

Another approach might be to ask whether any prospective juror would never award punitive damages to punish the defendant and to deter others from committing similar frauds, even if the evidence shows that the defendant intentionally committed fraud.[335.1]

335.1　*See, e.g.,* Ashcroft v. TAD Res. Int'l, 972 S.W.2d 502 (Mo. Ct. App. 1998) (plaintiff's attorney had right to ask jurors about attitude toward punitive damages).

Page 275

Add to text after subsection's first paragraph:

If there is reason to be concerned that jury members have been affected by industry publicity about frivolous lawsuits, consider telling the jury that you and your client dislike frivolous lawsuits. Then ask several members of the jury how they feel about frivolous lawsuits and whether any of them are members of a tort reform group. If any are, ask them to agree that the tort reform group is not against all lawsuits but just frivolous ones, and that it supports punitive damages in appropriate cases.

Add to text at end of subsection's second paragraph:

For example, if the defense is likely to stress an "as is" clause in the contract, effective *voir dire* questions might be whether any juror, in buying a car, had ever taken the time to read all the documents word for word, and how many of them had relied on the word of the salesman to know what was in the contract.

Add to text at end of subsection's third paragraph:

An alternative way to explore these issues is to ask if there is any member of the panel who would not mind it if they purchased a rebuilt wreck and that fact had not been disclosed to them. This more hypothetical question also has the advantage of conveying to the jury that the normal response is to be upset by the sale of an undisclosed wreck.

9.9.4 Countering Defense Arguments

Replace note 336 with:

336   *See* National Consumer Law Center, Unfair and Deceptive Acts and Practices § 4.2.11 (6th ed. 2004 and Supp.).

Page 276

Add to text after first sentence of subsection's sixth paragraph:

A useful *voir dire* question to address this concern is: "How many of you think there are too many lawsuits against car dealers for cheating people?"

Add note 338.1 to end of last sentence of subsection's third-to-last paragraph.

338.1   *See* Appx. I.7, *infra* (sample motion in limine seeking to bar references to consumer's prayer for attorney fees).

Page 277

9.9.5 Helping Fraud Victims Prepare for Testimony

Add to text at end of subsection's fourth paragraph:

Even a client who did not or could not read the contract may claim to have done so in order to please the examiner or because of fear of appearing stupid. These clients should be carefully prepared for testimony so that they can truthfully describe the facts.

9.9.5a Order of Witnesses

Add new subsection to text after § 9.9.5:

In presenting an automobile fraud case, remember that jurors remember best what they hear first and last. Some attorneys like to have the plaintiff or an expert for the plaintiff testify first, because then the jury gets an understanding of what the case is about. These witnesses will usually face vigorous cross-examination, however, and sometimes the plaintiff is inarticulate. Other attorneys prefer to call the defendant or an employee of the defendant first, to nail down the defendant's story so that it can be attacked throughout the trial. This strategy is particularly effective if the jury gets an early impression that the defendant is lying or unscrupulous. If there are good photos of wreck damage another effective approach is to blow them up, start with a witness who can identify them, and then keep them on an easel to refer to during the trial. Most attorneys wait to present evidence about damages until the last part of the trial.

Page 278

9.9.7 Should the Jury Be Told That Actual Damages Will Be Trebled?

Addition to note 352.

352   *Replace NCLC citation with*: National Consumer Law Center, Unfair and Deceptive Acts and Practices § 8.4.2.8 (6th ed. 2004 and Supp.).

9.10 Damage Awards

9.10.1 Direct Actual Damages

9.10.1.1 Benefit of the Bargain Versus Out-of-Pocket Damages

Replace note 354 with:

354   *See* National Consumer Law Center, Unfair and Deceptive Acts and Practices § 8.1 (6th ed. 2004 and Supp.).

Add to text after sentence containing note 357:

It is commonly used in UDAP cases as well.[357.1]

357.1　*See, e.g.,* Crowder v. Bob Oberling Enters., Inc., 499 N.E.2d 115 (Ill. App. Ct. 1986).

Page 279

Addition to note 358.

358　Blankenship v. Town & Country Ford, Inc., 622 S.E.2d 638 (N.C. Ct. App. 2005) (difference between amount paid and actual value, without offset for use, is proper measure of damages under state UDAP and damage disclosure statutes).

Add to text at end of subsection:

In some jurisdictions, the plaintiff is allowed to choose between the benefit of the bargain measure of damages and the out of pocket loss measure in cases of misrepresentation.[358.1]

358.1　Padgett's Used Cars and Leasing, Inc. v. Preston, 2005 WL 2290249 (Tex. App. Sept. 21, 2005) (unpublished, citation limited).

Page 280

9.10.1.3 Proving Diminished Value of Vehicle

Add to text after sentence containing note 364:

A vehicle may have only scrap value if poorly-repaired collision damage makes it dangerous to drive, as the owner of such a car could not in good faith sell it other than as scrap.

Addition to note 374.

374　Acheson v. Shafter, 107 Ariz. 576, 490 P.2d 832 (Ariz. 1971); King v. O'Rielly Motor Co., 16 Ariz. App. 518, 494 P.2d 718 (1972); Town & Country Chrysler Plymouth v. Porter, 11 Ariz. App. 369, 464 P.2d 815 (1970) (owner of rolled-back vehicle is competent to give opinion as to difference in value); Cash v. Styers, 2003 WL 129046 (Ark. Ct. App. Jan. 15, 2003); Razor v. Hyundai Motor Am., 2006 WL 240746, at *15 (Ill. Feb. 2, 2006) (affirming judgment for buyer who presented evidence of purchase price of car, its problems, and their effect on her, but left it to jury to quantify the diminution in value); JHC Ventures, Ltd. P'ship v. Fast Trucking, Inc., 94 S.W.3d 762, 49 U.C.C. Rep. Serv. 2d 167 (Tex. App. 2002) (buyer's testimony, based on commercial quotes for comparable product, sufficient evidence of value as warranted); Mayberry v. Volkswagen of Am., Inc., 692 N.W.2d 226 (Wis. 2005); Prather v. Crane, 675 N.W.2d 811 (Wis. Ct. App. 2004). *But see* Mitchell v. Backus Cadillac-Pontiac, Inc., 618 S.E.2d 87 (Ga. Ct. App. 2005) (affirming trial court's exclusion of owner's testimony because of insufficient foundation where owner's only sources of information about value of defective car were Internet research and talking to people in car business).

Add to text after sentence containing note 374:

The testimony should focus on market value rather than on the subjective value of the vehicle to the owner.[374.1]

374.1　Owens v. Mitsubishi Motor Sales, 2004 WL 2260619 (N.D. Ill. Oct. 4, 2004) (buyer's "belief" as to value too speculative); Kim v. Mercedes-Benz, U.S.A., Inc., 818 N.E.2d 713 (Ill. App. Ct. 2004) (plaintiff's testimony that he would not have bought an expensive new car if he had known of its problems insufficient to allow jury to set damages); Ford Motor Co. v. Cooper, 125 S.W.3d 794 (Tex. App. 2004); Momentum Motor Cars, Ltd. v. Williams, 2004 WL 2536844 (Tex. App. Nov. 10, 2004) (unpublished) (buyer's testimony legally insufficient when it related to value to him and current sale value, not to value at time of purchase).

Page 281

Addition to note 376.

376　*See* Owens v. Mitsubishi Motor Sales, 2004 WL 2260619 (N.D. Ill. Oct. 4, 2004) (buyer's "belief" as to value too speculative when buyer had no training, experience, or knowledge in vehicle values and had not reviewed any publications or consulted with any experts); Locascio v. Imports Unlimited, Inc., 309 F. Supp. 2d 267 (D. Conn. 2004) (finding consumer's "self-serving, after-the-fact speculations" about value of car unreliable because she lacked expertise, and awarding only statutory damages because of failure to prove actual damages); Mayberry v. Volkswagen of Am., Inc., 692 N.W.2d 226 (Wis. 2005) (while owner's testimony as to value at time of purchase is admissible, it may not be persuasive to jury when she resold the vehicle two years later for a higher price).

Add to text at end of subsection:

For these reasons, it is unwise to rely solely on the owner's testimony to prove diminished value. Some courts have gone farther and held that a foundation must be laid for the buyer's testimony before it will be admitted.[376.1]

376.1　Monroe v. Hyundai Motor Am., Inc., 606 S.E.2d 894 (Ga. Ct. App. 2004) (upholding trial court's exclusion of buyer's testimony because of insufficient foundation); Kim v. Mercedes-Benz, U.S.A., Inc., 818 N.E.2d 713 (Ill. App. Ct. 2004); Momentum Motor Cars, Ltd. v. Williams, 2004 WL 2536844 (Tex. App. Nov. 10, 2004) (unpublished) (buyer's testimony legally insufficient when it related to current value, not value at time of purchase, and he never testified that he was aware of its market value).

9.10.1.4 When to Utilize Used Car Valuation Guides

Add to text at end of subsection's second paragraph:

The Kelley Blue Book website states that, as a rule of thumb, fifty percent or more of a car's value should be deducted if it has a salvage title.[377.1]

377.1 Frequently asked questions (FAQ) section of Kelley Blue Book website, www.kbb.com (visited on Feb. 7, 2005).

9.10.2 Cancellation and Recovery of Amount Paid

9.10.2.1 General

Page 283

Replace note 391 with:

391 National Consumer Law Center, Unfair and Deceptive Acts and Practices § 8.3.9 (6th ed. 2004 and Supp.).

Addition to note 392.

392 Mitchell v. Backus Cadillac-Pontiac, Inc., 618 S.E.2d 87 (Ga. Ct. App. 2005).

9.10.2.2 Relation to Recovery for Diminished Value

Replace note 396 with:

396 *See* National Consumer Law Center, Unfair and Deceptive Acts and Practices § 9.5.8 (6th ed. 2004 and Supp.).

9.10.3 Incidental and Consequential Damages

9.10.3.1 General

Addition to notes 401, 402.

401 *Replace NCLC UDAP citation with*: National Consumer Law Center, Unfair and Deceptive Acts and Practices § 8.3.3 (6th ed. 2004 and Supp.).

402 Padgett's Used Cars and Leasing, Inc. v. Preston, 2005 WL 2290249 (Tex. App. Sept. 21, 2005) (unpublished, citation limited) (consumer may recover reasonable and necessary repair costs in addition to vehicle's reduced value, where repairs did not increase its value).

9.10.3.2 Emotional Distress Damages

Page 284

Addition to notes 405, 410, 417.

405 *Replace Campbell v. State Farm Mut. Auto. Ins. Co. citation with*: Campbell v. State Farm Mut. Auto. Ins. Co., 65 P.3d 1134 (Utah 2001) (emotional distress damages available on claim of fraud by insurer in refusing to settle claims; abrogates Turner v. Gen. Adjustment Bureau, 832 P.2d 62 (Utah Ct. App. 1992)), *rev'd on other grounds*, 538 U.S. 408 (2003) (reversing on punitive damages issues); *add*: Hoffman v. Stamper, 867 A.2d 276 (Md. 2005) (emotional distress damages are available for fraud as long as plaintiff shows objectively ascertainable injury).

Page 286

410 *Replace NCLC citation with*: National Consumer Law Center, Unfair and Deceptive Acts and Practices § 8.3.3.9 (6th ed. 2004 and Supp.).

Page 287

417 *See also* Hoffman v. Stamper, 867 A.2d 276 (Md. 2005) (plaintiff must show "physical" injury, broadly defined to include such objectively determinable symptoms as depression, loss of appetite, and irritability); Wilson v. Gen. Motors Acceptance Corp., 883 So. 2d 56 (Miss. 2004) (emotional distress damages are available for ordinary negligence only if plaintiff proves some sort of physical manifestation of injury or demonstrable physical harm).

9.10.4 Statutory Damages

Page 288

Replace note 424 with:

424 *See* National Consumer Law Center, Unfair and Deceptive Acts and Practices § 8.4.1 (6th ed. 2004 and Supp.).

9.10.5 Punitive Damages

Page 289

Addition to note 426.

426 *Replace NCLC citation with*: National Consumer Law Center, Unfair and Deceptive Acts and Practices § 8.4.1 (6th ed. 2004 and Supp.).

Replace note 427 with:

427   National Consumer Law Center, Unfair and Deceptive Acts and Practices § 9.2.5.3.3 (6th ed. 2004 and Supp.).

9.11 Settlement

9.11.1 Settlement Negotiations

Page 291

9.11.1.1 Nature of the Automobile Fraud Negotiation

Add to text at end of subsection's seventh paragraph:

"Take it or leave it" demands give the opponent little room to settle without losing face. The typical settlement dance of offers and counteroffers may seem like a charade but allows the opponent the sense of having negotiated a better deal than originally offered.

When defense counsel wants to discuss settlement right before trial some consumer attorneys follow a practice of having another attorney in the firm handle negotiations, giving that attorney the parameters for settlement and the goal number. This approach allows the lead lawyer to continue concentrating on trial preparation.

Add to text at end of subsection:

Often settlements are reached in the courthouse, either at a pre-trial conference or before or during trial. To prevent defendants from adding unbargained-for terms such as confidentiality clauses when drafting the settlement documents, it is helpful to recite the agreed terms on the record with a court reporter. After reciting the terms, the consumer's attorney should ask the opposing attorney, still on the record, whether the recitation is correct and includes everything. It is also a wise precaution to ask the judge to retain jurisdiction in case it is necessary to enforce the settlement. For settlements reached outside the courthouse many consumer attorneys offer to do the initial draft of the settlement documents, in order to minimize the opposing attorney's opportunity to include onerous, one-sided terms in the agreement.

Page 292

9.11.1.4 Dealing with Multiple Defendants and the Dealer's Insurer

Addition to note 441.

441   Nebraska Plastics, Inc. v. Holland Colors Americas, Inc., 408 F.3d 410 (8th Cir. 2005) (predicting that Nebraska would require dollar-for-dollar credit for settlement even where remaining defendant was intentional tortfeasor); *see also* Zivitz v. Greenberg, 279 F.3d 536 (7th Cir. 2002) (Ill. law) (no set-off when the damages awarded against non-settling defendant were not for identical injury). *But cf.* U.S. v. Contra Costa County Water Dist., 678 F.2d 90, 92 (9th Cir. 1982) (evidence of negotiations with other party is confidential and inadmissible to show amount of credit that should be applied to judgment).

Add note 442.1 after "misconduct" in sentence containing note 442.

442.1   Plath v. Schonrock, 64 P.3d 984 (Mont. 2003) (no set-off when settling defendant's liability was based on separate and distinct claim).

Addition to notes 443, 446.

443   Turner v. Firstar Bank, 2006 WL 539448 (Ill. App. Ct. Mar. 6, 2006) (plaintiff may recover punitive damages from one defendant even though she already recovered full compensatory damages plus punitive damages from another defendant).

446   *Replace Dynasty Hous., Inc. citation with*: 832 So. 2d 73 (Ala. Civ. App. 2001).

Page 293

9.11.1.5 Settlements Without Adequate Attorney Fees

Addition to notes 449, 451.

449   *Replace NCLC Consumer Law Pleadings citation with*: National Consumer Law Center, Consumer Law Pleadings No. 4, Ch. 8 (Cumulative CD-Rom and Index Guide).

451   *Replace NCLC citation with*: National Consumer Law Center, Unfair and Deceptive Acts and Practices § 8.8.11.3 (6th ed. 2004 and Supp.).

9.11.2 Settlement Terms

Page 294

9.11.2.1 Prompt Payment

Add to text at end of subsection's second paragraph:

If a judgment has been entered, the agreement can state that the consumer will refrain from execution so long as payments are made as scheduled, and that the consumer will have the judgment marked satisfied upon timely payment of the agreed-upon amounts.

Page 295

9.11.2.4 Confidentiality Agreements

Add to text after second-to-last sentence of subsection's third paragraph:

Another way to narrow the clause is to limit contacts with the press without otherwise requiring confidentiality.

Add new subsection to text after § 9.11.2.4:

9.11.2.4a Other Terms and Clauses

Sometimes a dealer, manufacturer, or insurer inserts an indemnification clause into the settlement agreement, requiring the consumer to indemnify it for any claims arising out of the sale, repair, or financing of the vehicle. Only in the rarest of cases should a consumer sign such a clause. Such a clause invites the defendant to sue the consumer if it has further legal problems with the vehicle. The defendant can not claim that it needs the indemnification clause to protect it from another suit by the consumer, because the release the consumer signs already accomplishes that objective.

If one of the defendants holds a note or installment contract signed by the consumer, the settlement agreement should require it to be returned to the consumer, marked paid or cancelled. Otherwise, there is a danger that it will be treated as a continuing obligation and assigned to another entity, and the consumer will be dunned for payment or even sued.

Any release should be mutual, with each party releasing the other from the same scope of claims. If only the consumer signs the release, the consumer is vulnerable to suit by the defendant.

9.11.2.6 Protecting Against the Defendant's Bankruptcy

Replace "A bankruptcy trustee" in subsection's second sentence with:

The suggestions made in § 9.11.2.1, *supra*, provide some protection against bankruptcy. Another concern is that a bankruptcy trustee

Replace note 460 with:

460   Archer v. Warner, 538 U.S. 314, 123 S. Ct. 1462, 155 L. Ed. 2d 454 (2003).

9.12 Attorney Fees in Automobile Fraud Cases

Page 296

9.12.1 Availability of Attorney Fees

Addition to note 464.

464   *Replace NCLC UDAP citation with*: National Consumer Law Center, Unfair and Deceptive Acts and Practices §§ 8.8, 9.2.5.3.2 (6th ed. 2004 and Supp.).

9.12.3 Standards for Determining Fees

Replace note 467 with:

467   *See* National Consumer Law Center, Truth in Lending § 8.9 (5th ed. 2003 and Supp.) (discussion of federal decisions on attorney fees).

Replace note 469 with:

469   *See* National Consumer Law Center, Unfair and Deceptive Acts and Practices §§ 8.8.11.3.1, 8.8.11.3.2 (6th ed. 2004 and Supp.) (discussion of the lodestar formula and the states that use it).

470   *See* National Consumer Law Center, Unfair and Deceptive Acts and Practices § 8.8.11.3.1 (6th ed. 2004 and Supp.) (state-by-state list of the standards used to calculate attorney fee awards).

Page 297

Add to text after subsection's third paragraph:

A punitive damages award is not a proper basis for reducing or denying an attorney fee award.[475.1] The purposes of the two awards are different: punitive damages are designed to punish offensive or unlawful conduct and deter it in the future, while fee shifting statutes are designed to encourage private enforcement.[475.2] Allowing attorney fees to be denied or reduced when the plaintiff wins substantial punitive damages would produce clearly irrational results:

- A consumer who loses gets no attorney fees;
- A consumer who wins a small recovery gets reduced attorney fees because of the reduced level of success;
- A consumer who wins a large judgment gets no attorney fees.

475.1   Grabinski v. Blue Springs Ford Sales, 203 F.3d 1024 (8th Cir. 2000). *See generally* National Consumer Law Center, Unfair and Deceptive Acts and Practices § 8.8.2.3 (6th ed. 2004 and Supp.).

475.2   Wilkins v. Peninsula Motor Cars, Inc., 587 S.E.2d 581 (Va. 2003) (consumer need not elect between fraud claim and UDAP claim, but may recover actual and punitive damages on the former and attorney fees on the latter).

9.12.4 Procedure for Requesting Fees

Addition to note 477.

477   *Replace NCLC citation with*: National Consumer Law Center, Unfair and Deceptive Acts and Practices § 8.8.12 (6th ed. 2004 and Supp.).

9.13 Collecting the Judgment

9.13.1 Collecting Against the Defendant's Assets

Page 298

9.13.1.1 Locating Dealer Bank Accounts

Add to text after second sentence of subsection's second paragraph:

The dealer's bank account can be located in the same way if someone has paid by check for repairs or parts from the dealer's service department.

Add to text at end of subsection:

The state's rules of civil procedure may allow the consumer's attorney to take a post-judgment examination of the judgment debtor. Useful documents to subpoena for such an examination include the operating reports that the dealer periodically makes to its authorized manufacturer, which show its assets and liabilities. The applications that the dealer has submitted for loans are also helpful because the dealer will be trying to look good to a lender and will therefore list assets that it might otherwise conceal. If the consumer's attorney is concerned that the dealer will clean out its bank accounts and sell its other assets immediately after being forced to reveal them, it may be helpful to bring a second person to the judgment debtor's examination. As soon as the location of the judgment debtor's bank account is determined, the second person leaves the examination, prepares garnishment papers, files them at the courthouse, and serves the bank.

9.13.1.3 Finding Hidden Dealer Assets

Add to text at beginning of subsection:

Manufacturers require franchised dealers to make periodic reports on their financial status. These reports can help locate assets. They are also a helpful way of verifying a claim by a dealer that it is on the brink of going out of business.

Add to text after fourth sentence of subsection's second paragraph:

When a dealer registers to attend an auction, it must fill out an on-line or paper form giving detailed information about its licensure and financial resources. Typically the form includes the identity of the dealer's bank account, wire transfer information, social security or federal tax identification number, and licensure information, plus photographs of the dealer's agents. Most auctions use the Auction Access registration form and database, and over 100,000 dealers have registered with that company. A blank copy of this registration form is reprinted in Appendix E.3, *infra*.

Page 300

9.13.3 Reaching the Dealer's Insurance Policy

Replace last sentence of subsection's first paragraph with:

The insurance may also cover liability incurred by a dealer for unknowingly selling a salvage vehicle when the brand was dropped from the title before the dealer acquired the car or may cover misstatements on the title more generally.[488.1]

If formal discovery to identify the dealer's insurance carrier is not possible, there are other ways to obtain this information. Many dealers purchase errors and omissions insurance from the same company they use to obtain their dealer bond, so the attorney could determine the name of the bonding company from state records and make a demand upon it. Court files of prior lawsuits against the dealer and the dealer's application for its state license may also include insurance information.

> 488.1   *See* Carr Chevrolet, Inc. v. Am. Hardware Mut. Ins. Co., 2003 WL 23590746 (D. Or. May 19, 2003) (title errors and omissions policy covered fraud damages for misstating mileage on title).

Addition to note 489.

> 489   *Accord* Erie Ins. Prop. & Cas. Co. v. Golub, 2005 WL 1845289 (S.D. W. Va. Aug. 2, 2005) (misrepresentation of history of vehicle not covered as "accident" by insurance policy; also, no coverage because no allegations of personal injury or property damage); *see also* Carr Chevrolet, Inc. v. Am. Hardware Mut. Ins. Co., 2003 WL 23590746 (D. Or. May 19, 2003) (odometer misrepresentation not covered as "accident").

Add to text at end of subsection:

Whether this sort of language covers unfair and deceptive acts and practices claims is discussed in another manual.[489.1]

If the dealer has gone out of business, it is important to find out what type of insurance coverage the dealer has. "Occurrence" policies provide coverage for events that occur while the policy is in effect. A "claims made" policy has to be in effect on the date a claim is made. A business with a "claims made" policy that is closing may buy "tail" coverage, which covers acts committed while the "claims made" policy was in effect.

> 489.1   National Consumer Law Center, Unfair and Deceptive Acts and Practices § 6.10.2 (6th ed. 2004 and Supp.).

9.13.4 Collecting on a State-Mandated Bond

9.13.4.1 General

Addition to notes 493, 494.

> 493   *Replace Ames citation with*: Ames v. Comm'r of Motor Vehicles, 839 A.2d 1250 (Conn. 2004). *Add*: Cooper v. Hartford Fin. Servs. Group, Inc., 2005 WL 1378907 (D.D.C. June 9, 2005) (bonding company's obligation is determined by statute, not by the words of the bond).
>
> 494   *Add at end of note*: See also True Heart Corp. v. River City Auto Sales, Inc., 82 P.3d 519 (Kan. Ct. App. 2003) (describing means of obtaining judicial review of state agency's decision on claim against bond).

Replace "dealer" in first sentence of subsection's fourth paragraph with:

dealer, especially one that was not entered by default,

Page 301

9.13.4.2 What Claimants Does the Dealer's Bond Protect?

Addition to notes 502, 503, 508.

> 502   Old Republic Sur. Co. v. GAC-MD, Inc., 2004 WL 34741 (Tex. App. Jan. 8, 2004) (unpublished) (dealer's bad check, issued to repurchase a vehicle from another dealer, was a payment to buy a motor vehicle and was thus covered by bond).

503   Old Republic Surety Co. v. Bonham State Bank, 172 S.W.3d 210 (Tex. App. 2005). *But see* Lawyers Sur. Corp. v. Riverbend Bank, 966 S.W.2d 182 (Tex. App. 1998) (bond that only covered bank drafts issued by dealers to buy vehicles not liable for floor plan financer's claim for dealer's nonpayment of promissory note).

508   *Replace Lawyers Sur. Corp. citation with*: 76 Ark. App. 415, 66 S.W.3d 669; *add*: *Cf.* Regional Acceptance Corp. v. Old Republic Sur. Co., 577 S.E.2d 391 (N.C. Ct. App. 2003) (entity that financed vehicle for buyers may make claim on bond when it is subrogated to buyers' rights).

Add to text at end of subsection's second paragraph:

A business partner who was cheated by the dealer out of his share of the proceeds of vehicle sales was not covered by a bond that protected retail or wholesale buyers and sellers, even though he bought vehicles for the dealer, as his relationship to the dealer was not that of a buyer or seller.[510.1]

510.1   True Heart Corp. v. River City Auto Sales, Inc., 82 P.3d 519 (Kan. Ct. App. 2003).

Page 302

9.13.4.3 Necessity to Prove Fraud or Specific Type of Conduct

Addition to notes 514, 527, 528.

514   *See also* True Heart Corp. v. River City Auto Sales, Inc., 82 P.3d 519 (Kan. Ct. App. 2003) (failing to pay business partner his share of proceeds of vehicle sales is a violation of law that would be covered by bond, but business partner is not within class of persons protected).

527   *Replace Ames citation with*: Ames v. Dep't of Motor Vehicles, 802 A.2d 126 (Conn. Ct. App. 2002) (commissioner may scrutinize judgment to determine how much of it is recoverable from the bond), *aff'd on other grounds*, 839 A.2d 1250 (Conn. 2004); *add*: Regional Acceptance Corp. v. Old Republic Sur. Co., 577 S.E.2d 391 (N.C. Ct. App. 2003); *see also* Rex, Inc. v. Manufactured Hous. Comm., 80 P.3d 470 (N.M. Ct. App. 2003) (collateral estoppel applies to bond forfeiture proceeding before administrative agency and precludes mobile home dealer from relitigating court's finding of misrepresentation); Old Republic Surety Co. v. Bonham State Bank, 172 S.W.3d 210, 214 (Tex. App. 2005) (motor vehicle bond is a judgment bond, so surety is bound by judgment in absence of fraud or collusion, unless judgment alters terms of bond by, for example, expanding its coverage). *But see* Lawyers Sur. Corp. v. Riverbend Bank, 966 S.W.2d 182 (Tex. App. 1998) (judgment has no effect if it alters the terms of the bond).

Page 303

528   Lawyers Sur. Corp. v. Riverbend Bank, 966 S.W.2d 182 (Tex. App. 1998).

9.13.4.4 Recovery of Different Types of Damages Under a Bond

Addition to notes 531, 533, 534.

531   *But see* State *ex rel.* Webb v. Hartford Cas. Ins. Co., 956 S.W.2d 272 (Mo. Ct. App. 1998) (bond for "any loss sustained" covers interest consumer incurred on car loan from credit union).

533   *Delete Ames citation.*

534   *Replace Ames citation with*: Ames v. Comm'r of Motor Vehicles, 839 A.2d 1250 (Conn. 2004) (UDAP treble damages not recoverable from bond); *add*: Cooper v. Hartford Fin. Servs. Group, Inc., 2005 WL 1378907 (D.D.C. June 9, 2005) (punitive damages not compensatory so not recoverable from mortgage lender's bond). *But cf.* Carr Chevrolet, Inc. v. Am. Hardware Mut. Ins. Co., 2003 WL 23590746 (D. Or. May 19, 2003) (coverage of punitive damages under liability insurance policy not against public policy unless defendant acted with subjective intent to cause harm).

Add to text after sentence containing note 536:

However, another court held that statutory damages under the Truth in Lending Act could be recovered from a mortgage lender's bond, as they were not punitive but intended to compensate the consumer for unlawful actions where the injury was non-pecuniary or difficult to calculate.[536.1]

536.1   Cooper v. Hartford Fin. Servs. Group, Inc., 2005 WL 1378907 (D.D.C. June 9, 2005).

Page 304

9.13.4.5 Attorney Fees Collectable Under the Bond

Addition to note 540.

540   *See, e.g.*, Va. Code Ann. § 46.2-1527.10 (Michie).

Add to text at end of subsection's first paragraph:

A general insurance law may also allow fees.[541.1]

541.1   *See* David Boland, Inc. v. Trans Coastal Roofing Co., 851 So. 2d 724 (Fla. 2003) (non-automobile case; Fla. Stat. Ann. § 627.428 (West), a general insurance law, allows recovery of attorney fees from surety in excess of construction performance bond's face amount, even without independent misconduct by surety).

Add to text after sentence containing note 545:

A court held that attorney fees could be collected against a mortgage company's bond where the mortgage lending statute allowed attorney fees as part of "damages," and the bond likewise covered "damages."[545.1]

545.1   Cooper v. Hartford Fin. Servs. Group, Inc., 2005 WL 1378907 (D.D.C. June 9, 2005).

Addition to notes 546, 549.

546   *Replace Ames citation with*: Ames v. Comm'r of Motor Vehicles, 839 A.2d 1250 (Conn. 2004) (attorney fees awarded under UDAP statute not recoverable against bond, which covered "any loss"); *replace Hubbel citation's parenthetical with*: (bond's coverage of "any loss" does not include attorney fees awarded on underlying UDAP claim; court declines to reach question whether fees might be allowed under general insurance statute, Fla. Stat. Ann. § 627.428 (West)). *Add: But cf.* Dallas Fire Ins. Co. v. Texas Contractors Sur. & Cas. Agency, 159 S.W.3d 895 (Tex. 2004) (suretyship is not insurance so state cause of action for unfair insurance practices does not apply).

549   *See* Garrido v. Star Ins. Co., Clearinghouse No. 55,611, No. 1 CA-CV 03-0648 (Ariz. Ct. App. Dec. 23, 2004) (consumer can assert bad faith tort claim against surety for unreasonable denial of claim on motor vehicle bond); *see also* Trustees of Plumbers & Pipefitters Union Local 525 Health & Welfare Trust Plan v. Developers Sur. & Indem. Co., 84 P.3d 59 (Nev. 2004) (surety may be liable for fees that exceed the bond amount if they are awarded in the injured party's suit against the surety over the bond). *But cf.* Dallas Fire Ins. Co. v. Texas Contractors Sur. & Cas. Agency, 159 S.W.3d 895 (Tex. 2004) (suretyship is not insurance so state cause of action for unfair insurance practices does not apply).

9.13.4.6 Bond Limitations on the Size of a Recovery

Addition to note 555.

555   *See also* Cooper v. Hartford Fin. Servs. Group, Inc., 2005 WL 1378907 (D.D.C. June 9, 2005) (construing mortgage lender's bond to be cumulative rather than continuous, so it was liable up to full amount for each year in which consumers suffered damages).

Page 307

Add new subsection to text after § 9.13.4.10:

9.13.4.11 Tips for Recovering Against a Bond

Motor vehicle dealer bonds are usually modest in amount and can be quickly exhausted if a dealer has cheated a number of consumers. In many states, bond proceeds are paid on a first-come, first-served basis. The first injured party to give notice may be first in line. At an early date, the consumer's attorney should determine what steps are necessary to put the consumer's claim in line for recovery under the bond.

If there are multiple claimants against the bond, the consumer's attorney should make sure that all are eligible claimants. Finance companies and floor plan financers may not be.[576.1]

When there are multiple claimants, the bonding company may file an interpleader action, seeking to deposit the money into court and let the claimants fight over it. In such a case, the bonding company's attorney may be entitled to payment from the proceeds of the bond, so it may be important to agree to whatever is necessary to minimize that attorney's work and involvement.

576.1   *See* § 9.13.4.2, *supra*.

9.13.5 Consumer Recovery Funds

Add to text at end of subsection's first paragraph:

After three years without claims, a dealer may choose between continuing to pay into the fund or maintaining a $100,000 bond.[578.1]

578.1   Va. Code Ann. §§ 46.2-1527.1, 46.2-1527.9 (Michie).

Federal Statutes

Page 318

A.2 Driver's Privacy Protection Act

Delete "and" from 18 U.S.C. § 2725(2).

Add to text after 18 U.S.C. § 2725(3):

    (4) "highly restricted personal information" means an individual's photograph or image, social security number, medical or disability information; and

    (5) "express consent" means consent in writing, including consent conveyed electronically that bears an electronic signature as defined in section 106(5) of Public Law 106-229.

A.3 National Motor Vehicle Title Information System

Replace "Automobile" in 49 U.S.C. § 30501(6) with:

Motor Vehicle

Page 319

Replace the first six words of 49 U.S.C. § 30502(a)(2) with:

In cooperation with the Secretary of Transportation

Page 320

Replace "Automobile" in first sentence of 49 U.S.C. § 30504(a)(1) with:

Motor Vehicle

Replace "in the business" in first sentence of 49 U.S.C. § 30504(b) with:

in business

Federal Regulations

B.2 Federal Motor Vehicle Theft Prevention Standard, 49 C.F.R. §§ 541.1–541.6

[Editor's Note: 49 C.F.R. Part 541 has been amended, effective September 1, 2006. See 69 Fed. Reg. 17,960 (Apr. 6, 2004); 69 Fed. Reg. 34,612 (June 22, 2004); 70 Fed. Reg. 28,843 (May 19, 2005). These Federal Register notices may be found on the CD-Rom accompanying this volume. Relevant amendments are reprinted below.]

Effective September 1, 2006, replace § 541.3 with:

Sec. 541.3 Application.

(a) Except as provided in paragraph (b) and (c) of this section, this standard applies to the following:

(1) Passenger motor vehicle parts identified in § 541.5(a) that are present in:

    (i) Passenger cars; and

    (ii) Multipurpose passenger vehicles with a gross vehicle weight rating of 6,000 pounds or less; and

    (iii) Light-duty trucks with a gross vehicle weight rating of 6,000 pounds or less, that NHTSA has determined to be high theft in accordance with 49 CFR 542.1; and

    (iv) Light duty trucks with a gross vehicle weight rating of 6,000 pounds or less, that NHTSA has determined to be subject to the requirements of this section in accordance with 49 CFR 542.2.

(2) Replacement passenger motor vehicle parts identified in § 541.5(a) for vehicles listed in paragraphs (1)(i) to (iv) of this section.

(b) *Exclusions.* This standard does not apply to the following:

(1) Passenger motor vehicle parts identified in § 541.5(a) that are present in vehicles manufactured by a motor vehicle manufacturer that manufactures fewer than 5,000 vehicles for sale in the United States each year.

(2) Passenger motor vehicle parts identified in § 541.5(a) that are present in a line with an annual production of not more than 3,500 vehicles.

(3) Passenger motor vehicle parts identified in § 541.5(a) that are present in light-duty trucks with a gross vehicle weight rating of 6,000 pounds or less, that NHTSA has determined to be subject to the requirements of this section in accordance with 49 CFR 542.2, if the vehicle line with which these light-duty trucks share majority of major interchangeable parts is exempt from parts marking requirements pursuant to part 543.

(c) For vehicles listed in subparagraphs (1)(i) to (iv) of this section that are (1) not subject to the requirements of this standard until September 1, 2006, and (2) manufactured between September 1, 2006 and August 31, 2007; a manufacturer needs to meet the requirements of this part only for lines representing at least 50% of a manufacturer's total production of these vehicles.

[59 FR 64168, Dec. 13, 1994; 69 FR 17967, April 6, 2004; 69 FR 34612, June 22, 2004; 70 FR 28851, May 19, 2005]

Effective September 1, 2006, replace § 541.5(e)(2) with:

(2) Each manufacturer subject to paragraph (e)(1) of this section shall, not later than 30 days before the line is introduced into commerce, inform NHTSA in writing of the target areas designated for each line subject to this standard. The information should be submitted to: Administrator, National Highway Traffic Safety Administration, 400 Seventh Street, SW, Washington, DC 20590.

Effective September 1, 2006, add to end of citation list for § 541.5:

[69 FR 17967, April 6, 2004]

Page 346

Appendix A to Part 541 Lines Subject to the Requirements of This Standard

Replace bracketed text with:

[*Not reprinted. This appendix is updated for each model year. For text of the appendix current through August 31, 2006, see 70 Fed. Reg. 20,483 (Apr. 20, 2005).*]

Effective September 1, 2006, replace Appendix A to Part 541 with:

Appendix A to Part 541 Light Duty Truck Lines Subject to the Requirements of This Standard

[*Not reprinted. This appendix is updated for each model year. For text of the appendix effective as of September 1, 2006, see 69 Fed. Reg. 17,967 (Apr. 6, 2004).*]

Replace title of Appendix A-I to Part 541 with:

Appendix A-I to Part 541 High-Theft Lines With Antitheft Devices Which are Exempted From the Parts-Marking Requirements of This Standard Pursuant to 49 CFR Part 543

Replace bracketed text with:

[*Not reprinted. This appendix is updated for each model year. For text of the appendix current through August 31, 2006, see 70 Fed. Reg. 20,483 (Apr. 20, 2005).*]

Effective September 1, 2006, replace Appendix A-I to Part 541 with:

Appendix A-I to Part 541 Lines with Antitheft Devices Which are Exempted From the Parts-Marking Requirements of This Standard Pursuant to 49 CFR Part 543

[*Not reprinted. This appendix is updated for each model year. For text of the appendix effective as of September 1, 2006, see 69 Fed. Reg. 17,967 (Apr. 6, 2004).*]

Appendix A-II to Part 541 High-Theft Lines With Antitheft Devices Which Are Exempted in Part From the Parts-Marking Requirements of This Standard Pursuant to 49 CFR Part 543

Replace bracketed text with:

[*Not reprinted. This appendix is updated for each model year. For text of the appendix current through the 2006 model year, see 69 Fed. Reg. 17,967 (Apr. 6, 2004).*]

Effective September 1, 2006, replace Appendix A-II to Part 541 with:

Appendix A-II to Part 541 Lines with Antitheft Devices Which are Exempted in Part From the Parts-Marking Requirements of This Standard Pursuant to 49 CFR Part 543

[*Not reprinted. This appendix is updated for each model year. For text of the appendix effective as of September 1, 2006, see 69 Fed. Reg. 17,967 (Apr. 6, 2004).*]

Effective September 1, 2006, replace Appendix B to Part 541 with:

Appendix B to Part 541 Light Duty Truck Lines With Theft Rates Below the 1990/91 Median Theft Rate, Subject to the Requirements of This Standard

[*Not reprinted.*]

Page 347

Effective September 1, 2006, replace Appendix C to Part 541 with:

Appendix C to Part 541 Criteria for Selecting Light Duty Truck Lines Likely to Have High Theft Rates

[*Not reprinted.*]

B.3 Vehicle Identification Number Requirements, 49 C.F.R. §§ 565.1–565.7

Replace § 565.3(j) with:

(j) *Model Year* means the year used to designate a discrete vehicle model, irrespective of the calendar year in which the vehicle was actually produced, provided that the production period does not exceed 24 months.

Add citation list to end of § 565.3:

[70 FR 23939, May 6, 2005]

Page 350

B.4 Certification, 49 C.F.R. §§ 567.1–567.7

[*Editor's Note: 49 C.F.R. Part 567 has been replaced, effective September 1, 2006. See 70 Fed. Reg. 7414 (Feb. 14, 2005). This* Federal Register *notice may be found on the CD-Rom accompanying this volume. The new regulation is reprinted after the following amendment to the existing version of section 567.4 (effective until August 31, 2006).*]

Page 352

Sec. 567.4 Requirements for manufacturers of motor vehicles.

Replace § 567.4(h)(2) with:

(2) (For multipurpose passenger vehicles, trucks, buses, trailers, and motorcycles) The manufacturer may, at its option, list more than one GVWR-GAWR-tire-rim combination on the label as long as the listing contains the tire-rim combination installed as original equipment on the vehicle by the vehicle manufacturer and conforms in content and format to the requirements for the tire-rim-inflation information set forth in § 571.110, § 571.120, § 571.129 and § 571.139 of this chapter.

Add to end of citation list for § 567.4:

[67 FR 69623, Nov. 18, 2002; 68 FR 33655, June 5, 2003]

Effective September 1, 2006 replace 49 C.F.R. Part 567 with:

PART 567—CERTIFICATION

Sec.
567.1 Purpose.
567.2 Application.
567.3 Definitions.
567.4 Requirements for manufacturers of motor vehicles.
567.5 Requirements for manufacturers of vehicles manufactured in two or more stages.
567.6 Requirements for persons who do not alter certified vehicles or do so with readily attachable components.
567.7 Requirements for persons who alter certified vehicles.

AUTHORITY: 49 U.S.C. 322, 30111, 30115, 30117, 30166, 32502, 32504, 33101–33104, 33108, and 33109; delegation of authority at 49 CFR 1.50.

SOURCE: 70 FR 7430, Feb. 14, 2005, unless otherwise noted.

Sec. 567.1 Purpose.

The purpose of this part is to specify the content and location of, and other requirements for, the certification label to be affixed to motor vehicles as required by the National Traffic and Motor Vehicle Safety Act, as amended (the Vehicle Safety Act) (49 U.S.C. 30115) and the Motor Vehicle Information and Cost Savings Act, as amended (the Cost Savings Act), (49 U.S.C. 30254 and 33109), to address certification-related duties and liabilities, and to provide the consumer with information to assist him or her in determining which of the Federal Motor Vehicle Safety Standards (part 571 of this chapter), Bumper Standards (part 581 of this chapter), and Federal Theft Prevention Standards (part 541 of this chapter), are applicable to the vehicle.

Sec. 567.2 Application.

(a) This part applies to manufacturers including alterers of motor vehicles to which one or more standards are applicable.

(b) In the case of imported motor vehicles that do not have the label required by 49 CFR 567.4, Registered Importers of vehicles admitted into the United States under 49 U.S.C. 30141–30147 and 49 CFR part 591 must affix a label as required by 49 CFR 567.4, after the vehicle has been brought into conformity with the applicable Safety, Bumper and Theft Prevention Standards.

Sec. 567.3 Definitions.

All terms that are defined in the Act and the rules and standards issued under its authority are used as defined therein. The term "bumper" has the meaning assigned to it in Title I of the Cost Savings Act and the rules and standards issued under its authority.

Addendum means the document described in § 568.5 of this chapter.

Altered vehicle means a completed vehicle previously certified in accordance with § 567.4 or § 567.5 that has been altered other than by the addition, substitution, or removal of readily attachable components, such as mirrors or tire and rim assemblies, or by minor finishing operations such as painting, before the first purchase of the vehicle other than for resale, in such a manner as may affect the conformity of the vehicle with one or more Federal Motor Vehicle Safety Standard(s) or the validity of the vehicle's stated weight ratings or vehicle type classification.

Alterer means a person who alters by addition, substitution, or removal of components (other than readily attachable components) a certified vehicle before the first purchase of the vehicle other than for resale.

Chassis-cab means an incomplete vehicle, with a completed occupant compartment, that requires only the addition of cargo-carrying, work-performing, or load-bearing components to perform its intended functions.

Completed vehicle means a vehicle that requires no further manufacturing operations to perform its intended function.

Final-stage manufacturer means a person who performs such manufacturing operations on an incomplete vehicle that it becomes a completed vehicle.

Incomplete trailer means a vehicle that is capable of being drawn and that consists, at a minimum, of a chassis (including the frame) structure and suspension system but needs further manufacturing operations performed on it to become a completed vehicle.

Incomplete vehicle means

(1) An assemblage consisting, at a minimum, of chassis (including the frame) structure, power train, steering system, suspension system, and braking system, in the state that

those systems are to be part of the completed vehicle, but requires further manufacturing operations to become a completed vehicle; or

(2) An incomplete trailer.

Incomplete vehicle document or *IVD* means the document described in 49 CFR 568.4(a) and (b).

Incomplete vehicle manufacturer means a person who manufactures an incomplete vehicle by assembling components none of which, taken separately, constitute an incomplete vehicle.

Intermediate manufacturer means a person, other than the incomplete vehicle manufacturer or the final-stage manufacturer, who performs manufacturing operations on a vehicle manufactured in two or more stages.

Sec. 567.4 Requirements for manufacturers of motor vehicles.

(a) Each manufacturer of motor vehicles (except vehicles manufactured in two or more stages) shall affix to each vehicle a label, of the type and in the manner described below, containing the statements specified in paragraph (g) of this section.

(b) The label shall be riveted or permanently affixed in such a manner that it cannot be removed without destroying or defacing it.

(c) Except for trailers and motorcycles, the label shall be affixed to either the hinge pillar, door-latch post, or the door edge that meets the door-latch post, next to the driver's seating position, or if none of these locations is practicable, to the left side of the instrument panel. If that location is also not practicable, the label shall be affixed to the inward-facing surface of the door next to the driver's seating position. If none of the preceding locations is practicable, notification of that fact, together with drawings or photographs showing a suggested alternate location in the same general area, shall be submitted for approval to the Administrator, National Highway Traffic Safety Administration, Washington, D.C. 20590. The location of the label shall be such that it is easily readable without moving any part of the vehicle except an outer door.

(d) The label for trailers shall be affixed to a location on the forward half of the left side, such that it is easily readable from outside the vehicle without moving any part of the vehicle.

(e) The label for motorcycles shall be affixed to a permanent member of the vehicle as close as is practicable to the intersection of the steering post with the handle bars, in a location such that it is easily readable without moving any part of the vehicle except the steering system.

(f) The lettering on the label shall be of a color that contrasts with the background of the label.

(g) The label shall contain the following statements, in the English language, lettered in block capitals and numerals not less than three thirty-seconds of an inch high, in the order shown:

(1) Name of manufacturer: Except as provided in paragraphs (g)(1)(i), (ii) and (iii) of this section, the full corporate or individual name of the actual assembler of the vehicle shall be spelled out, except that such abbreviations as "Co." or "Inc." and their foreign equivalents, and the first and middle initials of individuals, may be used. The name of the manufacturer shall be preceded by the words "Manufactured By" or "Mfd By." In the case of imported vehicles to which the label required by this section is affixed by the Registered Importer, the name of the Registered Importer shall also be placed on the label in the manner described in this paragraph, directly below the name of the actual assembler.

(i) If a vehicle is assembled by a corporation that is controlled by another corporation that assumes responsibility for conformity with the standards, the name of the controlling corporation may be used.

(ii) If a vehicle is fabricated and delivered in complete but unassembled form, such that it is designed to be assembled without special machinery or tools, the fabricator of the vehicle may affix the label and name itself as the manufacturer for the purposes of this section.

(iii) If a trailer is sold by a person who is not its manufacturer, but who is engaged in the manufacture of trailers and assumes legal responsibility for all duties and liabilities imposed by the Act with respect to that trailer, the name of that person may appear on the label as the manufacturer. In such a case the name shall be preceded by the words "Responsible Manufacturer" or "Resp Mfr."

(2) Month and year of manufacture: This shall be the time during which work was completed at the place of main assembly of the vehicle. It may be spelled out, as "June 2000", or expressed in numerals, as "6/00".

(3) "Gross Vehicle Weight Rating" or "GVWR" followed by the appropriate value in pounds, which shall not be less than the sum of the unloaded vehicle weight, rated cargo load, and 150 pounds times the number of the vehicle's designated seating positions. However, for school buses the minimum occupant weight allowance shall be 120 pounds per passenger and 150 pounds for the driver.

(4) "Gross Axle Weight Rating" or "GAWR," followed by the appropriate value in pounds, for each axle, identified in order from front to rear (e.g., front, first intermediate, second intermediate, rear). The ratings for any consecutive axles having identical gross axle weight ratings when equipped with tires having the same tire size designation may, at the option of the manufacturer, be stated as a single value, with the label indicating to which axles the ratings apply.

> *Examples of combined ratings:*
> GAWR:
>   (a) All axles—2,400 kg (5,290 lb) with LT245/75R16(E) tires.
>   (b) Front—5,215 kg (11,500 lb) with 295/75R22.5(G) tires.
>   First intermediate to rear—9,070 kg (20,000 lb) with 295/75R22.5(G) tires.

(5) One of the following statements, as appropriate:

   (i) For passenger cars, the statement: "This vehicle conforms to all applicable Federal motor vehicle safety, bumper, and theft prevention standards in effect on the date of manufacture shown above." The expression "U.S." or "U.S.A." may be inserted before the word "Federal".

   (ii) In the case of multipurpose passenger vehicles (MPVs) and trucks with a GVWR of 6,000 pounds or less, the statement: "This vehicle conforms to all applicable Federal motor vehicle safety and theft prevention standards in effect on the date of manufacture shown above." The expression "U.S." or "U.S.A." may be inserted before the (word "Federal").

   (iii) In the case of multipurpose passenger vehicles (MPVs) and trucks with a GVWR of over 6,000 pounds, the statement: "This vehicle conforms to all applicable Federal motor vehicle safety standards in effect on the date of manufacture shown above." The expression "U.S." or "U.S.A." may be inserted before the word "Federal".

(6) Vehicle identification number.

(7) The type classification of the vehicle as defined in § 571.3 of this chapter (e.g., truck, MPV, bus, trailer).

(h) *Multiple GVWR-GAWR ratings.*

(1) (For passenger cars only) In cases in which different tire sizes are offered as a customer option, a manufacturer may at its option list more than one set of values for GVWR and GAWR, to meet the requirements of paragraphs (g) (3) and (4) of this section. If the label shows more than one set of weight rating values, each value shall be followed by the phrase "with—tires," inserting the proper tire size designations. A manufacturer may, at its option, list one or more tire sizes where only one set of weight ratings is provided.

> *Example:* Passenger Car
> GVWR: 4,400 lb with P195/65R15 tires; 4,800 lb with P205/75R15 tires.
> GAWR: Front—2,000 lb with P195/65R15 tires at 24 psi; 2,200 lb with

P205/75R15 tires at 24 psi. Rear—2,400 lb with P195/65R15 tires at 28 psi; 2,600 lb with P205/75R15 tires at 28 psi.

(2) (For multipurpose passenger vehicles, trucks, buses, trailers, and motorcycles) The manufacturer may, at its option, list more than one GVWR-GAWR-tire-rim combination on the label, as long as the listing contains the tire-rim combination installed as original equipment on the vehicle by the manufacturer and conforms in content and format to the requirements for tire-rim-inflation information set forth in Standard Nos. 110, 120, 129 and 139 (§§ 571.110, 571.120, 571.129 and 571.139 of this chapter).

(3) At the option of the manufacturer, additional GVWR-GAWR ratings for operation of the vehicle at reduced speeds may be listed at the bottom of the certification label following any information that is required to be listed.

(i) [*Reserved*].

(j) A manufacturer may, at its option, provide information concerning which tables in the document that accompanies the vehicle pursuant to § 575.6(a) of this chapter apply to the vehicle. This information may not precede or interrupt the information required by paragraph (g) of this section.

(k) In the case of passenger cars imported into the United States under 49 CFR 591.5(f) to which the label required by this section has not been affixed by the original assembler of the passenger car, a label meeting the requirements of this paragraph shall be affixed before the vehicle is imported into the United States, if the car is from a line listed in Appendix A of 49 CFR part 541. This label shall be in addition to, and not in place of, the label required by paragraphs (a) through (j), inclusive, of this section.

(1) The label shall be riveted or permanently affixed in such a manner that it cannot be removed without destroying or defacing it.

(2) The label shall be affixed to either the hinge pillar, door-latch post, or the door edge that meets the door-latch post, next to the driver's seating position, or, if none of these locations is practicable, to the left side of the instrument panel. If that location is also not practicable, the label shall be affixed to the inward-facing surface of the door next to the driver's seating position. The location of the label shall be such that it is easily readable without moving any part of the vehicle except an outer door.

(3) The lettering on the label shall be of a color that contrasts with the background of the label.

(4) The label shall contain the following statements, in the English language, lettered in block capitals and numerals not less than three thirty-seconds of an inch high, in the order shown:

    (i) Model year (if applicable) or year of manufacture and line of the vehicle, as reported by the manufacturer that produced or assembled the vehicle. "Model year" is used as defined in § 565.3(h) of this chapter. "Line" is used as defined in § 541.4 of this chapter.

    (ii) Name of the importer. The full corporate or individual name of the importer of the vehicle shall be spelled out, except that such abbreviations as "Co." or "Inc." and their foreign equivalents and the middle initial of individuals, may be used. The name of the importer shall be preceded by the words "Imported By".

    (iii) The statement: "This vehicle conforms to the applicable Federal motor vehicle theft prevention standard in effect on the date of manufacture."

(*l*)(1) In the case of a passenger car imported into the United States under 49 CFR 591.5(f) which does not have a vehicle identification number that complies with 49 CFR 565.4 (b), (c), and (g) at the time of importation, the Registered Importer shall permanently affix a label to the vehicle in such a manner that, unless the label is riveted, it cannot be removed without being destroyed or defaced. The label shall be in addition to the label required by paragraph (a) of this section, and shall be affixed to the vehicle in a location specified in paragraph (c) of this section.

(2) The label shall contain the following statement, in the English language, lettered in block capitals and numerals not less than 4 mm high, with the location on the vehicle

of the original manufacturer's identification number provided in the blank: ORIGINAL MANUFACTURER'S IDENTIFICATION NUMBER SUBSTITUTING FOR U.S. VIN IS LOCATED————.

Sec. 567.5 Requirements for manufacturers of vehicles manufactured in two or more stages.

(a) *Location of information labels for incomplete vehicles.* Each incomplete vehicle manufacturer or intermediate vehicle manufacturer shall permanently affix a label to each incomplete vehicle, in the location and form specified in § 567.4, and in a manner that does not obscure other labels. If the locations specified in 49 CFR 567.4(c) are not practicable, the label may be provided as part of the IVD package so that it can be permanently affixed in the acceptable locations provided for in that subsection when the vehicle is sufficiently manufactured to allow placement in accordance therewith.

(b) *Incomplete vehicle manufacturers.*

(1) Except as provided in paragraph (f) of this section and notwithstanding the certification of a final-stage manufacturer under 49 CFR 567.5(d)(2)(v), each manufacturer of an incomplete vehicle assumes legal responsibility for all certification-related duties and liabilities under the Vehicle Safety Act with respect to:

    (i) Components and systems it installs or supplies for installation on the incomplete vehicle, unless changed by a subsequent manufacturer;

    (ii) The vehicle as further manufactured or completed by an intermediate or final-stage manufacturer, to the extent that the vehicle is completed in accordance with the IVD; and

    (iii) The accuracy of the information contained in the IVD.

(2) Except as provided in paragraph (f) of this section, each incomplete vehicle manufacturer shall affix an information label to each incomplete vehicle that contains the following statements:

    (i) Name of incomplete vehicle manufacturer preceded by the words "incomplete vehicle MANUFACTURED BY" or "incomplete vehicle MFD BY".

    (ii) Month and year of manufacture of the incomplete vehicle. This may be spelled out, as in "JUNE 2000", or expressed in numerals, as in "6/00". No preface is required.

    (iii) "Gross Vehicle Weight Rating" or "GVWR" followed by the appropriate value in kilograms and (pounds), which shall not be less than the sum of the unloaded vehicle weight, rated cargo load, and 150 pounds times the number of the vehicle's designated seating positions, if known. However, for school buses the minimum occupant weight allowance shall be 120 pounds per passenger and 150 pounds for the driver.

    (iv) "Gross Axle Weight Rating" or "GAWR," followed by the appropriate value in kilograms and (pounds) for each axle, identified in order from front to rear (*e.g.*, front, first intermediate, second intermediate, rear). The ratings for any consecutive axles having identical gross axle weight ratings when equipped with tires having the same tire size designation may be stated as a single value, with the label indicating to which axles the ratings apply.

    (v) Vehicle Identification Number.

(c) *Intermediate manufacturers.*

(1) Except as provided in paragraphs (f) and (g) of this section and notwithstanding the certification of a final-stage manufacturer under § 567.5(d)(2)(v), each intermediate manufacturer of a vehicle manufactured in two or more stages assumes legal responsibility for all certification-related duties and liabilities under the Vehicle Safety Act with respect to:

    (i) Components and systems it installs or supplies for installation on the incomplete vehicle, unless changed by a subsequent manufacturer;

(ii) The vehicle as further manufactured or completed by an intermediate or final-stage manufacturer, to the extent that the vehicle is completed in accordance with the addendum to the IVD furnished by the intermediate vehicle manufacturer;

(iii) Any work done by the intermediate manufacturer on the incomplete vehicle that was not performed in accordance with the IVD or an addendum of a prior intermediate manufacturer; and

(iv) The accuracy of the information in any addendum to the IVD furnished by the intermediate vehicle manufacturer.

(2) Except as provided in paragraphs (f) and (g) of this section, each intermediate manufacturer of an incomplete vehicle shall affix an information label, in a manner that does not obscure the labels applied by previous stage manufacturers, to each incomplete vehicle, which contains the following statements:

(i) Name of intermediate manufacturer, preceded by the words "INTERMEDIATE MANUFACTURE BY" or "INTERMEDIATE MFR".

(ii) Month and year in which the intermediate manufacturer performed its last manufacturing operation on the incomplete vehicle. This may be spelled out, as "JUNE 2000", or expressed as numerals, as "6/00". No preface is required.

(iii) "Gross Vehicle Weight Rating" or "GVWR", followed by the appropriate value in kilograms and (pounds), if different from that identified by the incomplete vehicle manufacturer.

(iv) "Gross Axle Weight Rating" or "GAWR" followed by the appropriate value in kilograms and (pounds), if different from that identified by the incomplete vehicle manufacturer.

(v) Vehicle identification number.

(d) *Final-stage manufacturers.*

(1) Except as provided in paragraphs (f) and (g) of this section, each final-stage manufacturer of a vehicle manufactured in two or more stages assumes legal responsibility for all certification-related duties and liabilities under the Vehicle Safety Act, except to the extent that the incomplete vehicle manufacturer or an intermediate manufacturer has provided equipment subject to a safety standard or expressly assumed responsibility for standards related to systems and components it supplied and except to the extent that the final-stage manufacturer completed the vehicle in accordance with the prior manufacturers' IVD or any addendum furnished pursuant to 49 CFR part 568, as to the Federal motor vehicle safety standards fully addressed therein.

(2) Except as provided in paragraphs (f) and (g) of this section, each final-stage manufacturer shall affix a certification label to each vehicle, in a manner that does not obscure the labels applied by previous stage manufacturers, and that contains the following statements:

(i) Name of final-stage manufacturer, preceded by the words "MANUFACTURED BY" or "MFD BY".

(ii) Month and year in which final-stage manufacture is completed. This may be spelled out, as in "JUNE 2000", or expressed in numerals, as in "6/00". No preface is required.

(iii) "Gross Vehicle Weight Rating" or "GVWR" followed by the appropriate value in kilograms and (pounds), which shall not be less than the sum of the unloaded vehicle weight, rated cargo load, and 150 pounds times the number of the vehicle's designated seating positions. However, for school buses the minimum occupant weight allowance shall be 120 pounds per passenger and 150 pounds for the driver.

(iv) "GROSS AXLE WEIGHT RATING" or "GAWR", followed by the appropriate value in kilograms and (pounds) for each axle, identified in order from front to rear (*e.g.*, front, first intermediate, second intermediate, rear). The ratings for any consecutive axles having identical gross axle weight ratings when equipped with tires having the same tire size designation may be stated as a single value, with the label indicating to which axles the ratings apply.

Examples of combined ratings:
    (a) All axles—2,400 kg (5,290 lb) with LT245/75R16(E) tires;
    (b) Front—5,215 kg (11,500 lb) with 295/75R22.5(G) tires;
    (c) First intermediate to rear—9,070 kg (20,000 lb) with 295/75R22.5(G) tires.

(v)(A) One of the following alternative certification statements:
    (1) "This vehicle conforms to all applicable Federal Motor Vehicle Safety Standards, [and Bumper and Theft Prevention Standards, if applicable] in effect in (month, year)."
    (2) "This vehicle has been completed in accordance with the prior manufacturers' IVD, where applicable. This vehicle conforms to all applicable Federal Motor Vehicle Safety Standards, [and Bumper and Theft Prevention Standards, if applicable] in effect in (month, year)."
    (3) "This vehicle has been completed in accordance with the prior manufacturers' IVD, where applicable, except for [insert FMVSS(s)]. This vehicle conforms to all applicable Federal Motor Vehicle Safety Standards, [and Bumper and Theft Prevention Standards if applicable] in effect in (month, year)."
    (B) The date shown in the statement required in paragraph (d)(2)(v)(A) of this section shall not be earlier than the manufacturing date provided by the incomplete or intermediate stage manufacturer and not later than the date of completion of the final-stage manufacture.
    (C) Notwithstanding the certification statements in paragraph (d)(2)(v)(A) of this section, the legal responsibilities and liabilities for certification under the Vehicle Safety Act shall be allocated among the vehicle manufacturers as provided in 567.5(b)(1), (c)(1), and (d)(1), and 49 CFR 568.4(a)(9).
(vi) Vehicle identification number.
(vii) The type classification of the vehicle as defined in 49 CFR 571.3 (e.g., truck, MPV, bus, trailer).

(e) More than one set of figures for GVWR and GAWR, and one or more tire sizes, may be listed in satisfaction of the requirements of paragraphs (d)(2)(iii) and (iv) of this section, as provided in § 567.4(h).

(f) If an incomplete vehicle manufacturer assumes legal responsibility for all duties and liabilities for certification under the Vehicle Safety Act, with respect to the vehicle as finally manufactured, the incomplete vehicle manufacturer shall ensure that a label is affixed to the final vehicle in conformity with paragraph (d) of this section, except that the name of the incomplete vehicle manufacturer shall appear instead of the name of the final-stage manufacturer after the words "MANUFACTURED BY" or "MFD BY" required by paragraph (d)(2)(i) of this section.

(g) If an intermediate manufacturer of a vehicle assumes legal responsibility for all duties and liabilities for certification under the Vehicle Safety Act, with respect to the vehicle as finally manufactured, the intermediate manufacturer shall ensure that a label is affixed to the final vehicle in conformity with paragraph (d) of this section, except that the name of the intermediate manufacturer shall appear instead of the name of the final-stage manufacturer after the words "MANUFACTURED BY" or "MFD BY" required by paragraph (f) of this section.

Sec. 567.6 Requirements for persons who do not alter certified vehicles or do so with readily attachable components.

A person who does not alter a motor vehicle or who alters such a vehicle only by the addition, substitution, or removal of readily attachable components such as mirrors or tires and rim assemblies, or minor finishing operations such as painting, in such a manner that the vehicle's stated weight ratings are still valid, need not affix a label to the vehicle, but shall allow a manufacturer's label that conforms to the requirements of this part to remain affixed to the vehicle. If such a person is a distributor of the motor vehicle, allowing the manufacturer's label to remain affixed to the vehicle shall satisfy the distributor's certification requirements under the Vehicle Safety Act.

Sec. 567.7 Requirements for persons who alter certified vehicles.

(a) With respect to the vehicle alterations it performs, an alterer:

(1) Has a duty to determine continued conformity of the altered vehicle with applicable Federal motor vehicle safety, Bumper, and Theft Prevention standards, and

(2) Assumes legal responsibility for all duties and liabilities for certification under the Vehicle Safety Act.

(b) The vehicle manufacturer's certification label and any information labels shall remain affixed to the vehicle and the alterer shall affix to the vehicle an additional label in the manner and location specified in § 567.4, in a manner that does not obscure any previously applied labels, and containing the following information:

(1) The statement: "This vehicle was altered by (individual or corporate name) in (month and year in which alterations were completed) and as altered it conforms to all applicable Federal Motor Vehicle Safety, Bumper and Theft Prevention Standards affected by the alteration and in effect in (month, year)." The second date shall be no earlier than the date of manufacture of the certified vehicle (as specified on the certification label), and no later than the date alterations were completed.

(2) If the gross vehicle weight rating or any of the gross axle weight ratings of the vehicle as altered are different from those shown on the original certification label, the modified values shall be provided in the form specified in § 567.4(g)(3) and (4).

(3) If the vehicle as altered has a different type classification from that shown on the original certification label, the type as modified shall be provided.

State Laws Relating to Automobile Fraud

Page 357

Replace citation to NCLC's UDAP manual in final sentence of Appendix's first paragraph with:

Unfair and Deceptive Acts and Practices Appxs. A, C.2 (6th ed. 2004)

Page 358

ALASKA

Add to text after State Bonding Statute *summary:*

***New Car Damage Disclosure*: Alaska Stat. § 45.25.510**
Disclosure of damage that exceeds greater of 5% of manufacturer's suggested list price or $1000.

Page 360

ARKANSAS

New Car Damage Disclosure

Replace "retail value" with:

sticker price

CALIFORNIA

State Salvage Vehicle Statute

In first sentence replace "insured it" with:

insured or is responsible for repairing it

New Car Damage Disclosures

Replace heading with:

***New Car Damage Disclosure*: Cal. Veh. Code §§ 9990–9993**

Page 361

COLORADO

State Salvage Vehicle Statute

Add to text after summary's fifth sentence:

This language must also be stamped on the vehicle itself.

Add to text after State Bonding Statute *summary:*

***New and Used Car Damage Disclosure*: Colo. Rev. Stat. § 6-1-708**
Deceptive practice to fail to disclose to purchaser prior to sale that a motor vehicle has sustained material damage at any one time from any one incident. Prohibition applies to persons acting in the course of their business, vocation, or occupation.

Add to text after State RICO Statute *summary:*

***Special Statutory Cause of Action for Automobile Fraud*: Colo. Rev. Stat. § 12-6-122(1)**
Allows consumer to sue dealer and salesperson for any fraud or fraudulent representations. Consumer may also sue bonding company.

DELAWARE

Add to text after State RICO Statute *summary:*

***Special Statutory Cause of Action for Automobile Fraud*: Del. Code Ann. tit. 21, § 6909(d)** Buyer has right to rescind contract at any time and receive full and complete refund of all purchase moneys, including interest and fees, if dealer fails to disclose in writing that a vehicle title has been branded "reconstructed," "flood damaged," "salvage," or as a former taxi.

DISTRICT OF COLUMBIA

Replace Automobile Auctions *summary with:*

***Automobile Auctions*: D.C. Code §§ 50-2402, 50-2421.10** (regulating public auction of abandoned vehicles)

GEORGIA

State Salvage Vehicle Statute

Replace summary's second sentence with:

Definition also includes certain imported vehicles damaged in shipment. Owner of vehicle that suffers certain specified damage must deliver title for cancellation. Owner who retains possession of salvage vehicle must obtain salvage certificate.

Add to text after summary's fifth sentence:

If vehicle is repaired by replacing less than two major component parts, title must be marked "salvage—repair." Title branding requirements apply to vehicles declared salvage after July 1, 2004, but metal plate is required for any vehicle restored after Nov. 1, 1982. Salvage vehicles must undergo state safety inspection before retitling.

Add to text after State RICO Statute *summary:*

***Special Statutory Cause of Action for Automobile Fraud*: Ga. Code Ann. §§ 43-47-15, 43-47-21**
Any person damaged by a violation may bring a private cause of action for actual, consequential, and punitive damages, plus attorney fees and court costs, against any licensed used vehicle dealer or used vehicle parts dealer who purchases or rebuilds a wrecked or salvage motor vehicle without complying with the state laws regarding titling and inspection.

IDAHO

Add to text after State RICO Statute *summary:*

***Special Statutory Cause of Action for Automobile Fraud*: Idaho Code Ann. §§ 49-1610, 49-1613**
Any person who suffers loss or damage by reason of any fraud, fraudulent representation, or violation of certain motor vehicle laws by a licensed dealer or a dealer's salesperson who is acting for the dealer has a private cause of action for damages and equitable relief. This cause of action applies to, inter alia, prohibitions against misleading or inaccurate advertising and knowing sale of a stolen vehicle.

ILLINOIS

State Lemon Laundering Statute

Replace citation with:

625 Ill. Comp. Stat. §§ 5/5-104.2, 5/5-104.3

Add to text after State UDAP Statute(s) *summary:*

***Special Statutory Cause of Action for Automobile Fraud*: 815 Ill. Comp. Stat. § 5/5-502**
Any person injured by a violation of the laws regarding vehicle dealers, transporters, wreckers, and rebuilders, or any interested person, may seek an injunction to prevent violations. This cause of action applies to the state's requirement that vehicle dealers disclose that a vehicle has been rebuilt (815 Ill. Comp. Stat. §§ 5/5-101(i)(5) (new vehicle dealers), 5/5-102(i)(5) (used vehicle dealers), 5/5-104.3), or is a lemon buyback (815 Ill. Comp. Stat. § 5/5-104.2).

Page 369

IOWA

Replace New and Used Car Damage Disclosure *summary with:*

***Used Car Damage Disclosure*: Iowa Code § 321.69**
Disclosure required if vehicle was damaged to the extent it met definition of wrecked or salvage vehicle.

Page 370

KANSAS

State Salvage Vehicle Statute

In summary's first sentence replace "one" with:

one more than six model years old

Replace summary's second sentence with:

Definition also includes vehicle six or fewer model years old if cost of repair is seventy-five percent or more of fair market value (except for merely exterior cosmetic damage resulting from windstorm or hail) and any motor vehicle if insurer determines it is a total loss and takes title. Owner of salvage vehicle must apply for salvage title before transferring car, as must any purchaser or insurance company that acquires salvage vehicle. If insurer settles claim but allows owner to keep car, it must notify owner of duty to apply for salvage title, and owner must do so. Lessee must inform lessor of salvage-level damage, and lessor must apply for salvage title.

KENTUCKY

State Salvage Vehicle Statute

Add to text after summary's third sentence:

Salvage title issued for out-of-state junk vehicle must be branded "salvage"; if rebuilt title is issued, title must be branded "rebuilt" and a metal plate must be affixed to the door frame.

New Car Damage Disclosure

Add to text at end of summary:

Buyer who suffers injury to business or property as result of violation has private cause of action for injunction, actual damages, costs, and attorney fees under Ky. Rev. Stat. Ann. § 190.062 (West).

Page 371

Add to text after State UDAP Statute(s) *summary:*

***Special Statutory Cause of Action for Automobile Fraud*: Ky. Rev. Stat. Ann. §§ 190.062, 190.071, 190.080 (West)**
Any person who suffers an injury to business or property as a result of a violation of certain motor vehicle laws has a private cause of action for an injunction against further violations, actual damages, costs, and attorney fees. This cause of action applies to Kentucky's prohibition against selling a used or demonstrator vehicle as new, its general prohibition against false or fraudulent representations in connection with the operation of a new motor vehicle dealership, its requirement that dealers disclose the identities of prior owners, and the state's new car damage disclosure requirement. Suit under this section must be filed in the Franklin Circuit Court.

LOUISIANA

State Salvage Vehicle Statute

Replace citation with:

La. Rev. Stat. Ann. §§ 32:702, 32:707, 32:707.3

Add to text at end of summary:	Special provisions requiring destruction of any total loss vehicle whose power train, computer, or electrical system was damaged by flooding as a result of a gubernatorially declared disaster or emergency.
Page 372	***New Car Damage Disclosure***
Replace citation with:	**La. Rev. Stat. Ann. § 32:1264**
Replace Automobile Auctions *summary with:*	***Automobile Auctions***: **La. Rev. Stat. Ann. § 32:771** (licensure); **La. Rev. Stat. Ann. § 33:2332** (disposition of vehicles recovered or seized by police)
Page 373	**MARYLAND**
	State Lemon Laundering Statute
Add to text at end of summary:	*See also* Md. Code Regs. 11.12.01.14(J) (details of disclosure requirements).
Add to text after State Bonding Statute *summary:*	***New Car Damage Disclosure***: **Md. Code Regs. 11.12.01.14(K)** Written disclosure of damage required if vehicle that has never been titled sustains either body damage or mechanical damage resulting in the replacement of major part or parts.
Page 376	**MISSISSIPPI**
	New Car Damage Disclosure
Replace citation with:	**50-014-003 Miss. Code R. § 1 (Weil)** (Motor Vehicle Comm'n)
Page 377	**MISSOURI**
	State Salvage Vehicle Statute
Replace citation with:	**Mo. Rev. Stat. §§ 301.010, 301.020, 301.190, 301.227, 301.573**
Replace summary's first sentence with:	A salvage vehicle is a vehicle 1) for which the cost of repairs exceeds seventy-five percent of the pre-accident fair market value; 2) which has been declared salvage by the owner, the holder of a security interest, or an insurance company; 3) which has a salvage title; or 4) which is abandoned property as defined by statute.
Add to text after summary's second sentence:	Owner of reconstructed or prior salvage vehicle must obtain branded title. Insurer must notify insured of this duty.
Replace "salvage" in summary's last sentence with:	reconstructed vehicle
Page 378	**NEBRASKA**
	State Salvage Vehicle Statute
Add to text after summary's third sentence:	If an insurance company acquires a salvage vehicle by paying a total loss settlement, it must obtain title, surrender it, and apply for salvage branded title; if owner elects to retain vehicle, insurer must notify department of motor vehicles, which must enter salvage brand onto computerized vehicle record, and owner must surrender title.

Add to text after State
UDAP Statute(s) *summary:*

Special Statutory Cause of Action for Automobile Fraud: **Neb. Rev. Stat. §§ 60-1440, 60-1411.03**
Any person injured by a violation of the state's motor vehicle industry licensing laws has a private cause of action for damages and equitable relief. These laws prohibit, inter alia, various types of false advertisements and representation of used vehicles as new.

NEVADA

Replace State Salvage
Vehicle Summary *with:*

State Salvage Vehicle Statute: **Nev. Rev. Stat. §§ 482.098, 482.245, 487.710 to 487.890**
A salvage vehicle is one that at any time has been declared a total loss vehicle, flood-damaged vehicle, or non-repairable vehicle, or has had "salvage" or a similar word or placed on any title. "Total loss vehicle" is one whose cost of repair is sixty-five percent or more of pre-damage fair market value, but definition excludes non-repairable vehicles (stripped vehicles, those with value only as scrap, and those that can not be restored to legal operation) and vehicles ten or more years old with only certain specified damage. Insurer that acquires salvage vehicle as result of settlement must surrender title and apply for salvage title, as must owner before transferring salvage vehicle. Any person who knowingly transfers an interest in a salvage vehicle must make written disclosure. Reconstructed salvage vehicles must be inspected for safety before registration. "Rebuilt" must appear on title for rebuilt vehicle and must be carried over onto later titles. A non-repairable vehicle must be processed as scrap, can not be rebuilt, can not receive a salvage title, and must be issued a non-repairable certificate before ownership is transferred.

State Lemon Laundering Statute: **2005 Nev. Stat. ch. 340**
Manufacturer who reacquires or assists lienholder in acquiring vehicle under state lemon law must cause it to be retitled in manufacturer's name, ask that certificate be branded "lemon law buyback," and place decal on vehicle. Manufacturer and any person who acquires such a vehicle for resale must make written disclosure to transferee. Manufacturer who acquires or assists lienholder in acquiring vehicle in response to express warranty claim by buyer must also provide disclosure to subsequent transferee. Confidentiality clauses in buyback agreements prohibited. Any person damaged by violation may sue for actual damages, punitive damages, costs, and attorney fees.

Add to text after State RICO
Statute *summary:*

Special Statutory Cause of Action for Automobile Fraud: **Nev. Rev. Stat. § 487.850**
Any person who, with intent to defraud, removes salvage or rebuilt indication on title or knowingly fails to disclose vehicle's salvage status before transfer is liable to person harmed for greater of treble damages, $5000, or actual damages, plus punitive damages. Prevailing purchaser or lessee may also recover attorney fees.

NEW HAMPSHIRE

State Salvage Vehicle Statute

*Add to text at beginning of
summary:*

A total loss vehicle is one that is so damaged that it is determined in connection with an insurance claim settlement that it is physically or practically impossible to repair the vehicle, or, for vehicles less than five model years old, the cost of repairing the vehicle is seventy-five percent or more of its fair market value.

*Replace "vehicle" in
summary's first sentence
with:*

total loss vehicle

*Delete parenthetical phrase
in summary's second
sentence.*

*In summary's last sentence
replace "salvage" with:*   salvage or rebuilt

Add to text after State
UDAP Statute(s) *summary:*   ***Special Statutory Cause of Action for Automobile Fraud***: **N.H. Rev. Stat. Ann. § 357-C:12**
Any person whose business or property is injured by a violation of certain state motor vehicle
laws has a private cause of action for actual damages, costs, and attorney fees. The substantive
prohibitions to which this private cause of action applies include sale of gray market vehicles
without disclosure.

Page 381   **NEW MEXICO**

Replace State Odometer
Statute *summary with:*   ***State Odometer Statute:*** **N.M. Stat. §§ 57-12-6, 66-3-101, 66-3-107**
Prohibited Acts: Person transferring a motor vehicle is required to record the actual mileage
of the vehicle as indicated on the odometer on a form provided by the motor vehicle
department. §§ 66-3-101, 66-3-107. Willful misrepresentation of the age of a motor vehicle
is a UDAP violation. § 57-12-6.
Criminal Penalties: Violation of § 57-12-6 is a misdemeanor.
Civil Penalties: None stated for violation of §§ 66-3-101, 66-3-107. For violation of
§ 57-12-6, buyer has UDAP remedies, including injunction, $100 penalty, the greater of treble
damages or $300 if willful, plus attorney fees and costs.

Replace State Salvage
Vehicle Statute *summary
with:*   ***State Salvage Vehicle Statute***: **N.M. Stat. §§ 66-1-4.12, 66-1-4.16, 66-3-4, 66-3-10.1**
A salvage vehicle is one other than a non-repairable vehicle that insurance company considers
uneconomical to repair and 1) that is in fact not repaired or 2) for which a total loss payment
is made if insurer obtained claimant's agreement to the amount of the payment and told the
claimant that title must be branded and submitted to state agency for issuance of salvage
certificate. Salvage vehicle can not be sold or conveyed unless title is branded. For a
non-repairable vehicle, that is, one that has no resale value except as scrap, insurer must stamp
title "nonrepairable," and owner must obtain non-repairable vehicle certificate before
keeping, selling, or disposing of vehicle. Such a vehicle can not be repaired, reconstructed,
or restored for highway operation and can only be sold to a wrecker.

Page 382

Add to text after State RICO
Statute *summary:*   ***Special Statutory Cause of Action for Automobile Fraud***: **N.M. Stat. §§ 57-16-4, 57-16-13**
Prohibits motor vehicle dealers from, *inter alia*, using any false, deceptive, or misleading
advertisements; willfully defrauding any retail buyer; failing to perform their obligations
under a manufacturer's warranty; and misrepresenting demonstrators or other used vehicles
as new. Consumer has a private cause of action for damages and attorney fees. If the
defendant acted maliciously, court or jury may award punitive damages of up to three times
actual damages.

Page 383   **NEW YORK**

Add to text after State RICO
Statute *summary:*   ***Special Statutory Cause of Action for Automobile Fraud***: **N.Y. Veh. & Traf. Law §§ 417-a,
471 (McKinney)**
Any person aggrieved by a dealer's sale of a gray market vehicle without a prominent label
disclosing that it was manufactured for distribution outside the United States may recover
"any additional margin obtained . . . on such purchase and resale." Consumer also has private
cause of action for treble damages or $100, whichever is greater, plus attorney fees, for failure
to disclose the principal prior use of a vehicle or its history as a lemon buyback.

NORTH CAROLINA

Used Car Damage Disclosure

Add to text at end of summary:

Statute incorporates remedies under N.C. Gen. Stat. § 20-348 ($1500 or treble damages, whichever is greater, plus costs and attorney fees).

Page 388

RHODE ISLAND

New Car Damage Disclosure

Add to text at end of summary:

Buyer has private cause of action for injunction, actual damages, costs, and reasonable attorney fee under R.I. Gen. Laws § 31-5.1-13.

Add to text after State RICO Statute *summary:*

Special Statutory Cause of Action for Automobile Fraud: R.I. Gen. Laws §§ 31-5.1-4, 31-5.1-13, 31-5.1-14

Any consumer who is injured by a violation of motor vehicle dealer, manufacturer, and distributor statutes may sue for an injunction against further violations and may seek actual damages, costs, and a reasonable attorney fee. These statutes broadly prohibit false or misleading advertisements by motor vehicle dealers, and actions that are arbitrary, in bad faith, or unconscionable, and that cause damage to any parties involved or to the public. In addition, any contract or portion of a contract that violates these laws is void and unenforceable.

Page 389

SOUTH CAROLINA

Add to text after State UDAP Statute(s) *summary:*

Special Statutory Cause of Action for Automobile Fraud: S.C. Code Ann. §§ 56-15-40, 56-15-110, 56-15-130

Prohibits any motor vehicle dealer from engaging in any action which is arbitrary, in bad faith, or unconscionable and which causes damage to any of the parties or to the public; engaging in false or misleading advertising; or representing and selling as new any motor vehicle that has been operated for demonstration purposes or is otherwise a used vehicle. Any contract in violation of these provisions is void and unenforceable. Any person injured "in his business or property" by a violation has a cause of action for double the actual damages plus costs and attorney fees, and additionally, if the defendant acted maliciously, punitive damages up to three times actual damages.

SOUTH DAKOTA

Replace State Salvage Vehicle Statute *summary with:*

State Salvage Vehicle Statute: S.D. Codified Laws §§ 32-3-12, 32-3-51.5, 32-3-51.6, 32-3-53, 32-3-53.2 (as amended by 2005 S.D. Laws 155)

Salvage vehicle is a vehicle that an insurer or self-insurer determines is a total loss due to damage caused by fire, vandalism, collision, weather, submersion in water, or flood, but vehicles more than six model years old or with a gross vehicle weight rating of more than 16,000 lbs. are exempt. Insurer who acquires ownership of salvage vehicle in settlement of total loss claim or self-insurer who acquires ownership of salvage vehicle must surrender title and obtain salvage title. An owner who retains the vehicle has this duty, and insurer or self-insurer must notify owner of this duty. If vehicle is restored to operation, vehicle may be issued a rebuilt title. Out-of-state vehicle with salvage or similar brand must receive salvage title or junking certificate.

Replace New *and Used Car Damage Disclosure* summary *with:*

New and Used Car Damage Disclosure: S.D. Codified Laws §§ 32-3-51.5 to 32-3-51.9, 32-3-51.18; S.D. Admin R. 64:28:03:04

Upon sale, transfer, or trade-in of motor vehicle, or licensing of vehicle titled in another state, seller must complete disclosure statement regarding any damage in excess of $5000. Vehicles more than six model years old or with a gross vehicle weight rating of more than 16,000 lbs. are exempt, and statute does not apply if a rebuilt title or junking certificate is sought. "Damage" includes that caused by fire, vandalism, collision, weather, submersion in water, or flood, but not normal wear and tear, glass damage, mechanical repairs, or electrical repairs that have not been caused by one of these events. Dealer must display sticker, decal, or notice on vehicle that discloses its damage; if dealer does not comply, buyer has right to rescind purchase up to ten days after receiving title.

TEXAS

Replace State Salvage Vehicle Statute *summary with:*

State Salvage Vehicle Statute: Tex. Transp. Code Ann. §§ 501.091 to 501.095, 501.097, 501.098, 501.100 to 501.103 (Vernon)

A salvage vehicle is a vehicle that has been damaged to the extent that the cost of repairs exceeds actual pre-damage cash value or is a vehicle that comes into the state with a salvage-type brand on its title. A non-repairable vehicle is a vehicle that has been so damaged, wrecked, or burned that its only residual value is as a source of parts or scrap metal, or is a vehicle that comes into the state with a non-repairable-type brand on its title. Insurer that acquires ownership or possession of salvage or non-repairable vehicle through payment of a claim must obtain salvage certificate or non-repairable title (similar requirements for self-insurers and buyers). Insurer may sell vehicle only to salvage vehicle dealer, out-of-state buyer, buyer in casual sale at auction, or metal recycler. If it does not acquire ownership it must file report with state motor vehicle department. Salvage vehicle may be issued regular title, branded "Rebuilt Salvage," after repairs. Non-repairable vehicle title must state that it may only be used for parts or scrap metal (with exceptions if title was issued before Sept. 1, 2003). Titles of out-of-state vehicles with salvage titles must be given a description that the motor vehicle department "considers appropriate."

State Lemon Laundering Statute

Replace citation with:

Tex. Occ. Code Ann. § 2301.610 (Vernon)

Add to text after summary's first sentence:

Disclosure statement must accompany vehicle through the first retail sale.

Add to text after State UDAP Statute(s) *summary:*

Special Statutory Cause of Action for Automobile Fraud: Tex. Occ. Code Ann. §§ 2301.351, 2301.805 (Vernon)

Any person damaged by a violation of certain motor vehicle laws, including a general prohibition against false, deceptive, or misleading advertising, may bring suit under the state UDAP statute.

UTAH

State Salvage Vehicle Statute

Add to text at end of summary:

Utah Code Ann. § 53-8-205 requires a salvage vehicle to pass a safety inspection before registration.

State Lemon Laundering Statute

Add to text at end of summary:

Violation is also a UDAP violation.

State Bonding Statute

Replace Amount *entry with:*

Amount: New and used motor vehicle dealers and special equipment dealers: $50,000 ($75,000 on or after July 1, 2006); motorcycle, off-highway vehicle, or small trailer dealers: $10,000; body shops: $20,000. Person making claim on the bond shall be awarded attorney fees in cases against surety or principal unless bond has been depleted.

Replace first sentence of Scope *entry with:*

Fraud, fraudulent representation, or violation of law requiring delivery of certificate of title or manufacturer's certificate of origin.

Add to text after State RICO Statute *summary:*

Special Statutory Cause of Action for Automobile Fraud: Utah Code Ann. § 41-3-702
Purchaser may maintain civil action for $1000 or treble damages, whichever is greater, plus reasonable attorney fees and costs, for violation of certain motor vehicle laws, including sale of a salvage vehicle without disclosure, false statements on a damage disclosure statement, and fraudulent certification that a vehicle is entitled to an unbranded title.

Page 394

VIRGINIA

State Bonding Statute

Replace citation with:

Va. Code Ann. §§ 46.2-1527.1 to 46.2-1527.10

Replace Persons Required to Post Bond *entry with:*

Persons Required to Post Bond: For first three years, dealer must post $25,000 bond and pay annual fee into Motor Vehicle Transaction Recovery Fund. After three years without claims, dealer applying for license renewal has the choice of either continuing to pay $100 per year into the fund, or maintaining a $100,000 bond. Consumers can recover from the recovery fund if the dealer is participating in it.

Replace Amount *entry with:*

Amount: $25,000 bond plus participation in recovery fund for first three years; after three years without claims, dealer has choice of continued participation in recovery fund or posting $100,000 bond. Maximum claim of one judgment creditor against the recovery fund is $20,000.

WASHINGTON

State Odometer Statute

Add to text at end of Private Civil Remedies *entry:*

See also Wash. Rev. Code §§ 46.70.180(5) (prohibiting odometer offenses), 46.70.190 (authorizing civil action for actual damages, costs, and attorney fees for any violation of chapter), 46.70.310 (any violation of chapter is UDAP violation).

Page 395

Add to text after State RICO Statute *summary:*

Special Statutory Cause of Action for Automobile Fraud: Wash. Rev. Code §§ 46.70.180, 46.70.310
Any person who suffers an injury to business or property because of a violation of the statutes regulating motor vehicle dealers and manufacturers has private cause of action for actual damages, costs, and attorney fees. Any violation is also a UDAP violation. The substantive prohibitions to which this cause of action applies include odometer offenses and a general prohibition against dissemination of false or deceptive statements.

WISCONSIN

State Salvage Vehicle Statute

Replace citation with: **Wis. Stat. §§ 342.01, 342.07, 342.10, 342.065** (see also Wis. Admin. Code Trans. § 139.04)

State Lemon Laundering Statute

Replace citation with: **Wis. Stat. §§ 218.015(2)(d), 218.0170(2)(d), 342.10, 342.15.1** (see also Wis. Admin. Code Trans. § 139.04)

State Bonding Statute

Replace Amount *entry with:*   *Amount*: Motor vehicle dealers: $50,000 or an irrevocable letter of credit in the same amount; wholesalers: $25,000 or an irrevocable letter of credit in the same amount; dealers in motorcycles and no other types of motor vehicles: $5000 or an irrevocable letter of credit in the same amount; if the licensor has reasonable cause to doubt applicant's financial responsibility or compliance with the statute, an additional bond of between $5000 and $100,000 may be required.

Add to text after State RICO Statute *summary:*   ***Special Statutory Cause of Action for Automobile Fraud***: **Wis. Stat. §§ 218.0116, 218.0163(2)**
Consumer has private cause of action for pecuniary loss caused by a licensed dealer's violation of certain provisions of the motor vehicle laws, including willful fraud; willful failure to perform any written agreement; fraudulent sales, leases, prelease agreements, repossessions, or transactions; fraudulent misrepresentation, circumvention, or concealment of certain material particulars of a transaction; unconscionable practices; and violation of various other motor vehicle laws. The consumer may also recover costs and attorney fees.

WYOMING

State Bonding Statute

Replace Amount *entry with:*   *Amount*: $25,000.

State-by-State Information on Requesting Title Histories

As described in Chapter 2, *supra*, a title history search from a state department of motor vehicles is often a critical step in an automobile fraud investigation. Because of the Driver Privacy Protection Act, applicants must indicate the use they will make of this data and must supply the state with other information. Most states have one or more forms to request a title search on a state website, other states have forms that are not posted on a website, and some states do not have forms, but require a letter or subpoena.

This Appendix first sets out for each state the address and website for the state department of motor vehicles. Then it indicates whether a form to request a title search can be found on the CD-Rom accompanying this manual and, if available, an Internet address to check to see if the form on the CD-Rom is still current. If a form is not available, the appendix details other information on the CD-Rom that will assist those seeking title searches. This Appendix also lists a second address for certain state department of motor vehicles if that address is a more appropriate one to use to obtain additional information on title searches.

The version of this Appendix on the CD-Rom accompanying this manual inludes live web links which, if clicked, provide direct access to the relevant state department of motor vehicles website. Finally, there are a number of websites which provide links to the websites of all fifty state departments of motor vehicles. These links may be found on the CD-Rom accompanying this manual and allow rapid access to the various states' websites: http://carprice.com/dmvdot, www.virtualgumshoe.com, and www.pimall.com/nais/dmv.html.

ALABAMA

Dept. of Revenue, Motor Vehicle Division, 1202 Gordon Persons Building, 50 N. Ripley St., P.O. Box 327610, Montgomery, AL 36132-7610, www.dps.state.al.us. The June 2004 form to apply for a title search is found on the CD-Rom accompanying this manual, and can also be obtained at www.ador.state.al.us/motorvehicle/mvforms/mvdppa1.pdf.

ALASKA

Division of Motor Vehicles, Attention: RESEARCH, 1300 W. Benson Blvd., Ste. 200, Anchorage, AK 99503-3600, www.state.ak.us/dmv. The June 2001 form to apply for a title search is found on the CD-Rom accompanying this manual, and can also be obtained at www.state.ak.us/local/akpages/admin/dmv/forms/pdfs/851.pdf.

ARIZONA

Motor Vehicle Division, P.O. Box 2100, Mail Drop 539M, Phoenix, AZ 85001, www.dot.state.az.us/MVD/mvd.htm. The August 2003 form to apply for a title search is found on the CD-Rom accompanying this manual, and the form may also be found on the department's website. A customer Service Guide and Drivers License Manual with some helpful information on title searches can be found at http://mvd.azdot.gov/mvd/formsandpub/mvd.asp. Additional information is available at Mail Drop 504M, Motor Vehicle Division, 1801 W Jefferson St., Phoenix, AZ 85007, (602) 255-0072, or toll free in Arizona at (800) 324-5425.

ARKANSAS

Dept. of Finance and Administration, Attn: Correspondence Desk, 1900 West Seven, Little Rock, AR 72201, www.accessarkansas.org/dfa/motorvehicle. No form is available from the state, but a search can be initiated using the following procedure. On company letterhead, send a detailed letter of outlining the request (vehicle identification number (VIN), make, model, certification, how far back into the history of the vehicle, and so forth), who you are, and how you will use the information. Additionally enclose a copy of a government-issued photo identification card and a check made payable to the Arkansas Department of Finance and Administration. Each record costs $1.00 per VIN AND $1.00 per page. To find out how much the total cost will be, call their office at (501) 682-4677, describe your request, and you will be given the total amount to include with your request. The research will begin once your request and payment are received. The request should be sent to Arkansas Department of Finance and Administration, P.O. Box 1272, Little Rock, AR 72203, Attention: Correspondence Desk. One can also set up an account with the Arkansas Department of Finance and Administration by calling (501) 682-4692 to request the form for setting up an account (they can not send it by e-mail or facsmile). You are required to send a check for $25.00 with the completed form.

CALIFORNIA

Dept. of Motor Vehicles, Office of Information Services, Public Operations, Unit-G199, P.O. Box 944247, Sacramento, CA 94244-2470, www.dmv.ca.gov. The form to apply for a title search is found on the CD-Rom accompanying this manual, but it presently is not available on the Department's website. The form found on the CD-Rom accompanying this manual has some unusual requirements, and it is best to contact the California Department of Motor Vehicles for instructions.

COLORADO

Dept. of Revenue, Motor Vehicle Division, 1881 Pierce St., Room 146, Lakewood, CO 80214, www.mv.state.co.us/mv.html. The August 1997 form is found on the CD-Rom accompanying this manual, and can also be obtained at www.revenue.state.co.us/MV_dir/formspdf/2539.pdf. Inquiries can be sent to Motor Vehicle Division, Traffic Records, Denver, CO 80261-0016.

CONNECTICUT

Title Section—Copy Record Unit, Dept. of Motor Vehicles, 60 State St., Wethersfield, CT 06109, (860) 263-5154, www.ct.gov/dmv/site/default.asp. The June 1997 form can be found on the CD-Rom accompanying this manual, but is not available on the department's website. You can request a form by going to www.dmvct.state.ct.us/j23form.htm or by mailing a request to Department of Motor Vehicles, Phone Center, 60 State St., Wethersfield, CT 06161 or by calling (860) 263-5700 (in the Hartford area or outside of Connecticut) or (800) 842-8222 (toll free within Connecticut only).

DELAWARE

Division of Motor Vehicles, Title Records Files, P.O. Box 698, Dover, DE 19903, www.delaware.gov/yahoo/DMV. The April 2001 form to request a title search is found on the CD-Rom accompanying this manual.

DISTRICT OF COLUMBIA

Dept. of Motor Vehicles, Title Records Files, 301 C St. NW, Room 1157A, Washington, DC 20001, http://dmv.washingtondc.gov/main.shtm. The October 2004 form to request a title search is found on the CD-Rom accompanying this manual, and can also be obtained at http://dmv.washingtondc.gov/info/forms/app-title_pdf.shtm.

FLORIDA

Division of Motor Vehicles, Neil Kirkman Bldg., 2900 Apalachee Parkway, Tallahassee, FL 32399-0500, www.hsmv.state.fl.us. The November 2004 form to request a title search is found on the CD-Rom accompanying this manual, and can also be obtained at http://www3.hsmv.state.fl.us/intranet/dmv/forms/btr/85054.pdf.

GEORGIA

Dept. of Public Safety, MVR Unit, P.O. Box 1456, Atlanta, GA 30371-2303, www.dmvs.ga.gov. The May 2002 form to request a title search is found on the CD-Rom accompanying this manual, and can also be obtained at www.dds.ga.gov/docs/forms/DS-18-SW.pdf. More information can be obtained by writing to the Department of Motor Vehicle Safety, Driver Services Division, Attn: MVR Unit, P.O. Box 80447, Conyers, GA 30013.

HAWAII

Hawaii has a number of county-wide addresses to contact concerning title information. For the County of Honolulu, the address is Department of Motor Vehicle Licensing, City & County of Honolulu, 1031 Nuuanu Ave., 2nd Floor, Honolulu, HI 96813, (808) 532-4311. For the outer islands (Hawaii County), contact Dept. of Finance, Treasury Division, Motor Vehicle Department, 101 Pauahi Street, Suite 5, Hilo, HI 96720, (808) 961-8351. For Maui County (islands of Maui, Molokai, Lanai), contact Department of Finance, Motor Vehicle Department, 70 E. Kaahumanu Avenue, Kahului, HI 96732, (808) 270-7841. For Kauai County,

contact Island of Kauai, Dept. of Finance, Treasury Division, Motor Vehicle Department, 444 Rice Street, A-466, Lihue, HI 96766, (808) 241-6577. The state-wide website address is www.co.honolulu.hi.us/csd/vehicle. Under state law, title searches can only be conducted in response to a subpoena request. The CD-Rom accompanying this manual contains a sample special proceeding to obtain a subpoena to request a title history in Hawaii.

IDAHO

Title Records, Transportation Dept., P.O. Box 7129, Boise, ID 83707-1129, http://itd.idaho.gov/dmv/index.htm. The June 2002 form to request a title search is found on the CD-Rom accompanying this manual, and can also be obtained at www.itd.idaho.gov/dmv/vehicleservices/3374.pdf. The website now requires the user to log in with a password. Additional information can be obtained from Vehicle Services/Special Plates, Idaho Transportation Department, P.O. Box 34, Boise, ID 83731-0034.

ILLINOIS

Office of the Secretary of State, Record Inquiry Section, 408 Howlett Building, Springfield, IL 62756, www.sos.state.il.us/depts/vehicles. A form to request a title search can be found on the CD-Rom accompanying this manual.

INDIANA

Bureau of Motor Vehicles, IGCN, Room N404, Vehicle Records Section, 100 North Senate Ave., Indianapolis, IN 46204. The September 1997 form to request a title search is found on the CD-Rom accompanying this manual, and can also be obtained at www.in.gov.bmv/forms/SF46449.pdf. More information can be obtained by writing to the Indiana Bureau of Motor Vehicles, IGCN, Room N404, Vehicle Records Section, 100 North Senate Avenue, Indianapolis, IN 46204.

IOWA

Title Section, Office of Vehicle Registration, Dept. of Transportation, Park Fair Mall, 100 Euclid Ave., P.O. Box 9204, Des Moines, IA 50306-9204, www.dot.state.ia.us/mvd/index.htm. The August 2000 form (form 431069) to request a title search is found on the CD-Rom accompanying this manual, and can also be obtained at www.iadotforms.dot.state.ia.us/iowadotforms/Library.aspx.

KANSAS

Dept. of Revenue, Titles and Registration Bureau, 915 S.W. Harrison, Docking State Office Building, 1st Floor, Room 159, Topeka, KS 66626-0001, www.accesskansas.org/living/cars-transportation.html. The March 2004 form to request a title search is found on the CD-Rom accompanying this manual, and can also be obtained at www.ksrevenue.org/pdf/forms/trdl302.pdf.

KENTUCKY

Transportation Cabinet, Division of Motor Vehicle Licensing, P.O. Box 2014, Frankfort, KY 40602-2014, Attn: Cathy, www.kytc.state.ky.us. The July 1998 form to request a title search is found on the CD-Rom accompanying this manual, and can also be obtained at http://mvl.ky.gov/MVLWeb/pdf/TC96-016.pdf.

LOUISIANA

Office of Motor Vehicles, 7979 Independence Blvd., Baton Rouge, LA 70806, http://omv.dps.state.la.us. The website has no form available, but the CD-Rom accompanying this manual contains a sample letter to request a title history drafted by a Louisiana consumer attorney.

MAINE

Title Examination & Information Unit, 29 State House Station, 101 Hospital Street, Augusta, ME 04333-0029, www.state.me.us/sos/bmv. The website has no form available, but a form used by the state for title search requests, along with accompanying documents and instructions, are found on the CD-Rom accompanying this manual.

MARYLAND

Title Files, Motor Vehicle Administration, 6601 Ritchie Hwy. NE, Glen Burnie, MD 21062, http://mva.state.md.us. The September 2000 form to request a title search is found on the CD-Rom accompanying this manual, and can also be obtained at http://mva.state.md.us/Resources/DR-057.pdf.

MASSACHUSETTS

Registry of Motor Vehicles, ATTN: Mail Listings Dept., P.O. Box 199100, Boston, MA 02119-9100, www.state.ma.us/rmv. The May 2002 form to request a title search is found on the CD-Rom accompanying this manual, and can also be obtained at www.state.ma.us/rmv/forms/21078.pdf.

MICHIGAN

Commercial Look-Up Unit, Dept. of State, 7064 Crowner Drive, Lansing, MI 48918-1540, www.michigan.gov/sos/. Michigan has two August 2003 forms to request a title search, both found on the CD-Rom accompanying this manual and at www.michigan.gov/documents/bdvr154_16269_7.pdf and www.michigan.gov/documents/bdvr153_16280_7.pdf. The BDVR-154 form is for those who are requesting a title history for a vehicle that does not belong them. The BDVR-153 form is for those who are requesting a title history for a vehicle they own. Requests for records can be made by mail, by phone (must have an account), or by facsimile (must have an account or pay with a credit card). To use the mail option, complete the BDVR 153 or 154 form in detail, meeting one of the thirteen permissible reasons if requesting a record other than your own vehicle's. Each record is $6.55 and may be charged to your Discover, Visa or Mastercard, or include a check or money order made payable to the State of Michigan. The telephone number to make a facsimile request is: (517) 322-1181.

MINNESOTA

Dept. of Public Safety, Driver and Vehicle Services, 445 Minnesota St., St. Paul, MN 55101, www.dps.state.mn.us/dvs. The latest form to request a title search is found on the CD-Rom accompanying this manual, and is also available on the department's website at www.dps.state.mn.us/dvs/MotorVehicle/Information/vehicle%20frame.htm.

MISSISSIPPI

Title Division, State Tax Commission, P.O. Box 1383, Jackson, MS 39205, www.mstc.state.ms.us/mvl/main.htm. The December 2002 form to request a title search is found on the CD-Rom accompanying this manual.

MISSOURI

Driver License Contact Information, 301 W. High St., Room 370, P.O. Box 100, Jefferson City, MO 65105, www.dor.state.mo.us/mvdl. Missouri has a two step process. The first step is to complete Form 4678, relating to the requester's qualifications under the Driver's Privacy Protection Act. The December 2003 version of Form 4678 is found on the CD-Rom accompanying this manual, but not on the state's website. Then one submits an application for a particular vehicle, found online at www.dor.mo.gov/mvdl/drivers/forms/5091.pdf. This February 2002 form is found on the CD-Rom accompanying this manual, but is not available on the state's website. One can also request Form 4678 (Request for MV/DL Records) by calling (573) 751-4509 or by visiting http://dort.state.mo.us/mvdl/formorder. One can also set up an account so that one can send requests by facsimile and be billed monthly, by calling (573) 751-4509 and requesting the appropriate forms. An example of a facsimile request used by a Missouri consumer attorney is found on the CD-Rom accompanying this manual.

MONTANA

Records and Driver Control Bureau, 2d Floor, Scott Hart Building, P.O. Box 201430, 303 N. Roberts, Helena, MT 59620-1430, www.doj.state.mt.us/department/motorvehicledivision.asp. The July 2004 form to request a title search is found on the CD-Rom accompanying this manual, and can also be obtained at www.doj.state.mt.us/driving/forms/mv210.pdf.

NEBRASKA

Title Section, Dept. of Motor Vehicles, P.O. Box 94789, Lincoln, NE 68509, www.dmv.state.ne.us. The July 2002 form to request title searches is found on the CD-Rom accompanying this manual and can also be obtained at www.dmv.state.ne.us/dvr/pdf/vehrecapp.pdf.

NEVADA

Records Section, Dept. of Motor Vehicles, 555 Wright Way, Carson City, NV 89711-0250, www.dmvstat.com. The September 2002 form to request title searches is found on the CD-Rom accompanying this manual and can also be obtained at www.dmvstat.com/pdfforms/ir002.pdf.

NEW HAMPSHIRE

Title Bureau, Dept. of Motor Vehicles, 10 Hazen Drive, Concord, NH 03305, www.state.nh.us/dmv. The July 2003 form to request a title search is found on the CD-Rom accompanying this manual, and can also be obtained at www.carcoresearch.com/pdf/DSMV_505.pdf.

NEW JERSEY

Motor Vehicle Services, P.O. Box 160, 225 East State St., Trenton,

NJ 08666, www.state.nj.us/mvc. The December 1997 form to request title searches is found on the CD-Rom accompanying this manual, but is not available on the state's website. To obtain a certified photocopy of a title (current owner information only): 1) visit the MVC Central Office in Trenton; 2) complete the Request for Title Search (Form ISM/DO-22A) to request a photocopy, and include the make, year, vehicle identification number, and reason for request; 3) present your driver license; and 4) pay the $10.50 fee, or mail the signed application, a copy of your driver license, and a check or money order for $10.50, to: Motor Vehicle Commission, Special Titles, 225 East State St., P.O. Box 017, Trenton, NJ 08666-0017.

NEW MEXICO

Vehicle Services Division, Dept. of Transportation, P.O. Box 1028, Santa Fe, NM 87504, www.state.nm.us/tax/mvd/mvd_home.htm. The September 1996 form to request title searches is found on the CD-Rom accompanying this manual, but is not available on the state's website.

NEW YORK

Abstract Unit, Public Services Bureau, Dept. of Motor Vehicles, Empire State Plaza, Albany, NY 12228, www.nydmv.state.ny.us. The May 2004 form to request a title search is found on the CD-Rom accompanying this manual, and can also be obtained at www.nydmv.state.ny.us/forms/mv15.pdf. For more information, contact MV-15 Processing, NYS Dept. of Motor Vehicles, 6 Empire State Plaza, Albany, NY 12228.

NORTH CAROLINA

Division of Motor Vehicles, 1100 New Bern Ave., Raleigh, NC 27697, www.dmv.dot.state.nc.us. The September 1999 form to request title searches is found on the CD-Rom accompanying this manual, and can also be obtained at www.ncdot.org/dmv/forms/vehicleregistration/download/mvr605a.pdf.

NORTH DAKOTA

Records, Vehicle Services Division, 608 East Blvd., Bismarck, ND 58505, www.state.nd.us/dot. The September 2002 form to request title searches is found on the CD-Rom accompanying this manual, and can also be obtained at www.state.nd.us/dot/docs/motorvehicle/sfn51269.pdf.

OHIO

Title Division, Bureau of Motor Vehicles, P.O. Box 16520, Columbus, OH 43266-0020, http://bmv.ohio.gov/bmv.html. An August 2002 form to request title searches is found on the CD-Rom accompanying this manual. Certain basic information is available on-line at the department's website. A more complicated process is required to obtain copies of the actual titles, because each county stores titles issued in that county. To begin your inquiry at www.ohiobmv.com, click the link for Online Title Inquiry and enter the vehicle identification number (VIN) or title number. A "hot print" provides a list of titles issued on that vehicle in Ohio. The county issuing each title is identified by the first two numbers of the title number, and "quick links" at www.ohiobmv.com list the codes for each county. Then request title information from the relevant counties, using the form found on the CD-Rom accompanying this manual and also at www.bmv.ohio.gov/pdf_forms/1173.pdf. It is possible to request the complete title jacket, which may include repossession affidavits, auction receipts, or other useful documentation.

OKLAHOMA

Tax Commission, Motor Vehicle Division, 2501 N. Lincoln Blvd., Oklahoma City, OK 73194, www.dps.state.ok.us/dls. The January 2004 form to request title searches is found on the CD-Rom accompanying this manual, and can also be obtained at www.oktax.state.ok.us/oktax/mvforms/769.pdf.

OREGON

Communications, Dept. of Motor Vehicles, 1905 Lane Ave., N.E., Salem, OR 97314, www.odot.state.or.us/dmv/index.htm. The October 2004 form to request title searches is found on the CD-Rom accompanying this manual, and can also be obtained at www.odot.state.or.us/forms/dmv/7122.pdf.

PENNSYLVANIA

Dept. of Transportation, Bureau of Driver Licensing, Vehicle Record Services, P.O. Box 68691, Harrisburg, PA 17106-8691, www.dmv.state.pa.us. The August 2004 form to request title searches is found on the CD-Rom accompanying this manual, and can also be obtained at www.dmv.state.pa.us/pdotforms/dl_forms/dl-135.pdf.

RHODE ISLAND

Division of Motor Vehicles, 286 Main St., Pawtucket, RI 02860, www.dmv.state.ri.us. A form to request a title search is found on the CD-Rom accompanying this manual, and can also be obtained at www.dmv.state.ri.us/forms/docs/titleinfo_request.pdf.

SOUTH CAROLINA

Title Section, Motor Vehicle Division, Dept. of Highways & Public Transportation, P.O. Box 1498, Columbia, SC 29216-0024, www.scdps.org. The January 2005 form to apply for a title search is found on the CD-Rom accompanying this manual, and can also be obtained at www.scdmvonline.com/forms/5027-A.pdf.

SOUTH DAKOTA

Motor Vehicle Division, 118 W. Capitol, Pierre, SD 57501-2080, www.state.sd.us/revenue/motorvcl.htm. The August 2003 form to request a title search is found on the CD-Rom accompanying this manual, and can also be obtained at https://www.state.sd.us/eforms/secure/eforms/EO821V1-DriversPrivacyAndProtection-Act.pdf. For more information, write SD Division of Motor Vehicles, Attn: Records Search Section, 445 East Capitol Ave., Pierre, SD 57501-3100.

TENNESSEE

Dept. of Safety, 1150 Foster Ave., Nashville, TN 37249, www.state.tn.us/safety. A form to request title searches is found on the CD-Rom accompanying this manual, but not on the state's website.

TEXAS

Dept. of Transportation, Vehicle Titles and Registration Division, 125 E. 11th St., Austin, TX 78779-0001, www.dot.state.tx.us/VTR/vtrreginfo.htm. The March 2004 form to request a title search is found on the CD-Rom accompanying this manual, but not on the state's website.

UTAH

State Tax Commission, Motor Vehicle Customer Service Division, 210 North 1950 West, Salt Lake City, UT 84134, www.dmv-utah.com. The July 2003 form to request title searches is found on the CD-Rom accompanying this manual, and can also be obtained at http://tax.utah.gov/forms/current/tc-890.pdf.

VERMONT

Registration Information, Dept. of Motor Vehicles, 120 State St., Montpelier, VT 05603, www.aot.state.vt.us/dmv/dmvhp.htm. The May 2004 form to request title searches is found on the CD-Rom accompanying this manual, and can also be obtained at www.aot.state.vt.us/dmv/documents/TA/Vg/Tavg116.pdf.

VIRGINIA

Title Research, Dept. of Motor Vehicles, P.O. Box 27412, Richmond, VA 23269, www.dmv.state.va.us. The April 2002 form to request a title search is found on the CD-Rom accompanying this manual and can be found online at www.dmv.state.va.us/webdoc/pdf/crd01.pdf.

WASHINGTON

Dept. of Licensing, Technical Services Unit, P.O. Box 9042, Olympia, WA 98507-9042, www.dol.wa.gov. The November 2000 form to request title searches is found on the CD-Rom accompanying this manual, and can also be obtained at www.dol.wa.gov/forms/420531.pdf.

WEST VIRGINIA

Division of Motor Vehicles, Information Services, 1606 Washington St. East, Charleston, WV 25311, www.wvdot.com. The November 1999 form to request title searches is found on the CD-Rom accompanying this manual, and can also be obtained at www.wvdot.com/6_motorists/dmv/downloads/DMV-ReqVInfo.pdf.

WISCONSIN

Vehicle Record Files, Room 100, Dept. of Transportation, P.O. Box 7911, Madison, WI 53707, www.dot.wisconsin.gov/drivers/index.htm. The January 2005 form to request a title search is found on the CD-Rom accompanying this manual, and also at www.dot.wisconsin.gov/drivers/forms/mv2896.pdf.

WYOMING

Dept. of Transportation, Driver Services-Driving Records, 5300 Bishop Blvd., Cheyenne, Wyoming 82009-3340, http://dot.state.wy.us. The January 2001 form to request title searches is found on the CD-Rom accompanying this manual, but is not available on the state's website.

State Automobile Dealer Licensing Offices

ALABAMA

Alabama Department of Revenue
Sales, Use & Business Tax Division
Severance & License Section
P.O. Box 327550
Montgomery, AL 36132-7550
Phone: (334) 353-7827 Fax: (334) 242-0770

ALASKA

State of Alaska
Division of Motor Vehicles
Attn: Dealer/Fleet
1300 W. Benson Boulevard, Suite 300
Anchorage, AK 99503-3691
Phone: (907) 269-3755 Fax: (907) 269-3762

ARIZONA

Arizona Department of Transportation
Motor Vehicle Division
Dealer Licensing Unit, M.D. 552M
2739 E. Washington St.
Phoenix, AZ 85034
Phone: (602) 712-7975 Fax: (602) 712-3268

ARKANSAS

Arkansas State Police
Regulatory Services Section
Vehicle Dealers License Administrator
No. 1 State Police Plaza Drive
Little Rock, AR 72209
Phone: (501) 618-8606 Fax: (501) 618-8621

CALIFORNIA

California Department of Motor Vehicles
Occupational Licensing Unit
P.O. Box 932342
Sacramento, CA 94232-3420
Phone: (916) 229-3126 Fax: (916) 229-4728

COLORADO

Colorado Department of Revenue
Auto Industry Licensing Division
1881 Pierce, #142
Lakewood, CO 80214
Phone: (303) 205-5732 Fax: (303) 205-5977

CONNECTICUT

Connecticut Department of Motor Vehicles
Dealers and Repairers Division
60 State Street
Wethersfield, CT 06161
Phone: (860) 263-5056 Fax: (860) 263-5554

DELAWARE

Delaware Motor Vehicle Division
Dealer Information
P.O. Box 698
Dover, DE 19903
Phone: (302) 744-2503 Fax: (302) 739-2602

DISTRICT OF COLUMBIA

Department of Consumer & Regulatory Affairs
Business Services Division
941 North Capitol, N.E.
Washington, DC 20002
Phone: (202) 442-4311 Fax: (202) 442-4523

FLORIDA

Florida Division of Motor Vehicles
Dealer Licensing
Neil Kirkman Building, Room A312
Tallahassee, FL 32399-0630
Phone: (850) 488-4958 Fax: (850) 922-9840

GEORGIA

Professional Licensing Boards Division
Used Motor Vehicle Dealers and Parts Dealers
237 Coliseum Drive
Macon, GA 31217-3858
Phone: (478) 207-1460 Fax: (478) 207-1468

HAWAII

Motor Vehicle Dealers
Professional & Vocational Licensing Division
Department of Commerce & Consumer Affairs
335 Merchant St.
Honolulu, HI 96813
Phone: (808) 586-3000

IDAHO

Idaho Transportation Department
Division of Motor Vehicles
Vehicle Services Section
P.O. Box 7129
Boise, ID 83707-1129
Phone: (208) 334-8681 Fax: (208) 334-8658

ILLINOIS

Illinois Secretary of State
Dealer Licensing Section
Howlett Building, Room 069
Springfield, IL 62756
Phone: (217) 782-7817 Fax: (217) 524-0120

INDIANA

Bureau of Motor Vehicles
Special Sales/Abandoned Vehicles Division
Dealer Department
6400 East 30th Street
Indianapolis, IN 46219
Phone: (317) 591-5311 Fax: (317) 591-5319

IOWA

Iowa Department of Transportation
Office of Vehicle Services
Park Fair Mall
100 Euclid Avenue
P.O. Box 9278
Des Moines, IA 50306-9278
Phone: (515) 237-3163 Fax: (515) 237-3181

KANSAS

Kansas Department of Revenue
Division of Motor Vehicles
Dealer Licensing Bureau
Docking State Office Building
Topeka, KS 66626-0001
Phone: (785) 296-3621 Fax: (785) 296-3852

KENTUCKY

Kentucky Motor Vehicle Commission
403 Wapping St.
Bush Building, Room 101
Frankfort, KY 40622
Phone: (502) 564-3750 Fax: (502) 564-5487

LOUISIANA

Used Motor Vehicle & Parts Commission
3132 Valley Creek Drive
Baton Rouge, LA 70808
Phone: (225) 925-3870 Fax: (225) 925-3869

Louisiana Motor Vehicle Commission
3519 12th St.

Metairie, LA 70002
Phone: (504) 838-5207 Fax: (504) 838-5416

MAINE

Maine Department of State
Bureau of Motor Vehicle
Dealer Section
State House Station #29
Augusta, ME 04333
Phone: (207) 624-9000 x52143 Fax: (207) 624-9037

MARYLAND

Maryland Motor Vehicle Dealer Licensing Department
6601 Ritchie Highway N.E., Room 146
Glen Burnie, MD 21062
Phone: (410) 787-2950 Fax: (410) 768-7167

MASSACHUSETTS

Contact city or town where the business is located.

MICHIGAN

Michigan Department of State
Bureau of Regulatory Services
Business Licensing Division
7707 Rickle St.
Lansing, MI 48918
Phone: (517) 373-9082 Fax: (517) 335-2810

MINNESOTA

Department of Public Safety
Dealers Division
445 Minnesota Street, Suite 186
St. Paul, MN 55101
Phone: (651) 296-2977 or (651) 296-6911
Fax: (651) 297-1480

MISSISSIPPI

Mississippi State Tax Commission
P.O. Box 1140
Jackson, MS 39215-1140
Phone: (601) 923-7100

MISSOURI

Missouri Motor Vehicle Bureau
Dealer Licensing Section
P.O. Box 43
Jefferson City, MO 65105
Phone: (573) 751-0527 Fax: (573) 751-4789

MONTANA

Department of Justice—Motor Vehicle Division
Dealer Services Section
1032 Buckskin Drive
Deer Lodge, MT 59722-2371
Phone: (406) 846-6000 Fax: (406) 846-6039

NEBRASKA

Motor Vehicle Industry Licensing Board
301 Centennial Mall South
P.O. Box 94697
Lincoln, NE 68509
Phone: (402) 471-2148 Fax: (402) 471-4563

NEVADA

Bureau of Enforcement
555 Wright Way
Carson City, NV 89711
Phone: (775) 684-4690 Fax: (775) 684-4691

NEW HAMPSHIRE

New Hampshire Department of Safety
Division of Motor Vehicles Dealer Desk
10 Hazen Drive
Concord, NH 03301
Phone: (603) 271-2330 Fax: (603) 271-8995

NEW JERSEY

New Jersey Division of Motor Vehicles
Dealer Licensing Section
225 East State Street, 4th Floor East
Trenton, NJ 08666
Phone: (609) 777-1690 Fax: (609) 292-5153

NEW MEXICO

Motor Vehicle Division
Dealer Licensing
5301 Central, N.E., Suite 1201
Albuquerque, NM 87108
Phone: (505) 841-6482 Fax: (505) 841-6420

NEW YORK

New York State Department of Motor Vehicles
Vehicle Safety
P.O. Box 2700-ESP
ESP (Empire State Plaza)
Albany, NY 12220-0700
Phone: (518) 474-2438 Fax: (518) 474-4702

NORTH CAROLINA

North Carolina Division of Motor Vehicles
Enforcement Section, Dealer Unit
1100 New Bern Avenue
Raleigh, NC 27697-0001
Phone: (919) 861-3182 Fax: (919) 861-3805

NORTH DAKOTA

NDDOT, Motor Vehicle Division
608 East Blvd.
Bismarck, ND 58505-0780
Phone: (701) 328-2725 Fax: (701) 328-1487

OHIO

Bureau of Motor Vehicles
Dealer Licensing Division
P.O. Box 16521
Columbus, OH 43266-0020
Phone: (614) 752-7636 Fax: (614) 752-7220

OKLAHOMA

Used Dealer Licensing
Oklahoma Used Motor Vehicle and Parts Commission
2401 N.W. 23rd, Suite 57
Oklahoma City, OK 73107
Phone: (405) 949-2626 Fax: (405) 949-9996

OREGON

Oregon Department of Transportation
Motor Vehicle Division
Business Licensing
1905 Lana Avenue N.E.
Salem, OR 97314
Phone: (503) 945-5052 Fax: (503) 945-5289

PENNSYLVANIA

[*Note: Complainants should contact both offices below.*]

Dealer Agent Services Group
Department of Transportation
Bureau of Motor Vehicles
1101 S. Front Street
Harrisburg, PA 17104
Phone: (717) 705-1162 Fax: (717) 787-9928

Department of State
Vehicle Licensing Board
2601 N. 3rd Street
Harrisburg, PA 17110
Phone: (717) 783-1697 Fax: (717) 787-0250

RHODE ISLAND

Rhode Island Motor Vehicle Dealers
License Commission
286 Main Street, Room 307
Pawtucket, RI 02860
Phone: (401) 721-2687 Fax: (401) 721-2697

SOUTH CAROLINA

Department of Motor Vehicles
Dealer License Section
P.O. Box 1498
Columbia, SC 29216-0023
Phone: (803) 737-1787 Fax: (803) 737-2098

SOUTH DAKOTA

South Dakota Department of Revenue
Division of Motor Vehicles
Anderson Building
445 East Capitol Avenue

Pierre, SD 57501-3185
Phone: (605) 773-3541 Fax: (605) 773-2549

TENNESSEE

Tennessee Motor Vehicle Commission
500 James Robertson Parkway, 2nd Floor
Nashville, TN 37243
Phone: (615) 741-2711 Fax: (615) 741-0651

TEXAS

Texas Department of Transportation (TDOT)
Motor Vehicle Division
Licensing Section
P.O. Box 2293
Austin, TX 78768
Phone: (512) 416-4800 or (877) 366-8887
Fax: (512) 416-4893

UTAH

Dealer Services
Utah State Tax Commission
Motor Vehicle Enforcement Division
210 North 1950 West
Salt Lake City, UT 84134
Phone: (801) 297-2600 Fax: (801) 297-2699

VERMONT

Vermont Motor Vehicle Department
Dealer Licensing
120 State Street
Montpelier, VT 05603
Phone: (802) 828-2038 Fax: (802) 828-2092

VIRGINIA

Motor Vehicle Dealer Board
Dealer Licensing Board
2201 West Broad Street
Richmond, VA 23220
Phone: (804) 367-0300 Fax: (804) 367-1053

WASHINGTON

Washington Department of Licensing
Dealer & Manufacturer Services
2000 4th Avenue, S.W.
Olympia, WA 98502
Phone: (360) 664-6466 Fax: (360) 386-6703

WEST VIRGINIA

West Virginia Department of Motor Vehicles
Dealer Services
1615 Washington Street, East
Charleston, WV 25317
Phone: (304) 558-3584 Fax: (304) 558-1013

WISCONSIN

DOT Dealer Section
4802 Sheboygan Avenue
Madison, WI 53707-7909
Phone: (608) 266-1425 Fax: (608) 267-0323

WYOMING

Wyoming Department of Transportation
Dealer Licensing
5300 Bishop Blvd.
Cheyenne, WY 82009-3340
Phone: (307) 777-4717 Fax: (307) 777-4772

Sample Complaints

Page 439

G.1 Complaints in the Appendix and on the CD-Rom

Replace note 1 with:

1   This complaint may also be found in National Consumer Law Center, Consumer Law Pleadings No. 2, § 6.2.1 (Cumulative CD-Rom and Index Guide).

Replace note 3 with:

3   This complaint may also be found in National Consumer Law Center, Consumer Law Pleadings No. 5, § 3.1 (Cumulative CD-Rom and Index Guide).

Replace note 4 with:

4   This complaint may also be found in National Consumer Law Center, Consumer Law Pleadings No. 9, § 5.1 (Cumulative CD-Rom and Index Guide).

Replace note 7 with:

7   This complaint may also be found in National Consumer Law Center, Consumer Law Pleadings No. 2, § 6.1.1 (Cumulative CD-Rom and Index Guide).

Replace note 8 with:

8   This complaint may also be found in National Consumer Law Center, Consumer Law Pleadings No. 6, § 11.1 (Cumulative CD-Rom and Index Guide).

Add to text at end of subsection:

- Complaint involving concealment of car's prior use by car rental agency.[8.1]
- Complaint involving concealment of car's salvage title.[8.2]
- Complaint involving undisclosed sale of lemon buyback recreational vehicle.[8.3]
- Complaint involving a rebuilt wreck.[8.4]

8.1   This complaint may also be found in National Consumer Law Center, Consumer Law Pleadings No. 9, § 5.3 (Cumulative CD-Rom and Index Guide).

8.2   This complaint may also be found in National Consumer Law Center, Consumer Law Pleadings No. 9, § 5.2 (Cumulative CD-Rom and Index Guide).

8.3   This complaint may also be found in National Consumer Law Center, Consumer Law Pleadings No. 10, § 2.1.1 (Cumulative CD-Rom and Index Guide).

8.4   This complaint may also be found in National Consumer Law Center, Consumer Law Pleadings No. 10, § 2.2 (Cumulative CD-Rom and Index Guide).

Page 443

G.3 Sample Complaint Against Dealer and Lender Relating to Odometer Misrepresentations and Lender's Supply of Information to Credit Reporting Agency

Replace note 11 with:

11   This complaint may also be found in National Consumer Law Center, Consumer Law Pleadings No. 2, § 6.2.1 (Cumulative CD-Rom and Index Guide).

Replace note 13 with:

13   This complaint may also be found in National Consumer Law Center, Consumer Law Pleadings No. 5, § 3.1 (Cumulative CD-Rom and Index Guide).

Page 450

G.5 Sample Complaint Against Dealer and Financer for Undisclosed Wreck History

Replace note 17 with:

17   This complaint may also be found in National Consumer Law Center, Consumer Law Pleadings No. 9, § 5.1 (Cumulative CD-Rom and Index Guide).

Replace note 20 with:

20   This complaint may also be found in National Consumer Law Center, Consumer Law Pleadings No. 2, § 6.2.1 (Cumulative CD-Rom and Index Guide).

Page 453

G.6 Sample Complaint in a Lemon Buyback Case

Replace NCLC Consumer Law Pleadings citation in introduction's second paragraph with:

Consumer Law Pleadings No. 2, § 6.1.1 (Cumulative CD-Rom and Index Guide)

Page 457

G.7 Sample Complaint Against Dealer for Concealment of Car's Prior Use

Replace note 25 with:

25   This complaint may also be found in National Consumer Law Center, Consumer Law Pleadings No. 9, § 5.1 (Cumulative CD-Rom and Index Guide).

Sample Discovery

H.2 Undisclosed Damage History

Page 464

Replace Appx. H.2.1 with:

H.2.1 Introduction

These discovery materials are intended solely as examples to be adapted to the facts and circumstances of a particular case and to the requirements of local rules and practices. Appendices H.2.2 and H.2.3, *infra*, are respectively interrogatories and a document request to the dealer in a case involving concealed damage. While the particular case involved flood damage, the discovery materials are easily adaptable to other types of damage. Appendix H.2.4, *infra*, is a document request to the prior owner of the vehicle. Finally, Appendix H.2.5, *infra*, is an outline for a deposition of the dealer. All of these materials are also found on the CD-Rom accompanying this manual.

In addition, the CD-Rom includes a number of other discovery materials for cases involving concealed wreck or other damage:

- Two sample document requests and interrogatories to the dealer in cases involving rebuilt wrecks.[5]
- A sample deposition outline for a rebuilt wreck case.[6]
- A sample report from an expert who examined a rebuilt wreck.[7]
- Depositions of a used car manager, a former used car manager, and a business manager in cases alleging the resale of rebuilt wrecked cars.

> 5   These discovery materials were drafted by Mark Steinbach, an attorney with O'Toole, Rothwell, Nassau & Steinbach in Washington D.C., who specializes in automobile fraud, and by Bernard E. Brown, an attorney in Kansas City, Missouri who specializes in automobile fraud.
>
> 6   This deposition outline was prepared by Attorney John Cole Gayle, who has a consumer law practice in Virginia.
>
> 7   This expert report was prepared for a case handled by Bernard E. Brown, an attorney in Kansas City, Missouri who specializes in automobile fraud.

H.3 Lemon Laundering

Page 471

H.3.1 Introduction

Add to text at end of subsection:

In addition, the CD-Rom contains discovery directed to the dealer, manufacturer, and bank in a case involving the undisclosed sale of a lemon buyback recreational vehicle.

Add new section to text after
Appx. H.5.

H.6 Request for Production of Documents to Floor Plan Financer

UNITED STATES DISTRICT COURT
DISTRICT OF ANY STATE

```
————————————————   )
                   )
PAUL PURCHASER,    )
         Plaintiff, )
                   )
v.                 )
                   )  Civil Action No.
                   )  90-123-ABC
FLOOR PLAN CREDIT, INC.,  )
et al.             )
        Defendants.  )
————————————————   )
```

FIRST REQUEST FOR PRODUCTION OF DOCUMENTS

Pursuant to Fed. R. Civ. P. 34 and 45, plaintiff requests that defendant Floor Plan Credit, Inc. produce the following documents at the office of plaintiff's attorney within thirty days hereof.

> [*The attorney may wish to add instructions and definitions similar to those found in Appx. H.2.4, supra.*]

1. Any floor plan agreement, bridge contract, or financing agreement covering assets or vehicles to be sold by Dealer.

2. Any monthly reports of vehicles coming into or leaving the floor plan from [*date*] to [*date*].

3. Any rules, guidelines, procedures, or instructions to Dealer regarding the means by which vehicles are brought into or leave the floor plan.

4. Any authorizations for Dealer's agents to buy vehicles under the floor plan covering [*date*] to [*date*].

5. Any document relating to any security interest, discharge of security interest, or payment for a [*description of plaintiff's vehicle and vehicle identification number (VIN)*].

6. The front and back of any drafts, checks, receipts, electronic wire transfer documents, money orders, cashier checks, draft envelopes, or other payment mechanisms, relating to [*description of plaintiff's vehicle and VIN*], and any ledger, statement, compilation, record, receipt, or report that contains information about any such payment.

7. The incoming and outgoing letters of collection relating to [*description of plaintiff's vehicle and VIN*].

8. The front and back of the title to [*description of plaintiff's vehicle and VIN*], or copies thereof if you no longer have the original.

9. All forms filled out, signed, or submitted to any state agency in connection with [*description of plaintiff's vehicle and VIN*], including title applications, title reassignment forms, odometer disclosure statements, power of attorney forms, and reports.

10. All certified mail receipts and courier receipts for letters or documents relating to [*description of plaintiff's vehicle and VIN*].

11. All checklists used in connection with the financing of [*description of plaintiff's vehicle and VIN*].

12. All reports, notes, or records of inspections of vehicles you provided floor plan financing for for Dealer from [*date*] to [*date*].

13. Any and all out of trust letters relating to Dealer.

14. Any and all documents pertaining to the debit, credit and adjustment of any account of Dealer from [*date*] to [*date*].

15. All letters, memoranda, notes, and correspondence to or from Dealer from [*date*] to [*date*].

16. All operating statements, accounting statements, and reserve account statements from [*date*] to [*date*].

17. All mail logs and telephone logs from [*date*] to [*date*].

18. All receipts for expenditures in connection with [*description of plaintiff's vehicle and VIN*], including titling receipts.

19. Any applications by Dealer for floor plan financing.

20. Any licenses you hold.

Attorney for Plaintiff

Appendix I   Sample Jury Trial Documents

Page 483

I.1 Documents Included in the Appendix and on the CD-Rom

Replace note 2 with:

2   This set of jury instructions may also be found in National Consumer Law Center, Consumer Law Pleadings No. 5, § 3.4 (Cumulative CD-Rom and Index Guide).

Replace note 4 with:

4   These instructions may also be found in National Consumer Law Center, Consumer Law Pleadings No. 5, § 6.3 (Cumulative CD-Rom and Index Guide).

Add to text at end of subsection:

- Consumer's pretrial disclosures, an expert's report on the vehicle, and jury instructions in an undisclosed sale of salvaged vehicle case.[5.1]
- Mediation presentation and a trial chart making parts and labor comparison in an undisclosed sale of lemon buyback recreational vehicle case.[5.2]
- Automotive expert's reports concerning diminished value of cars based on: undisclosed wreck damage, substandard repairs, prior use as a rental car, very high mileage, and excessive application of paint.[5.3]

5.1   These materials may also be found in National Consumer Law Center, Consumer Law Pleadings No. 2, § 6.2 (Cumulative CD-Rom and Index Guide).

5.2   These materials may also be found in National Consumer Law Center, Consumer Law Pleadings No. 10, § 2.1 (Cumulative CD-Rom and Index Guide).

5.3   These materials may also be found in National Consumer Law Center, Consumer Law Pleadings No. 11, Ch. 4 (Cumulative CD-Rom and Index Guide).

Page 495

I.8 Sample Jury Instructions in Odometer Case

Replace note 12 with:

12   These instructions may also be found in National Consumer Law Center, Consumer Law Pleadings No. 5, § 3.4 (Cumulative CD-Rom and Index Guide).

Replace NCLC citation in introduction's last sentence with:

National Consumer Law Center, Consumer Law Pleadings No. 5, § 6.3 (Cumulative CD-Rom and Index Guide)

Sample Motions and Briefs

A number of sample motions and briefs are included on the CD-Rom accompanying this manual:

- A motion for partial summary judgment and supporting memoranda in a case involving odometer disclosures that were inaccurate because the mileage exceeded the odometer's mechanical limits.[1]
- Memoranda in support of summary judgment for the consumer, and in opposition to summary judgment for an insurer, in an undisclosed wreck case.[2] These memos deal with the state salvage title law, breach of warranty, revocation of acceptance, fraud, and violations of the Magnuson-Moss Act and the state UDAP statute.
- A summary judgment brief and a reply brief discussing the dealer's violation of the federal odometer law and the state UDAP statute when it prevented the buyers from seeing a vehicle title that would have revealed the vehicle's history.[3]
- An appellate brief and a reply brief discussing the scope of a state dealer bond statute and whether the bond covers attorney fees and treble damages, and discussing a number of general principles that apply in interpreting dealer bond statutes.[4]
- A memorandum of law discussing the requirements of the federal odometer statute in opposition to a motion to dismiss a yo-yo sale case.[5]
- A trial brief in an undisclosed sale of salvaged vehicle case.[6]
- A trial brief in a rebuilt wreck case concerning pattern and expert evidence, and appropriate punitive damages.[7]

In addition, a sample motion *in limine*, seeking to preclude the presentation of evidence of settlement negotiations or attorney fees during the trial, may be found in Appendix I.7, *supra*. Sample motions and briefs in an automobile fraud class action are found in Appendices K.2 and K.3, *infra*: a sample motion, brief, and reply brief for class certification, and a sample motion for protective order with brief.

---

1   These documents were prepared by attorney Richard Feferman of Albuquerque, New Mexico, and may also be found in National Consumer Law Center, Consumer Law Pleadings No. 5, §§ 3.3.1 to 3.3.3 (Cumulative CD-Rom and Index Guide).

2   These memoranda, which were prepared by Dani K. Liblang, a Michigan attorney, are also found in National Consumer Law Center, Consumer Law Pleadings No. 5, §§ 6.1, 6.2 (Cumulative CD-Rom and Index Guide).

3   These briefs were prepared by attorney Richard Feferman of Albuquerque, New Mexico.

4   These briefs were prepared by attorney Joanne Faulkner of New Haven, Connecticut.

5   This memorandum, which was prepared by Tom Domonoske, a Virginia attorney, is also included in National Consumer Law Center, Consumer Law Pleadings No. 7, § 5.4 (Cumulative CD-Rom and Index Guide).

6   The brief was prepared by Bernard Brown of Kansas City, Missouri, and may also be found in National Consumer Law Center, Consumer Law Pleadings No. 2, § 6.2.6 (Cumulative CD-Rom and Index Guide).

7   These materials may also be found in National Consumer Law Center, Consumer Law Pleadings No. 11, Ch. 3 (Cumulative CD-Rom and Index Guide).

Appendix K	# Sample Class Action Pleadings in an Odometer Rollback Case

Page 503

K.1 Sample Class Action Complaint

In the caption replace "6. Marta Malfoy" with:

6. Narcissa Malfoy

In paragraph 8 replace "Marta Malfoy" with:

Narcissa Malfoy

In paragraph 12 replace "Marta Malfoy" with:

Narcissa Malfoy

Page 506

Replace note 4 with:

4 Plaintiffs ultimately decided not to seek class certification of this claim because of the need to prove reliance under Arizona's UDAP statute. *See* Appx. K.3.3, *infra* (reply brief in support of class certification).

K.3 Sample Class Certification Pleadings

Page 510

K.3.2 Sample Motion to Certify Class with Supporting Memorandum

In the caption replace "6. Marta Malfoy" with:

6. Narcissa Malfoy

In the final sentence of the first paragraph of Plaintiffs' Motion replace "Marta Malfoy" with:

Narcissa Malfoy

In the first sentence of the first paragraph of A. Overview *replace "Marta Malfoy" with:*

Narcissa Malfoy

Page 511

In the second sentence of the first paragraph of B. Procedural History *replace "Marta Malfoy" with:*

Narcissa Malfoy

K.3.3 Sample Reply Brief in Support of Class Certification

*In the caption replace "6.
Marta Malfoy" with:*

6. Narcissa Malfoy

K.3.3 Sample Reply Brief in Support of Class Certification

Sample Attorney Fee Papers

Page 531 **L.1 Introduction**

Add to text at end of section: Both sets of pleadings are also available on the CD-Rom accompanying this manual.

Appendix M

replacement appendix

Live web links can be found on the CD-Rom accompanying this volume.

Vehicle Title and Other History

www.e-autohistory.com (Experian Auto History)

www.carfaxreport.com or www.carfax.com (Carfax)

www.autocheck.com (AutoCheck)

www.choicepoint.net (CDB Infotek)

www.autotrackxp.com (AutoTrack)

www.carfraud.com (Carfraud.com)

www.carproof.com (Car Proof, which specializes in Canadian title information)

www.nicb.org (National Insurance Crime Bureau)

www.iso.com (ISO)

www.state.nj.us (lists of New Jersey lemon buybacks, flood-damaged vehicles, and salvage vehicles, by vehicle identification number)(click on Law and Public Safety, then on Division of Consumer Affairs, then on Lemon Law Unit)

http://myfloridalegal.com (Florida lemon buybacks list)

www.nsxprime.com (list of Acura NSX rebuilt wrecks)

www.pimall.com/nais/dmv.html (links to state motor vehicle departments' public records websites)

www.fleet.ford.com/maintenance/vin_tools/default.asp (decodes vehicle identification numbers)

Hurricane-Affected Vehicles

www.nicb.org (free search by VIN number for vehicles and watercraft affected by Hurricanes Katrina, Wilma, and Rita)

www.carfax.com/flood (free search by VIN number for vehicles with flood damage)

Government Information

www.nhtsa.dot.gov (National Highway Traffic and Safety Administration)

www.ftc.gov (Federal Trade Commission)

http://carprice.com/dmvdot/ and www.virtualgumshoe.com (links to state motor vehicle record departments) www.nass.org/sos/sos.html (links to state secretary of states' offices for corporate records)

www.sec.gov/edgar.shtml (information about publicly-traded companies from the Securities and Exchange Commission's EDGAR database)

www.residentagentinfo.com (contact information for every state to find registered agents for service of process)

http://pacer.psc.uscourts.gov (litigation database to find other lawsuits against a company or individual)

Car Pricing Guides

www.nadaguides.com (NADA guides, dealing with cars, trucks, watercraft, RVs, airplanes, classic vehicles, motorcycles, ATVs, snowmobiles, and manufactured homes)

www.kbb.com (Kelley Blue Book, dealing with new and used vehicles and motorcycles)

www.blackbookguides.com (National Auto Research publications, dealing with vehicles, motorcycles, watercraft, and snowmobiles)

www.carprice.com (Pace's Buyer's Guides)

www.edmunds.com (Edmunds)

www.autoweb.com

www.autosite.com (AutoSite)

www.intellichoice.com (CarCenter Intellichoice)

Vehicle Financing

www.FinanCenter.com

www.TValue.com

www.auto-loan.com

www.fairlanecredit.com

Consumer Organizations and Advocacy Groups

www.autosafety.org (Center for Auto Safety)

www.carconsumers.com (Consumers for Auto Reliability and Safety (CARS), a California-based organization, which includes a lemon index based on data auto manufacturers submit to California agencies, plus links to websites that rate auto safety)

www.consumerlaw.org (National Consumer Law Center)

www.naca.net (National Association of Consumer Advocates)

www.consumersunion.org (Consumers Union)

www.tlpj.org (Trial Lawyers for Public Justice)

www.atlanet.org (American Trial Lawyers Association)

www.notfea.org (National Odometer and Title Fraud Enforcement Association)

Industry Trade Associations

www.nada.org (National Automobile Dealers Association)

www.naaa.com (National Association of Automobile Auctions)

www.aspa.com (American Salvage Pool Association)

Others

www.alldata.com (offers on-line searches for technical service bulletins and recall notices, and also has a comprehensive set of links to other websites)

www.crashtest.com (compiles crash test results not only from NHTSA but from insurance sources and overseas governments; data can be retrieved by make and model; this website also retrieves NHTSA recall information)

www.autopedia.com (a vast amount of information about the car industry, including a list of the names and locations of dealers, the full text of each state's lemon law, links to state attorney general lemon law websites, and links to many other websites with information about the auto industry)

www.consumerworld.com (created by an attorney with a long-standing specialty in consumer law, this website is a public service non-commercial guide that catalogs over 1500 useful consumer resources; links allow the user to order many free or low-cost publications and newsletters)

www.cartalk.org (website of a weekly radio show about cars which includes repair reports about cars, and which compiles comments that car owners have submitted about good features and problems with their cars)

www.rv.org (website of a nonprofit organization for recreational vehicle owners which gathers information about buying, repairing, and troubleshooting)

www.autonews.com (website of *Automotive News*, which reports on enforcement actions)

www.AA1Car.com (links to technical resources, sources of service bulletins, service manuals, vehicle associations, organizations and manufacturers, and other automotive sites)

www.safecarguide.com (vehicle safety data and links)

www.internetautoguide.com (search feature for vehicle recalls)

Cumulative Index

This is a cumulative index. Only use this index, not the one in the main volume which is now superseded. When a section is referenced in this index, turn to that section in both the main volume and this Supplement. Section references followed by "S" are found only in the Supplement.

ACCIDENT REPORTS
see also PRIOR DAMAGE
DMV filings, 2.4.2.3
information source, 2.4.5.4.1
leased vehicles, 2.5.7

ACTIONS
breach of warranty, *see* WARRANTY CLAIMS
causes of action, selecting, 9.3.1
common law, *see* FRAUD CLAIMS
Odometer Act, *see* ENFORCEMENT ACTIONS (ODOMETER ACT)
RICO, *see* RICO CLAIMS
UDAP, *see* UDAP CLAIMS

ACTUAL DAMAGES
see DAMAGES, ACTUAL

ADD-ONS
dealer abuses, 1.3.6

ADDRESSES
helpful web addresses, 2.5.15, Appx. M
prior owners
    obtaining from DMV, 3.8, Appx. D
    obtaining from title search, 2.5.1

ADVERSE HISTORY
flood damage, *see* FLOOD DAMAGE
mechanical problems, *see* PREEXISTING MECHANICAL PROBLEMS
misrepresentations, *see* MISREPRESENTATIONS
NCLC auto fraud manual, scope, 1.2
nondisclosure, *see* NONDISCLOSURE
prior use, *see* PRIOR USE
stolen vehicle, *see* STOLEN VEHICLES
uncovering, *see* INVESTIGATORY TECHNIQUES
wreck damage, *see* WRECK DAMAGE

ADVERTISING
deceptive advertising
    analysis, 1.3.3
    license suspension, 6.5.7
    possible claims, 2.2.12

AGENTS
see also EMPLOYEES
knowledge imputed to, 8.4.4
misconduct, dealer liability, 7.4.2
odometer disclosures, liability, 4.6.2.2

potential defendant, 9.4.2
punitive damages, principal's liability, 7.10.7

AIRBAGS
state laws, 6.3bS
used cars, sold without, 2.8S

ALTERNATE TRANSPORTATION
actual damages claims, 5.8.1.7
CARS foundation assistance, 6.4.6, 8.2.7.7, 9.2.2

AMERICAN SALVAGE POOL ASSOCIATION
ethics and standards, 2.5.14
website, 2.5.15

APPRAISALS
see also PRICING
actual value, determination, 5.8.1.3
need to obtain, 9.2.1

ARBITRATION CLAUSES
avoiding, 9.3.5
defendants, strategic considerations, 9.4.1
enforceability, 9.3.5.1
non-signatory third parties, application, 9.3.5.5
punitive damages restrictions, 9.3.5.2, 9.3.5.3
tort claims, application, 9.3.5.4
written warranties, application, 9.3.5.6

"AS IS" CLAUSES
described, 7.8.2
disclosure requirements, 6.5.5, 8.2.4.3.5
fraud claims, effect, 7.8.2
implied warranty disclaimers
    effect, 8.2.4.3.1, 8.2.4.3.5
    Magnuson-Moss restrictions, 8.2.4.3.2
    state law restrictions, 8.2.4.3.3
    UCC restrictions, 8.2.4.3.4, 8.2.4.3.6
odometer violations, effect, 4.9
UDAP claims, effect, 8.4.3

ASSIGNMENTS
title, 2.4.2.1, 2.4.2.2, 3.2.4
    reassignment blocks and forms, 3.3.4
    transfers not requiring, 3.2.5

ATTORNEY FEES AND COSTS
availability, 9.12.1
bonds, recovering under, 9.13.4.5
expectations, explaining to client, 9.2.6
fee-shifting statutes, 9.12.6

References are to sections; references followed by "S" appear only in this Supplement

DISCLOSURE REGULATIONS (ODOMETERS) (*cont.*)
parties responsible
  agents, 4.6.2.2
  lessees, 4.6.2.3
  transferor and transferee, 4.6.2.2
power of attorney disclosures, 4.6.5.7, 5.3
reassignments, 4.6.5.6
records, retention, 3.3.2, 4.6.9
rental cars, 4.6.3.5
repossessions, 4.6.3.2
requirements
  generally, 4.6.1
  scope, 4.2.1, 4.6.2–3.6.4
reset odometers, 4.4, 4.6.6.8, 4.6.6.10
security interests, granting, 4.6.3.2
state request for alternative method, 4.6.5.8
statements as evidence, 9.8.7.1
supplementary information, selected excerpts, Appx. B.1.2
text, Appx. B.1.1
title documents, 3.6.2
transfers covered, 4.6.3
transfers exempted, 4.6.4
used cars, 3.6.2, 4.6.5.3, 4.6.5.4
violations
  certification as inaccurate, 4.6.6.4
  false statements, 4.5
  private right of action, 5.3
  remedies, 3.9.2
voluntary second set, 4.6.5.4
waiver of rights, 4.9

DISCOVERY
battles, preparing for, 9.5.4
  access to other cars sold by dealer, Appx. H.5
"contention questions," 9.5.5
deposition of consumer, 9.5.5
evidence of other bad acts, 9.8.1.1
formal discovery, 9.5.2
informal discovery prior to filing suit, 9.5.1
missing documents, dealing with, 9.5.7
sample discovery
  floor plan financer, Appx. H.6S
  lemon laundering, Appx. H.3
  net worth, Appx. H.4
  odometer misrepresentation, Appx. H.1
  undisclosed wreck history, Appx. H.2
techniques, 9.5.3
videotaping the deposition, 9.5.6
  advantages and disadvantages, 9.5.6.2
  right to, 9.5.6.1

DISCRIMINATION
automobile sales and credit, 1.3.12

DISTRIBUTORS
body shops as, 2.5.8
defined, 2.5.3, 3.5, 4.6.9
information source, 2.5.3
insurance companies as, 2.5.8, 4.6.9
manufacturers as, 2.5.9
Odometer Act, application, 4.2.1
records
  information source, 2.5.3
  inspection, 5.9.1.1
  odometer records, 2.5.3, 4.6.9

retention, 3.5, 4.6.9
  title records, 3.5
secured creditors as, 2.5.5, 4.6.9

DOCUMENTARY EVIDENCE
see under EVIDENCE

DOCUMENTARY FEES
dealer abuses, 1.3.6
state regulation, 6.5.6

DRIVER'S EDUCATION CAR
prior use, disclosure
  state law, 6.3
  UDAP claims, 8.4.8.4

DRIVER'S PRIVACY PROTECTION ACT (DPPA)
constitutionality, 3.8.4
effect, 3.8.1
identifying information
  disclosure restrictions, 3.3.6S, 3.8.2
  parallel state restrictions, 3.8.5
  safety situations, 3.8.3
overview, 3.8.1
text, Appx. A.2

ELECTION OF REMEDIES
common law fraud or statutory, 7.8.5
rescission or damages, 7.11.3

EMISSION TESTING RECORDS
DMV filings, 2.4.2.3

EMOTIONAL DISTRESS
damages for, 9.10.3.2
punitive damages, relationship, 7.10.6.3.3

EMPLOYEES
see also AGENTS
misconduct, dealer liability, 7.4.2
fraud by, punitive damage liability, 7.10.7
knowledge imputed to, 8.4.4
odometer disclosures, liability, 4.6.2.2

ENFORCEMENT ACTIONS (ODOMETER ACT)
see also DISCLOSURE REGULATIONS (ODOMETERS);
    ODOMETER ACT (FEDERAL)
arbitration clauses, effect, 9.3.5.2
attorney fees, *see* ATTORNEY FEES
buyers, against, 5.2.4
civil penalties, 5.9.1.2
class actions, 5.8.5
criminal penalties, 5.9.1.3
damages, 9.10.1.1
federal court jurisdiction, 5.5.1, 9.3.3.1
federal enforcement, 5.9.1
fraud claims, 9.3.3.3
indirect injuries, 5.2.5
injunctive relief, 5.9.1.4
intent requirements, 4.8.1, 5.3
  non-mileage disclosures, 3.9.2.2
  pleading, 5.7
jury trials, 5.5.3
leased vehicles, 5.2.6
lessee liability, 5.3
litigation aids, *see* LITIGATION AIDS
non-mileage disclosures, 3.9.2.2
other than current title owner, bringing, 5.2.2

References are to sections; references followed by "S" appear only in this Supplement

References are to sections; references followed by "S" appear only in this Supplement

References are to sections; references followed by "S" appear only in this Supplement

References are to sections; references followed by "S" appear only in this Supplement

References are to sections; references followed by "S" appear only in this Supplement

References are to sections; references followed by "S" appear only in this Supplement

References are to sections; references followed by "S" appear only in this Supplement

References are to sections; references followed by "S" appear only in this Supplement

Quick Reference to the Consumer Credit and Sales Legal Practice Series

References are to sections in *all* manuals in NCLC's Consumer Credit and Sales Legal Practice Series. References followed by "S" appear only in a Supplement.

Readers should also consider another search option available at *www.consumerlaw.org/keyword*. There, users can search all seventeen NCLC manuals for a case name, party name, statutory or regulatory citation, or *any* other word, phrase, or combination of terms. The search engine provides the title, page number and context of every occurrence of that word or phrase within each of the NCLC manuals. Further search instructions and tips are provided on the web site.

The Quick Reference to the Consumer Credit and Sales Legal Practice Series pinpoints where to find specific topics analyzed in the NCLC manuals. References are to individual manual or supplement sections. For more information on these volumes, see *What Your Library Should Contain* at the beginning of this volume, or go to www.consumerlaw.org.

This Quick Reference is a speedy means to locate key terms in the appropriate NCLC manual. More detailed indexes are found at the end of the individual NCLC volumes. Both the detailed contents pages and the detailed indexes for each manual are also available on NCLC's web site, www.consumerlaw.org.

NCLC *strongly recommends,* when searching for **PLEADINGS** on a particular subject, that users refer to the *Index Guide* accompanying *Consumer Law Pleadings on CD-Rom*, and *not* to this *Quick Reference.* Another option is to search for pleadings directly on the *Consumer Law Pleadings* CD-Rom or on the *Consumer Law in a Box* CD-Rom, using the finding tools that are provided on the CD-Roms themselves.

The finding tools found on *Consumer Law in a Box* are also an effective means to find statutes, regulations, agency interpretations, legislative history, and other primary source material found on NCLC's CD-Roms. Other search options are detailed in *Finding Aids and Search Tips, supra.*

Abbreviations

AUS	=	Access to Utility Service (3d ed. 2004 and 2006 Supp.)
Auto	=	Automobile Fraud (2d ed. 2003 and 2006 Supp.)
Arbit	=	Consumer Arbitration Agreements (4th ed. 2004 and 2005 Supp.)
CBPL	=	Consumer Banking and Payments Law (3d ed. 2005 and 2006 Supp.)
Bankr	=	Consumer Bankruptcy Law and Practice (7th ed. 2004 and 2005 Supp.)
CCA	=	Consumer Class Actions (6th ed. 2006)
CLP	=	Consumer Law Pleadings, Numbers One Through Eleven (2005)
COC	=	The Cost of Credit (3d ed. 2005 and 2006 Supp.)
CD	=	Credit Discrimination (4th ed. 2005 and 2006 Supp.)
FCR	=	Fair Credit Reporting (5th ed. 2002 and 2005 Supp.)
FDC	=	Fair Debt Collection (5th ed. 2004 and 2006 Supp.)
Fore	=	Foreclosures (2005)
Repo	=	Repossessions (6th ed. 2005)
Stud	=	Student Loan Law (2d ed. 2002 and 2005 Supp.)
TIL	=	Truth in Lending (5th ed. 2003 and 2005 Supp.)
UDAP	=	Unfair and Deceptive Acts and Practices (6th ed. 2004 and 2005 Supp.)
Warr	=	Consumer Warranty Law (3d ed. 2006)

References are to sections in *all* manuals in NCLC's Consumer Credit and Sales Legal Practice Series

References are to sections in *all* manuals in NCLC's Consumer Credit and Sales Legal Practice Series

References are to sections in *all* manuals in NCLC's Consumer Credit and Sales Legal Practice Series

References are to sections in *all* manuals in NCLC's Consumer Credit and Sales Legal Practice Series

References are to sections in *all* manuals in NCLC's Consumer Credit and Sales Legal Practice Series

References are to sections in *all* manuals in NCLC's Consumer Credit and Sales Legal Practice Series

References are to sections in *all* manuals in NCLC's Consumer Credit and Sales Legal Practice Series

Student Loans, Private Loans—Stud § 1.9S
Student Loans, Reinstating Eligibility—Stud Ch 8
Summary Judgment Briefs, Sample—FDC App J.1; CLP
Surety for Consumer Debtor—Repo § 12.9
Surety Liability for Seller's Actions—Auto § 9.13.4
Survey Evidence—FDC § 2.9.3
Surveys, Use in Litigation—CCA § 7.1.2.2.3
Target Marketing Lists—FCR §§ 2.3.3, 5.2.9.1, 5.3.8.4.2
Tax Abatement Laws, State Property, Summaries—Fore App G
Tax Collections—FDC §§ 4.2.8S, 13.2
Tax Consequences, Bankruptcy Discharge—Bankr § 14.6
Tax Form 1099-C—CCA § 12.5.2.3.6
Tax Implications of Damage Award—CCA § 12.5.2.3
Tax Implications to Client of Attorney Fees—CCA § 15.5
Tax Intercept—Bankr § 9.4.3
Tax Liens—Fore Ch 9
Tax Refund Intercepts—Stud § 5.2; FDC § 13.2
Tax Refunds—COC § 7.5.4
Tax Refunds in Bankruptcy—Bankr § 2.5.3
Tax Sales—Fore Ch 9
Taxis, Undisclosed Sale of—Auto § 2.4.5.6
Telechecks—UDAP §§ 5.1.10
Telecommunications Act of 1996—AUS Ch 2, App C
Telemarketing, Payment—CBPL §§ 2.3.5, 3.8
Telemarketing Fraud—UDAP § 5.9; FCR § 15.4
Telemarketing Fraud, Federal Statutes—UDAP App D
Telephone Cards, Prepaid—CBPL Ch 7
Telephone Companies as Credit Reporting Agencies—FCR § 2.6.9
Telephone Harassment—FDC § 9.3
Telephone Inside Wiring Maintenance Agreements—UDAP §§ 5.2.7.2, 5.6.10
Telephone Rates, Service—AUS Ch 2, App C
Telephone Service Contracts—UDAP §§ 5.2.7.2, 5.6.10
Telephone Slamming—AUS § 2.7.5.1; UDAP § 5.6.10
Teller's Checks—CBPL Ch 5
Tenant Approval Companies—FCR §§ 2.3.6.4, 2.6.1, 6.4.2.3.3, 13.3.2, 13.7.3
Tenant Ownership in Chapter 7 Liquidation—Bankr § 17.8.2
Tenant's Property Removed with Eviction—Repo § 15.7.4
Tenant's Rights When Landlord Files Bankruptcy—Bankr § 17.8; AUS § 4.5
Termination of Utility Service—AUS Chs 11, 12
Termite Control Services—UDAP § 5.6.3
Testers, Fair Housing—CD §§ 4.4.4, 11.2.2
Theft at ATM Machines, Bank Liability—CBPL § 3.5.4
Theft of Identity—FCR § 13.5.5
Third Party Liability Issues—AUS §§ 11.4, 11.5
Threats of Criminal Prosecution—FDC § 15.3
Tie-In Sale Between Mobile Home and Park Space—UDAP § 5.5.1.2
TIL—*See* Truth in Lending
Time Shares—UDAP § 5.5.5.10
Tire Identification—Auto § 2.2.3
Title, Automobile—Auto §§ 2.3, 2.4, Ch 3, Apps. D, E; UDAP § 5.4.5; Warr § 15.4.4
Tobacco—UDAP § 5.11.7
Tort Liability—FDC Ch 12
Tort Liability, Strict—Warr Ch 12
Tort Remedies, Unlawful Disconnections—AUS § 11.7.2
Tort Remedies, Wrongful Repossessions—Repo § 13.6
Towing—UDAP § 5.4.1.8; Repo Ch 15
Trade-in Cars—UDAP § 5.4.4.4
Trade Schools—Stud Ch 9; UDAP § 5.10.7
Trading Posts—UDAP § 5.1.1.5.5

Transcripts and Bankruptcy—Bankr § 14.5.5.2
Traveler's Checks—CBPL Ch 5, UDAP § 2.2.1.3
Travel Fraud—UDAP § 5.4.13
Treble Damages—UDAP § 8.4.2
Trebled, Disclosure to Jury that Damages Will Be—UDAP § 8.4.2.7.3
Trial Brief, Sample—FDC App J.4
Trial Documents, Sample—*See* Auto App I; FDC App J; Warr App M
Trustees in Bankruptcy—Bankr §§ 2.6, 2.7, 16.4.2, 17.7
Truth in Lending—TIL; COC §§ 2.3.4, 4.4.1; FDC § 9.4
Truth in Mileage Act—Auto Chs 3, 4, 5
Truth in Savings—CBPL § 4.5
Tuition Recovery Funds—Stud § 9.6
Typing Services—Bankr § 15.6
UCC Article 2—Warr
UCC Article 2 and Comments Reprinted—Warr App E
UCC Article 2A—Repo §§ 2.5.1.1, 14.1.3.1; Warr Ch 21, App E.5; UDAP § 5.4.8.5
UCC Articles 3 and 4—CBPL Chs 1, 2, App A
UCC Article 9—Repo
UCC Article 9, Revised—Repo App A
UCC Article 9 and Comments Reprinted—Repo App A
UDAP—UDAP; AUS § 1.7.2; Auto § 8.4; COC §§ 8.5.2.6, 12.5; FDC § 11.3; FCR § 10.4.2; Repo §§ 2.5.3.1, 13.4.3; Warr § 11.1
Unauthorized Card Use—TIL § 5.9.4
Unauthorized Practice of Law—FDC §§ 4.2.7.7, 5.6.2, 11.5; Bankr § 15.6; UDAP § 5.12.2
Unauthorized Use of Checks, Credit and Debit Cards—CBPL §§ 2.3, 3.3, 6.3
Unauthorized Use of Utility Service—AUS § 5.3
Unavailability of Advertised Items—UDAP § 4.6.2
Unconscionability—Warr §§ 11.2, 21.2.6; COC §§ 8.7.5, 12.7; UDAP §§ 4.4, 5.4.6.5; Auto § 8.7
Unconscionability of Arbitration Clauses—Arbit §§ 4.2, 4.3, 4.4
Unearned Interest—COC Ch 5
Unemployment Insurance—COC § 8.3.1.4
Unfair Insurance Practices Statutes—UDAP § 5.3; COC § 8.4.1.4
Unfair Practices Statutes—*See* UDAP
Unfairness—UDAP § 4.3
Uniform Arbitration Act – Arbit. Ch. 10
Uniform Commercial Code—*See* UCC
United States Trustee—Bankr §§ 2.7, 17.7.2
Universal Telephone Service—AUS Ch 2
Unlicensed Activities—COC § 9.2.4.5
Unpaid Refund Discharge of Student Loan—Stud § 6.4
Unsolicited Credit Cards—TIL § 5.9.2
Unsolicited Goods—UDAP § 5.8.4; FDC § 9.2
Unsubstantiated Claims—UDAP § 4.5
Used as New—UDAP § 4.9.4
Used Car Lemon Laws—Warr § 15.4.5
Used Car Rule—Warr § 15.8, App D; UDAP § 5.4.6.2, App B.6
Used Cars—Auto; Warr Ch 15, App K.3, App L.4; UDAP § 5.4.6
Used Cars, Assembled from Salvaged Parts—Auto §§ 1.4.3, 2.1.4
Used Cars, Financing—COC § 11.6
Used Cars, Undisclosed Sale of Wrecked Cars—Auto §§ 1.4.4, 2.1.4
Users of Consumer and Credit Reports—FCR Ch 5
Usury, Trying a Case—COC Ch 10
Utilities—AUS; CD §§ 2.2.2.3, 2.2.6.2; TIL § 2.4.6; UDAP §§ 2.3.2, 5.6.9
Utilities and Bankruptcy—AUS §§ 4.5, 12.1; Bankr § 9.8
Utilities as Credit Reporting Agencies—FCR § 2.6.9
Utility Commission Regulation—AUS § 1.3, App A

References are to sections in *all* manuals in NCLC's Consumer Credit and Sales Legal Practice Series

NOTES

220

NOTES

NOTES

NOTES

About the Companion CD-Rom

CD-Rom Supersedes All Prior CD-Roms

This CD-Rom supersedes the CD-Rom accompanying *Automobile Fraud* (2d ed. 2003) and its supplements. Discard all prior CDs. The 2006 CD-Rom contains everything found on the earlier CDs and contains much additional material.

What Is on the CD-Rom

For a detailed listing of the CD's contents, see the CD-Rom Contents section on page xxi of this book. Highlights and new additions include:

- 25 sample complaints concerning odometer fraud, undisclosed wreck history, lemon laundering, and grey-market vehicles;
- 30 sample discovery requests concerning odometer fraud, undisclosed wreck history, flood damage, lemon laundering, and grey-market vehicles;
- A series of expert reports regarding undisclosed wreck damage and diminished value;
- Sample *voir dire*, opening and closing statements, outline to examine expert witness, motion in limine for bifurcation, summary judgment memoranda, and jury instructions in an odometer case, a wrecked car case, and re missing evidence;
- 18 sample class action pleadings in odometer rollback cases, sample attorney fee documents, and a case study of successful rebuilt car litigation, including complaint and opening statement;
- The federal Odometer Act, its legislative history, and federal Odometer Act regulations;
- Certification regulations and the federal motor vehicle theft prevention standard, with updates and amendments;
- Review of state automobile fraud laws;
- NHTSA questions and answers, a NHTSA study of odometer fraud, and 40 NHTSA interpretation letters;
- State sources of title information, web links for requesting title histories, and the actual forms to apply for title information from most of the 50 states, updated for 2006;
- Sample title transfer documents and sample summary title history reports from Carfax and AutoCheck;
- A manufacturer lemon manual, a list of state dealer licensing offices, and sample documents to register a dealer with an automobile auction (with web link); and
- Links to key web sites related to automobile fraud.

How to Use the CD-Rom

The CD's pop-up menu quickly allows you to use the CD—just place the CD into its drive and click on the "Start NCLC CD" button that will pop up in the middle of the screen. You can also access the CD by clicking on a desktop icon that you can create using the pop-up menu.[1] For detailed installation instructions, see *One-Time Installation* below.

All the CD-Rom's information is available in PDF (Acrobat) format, making the information:

- Highly readable (identical to the printed pages in the book);
- Easily navigated (with bookmarks, "buttons," and Internet-style forward and backward searches);
- Easy to locate with keyword searches and other quick-search techniques across the whole CD-Rom; and
- Easy to paste into a word processor.

While much of the material is also found on the CD-Rom in word processing format, we strongly recommend you use the material in PDF format—not only because it is easiest to use, contains the most features, and includes more material, but also because you can easily switch back to a word processing format when you prefer.

Acrobat Reader 5.0.5 and 7.0.7 come free of charge with the CD-Rom. **We strongly recommend that new Acrobat users read the Acrobat tutorial on the Home Page. It takes two minutes and will really pay off.**

---

1 Alternatively, click on the D:\Start.pdf file on "My Computer" or open that file in Acrobat—always assuming "D:" is the CD-Rom drive on your computer.

How to Find Documents in Word Processing Format

Most pleadings and other practice aids are also available in Microsoft Word format to make them more easily adaptable for individual use. (Current versions of WordPerfect are able to convert the Word documents upon opening them.) The CD-Rom offers several ways to find those word processing documents. One option is simply to browse to the folder on the CD-Rom containing all the word processing files and open the desired document from your standard word processing program, such as Word or WordPerfect. All word processing documents are in the D:\WP_Files folder, if "D:" is the CD-Rom drive,[2] and are further organized by book title. Documents that appear in the book are named after the corresponding appendix; other documents have descriptive file names.

Another option is to navigate the CD in PDF format, and, when a particular document is on the screen, click on the corresponding bookmark for the "Word version of . . ." This will automatically run Word, WordPerfect for Windows, or *any other word processor* that is associated with the ".DOC" extension, and then open the word processing file that corresponds to the Acrobat document.[3]

Important Information Before Opening the CD-Rom Package

Before opening the CD-Rom package, please read this information. Opening the package constitutes acceptance of the following described terms. In addition, the *book* is not returnable once the seal to the *CD-Rom* has been broken.

The CD-Rom is copyrighted and all rights are reserved by the National Consumer Law Center, Inc. No copyright is claimed to the text of statutes, regulations, excerpts from court opinions, or any part of an original work prepared by a United States Government employee.

You may not commercially distribute the CD-Rom or otherwise reproduce, publish, distribute or use the disk in any manner that may infringe on any copyright or other proprietary right of the National Consumer Law Center. Nor may you otherwise transfer the CD-Rom or this agreement to any other party unless that party agrees to accept the terms and conditions of this agreement. You may use the CD-Rom on only one computer and by one user at a time.

The CD-Rom is warranted to be free of defects in materials and faulty workmanship under normal use for a period

of ninety days after purchase. If a defect is discovered in the CD-Rom during this warranty period, a replacement disk can be obtained at no charge by sending the defective disk, postage prepaid, with information identifying the purchaser, to National Consumer Law Center, Publications Department, 77 Summer Street, 10th Floor, Boston, MA 02110. After the ninety-day period, a replacement will be available on the same terms, but will also require a $20 prepayment.

The National Consumer Law Center makes no other warranty or representation, either express or implied, with respect to this disk, its quality, performance, merchantability, or fitness for a particular purpose. In no event will the National Consumer Law Center be liable for direct, indirect, special, incidental, or consequential damages arising out of the use or inability to use the disk. The exclusion of implied warranties is not effective in some states, and thus this exclusion may not apply to you.

System Requirements

Use of this CD-Rom requires a Windows-based PC with a CD-Rom drive. (Macintosh users report success using NCLC CDs, but the CD has been tested only on Windows-based PCs.) The CD-Rom's features are optimized with Acrobat Reader 5 or later. Acrobat Reader versions 5.0.5 and 7.0.7 are included free on this CD-Rom, and either will work with this CD-Rom as long as it is compatible with your version of Windows. Acrobat Reader 5 is compatible with Windows 95/98/Me/NT/2000/XP, while Acrobat Reader 7.0.7 is compatible with Windows 98SE/Me/NT/2000/XP. If you already have Acrobat Reader 6.0, we *highly* recommend you download and install the 6.0.1 update from Adobe's web site at www.adobe.com because a bug in version 6.0 interferes with optimum use of this CD-Rom. See the *Acrobat 6 Problem* button on the home page for details. The Microsoft Word versions of pleadings and practice aids can be used with any reasonably current word processor (1995 or later).

One-Time Installation

When the CD-Rom is inserted in its drive, a menu will pop up automatically. (Please be patient if you have a slow CD-Rom drive; this will only take a few moments.) If you do not already have Acrobat Reader 5.0.5 or later, first click the "Install Acrobat Reader" button. Do not reboot, but then click on the "Make Shortcut Icon" button. (You need not make another shortcut icon if you already have done so for another NCLC CD.) Then reboot and follow the *How to Use the CD-Rom* instructions above.

[*Note*: If the pop-up menu fails to appear, go to "My Computer," right-click "D:" if that is the CD-Rom drive, and select "Open." Then double-click on "Read_Me.txt" for alternate installation and use instructions.]

---

2 The CD-Rom drive could be any letter following "D:" depending on your computer's configuration.

3 For instructions on how to associate WordPerfect to the ".DOC" extension, go to the CD-Rom's home page and click on "How to Use/Help," then "Word Files."